lonely planet

AUSTRALIA

TOP SIGHTS, AUTHENTIC EXPERIENCES

Brett Atkinson,
Anthony H
Kate Morgan
Andy

Contents

Welcome to Australia

Australia is a wildly beautiful land, a vivid collusion of red outback sands, golden beaches and brightly coloured reefs – all of which set the stage for sophisticated urban indulgences and soulful Indigenous encounters.

Most Australians live along the coast, and most of these folks live in cities. It follows that urban life here is a lot of fun! Sydney is the glamorous poster child with world-class beaches and a glorious harbour. Melbourne is all arts, alleyways and stellar food. Brisbane is a subtropical town on the way up; Adelaide has festive grace and pubby poise. Boom-town Perth breathes West Coast optimism and Canberra showcases the nation's cultural treasures. Darwin, on the tropical northern frontier, and the chilly southern sandstone city of Hobart couldn't be more different.

Australia's landscapes are just as diverse, from lush tropical and temperate rainforests to the remote rocky outcrops of Uluru, Kakadu and the Kimberley. Beset with islands and deserted shores, Australia's coastline is wild and wonderful. Animating these splendid places is wildlife like nowhere else on the planet: kangaroos, crocodiles, wombats, wallabies, platypus, crocodiles, dingoes and 700-plus bird species.

Hungry yet? Australia plates up a multicultural fusion of European techniques and fresh Pacific-rim ingredients – aka 'Mod Oz' (Modern Australian). Seafood plays a starring role, though you'll always find beef, lamb and chicken at Aussie barbecues. To wash all it down, Australian beers, wines and whiskies are world-beaters.

Beset with islands and deserted shores, Australia's coastline is wild and wonderful.

Bondi Beach, Sydney (p44)

INDONESIA
Savu Sea
Timor Sea
Melville Island
Bathurst Island
Darwin
Jabiru
KAKADU NATIONA
p239
Joseph Bonaparte Gulf
Katherine
INDIAN OCEAN
Kununurra
Daly Waters
Cape Leveque
The Kimberley
Broome
Tennant Creek
Port Hedland
NORTHERN TERRITORY
The Pilbara
Karratha
North West Cape
Exmouth
Gibson Desert
ULURU & THE OUTBACK
p223
Alice
Little Sandy Desert
Yulara
Uluru-Kata Tjuta National Park
Shark Bay
WESTERN AUSTRALIA
Great Victoria Desert
Mt Magnet
Coober Pedy
Geraldton
Nullarbor
Plain
Kalgoorlie-Boulder
Eucla
PERTH & FREMANTLE
p257
Perth
Fremantle
Great Australian Bight
Bunbury
Esperance
Margaret River
Albany
SOUTHERN OCEAN
0 500 km
0 250 miles

Torres Strait
Thursday Island
Cape York
PAPUA NEW GUINEA
Weipa
Coral Sea
SOUTH PACIFIC OCEAN
L PARK
Gulf of Carpentaria
Cape York Peninsula
Daintree National Park
Great Barrier Reef
Port Douglas
Cairns
GREAT BARRIER REEF & THE DAINTREE p107
Townsville
THE WHITSUNDAYS p129
Mt Isa
Airlie Beach
Mackay
Great Barrier Reef
Winton
QUEENSLAND
Rockhampton
Simpson Desert
Birdsville
Bundaberg
Fraser Island
Charleville
Noosa
Lake Eyre North
BRISBANE
Lake Eyre South
BYRON BAY p95
Bourke
GREAT DIVIDING RANGE
Coffs Harbour
Tamworth
Port Augusta
Broken Hill
NEW SOUTH WALES
Port Macquarie
Newcastle
Lord Howe Island (NSW)
Mildura
Adelaide
Hay
SYDNEY p35
CANBERRA p81
Albury
ACT
Mt Kosciuszko
VICTORIA
Ballarat
Geelong
MELBOURNE p141
AT OCEAN ROAD p167
Tasman Sea
King Island
Bass Strait
Flinders Island
Launceston
TASMANIA
HOBART p179

BSCHUITDESIGN/GETTY IMAGES ©

Plan Your Trip
Australia's Top 12

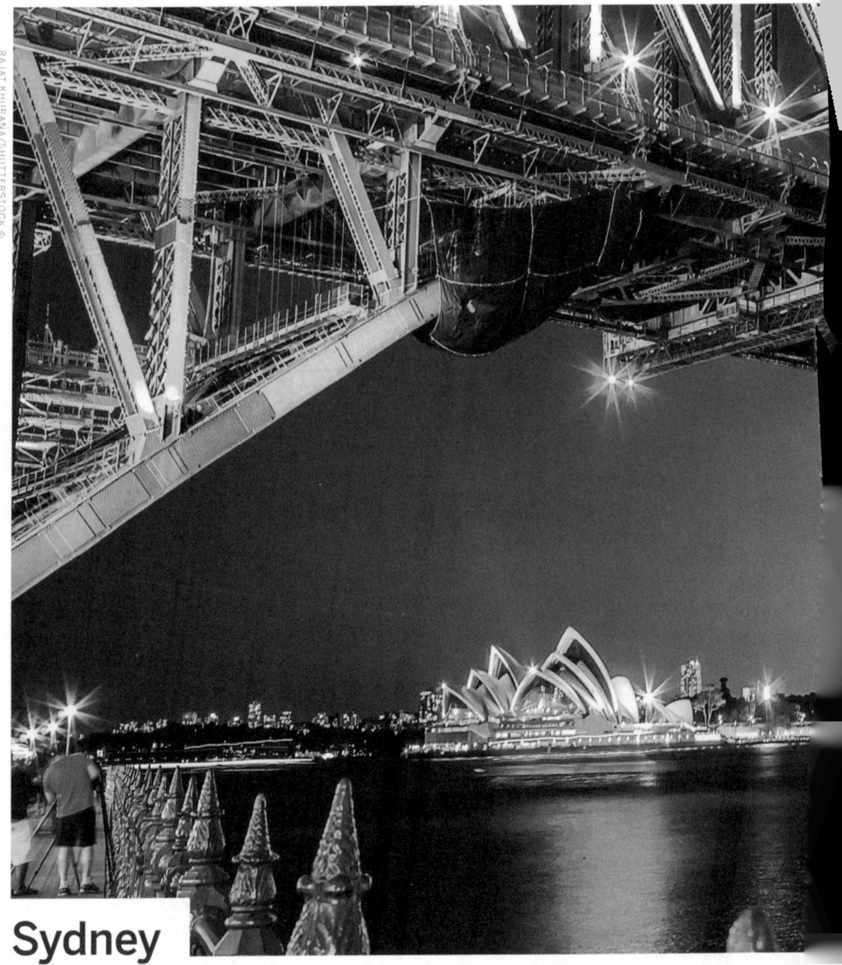

Sydney

Australia's iconic city is beachy and beautiful

The big-ticket sights in Sydney (p35) – the Sydney Opera House, the Rocks and Sydney Harbour Bridge – top most people's lists. But to really catch Sydney's vibe, spend a day at the beach. Stake out some sand at Bondi Beach and plunge into the surf; or hop on a harbour ferry to Manly for a swim, a surf or a walk along the sea-sprayed promenade to Shelly Beach. *Ahhh,* this is the life!

1

SUNFLOWEREY/SHUTTERSTOCK ©

Canberra

Australia's cultural and political heart

2

The major drawcard in Australia's purpose-built capital city (p81) is a portfolio of lavishly endowed museums and galleries. Institutions such as the National Gallery of Australia, National Museum of Australia, National Portrait Gallery and Australian War Memorial offer visitors a fascinating insight into the country's history and culture, both ancient and modern. Australian War Memorial (p85)

DARREN TIERNEY/SHUTTERSTOCK ©

Byron Bay

Counter-cultural mecca by the sea

3

Australia's most easterly point, big-hearted Byron Bay (p95) is an enduring icon of Australian culture. Families on holiday, hippies, surfers and sunseekers from across the globe gather by the foreshore at sunset, drawn to this spot by fabulous restaurants, a chilled pace of life and an astonishing range of activities on offer. But mostly they're here because this is one of Australia's most beautiful stretches of coast.

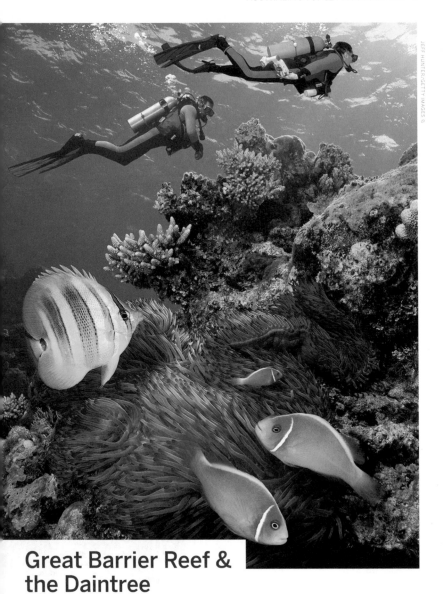

Great Barrier Reef & the Daintree

Kaleidoscopic coral and ancient rainforest

The Unesco World Heritage–listed Great Barrier Reef (p110) is a 2000km-long ecosystem populated with dazzling coral and tropical fish. Underwater nirvana! Back on dry land, the Daintree (p116) is another Unesco darling, enveloping visitors in prehistoric ferns and twisted mangroves spilling onto brilliant white-sand beaches.

5

The Whitsundays

Set sail through a tropical archipelago

You can hop around a whole stack of tropical islands in this seafaring life and never find anywhere with the sheer beauty of Queensland's Whitsundays (p129). Travellers of all monetary persuasions launch yachts from party-town Airlie Beach or from sprawling Hamilton Island and drift between these lush green isles in a slow search for paradise (you'll probably find it in more than one place).

Whitehaven Beach, Whitsunday Island (p138)

Melbourne

Soul, style and substance down south

Why the queue? Oh, that's just the line to get into the latest hot 'no bookings' restaurant in Melbourne (p141). The next best restaurant/chef/cafe/barista/bar/food truck may be the talk of the town, but there are things here the locals would never change: the leafy parks and gardens, the crowded trams and the passionate sporting allegiances. On alleyway walls, the city's world-renowned street-art scene expresses Melbourne's fears, frustrations and joys.

Degraves St (p150)

MATT MUNRO/LONELY PLANET ©

JOON WEI OOI/500PX ©

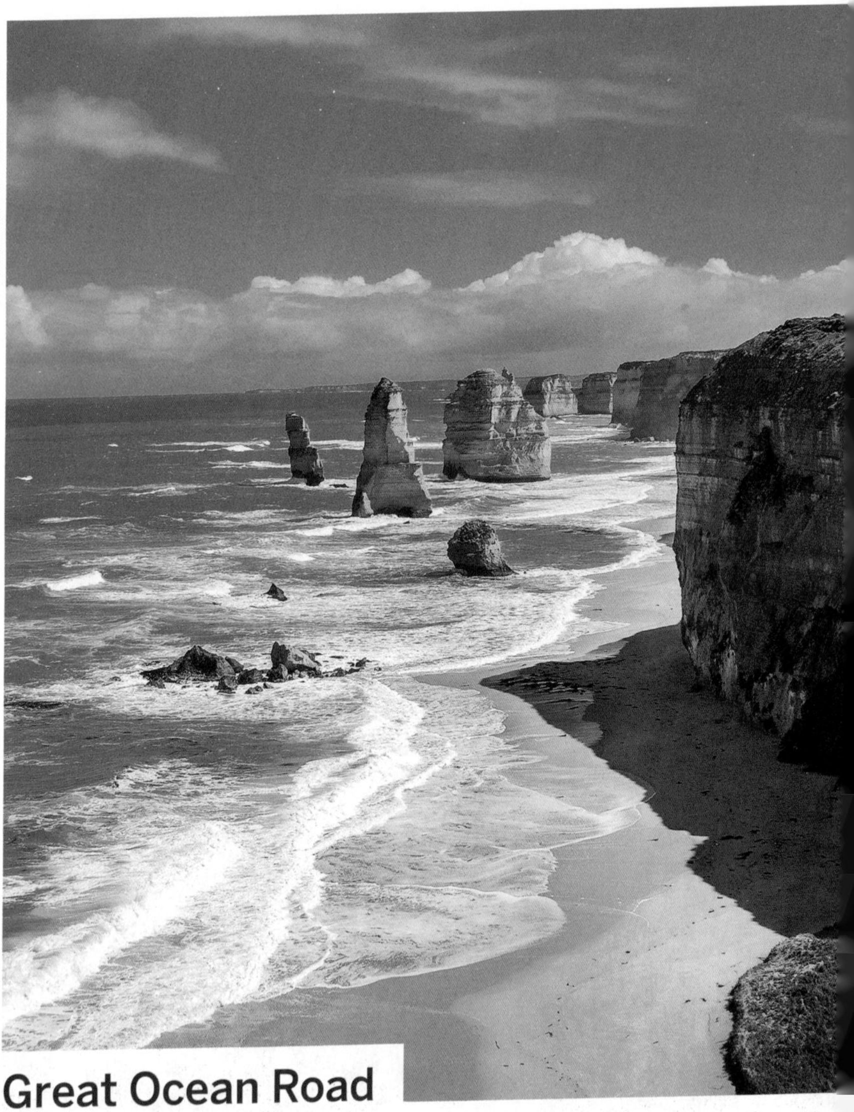

KAMALA SAKORNMANEESUP/SHUTTERSTOCK ©

Great Ocean Road

A classic Australian road trip

The Twelve Apostles – craggy rock formations jutting out of wild waters – are one of Victoria's most vivid sights, but it's the 'getting there' journey along the Great Ocean Road (p167) that doubles their impact. Drive slowly along roads that curl beside spectacular Bass Strait beaches and holiday villages, then whip inland through temperate rainforest studded with small towns and big trees.

Twelve Apostles (p170)

7

MONA/REMI CHAUVIN. IMAGE COURTESY MONA, MUSEUM OF OLD AND NEW ART, HOBART ©

Hobart

History and hip culture hand-in-hand

Hobart (p179) is Australia's second-oldest city, and perhaps its prettiest. The city's idiosyncratic island culture has been boosted of late by flourishing food and arts scenes, with MONA at the helm – an innovative, world-class museum described by its owner as a 'subversive adult Disneyland'. But Hobart's antique vibes endure: Salamanca Place and Battery Point evoke colonial days that somehow don't seem so far gone. MONA (p182)

WENDY MEDER/SHUTTERSTOCK ©

MILLEFIORE IMAGES/SHUTTERSTOCK ©

KJUUURS/SHUTTERSTOCK ©

Adelaide & South Australia's Wine Regions

Fine wines and refined urban vibes

Flying enticingly under the tourist radar, 'SA' is home to Adelaide (p208) – a charming city with burgeoning arts, food and laneway bar scenes – and a cavalcade of world-class wine regions. Sip shiraz in the Barossa Valley (p202) or McLaren Vale (p204), or pinot noir in the cool Adelaide Hills (p206). Happy days!

Uluru & the Outback

Big boulders and endless desert skies

No matter how many times you've seen it on postcards, nothing prepares you for the burnished grandeur of Uluru (p226) as it first appears on the outback horizon. With its remote desert location, deep cultural significance and dazzling natural beauty, Uluru is an essential Australian pilgrimage. Equally captivating is Kata Tjuta (p230), with mystical walks, sublime sunsets and ancient desert cultures.

10

12

Perth & Fremantle

Bright city lights and harbourside nights

Way out west is ebullient, optimistic Perth (p262), closer to Singapore than Sydney and one of the world's most remote cities of this size. Just down the Swan River is Fremantle (p267) – Western Australia's major port – a raffish, artsy, student-filled harbour town, defined by a classic cache of Victorian architecture. Like any port, the world washes in on the tide and washes out again, leaving the locals buzzing with global zeitgeist. Perth

PETER EVE/TOURISM NT ©

11

Kakadu National Park

Wilds in the tropical Top End

Kakadu (p239) is like another world. This staggering array of Aboriginal art (and living Aboriginal culture), lush wetlands, ancient gorges and abundant wildlife is spread across nearly 20,000 sq km of Australia's Top End. Visitors – whether they choose to simply dip in with a day's guided tour or take the plunge on a longer camping trek – find it hard to shake this land that time forgot.

CATHERINE SUTHERLAND/LONELY PLANET ©

Plan Your Trip
Need to Know

When to Go

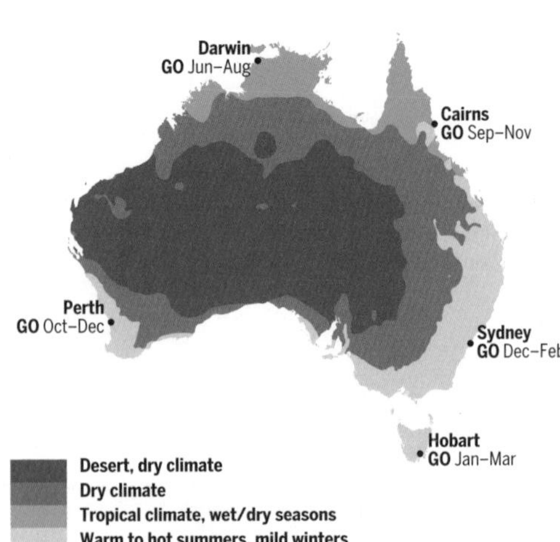

High Season (Dec–Feb)

- Summertime: local holidays, busy beaches.
- Prices rise 25% for big-city accommodation.
- Outdoor concerts, film screenings and food festivals.

Shoulder (Mar–May & Sep–Nov)

- Warm sun, clear skies, shorter queues.
- Easter is busy with travelling Aussie families.
- Atmospheric autumn leaves in southeastern states.

Low Season (Jun–Aug)

- Cool and rainy down south; mild and sunny up north.
- Low tourist numbers; attractions keep shorter hours.
- Head for the desert, the tropical north or the snow.

Currency

Australian dollar ($)

Language

English

Visas

All visitors to Australia need a visa, except New Zealanders. Apply online for an ETA or eVisitor visa, each allowing a three-month stay: www.border.gov.au.

Money

ATMs widely available in cities and larger towns. Credit cards accepted for hotels, restaurants, transport and activity bookings.

Mobile Phones

European phones work on Australia's network, but not most North American or Japanese phones. Use global roaming or a local SIM card and a prepaid account.

Time

Australia has three main time zones: Australian Eastern, Central and Western Standard Time. Sydney is on AEST, which is GMT/UCT plus 10 hours.

Daily Costs

Budget: Less than $150

- Hostel dorm bed: $28–40
- Simple main meal: $15–25
- Short bus or tram ride: $4

Midrange: $150–300

- Double room in a motel, B&B or hotel: $130–250
- Brunch in a good cafe: $25–40
- Short taxi ride: $25

Top End: More than $300

- Double room in a top-end hotel: from $250
- Three-course restaurant meal: from $100
- Domestic flight Sydney to Melbourne: from $100

Useful Websites

Tourism Australia (www.australia.com) Glossy main government tourism site with visitor info.

Bureau of Meteorology (www.bom.gov.au) Nationwide weather forecasts.

The Guardian (www.theguardian.com/australia-news) Australian online edition of the *Guardian* with nationwide news.

Parks Australia (www.environment.gov.au/topics/national-parks) Australia's national parks and reserves.

Exchange Rates (www.xe.com) Current exchange rates.

Lonely Planet (www.lonelyplanet.com/australia) Destination information, hotel bookings, traveller forum and more.

Opening Hours

Business hours vary from state to state; the following is a guide.

Banks 9.30am to 4pm Monday to Thursday; until 5pm Friday.

Cafes 7am to 5pm.

Pubs 11am to midnight.

Restaurants Noon to 2.30pm for lunch; 6pm to 9.30pm for dinner.

Shops 9am to 5pm or 6pm Monday to Sunday.

Supermarkets 7am until at least 8pm; some open 24 hours.

Arriving in Australia

Sydney Airport (p70) AirportLink trains run to the city centre every 10 minutes, 5am to 1am (20 minutes). Prebooked shuttle buses service city hotels. A taxi into the city costs $55 (30 minutes).

Melbourne Airport (p163) SkyBus services run to the city (20 minutes) every 10 to 30 minutes round the clock. A taxi into the city could cost from $55 to $75 (including surcharges and tolls) depending on traffic and time of day.

Getting Around

Australia is the sixth-largest country in the world: getting from A to B requires some thought.

Bus Reliable, frequent long-haul services around the country. Not always cheaper than flying.

Car Travel at your own tempo and explore remote areas. Drive on the left.

Air Fast track your holiday: affordable, frequent flights between cities.

Train Slow, expensive and infrequent...but the scenery is great!

For more on **getting around**, see p312 

Plan Your Trip

Hot Spots For...

STRUCTURESXX / SHUTTERSTOCK ©

Beaches

With this much coastline to play with, it's no surprise that daily life for many Australians involves a trip to the beach. Enjoy!

Sydney (p35)
Sydney's fab beaches range from surf-strewn bays to sheltered harbour swim-spots: irresistible!

Bondi Beach
Sydney's biggest, best and most 'braggadocious' (p44).

Byron Bay (p95)
Everyone comes to Byron for the beaches, from wild ocean shores to sheltered sandy nooks.

Watego's Beach
Chill on the sand at hidden Watego's Beach (p100).

Great Ocean Road (p167)
Along Victoria's photogenic Great Ocean Road are a string of amazing surf beaches (bring your wetsuit).

Bells Beach
Enjoy riding Bells' point break – an epic right-hander (p172).

TANYA ANN PHOTOGRAPHY / GETTY IMAGES ©

Islands

Australia has thousands of islands...8222 of them, in fact! From tropical to windswept, there's one waiting for every kind of traveller.

The Whitsundays (p129)
Check yourself into a resort or go sailing around this pristine Queensland archipelago.

Hayman Island
Reigns supreme in the luxe resort scene here (p139).

Southern Reef Islands (p118)
The northern Great Barrier Reef gets all the press, but its southern isles are low-key and lovely.

Lady Musgrave Island
Offers brilliant snorkelling and castaway vibes (p118).

Fremantle (p267)
You could argue that 'Freo' is an island of culture...but a short ferry ride away lies a true island gem.

Rottnest Island
Meet cute quokkas at this endearing holiday haunt (p263).

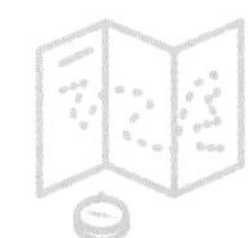

Indigenous Culture

With artefacts dating back more than 50,000 years, Australia's Indigenous culture is ancient, rich and varied.

PARKS AUSTRALIA ©

Uluru-Kata Tjuta National Park (p223)
Much more than big boulders: learn about local Aboriginal mythology, laws, customs and religion.

Cultural Centre
Book an Indigenous guide for a tour of the Rock (p226).

Kakadu National Park (p239)
Discover ancient Aboriginal rock-art galleries and experience 'bush tucker' on an Indigenous-led tour.

Kakadu Rock Art
Visits Kakadu's famous rock-art galleries (p242).

Alice Springs (p233)
Alice is the epicentre for authentic Aboriginal arts from right across central Australia.

Araluen Arts Centre
Excellent galleries and a performance theatre (p233).

Wildlife

From marine mammals to marsupials, birds and reptiles, Australia overflows with native wildlife. Meeting these locals is worth planning your trip around.

HUGH LANSDOWN / SHUTTERSTOCK ©

Great Barrier Reef (p110)
Turtles, dugongs, sharks, manta rays, crabs, eels and unbelievable numbers of tropical fish.

Sealife Spotting
Head out to the reef from Cairns or Port Douglas (p124).

The Daintree Rainforest (p116)
Queensland's tropical Daintree buzzes with birds, frogs, insects, even wandering cassowaries.

Crocodile Spotting
Crocodile Express runs Daintree River tours (p126).

Sydney (p35)
Experience Australia's eccentric wildlife at Sydney's excellent, accessible zoos and aquariums.

Taronga Zoo
This zoo is worth a visit for the ferry ride alone (p55).

Plan Your Trip
Local Life

LEXTER YAP/SHUTTERSTOCK ©

Activities

As Australia's national anthem will melodiously inform you, this land is 'girt by sea'. Surfing, fishing, sailing, diving and snorkelling are what people do here – national pastimes one and all. Marine-mammal-watching trips have also become popular in recent years. Inland there are vast lakes and meandering rivers, offering rafting, canoeing, kayaking and (yet more) fishing opportunities.

Back on dry land, bushwalking (aka hiking) is a major pastime in all Australian states and territories. Cycling is a great way to get around, despite the mammoth distances sometimes involved. There's also skiing in the mountains and wildlife watching pretty much everywhere.

Shopping

Australia's big cities can satisfy most consumer appetites with everything from high-fashion boutiques to secondhand emporia, while many smaller places tend towards speciality retail, be it home-grown produce, antiques or arts and crafts. Markets are a great place to shop – most cities have at least one permanent bazaar.

An Aboriginal artwork or artefact makes an evocative reminder of your trip. The best places to buy artefacts are either directly from the communities that have art-and-craft centres or from galleries and outlets that are owned, operated or supported by Aboriginal communities – the general standard in such places is that the artist receives around half of the proceeds from any sale of their work.

Entertainment

Australia's dynamic and richly varied cultural life is reflected in its entertainment options, which range from epic sporting events and thriving live-music scenes in the major cities to arts festivals, classical music and ballet.

POMINOZ/SHUTTERSTOCK ©

Eating

Australia's culinary scene is almost unrecognisable from a couple of decades ago. Back then, here was a place of simple and largely unimaginative tastes imported from the US and UK, with pasta and pizza the extent of the variety. To see what it once was like, venture to an outback roadhouse and order the special – typically as rich in grease as it is uninspiring in ambition. But just about everywhere else, the country's culinary offerings are filled with flavour and innovation, informed by a commitment to fresh ingredients and bequeathed endless variety by the extraordinary diversity of peoples who have come here from around the world (bringing their recipes with them) and now call Australia home.

Drinking & Nightlife

Australians enjoy a drink almost as much as they like to go out with friends – a winning combination if you're looking for nightlife. Pubs are the reliable workhorses of the drinking-and-nightlife scene, but slick nightclubs and classy wine bars serving craft beers and world-class wines are now as much a part of Australian life as VB or XXXX beer. Venues with great views and/or open-air beer gardens provide the perfect Aussie backdrop to quench your thirst. You'll also find whisky bars here, serving Australian gins and fine whiskies from Tasmania's chilly (and rather Scotland-like) central highlands.

★ Best Eating Experiences

Quay (p59)

Lorne Beach Pavilion (p174)

Attica (p159)

Sounds of Silence (p229)

Templo (p193)

From left: Bushwalking, Blue Mountains (p74); Indigenous dancers, Sydney

Plan Your Trip
Month by Month

January

January yawns into action as Australia recovers from its Christmas hangover. The festival season kicks in with outdoor music festivals; Melbourne hosts the Australian Open tennis. Wet season in the Top End.

Sydney Festival

'It's big' says the promo material. Indeed, this fab affiliation of music, dance, talks, theatre and visual arts is an artistic behemoth (www.sydneyfestival.org.au).

MONA FOMA

In Hobart, MONA FOMA (www.mofo.net.au) is MONA's Festival of Music & Art: it's edgy, progressive and unexpected.

Australia Day

26 January is Australia's 'birthday' (www.australiaday.org.au) – the date when the First Fleet landed in 1788. Australians celebrate with picnics, barbecues, fireworks and, increasingly, nationalistic chest-beating.

February

February is usually Australia's warmest month: hot and sticky up north as the wet season continues, but divine down south.

Adelaide Fringe

Acts that don't make the cut for the more highbrow Adelaide Festival end up in the month-long Fringe (www.adelaidefringe.com.au), second only to Edinburgh's version.

Sydney Gay & Lesbian Mardi Gras

Mardi Gras (www.mardigras.org.au) is a month-long arts festival running deep into March and culminating in a flamboyant parade along Sydney's Oxford St.

☆ Tropfest

The world's largest short-film festival (www.tropfest.org.au) happens in Sydney's west.

Above: Horse racing, Melbourne

March

March is harvest time in Australia's vineyards. Melbourne's streets jam up with the Formula One Grand Prix.

☆ WOMADelaide

This annual festival of world music, arts, food and dance (www.womadelaide.com.au) happens in Adelaide's Botanic Park.

April

Melbourne and the Adelaide Hills are atmospheric as European trees change hue. Up north the rain is abating. Easter means pricey accommodation.

☆ Byron Bay Bluesfest

Music erupts over the Easter weekend (www.bluesfest.com.au) when 20,000 festival goers swamp Byron Bay to hear blues-and-roots bands from all over the world (Ben Harper, Neil Young, Bonnie Raitt...).

★ Best Festivals

MONA FOMA, January

Adelaide Fringe, February

Sydney Gay & Lesbian Mardi Gras, February

Byron Bay Bluesfest, April

Melbourne International Film Festival, July

May

The dry season begins in the Northern Territory, northern Western Australia and Far North Queensland: relief from humidity. A great time to visit Uluru.

Noosa Food & Wine

One of Australia's best regional culinary fests (www.noosafoodandwine.com.au), with cooking demonstrations, wine tastings, feasting and live concerts.

Above: Sydney Gay & Lesbian Mardi Gras

June

Winter begins: snow falls across the Southern Alps ski resorts and football season fills grandstands. Peak season in the tropical north.

July

Pubs with open fires, cosy cafes and empty beaches down south; packed markets, tours and accommodation up north.

☆ Melbourne International Film Festival

Right up there with Toronto and Cannes, MIFF (www.miff.com.au) is wildly popular. Short films, feature-length spectaculars and documentaries flicker across city screens.

August

Southerners, sick of winter's grey-sky drear, head to Queensland for some sun. Last chance (almost) to head to the tropical Top End or outback before things get too hot and wet.

Cairns Festival

This massive art-and-culture fest (www.cairns.qld.gov.au/festival) delivers music, theatre, dance, comedy, film, Indigenous art and public exhibitions.

September

Spring brings rampant wildflower blooms across outback WA and SA. Football finishes and the spring horse-racing carnival begins.

Floriade

A florid display of spring flowers in Canberra (www.floriadeaustralia.com). Locals shake off the winter chills with a look at some blooms.

☆ AFL Grand Final

The pinnacle of the Australian Football League (AFL; www.afl.com.au) season is this high-flying spectacle in Melbourne, watched (on TV) by millions of rabid fans.

October

The weather avoids extremes everywhere: a good time to go camping or to hang out at some vineyards (it's a dirty job, but someone's gotta do it...).

Melbourne Festival

This annual arts festival offers some of the best of opera, theatre, dance and visual arts from around the world (www.melbournefestival.com.au).

November

Northern beaches may close due to 'stingers' – jellyfish – in the shallow waters off north Queensland, the NT and WA. Outdoor events ramp up.

☆ Melbourne Cup

On the first Tuesday in November, Australia's premier horse race chews up the turf in Melbourne (www.melbournecup.com). The whole country pauses to watch the 'race that stops a nation'.

Margaret River Gourmet Escape

The culinary world's heavy hitters descend on Margaret River in WA for four days of culinary inspiration (www.gourmetescape.com.au).

Sculpture by the Sea

The cliff-top trail from Bondi Beach to Tamarama in Sydney transforms into an exquisite sculpture garden (www.sculpturebythesea.com).

December

School's out! Holidays begin two weeks before Christmas. Cities fill with shoppers and the weather hots up.

Sydney to Hobart Yacht Race

The world's most arduous open-ocean yacht race (www.rolexsydneyhobart.com) departs Sydney Harbour on Boxing Day.

Plan Your Trip
Get Inspired

Read

The Narrow Road to the Deep North (Richard Flanagan; 2014) From Hobart to the Thai-Burma Death Railway.

The Bodysurfers (Robert Drewe; 1983) Seductive tales from Sydney's northern beaches.

True History of the Kelly Gang (Peter Carey; 2000) Fictionalised recreation of Australia's favourite bushranger.

The Secret River (Kate Grenville; 2005) Convict life near Sydney in the 19th century.

Dirt Music (Tim Winton; 2002) Guitar-strung Western Australian page-turner.

The Red Highway (Nicholas Rothwell; 2009) A lyrical exploration of Australia's interior.

Watch

Gallipoli (director Peter Weir; 1981) Nationhood in the crucible of WWI.

Lantana (director Ray Lawrence; 2001) A moving meditation on love, truth and grief.

Australia (director Baz Luhrmann; 2008) Over-the-top period romance in northern Australia.

Mad Max (director George Miller; 1979) Mel Gibson gets angry and creates an Aussie legend.

The Hunter (director Daniel Nettheim; 2011) Grumpy Willem Dafoe goes hunting for the last Tasmanian tiger.

Listen

Back in Black (AC/DC; 1980) Classic hard rock from the masters of the genre.

The Rubens (The Rubens; 2012) Croony and catchy; key track 'Lay it Down'.

Internationalist (Powderfinger; 1998) Brisbane's best; key track 'Passenger'.

This is Acting (Sia; 2016) Global star from Adelaide whose 2016 offering includes the worldwide hit 'Cheap Thrills'.

Diesel & Dust (Midnight Oil; 1987) Includes 'Beds Are Burning', an Aboriginal land-rights anthem.

Plan Your Trip
Five-Day Itineraries

Way Out West

Plenty of Australians have never been to Western Australia – it's so far from the east coast it could be another country! Spend five days checking out Perth and Fremantle, with a day-trip ferry ride out to bike and swim on Rottnest Island.

1 Perth (p262) Bright and perky, Perth is an upbeat city a long way from anywhere but perfectly self-contained. 🚗 30 mins to Fremantle

2 Fremantle (p267) 'Freo' is a raffish port town full of musicians, students and artists = good times! ⛴ 30 mins to Rottnest Island

3 Rottnest Island (p263) A ferry jaunt from Fremantle, 'Rotto' is a beautiful car-free isle with a chequered history. Discover hidden beaches on a bike.

Southern Scenic

Culture and coffee; sport and street art – Melbourne is Australia's hippest city. Further south, the scenic Great Ocean Road tracks west – a classic Aussie road trip. Keep driving and you'll hit impressive Adelaide, with world-beating wine regions on tap.

Adelaide (p208) Spend a day in underrated Adelaide, a sassy city with brilliant bars and even better restaurants.

🚗 1 hr to McLaren Vale Wine Region

McLaren Vale Wine Region (p204) Daytrip south of Adelaide to our fave SA wine region: McLaren Vale's Mediterranean-like vineyards produce Australia's best shiraz.

Melbourne (p141) Ride Melbourne's trams between the MCG, jazzy laneway bars, Chinatown and top-flight restaurants.

🚗 1½ hrs to Great Ocean Road

Great Ocean Road (p167) This photogenic surf-coast route passes tall forests, beach towns and amazing rock formations – allow two days.

🚗 6½ hrs to Adelaide

Plan Your Trip
10-Day Itinerary

Cities Big & Small

Over 10 days you can experience the best of Sydney, Australia's brightest big city, and the gorgeous Blue Mountains. Short flights away are two of Australia's most beguiling small cities – Canberra and Hobart – with the arts and history at the fore.

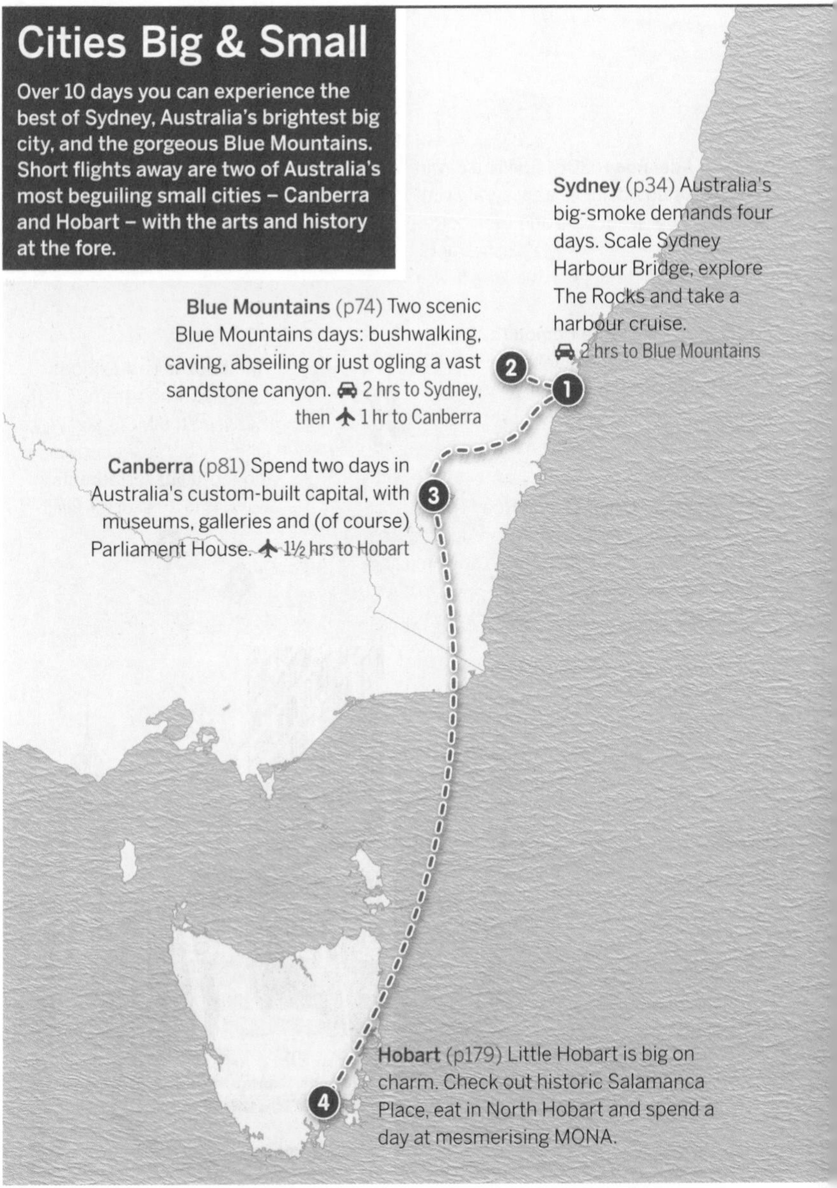

1 Sydney (p34) Australia's big-smoke demands four days. Scale Sydney Harbour Bridge, explore The Rocks and take a harbour cruise. 🚗 2 hrs to Blue Mountains

2 Blue Mountains (p74) Two scenic Blue Mountains days: bushwalking, caving, abseiling or just ogling a vast sandstone canyon. 🚗 2 hrs to Sydney, then ✈ 1 hr to Canberra

3 Canberra (p81) Spend two days in Australia's custom-built capital, with museums, galleries and (of course) Parliament House. ✈ 1½ hrs to Hobart

4 Hobart (p179) Little Hobart is big on charm. Check out historic Salamanca Place, eat in North Hobart and spend a day at mesmerising MONA.

FROM LEFT: DAVIDF/GETTY IMAGES ©, M LETSCHERT/SHUTTERSTOCK ©, PHILLIP MINNIS/SHUTTERSTOCK ©

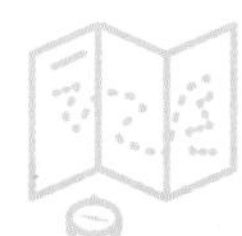

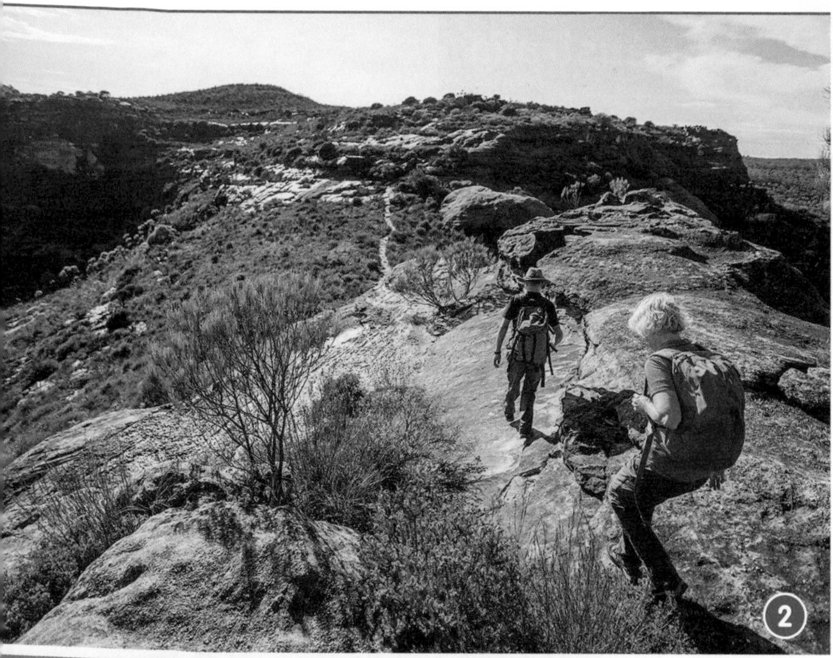

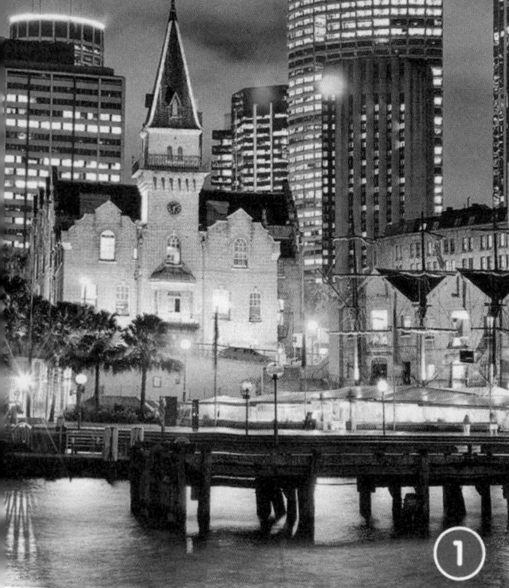

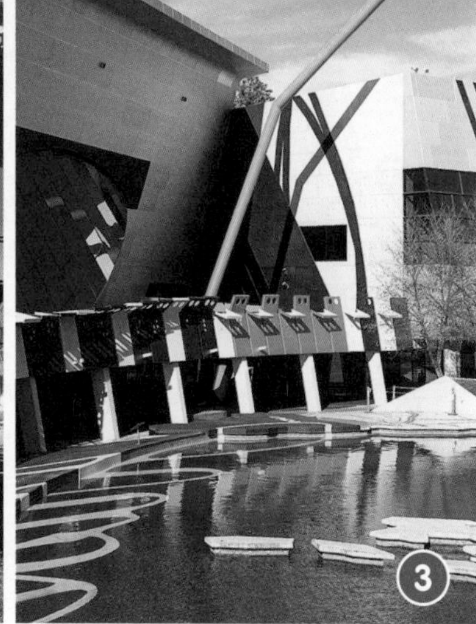

Plan Your Trip
Two Week Itinerary

Best of Australia

Two weeks to explore one of the largest countries on the planet will never be enough, but if you plan carefully and don't mind flying, you can get a taste of Australia's greatest hits: the reef, the rock, the wildlife and the big-city lights.

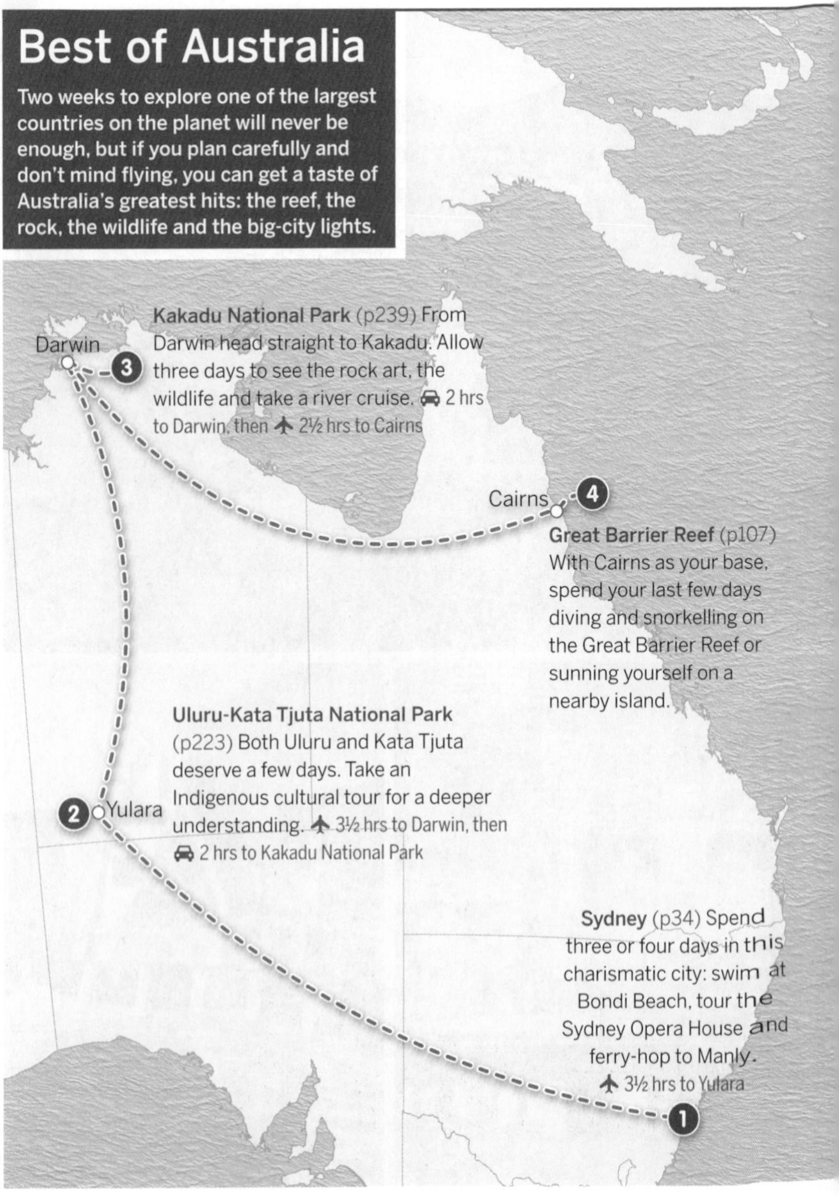

Darwin

3 **Kakadu National Park** (p239) From Darwin head straight to Kakadu. Allow three days to see the rock art, the wildlife and take a river cruise. 2 hrs to Darwin, then 2½ hrs to Cairns

Cairns

4 **Great Barrier Reef** (p107) With Cairns as your base, spend your last few days diving and snorkelling on the Great Barrier Reef or sunning yourself on a nearby island.

Yulara

2 **Uluru-Kata Tjuta National Park** (p223) Both Uluru and Kata Tjuta deserve a few days. Take an Indigenous cultural tour for a deeper understanding. 3½ hrs to Darwin, then 2 hrs to Kakadu National Park

1 **Sydney** (p34) Spend three or four days in this charismatic city: swim at Bondi Beach, tour the Sydney Opera House and ferry-hop to Manly. 3½ hrs to Yulara

4

3

2

FROM LEFT: JEFF HUNTER/GETTY IMAGES ©, PARKS AUSTRALIA ©, MAURIZIO DE MATTEI/SHUTTERSTOCK ©

Plan Your Trip
Family Travel

OLGA KASHUBIN/SHUTTERSTOCK ©

Australia for Kids

Don't underestimate the vast distances in Australia: the open road may be just the tonic for stressed-out parents, but it's probably not numero uno on the kids' hit list. Australia's cities, however, abound with attractions designed for bright young minds and bodies of boundless energy: museums, zoos, aquariums, interactive technology centres, amusement parks...

Lonely Planet's *Travel with Children* contains a wealth of useful information, hints and tips.

Sleeping & Eating

Top-end hotels and many (but not all) midrange hotels cater for children. B&Bs, however, often market themselves as sanctuaries from all things child related.

Dining with children in Australia is relatively easy. At all but the flashiest places children are commonly seen. Kids are usually more than welcome at cafes, while bistros and clubs often see families dining early. Many fine-dining restaurants discourage small children (assuming that they're all ill-behaved).

Most places that do welcome children don't have kids' menus, and those that do usually offer everything straight from the deep fryer – crumbed chicken and chips etc. You might be best finding something on the normal menu (say a pasta or salad) and asking the kitchen to adapt it to your child's needs.

Medical & Safety

Australia has high-standard medical services and facilities: items such as baby formula and disposable nappies are widely available.

Major hire-car companies will supply and fit child safety seats, charging a one-off fee of around $25 or a per-day rate. Call taxi companies in advance to organise child safety seats. The rules for travelling in taxis with kids vary from state to state: in most places safety seats aren't legally required, but must be used if available.

MARTIN VALIGURSKY/SHUTTERSTOCK ©

Change Facilities & Babysitters

Most shopping centres and all cities and major towns have public baby change facilities; ask the local tourist office or city council for details. It is your legal right to publicly breastfeed anywhere in Australia.

If you want to leave Junior behind for a few hours, many of Australia's licensed childcare agencies offer casual care. Search for 'Baby Sitters' and 'Child Care Centres' in the online *Yellow Pages*, or contact the local council for listings.

Kids' Discounts

Child and family concessions often apply to accommodation, tours, admission fees and transport, with discounts as high as 50% off the adult rate. However, the definition of 'child' varies from under 12 to under 18 years. Accommodation concessions generally apply to children under 12 years sharing the same room as adults. On the major airlines, infants travel free provided they don't occupy a seat – child fares usually apply between the ages of two and 11 years.

★ Best for Kids

Sydney Sea Life Aquarium (p52)

AFL footy at the Melbourne Cricket Ground (p148)

Territory Wildlife Park (p249)

Salamanca Market (p185)

Taronga Zoo (p55)

From left: Taronga Zoo (p55), Sydney; Gold Coast, Queensland

Sydney Opera House (p38)
Royal Botanic Garden (p48)

Bondi Icebergs Pool (p45)

Arriving in Sydney

Sydney Airport (p70) Most visitors arrive at the international airport, 10km south of the city centre. Airport shuttles ($20), taxis ($55) and trains (around $16) head into the city.

Central Station (p71) Interstate trains arrive at this hub in the CBD.

Sydney Coach Terminal (p70) Long-haul buses arrive at this terminal adjacent to Central Station.

Where to Stay

Your choice of neighbourhood will inform the tone of your Sydney experience. Circular Quay, the Rocks and the city centre have famous sights and myriad eating and drinking options. Surry Hills and Darlinghurst are much hipper, with fab bars and gay clubs. Glebe and Newtown are grungier and bookish, while Bondi and the beach 'burbs are backpacker/surfer central. For more information on the best neighbourhoods to stay, see p73.

Sydney Opera House

Come face to face with Sydney's number-one symbol. On a sunny day it's postcard-perfect, its curves a pinnacle of architectural expression.

Great For...

☑ Don't Miss

Catch a show: take a glass of bubbles outside during interval and admire the harbour.

Design & Construction

Danish architect Jørn Utzon's competition-winning 1956 design is Australia's most recognisable visual image. It's said to have been inspired by billowing sails, orange segments, palm fronds and Mayan temples, and has been poetically likened to nuns in a rugby scrum, a typewriter stuffed with scallop shells and the sexual congress of turtles. It's not until you get close that you realise that the seemingly solid expanse of white is actually composed of tiles – 1,056,000 self-cleaning cream-coloured Swedish tiles, to be exact.

The Opera House's construction was itself truly operatic – so much so, it was dramatised as *The Eighth Wonder*, performed here by Opera Australia in 1995. The predicted four-year construction started in 1959. After a tumultuous clash

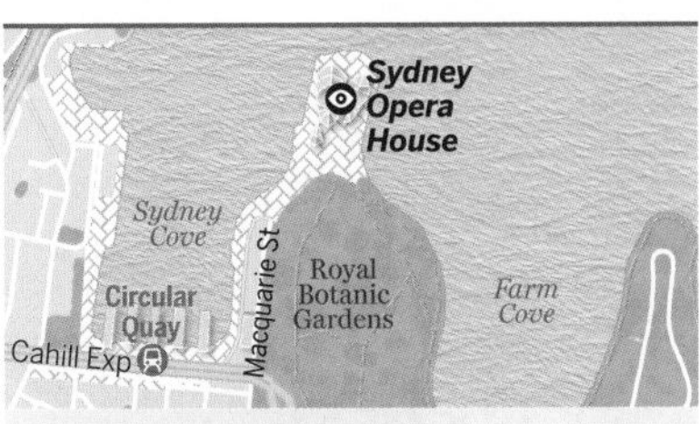

of egos, delays, politicking, death and cost blow-outs, Utzon quit in disgust in 1966. The Opera House finally opened in 1973. Utzon and his son Jan were commissioned for renovations in 2004, but Utzon died in 2008 having never seen his finished masterpiece in the flesh.

Tours

One-hour guided tours depart throughout the day: you're more likely to see everything if you go early (some spaces close for rehearsals). A highlight is the **Utzon Room**, the only part of the Opera House to have an interior designed by the great man himself. The two-hour 7am backstage tour ($165) includes the Green Room, stars' dressing rooms, stage and orchestra pit.

Need to Know

Map p50; 02-9250 7777; www.sydneyopera house.com; Bennelong Point; tours adult/child $37/20; tours 9am-5pm; Circular Quay

Take a Break

Opera Bar (p65) has the best views in the business.

★ Top Tip

Most events (more than 2400 of them annually!) sell out quickly, but partial-view tickets are often available on short notice.

Performances

Inside, dance, concerts, opera and theatre are staged in the **Concert Hall**, **Joan Sutherland Theatre**, **Drama Theatre** and **Playhouse**, while more intimate and left-of-centre shows inhabit the **Studio**. Companies regularly performing here include the following:

Australian Ballet (1300 369 741; www.australianballet.com.au; tickets $39-289)

Australian Chamber Orchestra (02-8274 3888; www.aco.com.au; tickets $46-127)

Bangarra Dance Theatre (Map p50; 02-9251 5333; www.bangarra.com.au; Pier 4/5, 15 Hickson Rd; 324, 325, 998, Circular Quay)

Opera Australia (02-9318 8200; www.opera-australia.org.au; Sydney Opera House; tickets $49-199; Circular Quay)

Sydney Symphony Orchestra (02-8215 4600; www.sydneysymphony.com)

Sydney Theatre Company (p69)

Check the free monthly *What's On* brochure for upcoming events, including *Kids at the House* for children's entertainment.

BridgeClimb

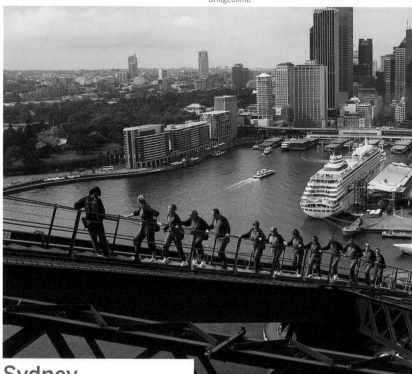

GREG ELMS/GETTY IMAGES ©

Sydney Harbour Bridge

Sydney's second-most-loved construction embodies both practicality and beauty. Views from the big steel rainbow are sublime, whether you're on foot or on a BridgeClimb.

Great For...

☑ Don't Miss

Walking across the 'coathanger' north to south, with Opera House views.

The Structure

At 134m high, 1149m long, 49m wide and 52,800 tonnes, the Sydney Harbour Bridge is the world's largest and heaviest (but not longest) steel arch. It links the Rocks with North Sydney, crossing the harbour at a narrow point.

The two halves of chief engineer JJC Bradfield's mighty arch were built outwards from each shore. In 1930, after seven years of merciless toil by 1400 workers, the two arches were centimetres apart when 100km/h winds set them swaying. The 'coathanger' hung tough, and the bridge finally opened to the public two years later.

The bridge is the centrepiece of Sydney's major celebrations, particularly the New Year's Eve fireworks.

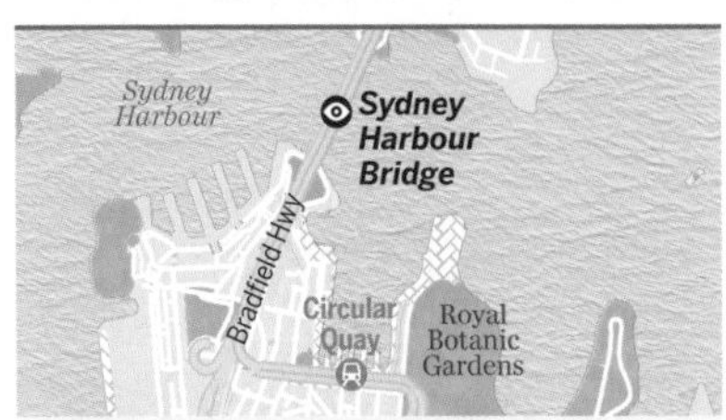

Need to Know

Map p50; Circular Quay

Take a Break

Try the rooftop at the Glenmore (p65) pub for a post-bridge beverage.

Top Tip

Vertigo? The track over the arch is wide enough for you to never see straight down.

BridgeClimb

Once only painters and daredevils scaled the Harbour Bridge – now anyone can do it. Make your way through the **BridgeClimb** (Map p50; 02-8274 7777; www.bridgeclimb.com; 3 Cumberland St; adult $248-383, child $168-273) departure lounge and the extensive training session, don your headset, an umbilical safety cord and a dandy grey jumpsuit and up you go.

Tours last 2¼ to 3½ hours – a preclimb toilet stop is a smart idea. If you're uncertain whether your nerve or bladder will hold that long, a 90-minute sampler is available but it only goes halfway and never reaches the summit. The priciest climbs are at dawn and sunset.

Crossing on Foot

The best way to experience the bridge is on foot – don't expect much of a view crossing by train or car (driving south there's a toll). Staircases access the bridge from both shores; a footpath runs along its eastern side and a cycleway along the west.

Pylon Lookout

The bridge's hefty pylons may look as though they're shouldering all the weight, but they're largely decorative – right down to their granite facing. There are awesome views from the top of the **Pylon Lookout** (Map p50; 02-9240 1100; www.pylonlookout.com.au; adult/child $15/10; 10am-5pm), atop the southeast pylon, 200 steps above the bridge's footpath. Inside the pylon there are exhibits about the bridge's construction, including an eight-minute film which screens every 15 minutes.

Sydney Harbour

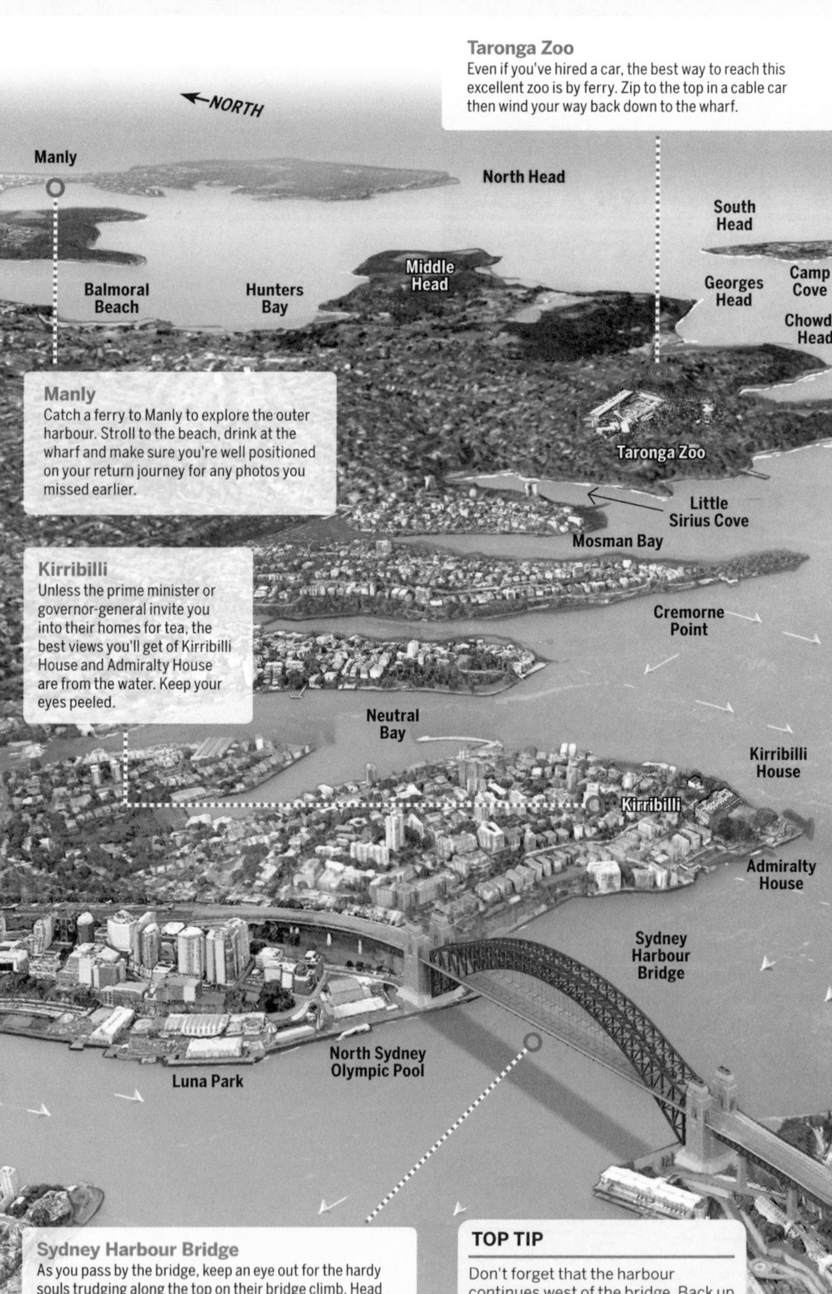
Taronga Zoo
Even if you've hired a car, the best way to reach this excellent zoo is by ferry. Zip to the top in a cable car then wind your way back down to the wharf.
NORTH
Manly
North Head
South Head
Middle Head
Balmoral Beach
Hunters Bay
Georges Head
Camp Cove
Chowder Head
Manly
Catch a ferry to Manly to explore the outer harbour. Stroll to the beach, drink at the wharf and make sure you're well positioned on your return journey for any photos you missed earlier.
Taronga Zoo
Little Sirius Cove
Mosman Bay
Kirribilli
Unless the prime minister or governor-general invite you into their homes for tea, the best views you'll get of Kirribilli House and Admiralty House are from the water. Keep your eyes peeled.
Cremorne Point
Neutral Bay
Kirribilli House
Kirribilli
Admiralty House
Sydney Harbour Bridge
North Sydney Olympic Pool
Luna Park
Sydney Harbour Bridge
As you pass by the bridge, keep an eye out for the hardy souls trudging along the top on their bridge climb. Head here at sunrise or sunset for golden harbour views.
TOP TIP
Don't forget that the harbour continues west of the bridge. Back up a Manly trip with a river ferry service.

Watsons Bay
Imagine Watsons Bay as the isolated fishing village it once was as you pull into its sheltered wharf. Stroll around South Head for views up the harbour and over ocean-battered cliffs.
Fort Denison
Known as Pinchgut, this fortified speck was once a place of fearsome punishment. The bodies of executed convicts were left to hang here as a grisly warning to all; the local Aborigines were horrified.
DINOZZAVER/SHUTTERSTOCK ©
FERRIES
Circular Quay is the hub for state-run Sydney Ferries; nine separate routes leave from here, journeying to 38 different wharves.
Watsons Bay
Vaucluse Bay
Shark Bay
Macquarie Lighthouse
Rose Bay
Bradleys Head
Shark Island
Point Piper
Double Bay
Darling Point
Clark Island
Garden Island
Naval Base
Elizabeth Bay
Fort Denison
Mrs Macquaries Point
Potts Point
Woolloomooloo Finger Wharf
Government House
Sydney Opera House
Farm Cove
Royal Botanic Garden
Circular Quay
The Rocks
Sydney Opera House
You can clamber all over it and walk around it, but nothing beats the perspective you get as your ferry glides past the Opera House's dazzling sails. Have your camera at the ready.
Circular Quay
Circular Quay has been at the centre of Sydney life since the First Fleet dropped anchor here in 1788. Book your ferry ticket, check the indicator boards for the correct pier and get on board.

Bondi Icebergs Pool

Bondi Beach

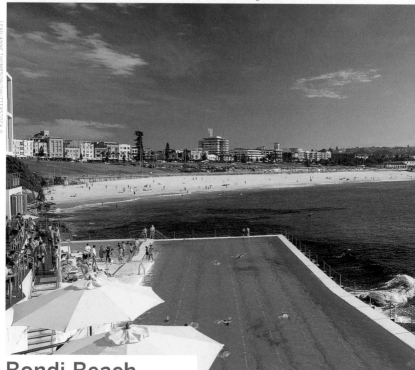

Definitively Sydney, Bondi is one of the world's great beaches: ocean and land collide, the Pacific arrives in great foaming swells and all people are equal, as democratic as sand.

Great For...

☑ **Don't Miss**

A quick dip in the Bondi Icebergs Pool

A Day at the Beach

Bondi is the closest ocean beach to the city centre (8km away), has consistently good (though crowded) waves, and is great for a rough-and-tumble swim. Surfers carve up sandbar breaks at either end of the beach. Two surf clubs – Bondi and North Bondi – patrol the water between sets of red-and-yellow flags, positioned to avoid the worst rips and holes. Thousands of unfortunates have to be rescued from the surf each year (enough to make a TV show about it) – don't become a statistic! If the sea's angry or you have small children in tow, try the saltwater sea baths at either end of the beach.

North Bondi is a great place to learn to surf, and well-established surf school **Let's Go Surfing** (☎02-9365 1800; www.letsgosurfing.com.au; 128 Ramsgate Ave,

Bondi; board & wetsuit hire 1hr/2hr/day/week $25/30/50/200; 9am-5pm) offers lessons catering to practically everyone. There are classes for grommets aged seven to 16 (1½ hours, $49) and adults (two hours, $110; women-only classes available), or you can book a private tutor (1½ hours, $195/284 for one/two people). Prices drop outside summer.

Prefer wheels to fins? There's a **skate ramp** (Queen Elizabeth Dr) at the beach's southern end. If posing in your budgie smugglers (Speedos) isn't having enough impact, there's an outdoor **workout area** (Queen Elizabeth Dr) FREE near the North Bondi Surf Club. Coincidentally (or perhaps not), this is the part of the beach where the gay guys hang out.

Need to Know

Campbell Pde, Bondi Beach; 333, 380-2

Take a Break

Grab a delicious bagel from Lox, Stock & Barrel (p64).

Top Tip

Swim between the red-and-yellow flags, indicating safe sections of beach patrolled by lifeguards.

What's Nearby?

Bondi Pavilion Notable Building

(www.waverley.nsw.gov.au; Queen Elizabeth Dr; 9am-5pm) FREE Built in the Mediterranean Georgian Revival style in 1929, 'The Pav' is more a cultural centre than a changing shed. There's a free art gallery upstairs, a theatre out the back and various cafes and a bar lining the ocean frontage.

Bronte Beach Beach

(Bronte Rd, Bronte; 378) A winning family-oriented beach hemmed in by sandstone cliffs and a grassy park, Bronte lays claim to the title of the oldest surf lifesaving club in the world (1903).

Bondi Icebergs Pool Swimming

(02-9130 4804; www.icebergs.com.au; 1 Notts Ave; adult/child $6.50/4.50; 6am-6.30pm Mon-Wed & Fri, 6.30am-6.30pm Sat & Sun) Sydney's most famous pool commands the best view in Bondi and has a cute little cafe. It's a saltwater pool that's regularly doused by the bigger breakers. There's a more sheltered pool for kids.

Bondi to Coogee Clifftop Trail

Sydney's most scenic walk, this sublime coastal path is a must. Both ends are serviced by bus routes, and there are plenty of places to eat and swim en route.

Start Bondi Beach
Distance 6km
Duration Three hours

2 Small but perfectly formed, **Tamarama Beach** has a deep reach of sand, totally disproportionate to its width.

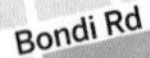

3 Descend from the clifftops onto **Bronte Beach** (p45) and take a dip, or head to a cafe for a caffeine hit.

Take a Break...
The best lunch option is Bronte's **Three Blue Ducks** (p64).

6 Beyond Cliffbrook Pde, take the steps down to **Gordons Bay**, one of Sydney's best dive spots.

Alison Rd

Alison Rd

Randwick Racecourse

7 The trail ends on glorious **Coogee Beach**. Swagger up to the rooftop of the **Coogee Pavilion** and toast your efforts.

N 0 — 1 km
0 — 0.5 miles

Curlewis St
Bondi Park
NORTH BONDI
Campbell Pde
Hall St
BONDI BEACH
Bondi Bay
Francis St
Notts Ave
Bondi Rd
BONDI
Sandridge St
Mackenzies Bay
Tamarama Park
TAMARAMA
Tamarama Bay
Hewlett St
Bronte Park
Bronte Rd
BRONTE
Macpherson St
Three Blue Ducks
Boundary St E
CLOVELLY
Burrows Park
Clovelly Rd
Gordons Bay
Moore St
COOGEE
Arden St
Coogee Bay Rd
Coogee Bay
Wedding Cake Island
SOUTH PACIFIC OCEAN

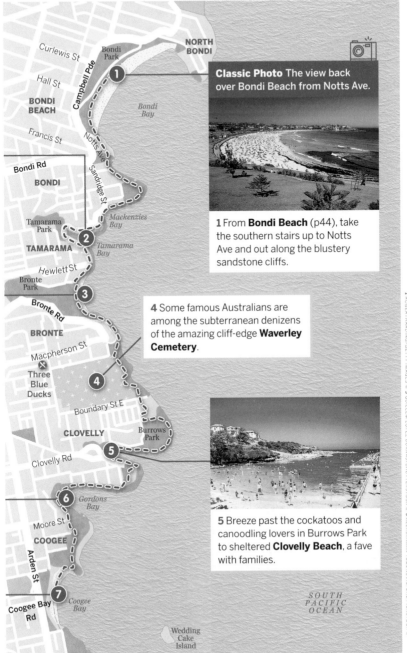

Classic Photo The view back over Bondi Beach from Notts Ave.

1 From **Bondi Beach** (p44), take the southern stairs up to Notts Ave and out along the blustery sandstone cliffs.

4 Some famous Australians are among the subterranean denizens of the amazing cliff-edge **Waverley Cemetery**.

5 Breeze past the cockatoos and canoodling lovers in Burrows Park to sheltered **Clovelly Beach**, a fave with families.

SIGHTS

Circular Quay & the Rocks

Join the tourist pilgrimage to the Opera House and Harbour Bridge then grab a schooner at a convict-era pub in the Rocks.

Royal Botanic Garden Gardens

(Map p50; 02-9231 8111; www.rbgsyd.nsw.gov.au; Mrs Macquaries Rd; 7am-dusk; Circular Quay) FREE These expansive gardens are the city's favourite picnic destination, jogging route and snuggling spot. Bordering Farm Cove, east of the Opera House, the gardens were established in 1816 and feature plant life from Australia and around the world.

Museum of Contemporary Art Gallery

(MCA; Map p50; 02-9245 2400; www.mca.com.au; 140 George St; 10am-5pm Fri-Wed, to 9pm Thu; Circular Quay) FREE By the harbour, the MCA is a showcase for Australian and international contemporary art, with a rotating permanent collection and temporary exhibitions. The Gotham City–style art deco building has had a modern gallery space grafted on to it, the highlight of which is the rooftop cafe. Free guided tours daily.

Rocks Discovery Museum Museum

(Map p50; 02-9240 8680; www.therocks.com; Kendall Lane; 10am-5pm; Circular Quay) FREE Divided into four chronological displays – Warrane (pre-1788), Colony (1788–1820), Port (1820–1900) and Transformations (1900 to the present) – this small, excellent museum tucked away down a Rocks laneway digs deep into the area's history and leads you on an artefact-rich tour.

Sydney Observatory Observatory

(Map p50; 02-9217 0111; www.maas.museum/sydney-observatory; 1003 Upper Fort St; 10am-5pm; Circular Quay) FREE Built in the 1850s, Sydney's copper-domed, Italianate sandstone observatory squats atop pretty **Observatory Hill**, overlooking the harbour. Inside is a collection of vintage apparatus, including Australia's oldest working telescope (1874). Also on offer are entertaining tours (adult/child $10/8), which include a planetarium show.

From left: Royal Botanic Garden; Sydney Observatory; Sydney Tower Eye (p51); Chinatown (p51)

LEONID ANDRONOV/SHUTTERSTOCK ©

GORDON BELL/SHUTTERSTOCK ©

City Centre

Sydney's CBD features gracious colonial buildings scattered among the skyscrapers, with orderly parks providing breathing space. Rambunctious Haymarket and Chinatown are here too.

Art Gallery of NSW Gallery

(Map p54; ☎1800 679 278; www.artgallery.nsw.gov.au; Art Gallery Rd; ⏲10am-5pm Thu-Tue, to 10pm Wed; 📶; 🚌441; 🚉St James) **FREE** With its neoclassical Greek frontage and modern rear end, this much-loved institution plays a prominent and gregarious role in Sydney society. Blockbuster international touring exhibitions arrive regularly and there's an outstanding permanent collection of Australian art, including a substantial Indigenous section. Free guided tours.

Hyde Park Barracks Museum Museum

(Map p50; ☎02-8239 2311; www.sydneylivingmuseums.com.au; Queens Sq, Macquarie St; adult/child $12/8; ⏲10am-5pm; 🚉St James) Convict architect Francis Greenway designed this squarish, decorously Georgian structure (1819) as convict quarters. Fifty thousand men and boys sentenced to transportation passed through here in

Sydney for Kids

Organised kids' activities ramp up during school holidays (December/January, April, July and September); check www.sydneyforkids.com.au, www.ellaslist.com.au and www.childmags.com.au for listings.

Most kids love the Sydney Sea Life Aquarium (p52), Wild Life Sydney Zoo (p52) and Australian National Maritime Museum (p52) at Darling Harbour, and the Powerhouse Museum (p52) in neighbouring Ultimo. Also worth investigating are the 'Tours for Tots' and 'Gallery Kids Sunday Performance' at the Art Gallery of NSW (p49) – details are on the gallery's website.

Elsewhere, Taronga Zoo (p55) and Luna Park (p56) are sure to please. Or just take them to the beach!

CHAMELEONSEYEL/SHUTTERSTOCK ©

TOOYKRUB/SHUTTERSTOCK ©

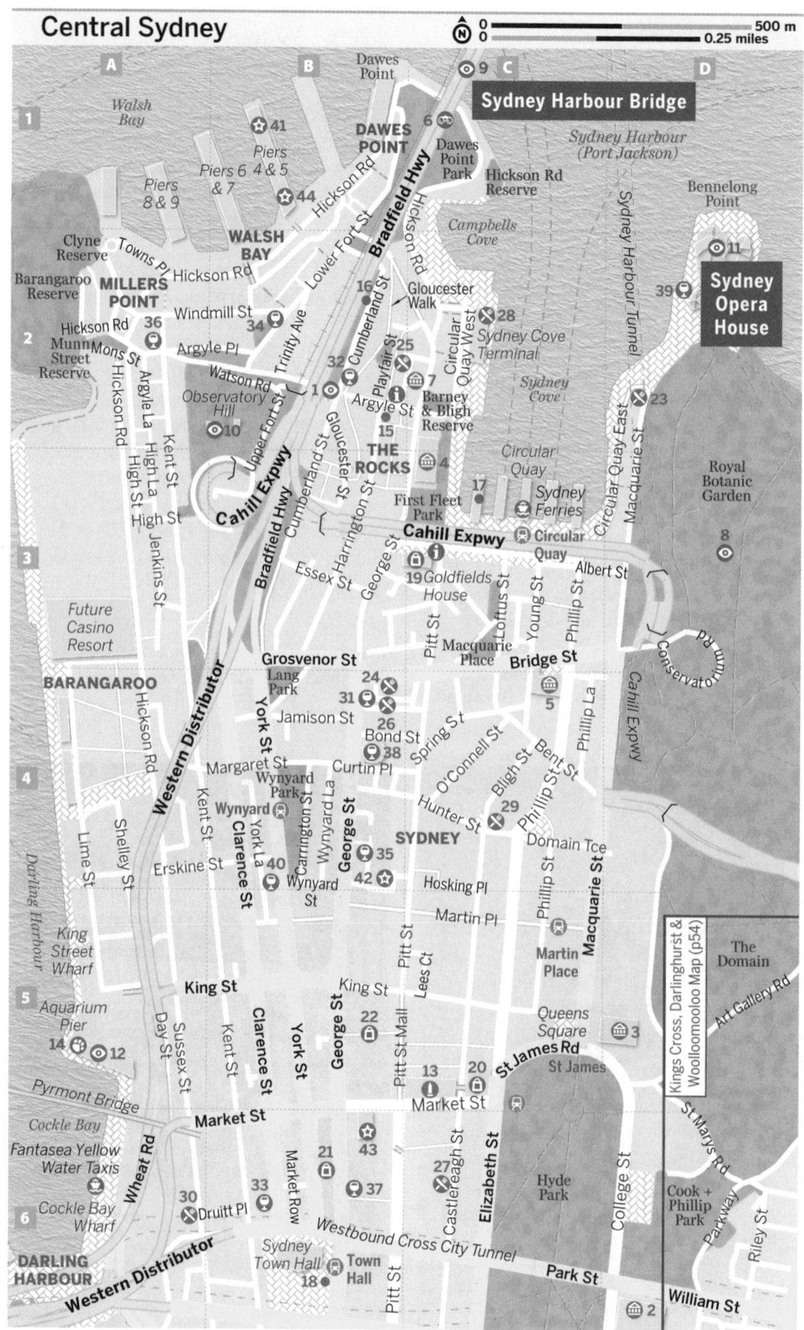
Central Sydney
500 m
0.25 miles
Sydney Harbour Bridge
Sydney Opera House
Walsh Bay
Dawes Point
DAWES POINT
Piers 4 & 5
Piers 6 & 7
Piers 8 & 9
WALSH BAY
MILLERS POINT
Clyne Reserve
Barangaroo Reserve
Munn Street Reserve
Observatory Hill
THE ROCKS
Dawes Point Park
Hickson Rd Reserve
Campbells Cove
Sydney Harbour (Port Jackson)
Bennelong Point
Sydney Cove Terminal
Sydney Cove
Circular Quay
Barney & Bligh Reserve
First Fleet Park
Sydney Ferries
Circular Quay
Royal Botanic Garden
Goldfields House
Macquarie Place
Lang Park
Future Casino Resort
BARANGAROO
Wynyard Park
Wynyard
SYDNEY
Martin Place
Queens Square
St James
Darling Harbour
King Street Wharf
Aquarium Pier
Pyrmont Bridge
Cockle Bay
Fantasea Yellow Water Taxis
Cockle Bay Wharf
DARLING HARBOUR
Sydney Town Hall
Town Hall
Hyde Park
The Domain
Cook + Phillip Park
Kings Cross, Darlinghurst & Woolloomooloo Map (p54)
Hickson Rd
Towns Pl
Windmill St
Argyle Pl
Mons St
Watson Rd
Lower Fort St
Upper Fort St
Trinity Ave
Bradfield Hwy
Cahill Expwy
Cumberland St
Gloucester Walk
Gloucester St
Playfair St
Argyle St
Harrington St
George St
Essex St
Kent St
High St
High La
Argyle La
Jenkins St
Circular Quay West
Circular Quay East
Sydney Harbour Tunnel
Macquarie St
Albert St
Loftus St
Young St
Phillip St
Pitt St
Bridge St
Conservatorium Rd
Grosvenor St
Western Distributor
York St
Jamison St
Bond St
Spring St
O'Connell St
Bligh St
Bent St
Phillip La
Margaret St
Curtin Pl
Hunter St
Domain Tce
Carrington St
Wynyard La
York La
Clarence St
Erskine St
Wynyard St
Hosking Pl
Martin Pl
Lime St
Shelley St
King St
Lees Ct
Day St
Sussex St
Pitt St Mall
St James Rd
Market St
Art Gallery Rd
St Marys Rd
Wheat Rd
Market Row
Castlereagh St
Elizabeth St
College St
Druitt Pl
Westbound Cross City Tunnel
Park St
William St
Parkway
Riley St
A
B
C
D
1
2
3
4
5
6

Central Sydney

Sights

1	Argyle Cut	B2
2	Australian Museum	D6
3	Hyde Park Barracks Museum	D5
4	Museum of Contemporary Art	C3
5	Museum of Sydney	C4
6	Pylon Lookout	C1
7	Rocks Discovery Museum	C2
8	Royal Botanic Garden	D3
9	Sydney Harbour Bridge	C1
10	Sydney Observatory	B2
11	Sydney Opera House	D2
12	Sydney Sea Life Aquarium	A5
13	Sydney Tower Eye	C5
14	Wild Life Sydney Zoo	A5

Activities, Courses & Tours

15	Bonza Bike Tours	B2
16	BridgeClimb	B2
17	Captain Cook Cruises	C3
18	I'm Free	B6

Shopping

19	Australian Wine Centre	C3
20	David Jones	C5
21	Queen Victoria Building	B6
22	Strand Arcade	B5

Eating

23	Aria	D2
24	Eleven Bridge	B4
25	Fine Food Store	B2
26	Mr Wong	B4
27	Pablo & Rusty's	C6
28	Quay	C2
29	Rockpool Bar & Grill	C4
30	Sepia	A6
	Spice Temple	(see 29)

Drinking & Nightlife

31	Establishment	B4
32	Glenmore	B2
33	Grandma's	B6
34	Hero of Waterloo	B2
35	Ivy	B4
36	Lord Nelson Brewery Hotel	A2
37	Marble Bar	B6
38	O Bar	B4
39	Opera Bar	D2
40	Uncle Ming's	B4

Entertainment

41	Bangarra Dance Theatre	B1
42	City Recital Hall	B4
43	State Theatre	B6
44	Sydney Theatre Company	B1

30 years. It later became an immigration depot, a women's asylum and a law court. These days it's a fascinating museum.

Museum of Sydney Museum

(MoS; Map p50; ☎02-9251 5988; www.sydneylivingmuseums.com.au; cnr Phillip & Bridge Sts; adult/child $12/8; ⏰10am-5pm; 📶; 🚆Circular Quay) Built on the site of Sydney's first Government House, the MoS is a fragmented, storytelling museum, which uses installations to explore the city's history. The area's long Indigenous past is highlighted, while key figures in Sydney's planning and architecture are brought to life.

Sydney Tower Eye Tower

(Map p50; ☎1800 258 693; www.sydneytowereye.com.au; level 5, Westfield Sydney, 188 Pitt St; adult/child $26.50/17, Skywalk $70/49; ⏰9am-9.30pm May-Sep, to 10pm Oct-Apr; 🚆St James) The 309m-tall Sydney Tower (1981) offers unbeatable 360-degree views from the observation level 250m up – and even better ones for the daredevils braving the Skywalk on its roof.

Chinatown Area

(www.sydney-chinatown.info; 🚊Paddy's Markets, 🚆Town Hall) With a discordant soundtrack of blaring Canto pop, Dixon St is the heart of Chinatown: a narrow, shady pedestrian mall with a string of restaurants and insistent spruikers. It's a fabulous eating district, which effectively extends for several blocks north and south of here, and segues into Koreatown and Thaitown to the east.

Darling Harbour & Pymont

Dotted between the flyovers and fountains of Sydney's purpose-built tourist hub are some of the city's highest-profile attractions. In Pyrmont, on the harbour's western shore, the Star casino complex has had an expensive do-over.

LEMBIBUCHANAN/GETTY IMAGES ©

From left: Sydney Sea Life Aquarium; Australian National Maritime Museum; Sydney Fish Market

MEZAIRI/SHUTTERSTOCK ©

Wild Life Sydney Zoo Zoo

(Map p50; ☎02-9333 9245; www.wildlifesydney.com.au; Aquarium Pier; adult/child $40/28; ⏰9.30am-5pm Apr-Sep, to 7pm Oct-Mar, last entry 1hr before closing; 🚆Town Hall) Complementing its sister and neighbour, Sea Life, this large complex houses an impressive collection of Australian native reptiles, butterflies, spiders, snakes and mammals (including kangaroos and koalas). The nocturnal section is particularly good.

Sydney Sea Life Aquarium Aquarium

(Map p50; ☎02-8251 7800; www.sydneyaquarium.com.au; Aquarium Pier; adult/child $40/28; ⏰9.30am-6pm Mon-Thu, to 7pm Fri-Sun & school holidays, last entry 1hr earlier; 🚆Town Hall) As well as regular wall-mounted tanks and ground-level enclosures, this impressive complex has two large pools that you can walk through, safely enclosed in Perspex tunnels, as an intimidating array of sharks and rays pass overhead. Other highlights include clownfish (howdy Nemo), platypuses, moon jellyfish (in a disco-lit tube), sea dragons and the swoon-worthy finale: the two-million-litre Great Barrier Reef tank.

Australian National Maritime Museum Museum

(☎02-9298 3777; www.anmm.gov.au; 2 Murray St; permanent collection free, temporary exhibitions adult/child $20/free; ⏰9.30am-5pm, to 6pm Jan; 🚊Pyrmont Bay) FREE Beneath a soaring roof, the Maritime Museum sails through Australia's inextricable relationship with the sea. Exhibitions range from Indigenous canoes to surf culture, immigration to the navy. Excellent free guided tours.

Powerhouse Museum Museum

(Museum of Applied Arts & Sciences, MAAS; ☎02-9217 0111; www.powerhousemuseum.com; 500 Harris St, Ultimo; adult/child $15/8; ⏰10am-5pm; 📶; 🚊Exhibition Centre) A short walk from Darling Harbour, this cavernous science and design museum whirs away inside the former power station for Sydney's defunct, original tram network. The collection and temporary exhibitions cover everything from robots and life on Mars to steam trains to climate change to atoms to

KOBOZAA/SHUTTERSTOCK ©

fashion, industrial design and avant-garde art installations.

Sydney Fish Market Market
(☎02-9004 1108; www.sydneyfishmarket.com.au; Bank St; ⏰7am-4pm; Fish Market) This piscatorial precinct on Blackwattle Bay shifts over 15 million kilograms of seafood annually, and has retail outlets, restaurants, a sushi bar, an oyster bar, and a highly regarded cooking school. Check it out on a behind-the-scenes tour (adult/child $35/10).

Surry Hills & Darlinghurst

Surry Hills is liberally scattered with corner pubs, fantastic eateries and quirky cafes and bars. Neighbouring Darlinghurst is synonymous with Sydney's gay community: the lower end of Oxford St is home to most of the city's gay bars.

Australian Museum Museum
(Map p50; ☎02-9320 6000; www.australianmuseum.net.au; 6 College St, Darlinghurst; adult/child $15/free; ⏰9.30am-5pm; ; Museum) Under an ongoing process of modernisation,

Kings Cross

Crowned by a huge illuminated **Coca-Cola Sign** (Map p54; Darlinghurst Rd; Kings Cross), the 'Cross' has long been the home of Sydney vice. Although once home to grand estates and stylish apartments, the suburb underwent a radical change in the 1930s, when wine-soaked intellectuals, artists and ne'er-do-wells rowdily claimed the streets. The neighbourhood's reputation was sealed during the Vietnam War, when American sailors based at nearby Garden Island flooded the Cross with a tide of drug-fuelled debauchery. The streets retain an air of seedy hedonism, although major building programs have accelerated gentrification.

It's a 15-minute walk to the Cross from the city, or you could hop on a train. Buses 311 and 323–6 from the city also pass through here.

Kings Cross, Darlinghurst & Woolloomooloo

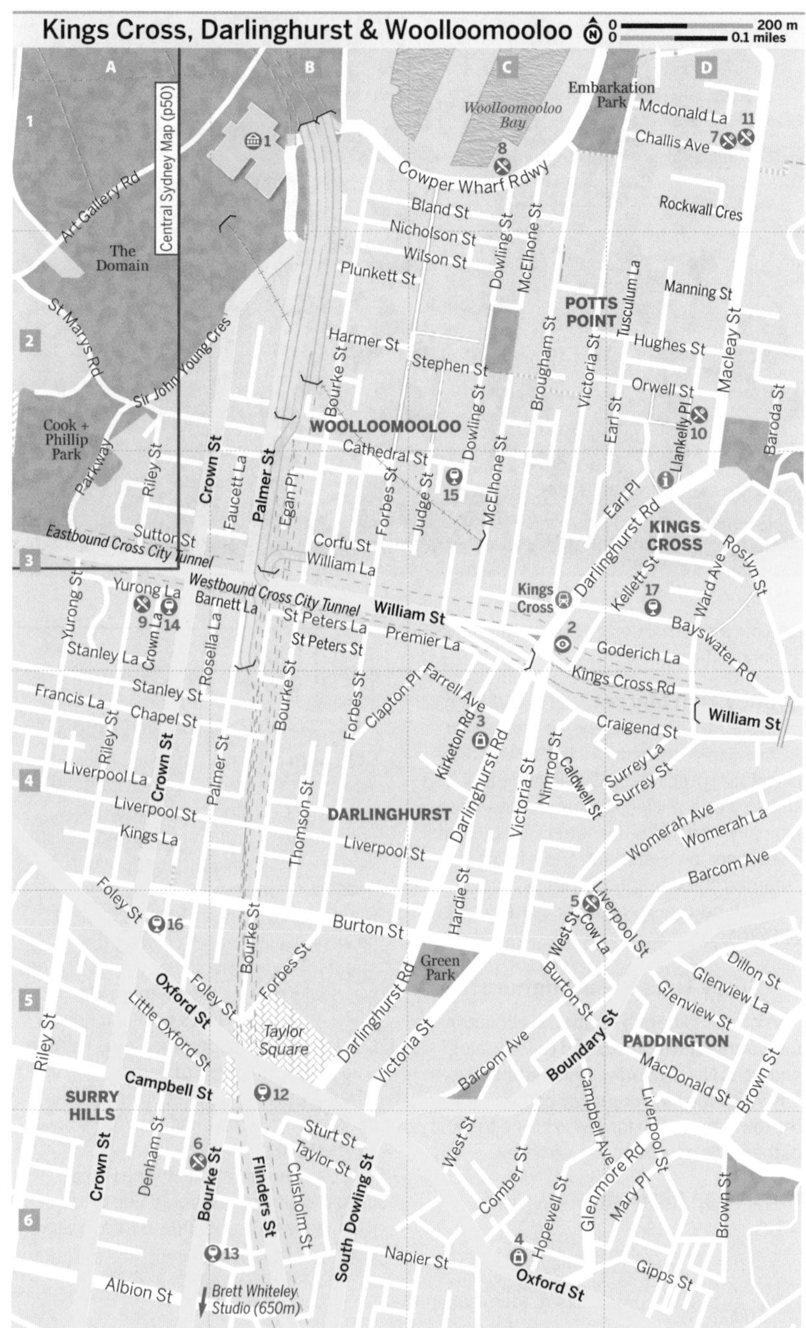
0 200 m
0 0.1 miles
N
A
B
C
D
1
2
3
4
5
6
Central Sydney Map (p50)
Woolloomooloo Bay
Embarkation Park
Mcdonald La
Challis Ave
Cowper Wharf Rdwy
Art Gallery Rd
The Domain
Bland St
Nicholson St
Wilson St
Plunkett St
Rockwall Cres
Dowling St
McElhone St
Tusculum La
Manning St
POTTS POINT
St Marys Rd
Sir John Young Cres
Harmer St
Stephen St
Brougham St
Victoria St
Hughes St
Macleay St
Orwell St
Earl St
Llankelly Pl
Baroda St
Cook + Phillip Park
Parkway
Riley St
Crown St
Faucett La
Palmer St
Egan Pl
Bourke St
WOOLLOOMOOLOO
Cathedral St
Forbes St
Judge St
McElhone St
Earl Pl
Darlinghurst Rd
KINGS CROSS
Roslyn St
Sutton St
Eastbound Cross City Tunnel
Corfu St
William La
Yurong St
Yurong La
Barnett La
Westbound Cross City Tunnel
William St
St Peters La
St Peters St
Premier La
Kings Cross
Kellett St
Ward Ave
Bayswater Rd
Goderich La
Kings Cross Rd
Stanley La
Crown La
Rosella La
Stanley St
Francis La
Chapel St
Clapton Pl
Farrell Ave
Kirketon Rd
Craigend St
William St
Riley St
Liverpool La
Palmer St
Thomson St
Nimrod St
Caldwell St
Surrey La
Surrey St
Liverpool St
DARLINGHURST
Kings La
Liverpool St
Womerah Ave
Womerah La
Barcom Ave
Foley St
Hardie St
Burton St
West St
Cow La
Liverpool St
Green Park
Dillon St
Glenview La
Glenview St
Oxford St
Foley St
Little Oxford St
Forbes St
Taylor Square
Riley St
Victoria St
Burton St
Boundary St
PADDINGTON
Barcom Ave
MacDonald St
Brown St
SURRY HILLS
Campbell St
Sturt St
Taylor St
West St
Campbell Ave
Liverpool St
Glenmore Rd
Denham St
Crown St
Bourke St
Flinders St
Chisholm St
South Dowling St
Comber St
Hopewell St
Mary Pl
Brown St
Napier St
Oxford St
Gipps St
Albion St
Brett Whiteley Studio (650m)
1
2
3
4
5
6
7
8
9
10
11
12
13
14
15
16
17

Kings Cross, Darlinghurst & Woolloomooloo

Sights
1 Art Gallery of NSW ... B1
2 Coca-Cola Sign ... C3

Shopping
3 Artery ... C4
4 Capital L ... C6

Eating
5 bills ... C5
6 Dead Ringer ... A6
7 Fratelli Paradiso ... D1
8 Harry's Cafe de Wheels ... C1
9 Red Lantern on Riley ... A3
10 Room 10 ... D2
11 Yellow ... D1

Drinking & Nightlife
12 Arq ... B5
13 Beresford Hotel ... B6
14 Love, Tilly Devine ... A3
15 Old Fitzroy Hotel ... C3
16 Shady Pines Saloon ... A5
17 World Bar ... D3

Entertainment
Old Fitz Theatre ... (see 15)

this museum, established just 40 years after the First Fleet dropped anchor, is doing a brilliant job of it. Standouts include the Indigenous Australians section, natural history section and excellent dinosaur gallery.

Brett Whiteley Studio — Gallery

(02-9225 1881; www.artgallery.nsw.gov.au/brett-whiteley-studio; 2 Raper St, Surry Hills; 10am-4pm Fri-Sun; Central) FREE Acclaimed local artist Brett Whiteley (1939–92) lived fast and without restraint. His hard-to-find studio (look for the signs on Devonshire St) has been preserved as a gallery for some of his best work.

Paddington & Centennial Park

Paddington, aka 'Paddo', is an upmarket residential suburb of restored Victorian-era terrace houses and jacaranda-lined streets. Visit on a Saturday to see the Paddington Markets (p58).

East of Paddington is the 220-hectare **Centennial Park** (02-9339 6699; www.centennialparklands.com.au; Oxford St; Bondi Junction), which has running, cycling, skating and horse-riding tracks, duck ponds, barbecue sites and sports pitches.

Manly & the North Shore

With both a harbour side and a glorious ocean beach, Manly is Sydney's only ferry destination with surf. Worth visiting for the ferry ride alone.

Still on the North Shore, just east of the Harbour Bridge is the stately Kirribilli, home to **Admiralty House** (www.gg.gov.au; Kirribilli Ave; Milsons Point) and **Kirribilli House** (Kirribilli Ave), the Sydney residences of the governor-general and prime minister respectively.

Manly Beach — Beach

(Manly) Sydney's second most famous beach stretches for nearly two golden kilometres, lined by Norfolk Island pines and midrise apartment blocks. Surf's up!

Taronga Zoo — Zoo

(02-9969 2777; www.taronga.org.au; Bradleys Head Rd, Mosman; adult/child $46/26; 9.30am-5pm Sep-Apr, 9.30am-4.30pm May-Aug; 247, Taronga Zoo) A 12-minute ferry ride from Circular Quay, this bushy harbour hillside is full of kangaroos, koalas and similarly hirsute Australians, plus numerous imported guests. The zoo's critters have million-dollar harbour views, but seem blissfully unaware of the privilege. Feedings and encounters happen throughout the day, while in summer, twilight concerts (www.twilightattaronga.org.au) jazz things up.

North Head — National Park

(North Head Scenic Dr; 135) About 3km south of Manly, spectacular, chunky North Head offers dramatic cliffs, lookouts and sweeping views of the ocean, the harbour and the city; hire a bike and go exploring.

Luna Park Amusement Park

(☎02-9922 6644; www.lunaparksydney.com; 1 Olympic Dr, Milsons Point; ⏰11am-10pm Fri & Sat, 10am-6pm Sun, 11am-4pm Mon; ⛴Milsons Point) FREE A sinister chip-toothed clown face (50 times life-sized) forms the entrance to this old-fashioned amusement park overlooking Sydney Harbour. You can purchase a two-ride pass ($20), or buy a height-based unlimited-ride pass (adults $52, kids $22 to $45; cheaper if purchased online).

ACTIVITIES

Surf spots on the South Shore include Bondi, Tamarama, Coogee, Maroubra and Cronulla. The North Shore is home to a dozen surf beaches between Manly and Palm Beach, including Curl Curl, Dee Why, Narrabeen, Mona Vale and Newport. For updates on what's breaking where, see www.coastalwatch.com or www.magicseaweed.com.

There are 100-plus public swimming pools in Sydney, and many beaches have protected rock pools. Harbour beaches offer sheltered and shark-netted swimming.

Manly Scenic Walkway Walking

(www.manly.nsw.gov.au; ⛴Manly) This epic walk has two major components: the 10km western stretch between Manly and Spit Bridge, and the 9.5km eastern loop around North Head. Either download a map or pick one up from the information centre near the wharf.

Dive Centre Bondi Diving

(☎02-9369 3855; www.divebondi.com.au; 198 Bondi Rd, Bondi; ⏰9am-6pm Mon-Fri, 8am-6pm Sat & Sun; 🚌333) Friendly and professional, this centre offers guided dives from shore ($155 for two) or boat ($185 for two) as well as equipment hire and PADI courses.

Manly Surf School Surfing

(☎02-9932 7000; www.manlysurfschool.com; North Steyne Surf Club, Manly; 🚌139, ⛴Manly) Reliable and well-established, this school offers two-hour surf lessons year-round (adult/child $70/55), as well as private tuition. It's a fair bit cheaper if you book a multi-class package.

From left: Manly Beach (p55); Taronga Zoo (p55); Luna Park; Manly Surf School

YUNSUN_KIM/SHUTTERSTOCK ©

A F GOSS/SHUTTERSTOCK ©

Andrew (Boy) Charlton Pool Swimming

(02-9358 6686; www.abcpool.org; 1c Mrs Macquaries Rd; adult/child $7.40/5.60; 6am-8pm; Martin Place) Sydney's best saltwater pool – smack bang next to the harbour – is a magnet for water-loving gays, straights, parents and fashionistas. Serious lap swimmers rule the pool, so maintain your lane.

 TOURS

Sydney Architecture Walks Walking

(0403 888 390; www.sydneyarchitecture.org; adult walks $49-59, cycle incl bike $120) These bright young archi-buffs run two 3½-hour cycling tours and five themed two-hour walking tours (The City; Utzon and the Sydney Opera House; Harbourings; Art, Place and Landscape; and Modern Sydney).

Bonza Bike Tours Cycling

(Map p50; 02-9247 8800; www.bonzabiketours.com; 30 Harrington St; office 9am-5pm; Circular Quay) These bike boffins run a 2½-hour Sydney Highlights tour (adult/child $79/99) and a four-hour Sydney Classic tour ($119/99). Other tours include the Harbour Bridge and Manly. It also hires bikes (per hour/half-day/day/week $10/19/29/125).

Captain Cook Cruises Cruise

(Map p50; 02-9206 1111; www.captaincook.com.au; Wharf 6, Circular Quay; Circular Quay) As well as ritzy lunch and dinner cruises and whale watching, this crew offers an aquatic version of a hop-on, hop-off bus tour, stopping at Watsons Bay, Taronga Zoo, Fort Denison, Garden Island, Shark Island, Manly, Circular Quay, Luna Park and Darling Harbour. It costs $45/25 for adults/children and includes some commentary.

Sydney Harbour Kayaks Kayaking

(02-9960 4590; www.sydneyharbourkayaks.com.au; Smiths Boat Shed, 81 Parriwi Rd, Mosman; 9am-5pm Mon-Fri, 7.30am-5pm Sat & Sun; 173-180) Rents kayaks (from $20 per hour) and stand-up paddleboards (from $25), and leads excellent four-hour eco-tours ($125) from near the Spit Bridge.

ALEKSANDAR TODOROVIC/SHUTTERSTOCK ©

ANDREW WATSON/GETTY IMAGES ©

Weekend Markets

Carriageworks Farmers Market (www.carriageworks.com.au; Carriageworks, 245 Wilson St, Eveleigh; 8am-1pm Sat; Redfern) Over 70 regular stallholders sell their goodies at Sydney's best farmers market, held in a heritage-listed railway workshop.

Paddington Markets (02-9331 2923; www.paddingtonmarkets.com.au; 395 Oxford St, Paddington; 10am-4pm Sat; 333, 380) Originating in the hippie 1970s, these markets are considerably more mainstream these days. They are still worth exploring for their new and vintage clothing, arts, crafts and jewellery.

Glebe Markets (www.glebemarkets.com.au; Glebe Public School, cnr Glebe Point Rd & Derby Pl, Glebe; 10am-4pm Sat; 431, 433, Glebe) The best of the west; Sydney's dreadlocked, shoeless, inner-city contingent beats a course to this crowded hippie-ish market.

Paddington Markets
KOKKAI NG/GETTY IMAGES ©

I'm Free Walking
(Map p50; 0405 515 654; www.imfree.com.au; 483 George St; 10.30am & 2.30pm; Town Hall) FREE Departing twice daily from the square off George St between the Town Hall and St Andrew's Cathedral (no bookings taken – just show up), these highly rated three-hour tours are run by enthusiastic young guides for tips. The route takes in the Rocks, Circular Quay, Martin Place, Pitt St and Hyde Park.

SHOPPING

Queen Victoria Building Shopping Centre
(QVB; Map p50; 02-9265 6800; www.qvb.com.au; 455 George St; 9am-6pm Mon-Wed, Fri & Sat, 9am-9pm Thu, 11am-5pm Sun; Town Hall) The magnificent QVB takes up a whole block and boasts nearly 200 shops on five levels. It's a High Victorian masterpiece – without doubt Sydney's most beautiful shopping centre.

Australian Wine Centre Wine
(Map p50; 02-9247 2755; www.australianwinecentre.com; Goldfields House, 1 Alfred St; 10am-7pm Sun & Mon, 9.30am-8pm Tue-Thu & Sat, 9.30am-9pm Fri; Circular Quay) This multilingual basement store is packed with quality Australian wine, beer and spirits. Despite its location, it's no tourist trap: smaller producers are well represented. International shipping can be arranged.

Strand Arcade Shopping Centre
(Map p50; www.strandarcade.com.au; 412 George St; 9am-5.30pm Mon-Wed & Fri, 9am-9pm Thu, 9am-4pm Sat, 11am-4pm Sun; Town Hall) Constructed in 1891, the Strand rivals the Queen Victoria Building in the ornateness stakes. The three floors of designer fashions, Australiana and old-world coffee shops will make your short-cut through here considerably longer.

David Jones Department Store
(Map p50; 02-9266 5544; www.davidjones.com.au; 86-108 Castlereagh St; 9.30am-7pm Sun-Wed, 9.30am-9pm Thu & Fri, 9am-7pm Sat; St James) DJs is Sydney's premier department store, occupying two enormous city buildings. The Castlereagh St store has women's and children's clothing; Market St has menswear, electrical goods and a high-brow food court.

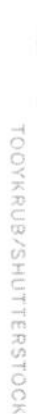

Queen Victoria Building

Gleebooks Books
(02-9660 2333; www.gleebooks.com.au; 49 Glebe Point Rd, Glebe; 9am-7pm Sun-Wed, to 9pm Thu-Sat; Glebe) One of Sydney's best bookshops, Gleebooks' aisles are full of politics, arts and general fiction, and staff really know their stuff.

Capital L Fashion & Accessories
(Map p54; 02-9361 0111; www.capital-l.com; 100 Oxford St, Paddington; 10.30am-6pm; Kings Cross) This attractive boutique stocks women's clothing by up-and-coming Australian designers. Hip sales staff break from tradition and actually help you find and try on clothes.

Artery Art
(Map p54; 02-9380 8234; www.artery.com.au; 221 Darlinghurst Rd, Darlinghurst; 10am-6pm Mon-Fri, 10am-4pm Sat & Sun; Kings Cross) Step into a world of mesmerising dots and swirls at this small gallery devoted to Aboriginal art. Artery's motto is 'ethical, contemporary, affordable'.

EATING

Circular Quay & the Rocks

Fine Food Store Cafe $
(Map p50; 02-9252 1196; www.finefood store.com; cnr Mill & Kendall Lanes; light meals $9-15; 7am-4.30pm Mon-Sat, 7.30am-4.30pm Sun; ; Circular Quay) The Rocks sometimes seems all pubs, so it's a delight to find this tucked-away contemporary cafe that works for a sightseeing stopover or a better, cheaper breakfast than your hotel. Staff are genuinely welcoming, make very respectable coffee, and offer delicious panini, sandwiches and other breakfast and lunch fare.

Quay Modern Australian $$$
(Map p50; 02-9251 5600; www.quay.com.au; Level 3, Overseas Passenger Terminal; 4/8 courses $175/235; 6-9.30pm Mon-Thu, noon-1.30pm & 6-9.30pm Fri-Sun; Circular Quay) Quay is shamelessly guilty of breaking the rule that good views make for bad food. Chef Peter Gilmore never rests on his laurels, consistently delivering the exquisitely

★ Top Five Sydney Dining

Quay (p59)

Tetsuya's (p60)

Mr Wong (p60)

Ester (p61)

Bourke Street Bakery (p62)

From left: Bourke Street Bakery (p62); Strand Arcade (p58); Peter Gilmore at Quay (p59)

crafted, adventurous cuisine which has landed Quay on the prestigious World's Best Restaurants list. And the view? Like dining in a postcard.

City Centre

Mr Wong Chinese **$$**

(Map p50; ☎02-9240 3000; www.merivale.com.au/mrwong; 3 Bridge Lane; mains $26-38; ⌚noon-3pm & 5.30-11pm Mon-Wed, noon-3pm & 5.30pm-midnight Thu & Fri, 10.30am-3pm & 5.30pm-midnight Sat, 10.30am-3pm & 5.30-10pm Sun; ; Wynyard) Classy but comfortable in an attractive low-lit space on a CBD laneway, Mr Wong has exposed-brick colonial warehouse chic and a huge team of staff and hanging ducks in the open kitchen. Lunchtime dim sum offerings bristle with flavour and the 'textured' chicken and jellyfish salad is a mouth-freshening sensation. Mains such as crispy pork hock are sinfully sticky, while Peking duck rolls are legendary.

Pablo & Rusty's Cafe **$$**

(Map p50; ☎02-9283 9543; www.pabloandrustys.com.au; 161 Castlereagh St; light meals $10-25; ⌚6.30am-5pm Mon-Fri, 8am-3pm Sat; ; Town Hall) Pablo & Rusty's inviting wood-and-brick decor and seriously good coffee (several single origins available daily) are complemented by a range of appealing specials, ranging from sandwiches to wholesome Mediterranean- and Asian-influenced combos such as tuna poke with brown rice or lychee and ginger tapioca.

Rockpool Bar & Grill Steak **$$$**

(Map p50; ☎02-8078 1900; www.rockpool.com; 66 Hunter St; mains $45-59, bar mains $18-32; ⌚noon-3pm & 6-11pm Mon-Fri, 6-11pm Sat, 5.30-10.30pm Sun; Martin Place) You'll feel like a 1930s Manhattan stockbroker when you dine at this sleek operation in the art deco City Mutual Building. The bar is famous for its dry-aged, full-blood Wagyu burger (make sure you order a side of the hand-cut fat chips).

Tetsuya's French, Japanese **$$$**

(☎02-9267 2900; www.tetsuyas.com; 529 Kent St; degustation $230, matching wines $110; ⌚5.30-10pm Tue-Fri, noon-3pm & 5.30-10pm Sat; Town Hall) Concealed in a villa behind

BLOOMBERG/GETTY IMAGES ©

a historic cottage amid the high-rises, this extraordinary restaurant is for those seeking a culinary journey rather than a simple stuffed belly. Settle in for 10-plus courses of French- and Japanese-inflected food from the creative genius of Japanese-born Tetsuya Wakuda. Book way ahead.

Sepia Japanese, Fusion **$$$**

(Map p50; 02-9283 1990; www.sepiarestaurant.com.au; 201 Sussex St; degustation $215, matching wines $135; noon-3pm Fri & Sat, 6-10pm Tue-Sat; Town Hall) A Japanese sensibility permeates the boundary-pushing menu at what is sometimes said to be Australia's best restaurant. Sensational seafood and exquisite bursts of flavour make the palate sing. The atmosphere is plush, low-lit and fairly formal; there's also a wine bar.

Inner West

Black Star Pastry Bakery **$**

(02-9557 8656; www.blackstarpastry.com.au; 277 Australia St, Newtown; snacks $4-10; 7am-5pm; ; Newtown) Wise folks follow the black star to pay homage to excellent coffee, a large selection of sweet things and a few very good savoury things (gourmet pies and the like). There are only a couple of tables; it's more a snack-and-run or picnic-in-the-park kind of place.

Thanh Binh Vietnamese **$$**

(02-9557 1175; www.thanhbinh.com.au; 111 King St, Newtown; mains $18-28; 5-11pm Mon-Fri, noon-11pm Sat & Sun; ; Macdonaldtown) This old Vietnamese favourite isn't top of the trendmeter any more, but it should be for its wide range of consistently delicious dishes. Favourites are soft-shell crab on papaya salad or sinful pork belly and quail eggs in stock.

Ester Modern Australian **$$$**

(02-8068 8279; www.ester-restaurant.com.au; 46/52 Meagher St, Chippendale; mains $32-49; 6-10pm Mon-Thu, noon-3pm & 6-11pm Fri, 6-11pm Sat, noon-5pm Sun; ; Redfern) Ester breaks the trend for hip eateries by accepting bookings, but in other respects it exemplifies Sydney's contemporary dining scene: informal but not sloppy; innovative without being overly gimmicky; hip, but never try-hard.

Sydney's Celebrity Chefs

Bill Granger

Author of 10 cookbooks; owner of the legendary **bills** (Map p54; 02-9360 9631; www.bills.com.au; 433 Liverpool St, Darlinghurst; mains $15-29; 7.30am-3pm Mon-Sat, 8am-3pm Sun; ; Kings Cross).

Luke Nguyen

Presents TV programs, pens cookbooks and plates up Vietnamese delights at **Red Lantern on Riley** (Map p54; 02-9698 4355; www.redlantern.com.au; 60 Riley St, Darlinghurst; mains $40-43; 6-10pm Sun-Thu, noon-3pm & 6-11pm Fri, 6-11pm Sat; ; Museum).

Matt Moran

Boasting **Aria** (Map p50; 02-9240 2255; www.ariarestaurant.com; 1 Macquarie St; 2-/3-/4-course dinner $115/145/170, degustation $205; noon-2.15pm & 5.30-10.30pm Mon-Fri, noon-1.45pm & 5-10.30pm Sat, noon-2.15pm & 5.30-8.30pm Sun; Circular Quay), **Chiswick Restaurant** (02-8388 8688; www.chiswickrestaurant.com.au; 65 Ocean St, Woollahra; mains $30-38; noon-2.30pm & 6-10pm Mon-Thu, noon-3pm & 6-10pm Fri & Sat, noon-3pm & 6-9pm Sun; ; 389) and **Opera Bar** (p65), Matt graces the TV screen on *MasterChef Australia*.

Neil Perry

The city's original rock-star chef (with ponytail) heads up **Rockpool Bar & Grill** (p60), **Eleven Bridge** (Map p50; 02-9252 1888; www.rockpool.com; 11 Bridge St; mains $52-72; noon-3pm & 6-10pm Mon-Fri, 6-11pm Sat; Circular Quay) and **Spice Temple** (Map p50; 02-8078 1888; www.rockpool.com; 10 Bligh St; dishes $30-50; noon-3pm & 6-10.30pm Mon-Fri, 6-10.30pm Sat, 5.30-10pm Sun; ; Martin Place).

Influences straddle continents and dishes are made to be shared.

Surry Hills & Darlinghurst

Bourke Street Bakery Bakery $

(02-9699 1011; www.bourkestreetbakery.com.au; 633 Bourke St, Surry Hills; items $5-14; 7am-6pm Mon-Fri, to 5pm Sat & Sun; ; 301, Central) Queuing outside this teensy bakery is an essential Surry Hills experience. It sells a tempting selection of pastries, cakes, bread and sandwiches, along with sausage rolls which are near legendary in these parts.

Le Monde Cafe $

(02-9211 3568; www.lemondecafe.com.au; 83 Foveaux St, Surry Hills; dishes $10-16; 6.30am-4pm Mon-Fri, 7am-2pm Sat; ; Central) Some of Sydney's best breakfasts are served between the demure dark wooden walls of this small street-side cafe. Top-notch coffee and a terrific selection of tea will gear you up to face the world, while dishes such as truffled poached eggs or confit pork belly make it worth walking up the hill for.

Dead Ringer Tapas $$

(Map p54; 02-9331 3560; www.deadringer.wtf; 413 Bourke St, Surry Hills; dishes $18-33; 5pm-midnight Mon-Fri, noon-midnight Sat & Sun; ; 333, 380) Barstool it or grab an outdoor table and graze on Dead Ringer's short menu that changes slightly daily and runs from bar snacks through tapas to mains. There's always something interesting by the glass to accompany.

Devonshire Modern European $$$

(02-9698 9427; www.thedevonshire.com.au; 204 Devonshire St, Surry Hills; degustation $95, matching wines $55, mains $37; noon-2.30pm Fri, 6-10pm Tue-Sat; Central) Chef Jeremy Bentley's food is simply extraordinary – complex, precisely presented and full of flavour. And while there's white linen on the tables, the atmosphere isn't the least bit starchy.

Kings Cross, Potts Point & Woolloomooloo

Harry's Cafe de Wheels Fast Food $

(Map p54; 02-9357 3074; www.harryscafedewheels.com.au; Cowper Wharf Roadway, Woolloomooloo; pies $5-8; 8.30am-2am Mon & Tue, 8.30am-3am Wed & Thu, 8.30am-4am Fri, 9am-4am Sat, 9am-1am Sun; 311, Kings Cross) Open since 1938, Harry's has been serving meat pies to everyone from Pamela Anderson to Frank Sinatra and Colonel Sanders. You can't leave without trying a Tiger: a hot meat pie with sloppy peas, mashed potato, gravy and tomato sauce.

Room 10 Cafe $

(Map p54; 02-8318 0454; www.facebook.com/room10espresso; 10 Llankelly Pl, Kings Cross; mains $8-14; 7am-4pm Mon-Fri, 8am-4pm Sat & Sun; ; Kings Cross) Genuinely warm and welcoming, this tiny cafe is the sort of place where staff know all the locals by name. The coffee is delicious and the food's limited to sandwiches, salads and such – tasty and uncomplicated.

Fratelli Paradiso Italian $$

(Map p54; 02-9357 1744; www.fratelliparadiso.com; 12-16 Challis Ave, Potts Point; breakfast $12-14, mains $22-38; 7am-11pm Mon-Sat, to 10pm Sun; Kings Cross) This underlit trattoria has them queuing at the door (especially on weekends). The intimate room showcases seasonal Italian dishes cooked with Mediterranean zing. Lots of busy black-clad waiters, lots of Italian chatter, lots of oversized sunglasses.

Yellow Vegetarian $$

(Map p54; 02-9332 2344; www.yellowsydney.com.au; 57 Macleay St, Potts Point; degustation menu $70; 6-11pm Mon-Fri, 8am-3pm & 6-11pm Sat & Sun; ; Kings Cross) Once a sunflower-yellow symbol of all things Bohemian, this former artists' residence is now a top-notch contemporary vegetarian restaurant. The tasting menus (including a vegan one) take the Sydney non-meat scene to new levels.

bills by Bill Granger

Paddington

Four in Hand Modern Australian $$

(☎02-9326 2254; www.fourinhand.com.au; 105 Sutherland St; mains $28-38; ⏰5.30-9.30pm Mon-Wed, noon-3pm & 5.30-9.30pm Thu-Sun; 🚌389) You can't go far in Paddington without tripping over a beautiful old pub with amazing food. This is among the best: quality meats and seafood are given confident treatment and exotic garnishes, never losing sight of the gastropub idea.

Eastern Beaches

Lox, Stock & Barrel Cafe, Jewish $

(☎02-9300 0368; www.loxstockandbarrel.com.au; 140 Glenayr Ave, Bondi Beach; breakfast & lunch dishes $10-22, dinner $18-29; ⏰7am-3.30pm Sun-Tue, 7am-3.30pm & 6-10pm Wed & Thu, 7am-3.30pm & 6-11pm Fri & Sat; 📶🌱; 🚌389) Stare down the barrel of a smoking hot bagel and ask yourself one question: Wagyu corned-beef Reuben, or homemade pastrami and Russian coleslaw?

Three Blue Ducks Cafe $$

(☎02-9389 0010; www.threeblueducks.com; 141-143 Macpherson St, Bronte; breakfast $14-22, lunch $20-32, dinner $28-38; ⏰6.30am-2.30pm Sun-Tue, 6.30am-2.30pm & 5-11pm Wed-Sat; 📶🌱; 🚌378) 🍃 These ducks are a fair waddle from the water, but that doesn't stop queues forming outside the graffiti-covered walls for weekend breakfasts across two seating areas. The adventurous chefs have a strong commitment to using local, organic and fair-trade food whenever possible.

Icebergs Dining Room Italian $$$

(☎02-9365 9000; www.idrb.com; 1 Notts Ave, Bondi; mains $46-52; ⏰noon-3pm & 6.30-11pm Tue-Sun; 🚌333, 380) 🍃 Poised above the famous Icebergs swimming pool, Icebergs' views sweep across the Bondi Beach arc to the sea. Inside, bow-tied waiters deliver fresh, sustainably sourced seafood and steaks cooked with élan. There's also an elegant cocktail bar.

Opera Bar

DRINKING & NIGHTLIFE

Circular Quay & the Rocks

Opera Bar — Bar

(Map p50; 02-9247 1666; www.operabar.com.au; lower concourse, Sydney Opera House; 9am-midnight Sun-Thu, 9am-1am Fri & Sat; Circular Quay) Right on the harbour with the Opera House on one side and the Harbour Bridge on the other, this perfectly positioned terrace manages a very Sydney marriage of the laid-back and the sophisticated. There's live music or DJs most nights.

Glenmore — Pub

(Map p50; 02-9247 4794; www.theglenmore.com.au; 96 Cumberland St; 10am-midnight Sun-Thu, to 1am Fri & Sat; ; Circular Quay) Downstairs it's a predictably nice old Rocks pub, but head up to the rooftop and the views are beyond fabulous: Opera House (until a cruise ship docks), harbour and city skyline all present and accounted for.

Hero of Waterloo — Pub

(Map p50; 02-9252 4553; www.heroofwaterloo.com.au; 81 Lower Fort St; 10am-11.30pm Mon-Wed, 10am-midnight Thu-Sat, 10am-10pm Sun; Circular Quay) Enter this rough-hewn 1843 sandstone pub to meet some locals, chat up the Irish bar staff and grab an earful of the swing, folk and Celtic bands (Friday to Sunday).

Lord Nelson Brewery Hotel — Brewery

(Map p50; 02-9251 4044; 19 Kent St; 11am-11pm Mon-Sat, noon-10pm Sun; Circular Quay) Built in 1836 and converted into a pub in 1841, this atmospheric sandstone boozer is one of three claiming to be Sydney's oldest (all using slightly different criteria). The on-site brewery cooks up its own natural ales (try the Old Admiral).

City Centre

Grandma's — Cocktail Bar

(Map p50; 02-9264 3004; www.grandmasbarsydney.com; basement, 275 Clarence St; 3pm-midnight Mon-Fri, 5pm-1am Sat; Town Hall) Billing itself as a 'retrosexual haven of cosmopolitan kitsch and faded granny glamour', Grandma's hits the mark. It's very quirky, and very relaxed and casual for a CBD venue. Toasted sandwiches provide sustenance.

Swanky Downtown Bars

Ivy (Map p50; 02-9254 8100; www.merivale.com/ivy; Level 1, 330 George St; noon-late Mon-Fri, 6.30pm-3.30am Sat; ; Wynyard) Hidden down a lane off George St, Ivy is a fashionable complex of bars, restaurants...even a swimming pool. It's also Sydney's most hyped venue; expect lengthy queues of suburban kids waiting to shed $40 on a Saturday for entry to Sydney's hottest club night, Pacha.

Marble Bar (Map p50; 02-9266 2000; www.marblebarsydney.com.au; basement, 488 George St; 4pm-midnight Sun-Thu, to 2am Fri & Sat; ; Town Hall) Built for a staggering £32,000 in 1893 as part of the Adams Hotel on Pitt St, this ornate underground bar is one of the best places in town for putting on the ritz (even if this is the Hilton). Musos play anything from jazz to funk, Thursday to Saturday.

O Bar (Map p50; 02-9247 9777; www.obardining.com.au; Level 47, Australia Square, 264 George St; 5pm-late Sat-Thu, noon-late Fri; ; Wynyard) The cocktails at this 47th-floor revolving bar aren't cheap, but the views are truly wonderful. Get up there shortly after opening time, and kick back to enjoy the sunset and transition into night.

Gay & Lesbian Sydney

Gay and lesbian culture forms a vocal and vital part of Sydney's social fabric. Oxford St, Darlinghurst, has long been the locus of the gay scene and every year, tens of thousands of spectators line the street for the famous **Sydney Gay & Lesbian Mardi Gras** (www.mardigras.org.au; Feb-Mar) parade.

Free gay media includes *SX* (www.gaynewsnetwork.com.au), the *Star Observer* (www.starobserver.com.au) and *Lesbians on the Loose* (www.lotl.com).

Most hotels, restaurants and bars in Darlinghurst, Surry Hills and Newtown are very gay-friendly. To party, check out the following:

Beresford Hotel (Map p54; 02-9240 3000; www.merivale.com.au/theberesfordhotel; 354 Bourke St, Surry Hills; noon-1am; 374, 397, 399) Bold and beautiful on Sunday afternoons.

Sly Fox (02-9557 2917; www.slyfox.sydney; 199 Enmore Rd, Enmore; 2pm-midnight Sun & Tue, 2pm-3am Wed & Thu, 2pm-6am Fri & Sat; Newtown) Lesbian night in Enmore.

Arq (Map p54; 02-9380 8700; www.arqsydney.com.au; 16 Flinders St, Darlinghurst; 9pm-3am Thu-Sun; 333, 380) One of the city's best clubs, gay or straight.

Imperial Hotel (02-9516 1766; www.imperialsydney.com.au; 35 Erskineville Rd, Erskineville; admission free-$15; 3pm-midnight Sun, Wed & Thu, to 5am Fri & Sat; Erskineville) Cabaret, pool and cruising.

Sydney Gay & Lesbian Mardi Gras

Uncle Ming's Cocktail Bar

(Map p50; www.unclemings.com.au; 55 York St; noon-midnight Mon-Fri, 4pm-midnight Sat; Wynyard) We love the dark romantic opium-den atmosphere of this small bar secreted away in a basement by a shirt shop. It also does an excellent line in dumplings and usually has very welcoming bar staff.

Establishment Bar

(Map p50; 02-9240 3100; www.merivale.com/establishmentbar; 252 George St; 11am-late Mon-Fri, noon-late Sat, noon-10pm Sun; ; Wynyard) Establishment's cashed-up crush proves that the art of swilling cocktails after a hard city day is not lost. Sit at the majestic marble bar or in the swish courtyard, or be absorbed by a leather lounge.

Inner West

Courthouse Hotel Pub

(02-9519 8273; 202 Australia St, Newtown; 10am-midnight Mon-Sat, to 10pm Sun; Newtown) A block back from the King St fray, the 150-year-old Courthouse is one of Newtown's best pubs, the kind of place where everyone from pool-playing goth lesbians to magistrates can have a beer and feel right at home.

Earl's Juke Joint Bar

(www.facebook.com/earlsjukejoint; 407 King St, Newtown; 4pm-midnight; Newtown) The current it-bar of the minute, swinging Earl's serves craft beers and killer cocktails to the Newtown hiperati. It's hidden behind the down-at-heel facade of the butcher's shop it used to be, but once in, you're in swinging New Orleans, with a bar as long as the Mississippi.

Young Henry's Brewery

(02-9519 0048; www.younghenrys.com; 76 Wilford St, Newtown; noon-7pm Mon-Fri, 10am-7pm Sat, 11am-7pm Sun; Newtown) Conviviality is assured in this craft brewery bar, where the beer is as fresh as you'll get. Basically, it's filled a bit of warehouse with high tables, a loud stereo system and a counter to serve its delicious beer, opened the roller door and filled it with happy locals.

Surry Hills & Darlinghurst

Shakespeare Hotel Pub

(02-9319 6883; www.shakespearehotel.com.au; 200 Devonshire St, Surry Hills; 10am-midnight Mon-Sat, 11am-10pm Sun; Central) This is a classic Sydney pub (1879) with art nouveau tiled walls, skuzzy carpet, the horses on the TV and cheap bar meals. It's a proper convivial all-welcome place that's the antithesis of the more gentrified Surry Hills drinking establishments.

Love, Tilly Devine Wine Bar

(Map p54; 02-9326 9297; www.lovetillydevine.com; 91 Crown Lane, Darlinghurst; 5pm-midnight Mon-Sat, 5-10pm Sun; Museum) This split-level laneway bar is pretty compact, but the wine list certainly isn't. It's an extraordinary document, with some exceptionally well-chosen wines.

Shady Pines Saloon Bar

(Map p54; 0405 624 944; www.shadypinessaloon.com; shop 4, 256 Crown St, Darlinghurst; 4pm-midnight; Museum) With no sign or street number on the door and entry via a shady back lane, this subterranean honky-tonk bar caters to the urban boho. Sip whisky and rye with the good ole hipster boys amid Western memorabilia and taxidermy.

Wild Rover Bar

(02-9280 2235; www.thewildrover.com.au; 75 Campbell St, Surry Hills; 4pm-midnight Mon-Sat; Central) Look for the unsigned wide door and enter this supremely cool brick-lined speakeasy, where a big range of craft beer is served in chrome steins and jungle animals peer benevolently from the green walls. The upstairs bar opens for trivia and live bands.

Kings Cross, Potts Point & Woolloomooloo

Old Fitzroy Hotel Pub

(Map p54; 02-9356 3848; www.oldfitzroy.com.au; 129 Dowling St, Woolloomooloo; 11am-midnight Mon-Fri, noon-midnight Sat, 3-10pm Sun; ; Kings Cross) Islington

Love, Tilly Devine

meets Melbourne in the backstreets of Woolloomooloo: this totally unpretentious **theatre pub** (www.oldfitztheatre.com) is also a decent old-fashioned boozer in its own right, with a great variety of beers on tap and a convivial welcome.

World Bar Bar, Club

(Map p54; 02-9357 7700; www.theworldbar.com; 24 Bayswater Rd, Kings Cross; 2pm-midnight Sun & Mon, 2pm-3am Tue-Sat; ; Kings Cross) World Bar (a reformed bordello) is an unpretentious grungy club with three floors to lure in the backpackers and cheap drinks to loosen things up. DJs play indie, hip hop, power pop and house nightly. Wednesday (The Wall) and Saturday (Cakes) are the big nights.

Eastern Beaches

Anchor Bar

(02-8084 3145; www.anchorbarbondi.com; 8 Campbell Pde, Bondi Beach; 5pm-midnight Tue-Fri, 12.30pm-midnight Sat & Sun; ; 333, 380-382) Surfers, backpackers and the local cool kids slurp down icy margaritas at this bustling bar at the south end of the strip. The two-hour happy hour from 5pm weekdays is a great way to start the post-surf debrief.

Manly

Manly Wharf Hotel Pub

(02-9977 1266; www.manlywharfhotel.com.au; East Esplanade; 11.30am-midnight Mon-Fri, 11am-midnight Sat, 11am-10pm Sun; ; Manly) Just along the wharf from the ferry, this remodelled pub is all glass and water vistas, with loads of seating so you've a good chance of grabbing a share of the view. It's a perfect spot for sunny afternoon beers.

ENTERTAINMENT

City Recital Hall Classical Music

(Map p50; 02-8256 2222; www.cityrecitalhall.com; 2 Angel Pl; box office 9am-5pm Mon-Fri; Wynyard) Based on the classic configuration of the 19th-century European concert hall, this custom-built 1200-seat venue boasts near-perfect acoustics. Catch top-flight companies such as Musica Viva, the Australian Brandenburg

From left: Manly Wharf Hotel; City Recital Hall; Belvoir St Theatre; Sydney Theatre Company

ANDREW WATSON/GETTY IMAGES ©

OLIVER STREWE/GETTY IMAGES ©

Orchestra and the Australian Chamber Orchestra here.

Metro Theatre Live Music
(☎02-9550 3666; www.metrotheatre.com.au; 624 George St; Town Hall) The Metro is easily Sydney's best venue for catching local and alternative international acts in intimate, well-ventilated, easy-seeing comfort. Other offerings include comedy, cabaret and dance parties.

Belvoir St Theatre Theatre
(☎02-9699 3444; www.belvoir.com.au; 25 Belvoir St, Surry Hills; 372, Central) In a quiet corner of Surry Hills, this intimate venue with two small stages is the home of an often-experimental and consistently excellent theatre company that specialises in quality Australian drama. It often commissions new works and is a vital cog in the Sydney theatre scene.

Golden Age Cinema & Bar Cinema
(☎02-9211 1556; www.ourgoldenage.com.au; 80 Commonwealth St, Surry Hills; tickets $20; 4pm-midnight Wed-Fri, 2.30pm-midnight Sat & Sun; Central) In what was once the Sydney HQ of Paramount pictures, a heart-warming small cinema shows old favourites, art-house classics and a few recherché gems. There's a great small bar here too.

Moonlight Cinema Cinema
(www.moonlight.com.au; Belvedere Amphitheatre, cnr Loch & Broome Aves, Centennial Park; adult/child $19/14.50; sunset Dec-Mar; Bondi Junction) Take a picnic and join the bats under the stars in magnificent Centennial Park; enter via the Woollahra Gate on Oxford St. A mix of new-release blockbuster, art-house and classic films is screened.

Sydney Theatre Company Theatre
(STC; Map p50; ☎02-9250 1777; www.sydneytheatre.com.au; Pier 4/5, 15 Hickson Rd, Walsh Bay; box office 9am-7.30pm Mon, 9am-8.30pm Tue-Fri, 11am-8.30pm Sat, 2hr before show Sun; 324, 325, 998, Circular Quay) Established in 1978, the STC is Sydney theatre's top dog and has played an important part in the careers of many famous Australian actors

OLIVER STREWE/GETTY IMAGES ©

CORNFIELD/SHUTTERSTOCK ©

Spectator Sports

Sydneysiders are passionate about the **National Rugby League** (NRL; www.nrl.com). The season kicks off in March in suburban stadiums, with the grand final in early October.

Over the same period, hometown favourites the Sydney Swans and Greater Western Sydney Giants play in the **Australian Football League** (AFL; www.afl.com.au). The Swans play at the **Sydney Cricket Ground** (SCG; 02-9360 6601; www.sydneycricketground.com.au; Driver Ave, Moore Park; 373-377) and the Giants at the Sydney Showground Stadium in Sydney's Olympic Park.

The **cricket** (www.cricket.com.au) season runs from October to March, with the SCG hosting interstate Sheffield Shield and sell-out international Test, Twenty20 and One Day International matches.

Sydney Cricket Ground
SINGH_LENS/SHUTTERSTOCK ©

(especially Cate Blanchett, who was co-artistic director from 2008 to 2013).

State Theatre Theatre
(Map p50; 02-9373 6655; www.statetheatre.com.au; 49 Market St; Town Hall) The beautiful 2000-seat State Theatre is a lavish, gilt-ridden, chandelier-dangling palace. It hosts the Sydney Film Festival, concerts, comedy, opera, musicals and the odd celebrity chef.

INFORMATION

MEDICAL SERVICES

Hospitals with 24-hour accident and emergency departments include the following:

St Vincent's Hospital (02-8382 1111; www.svhs.org.au; 390 Victoria St, Darlinghurst; Kings Cross)

Sydney Hospital (02-9382 7111; www.seslhd.health.nsw.gov.au/SHSEH; 8 Macquarie St; Martin Place)

Kings Cross Clinic (02-9358 3066; www.kingscrossclinic.com.au; 13 Springfield Ave, Kings Cross; 9am-1pm & 2.30-6pm Mon-Fri, 10am-1pm Sat; Kings Cross) Offers general and travel-related medical services.

TOURIST INFORMATION

Sydney Visitor Centres (02-8273 0000; www.sydney.com) Have a wide range of brochures, and staff can book accommodation, tours and attractions. Branches:

Rocks (Map p50; cnr Argyle & Playfair Sts; 9.30am-5.30pm; Circular Quay)

Darling Harbour (Palm Grove, Darling Harbour; 9.30am-5.30pm; Town Hall)

City Host Information Kiosks (www.cityofsydney.nsw.gov.au) Branches:

Circular Quay (Map p50; cnr Pitt & Alfred Sts; 9am-5pm; Circular Quay)

Chinatown (Dixon St; 11am-5pm; Town Hall)

Kings Cross (Map p54; cnr Darlinghurst Rd & Springfield Ave; 9am-5pm; Kings Cross).

GETTING THERE & AWAY

AIR

Sydney Airport (02-9667 9111; www.sydneyairport.com.au; Airport Dr, Mascot) has separate international (T1) and domestic (T2 and T3) sections, 4km apart.

BUS

Long-distance coaches arrive at **Sydney Coach Terminal** (02-9281 9366; www.sydneycoachterminal.com.au; Eddy Ave; 8am-6pm, from

6am summer; Central), underneath Central Station.

TRAIN

Intercity trains pull into Sydney's historic **Central Station** (Eddy Ave; Central), in the Haymarket area of the city.

GETTING AROUND

TO/FROM THE AIRPORT

Airport shuttles head to hotels and hostels in the city centre, and some reach surrounding suburbs and beach destinations. Operators include **KST Airporter** (02-8339 0155; www.kst.com.au; airport to CBD adult/child $17/12), **Airport Shuttle North** (02-9997 7767; www.asntransfers.com; airport to Manly 1/2/3 people $41/51/61) and **Manly Express** (02-8068 8473; www.manlyexpress.com.au; airport to Manly 1/2/3 people $40/55/65).

Taxi fares from the airport are approximately $25 to $55 to the city centre, $55 to $65 to North Sydney and $90 to $100 to Manly.

Trains from both the domestic and international terminals, connecting into the main train network, are run by **Airport Link** (www.airportlink.com.au; adult/child $13.40/12 plus normal rail fare; 5am-11.45pm, extended on Fri & Sat night). They're frequent (every 10 minutes), quick (13 minutes to Central) and easy to use.

PUBLIC TRANSPORT

Transport NSW (131 500; www.transportnsw.info) is the body that coordinates all of the state-run bus, ferry, train and light rail services. You'll find a useful journey planner on its website.

BUS

Sydney Buses (131 500; www.sydneybuses.info) has an extensive network, operating from around 5am to midnight when less frequent NightRide services commence. Tap on/off with your Opal card.

FERRY

Most **Sydney Ferries** (Map p50; 131 500; www.transportnsw.info) operate between 6am and midnight. The standard Opal Card single fare for most harbour destinations is $5.74; ferries to Manly cost $7.18.

Private company **Manly Fast Ferry** (02-9583 1199; www.manlyfastferry.com.au; adult one-way off-peak/peak $8.70/7.80) offers boats that blast from Circular Quay to Manly in 18 minutes.

LIGHT RAIL

Tram services run between Central Station and Dulwich Hill, stopping at Chinatown, Darling Harbour, The Star casino, Sydney Fish Market, Glebe and Leichhardt en route. Opal card fares cost $2.10 for a short journey and $3.50 for a longer one.

TRAIN

Sydney Trains (13 15 00; www.sydneytrains.info) has a large suburban railway web with relatively frequent services, although there are no lines to the northern or eastern beaches. Trains run from around 5am to midnight. A short one-way trip costs $3.38 with an Opal card, or $2.36 off-peak.

CAR & MOTORCYCLE

Avoid driving in central Sydney if you can: there's a confusing one-way street system, parking is elusive and expensive (even at hotels), and parking inspectors, tolls and tow-away zones proliferate. Conversely, a car is handy for accessing Sydney's outer reaches (particularly the beaches) and for day trips.

Online Resources

Destination NSW (www.sydney.com) Official visitors' guide.

City of Sydney (www.cityofsydney.nsw.gov.au) Council-run site for visitor information.

Sydney Morning Herald (www.smh.com.au) Daily newspaper.

Lonely Planet (www.lonelyplanet.com/australia/sydney) Destination information.

Opal Cards

Sydney's public transport network runs on a smartcard system called **Opal** (www.opal.com.au). The card can be obtained (for free) and loaded with credit (minimum $10) at newsagencies and convenience stores across Sydney. When commencing a journey you touch the card to an electronic reader, located at train station gates, near bus and light rail doors and at ferry wharves. You then touch a reader when you complete your journey so that the system can deduct the correct fare. Daily charges are capped at $15 ($2.50 on Sundays).

You can still buy single tickets (Opal single trip tickets) from machines at train stations, ferry wharves and light rail stops, or from bus drivers, but they're more expensive than Opal card fares.

TOLL ROADS

There are hefty tolls on most of Sydney's motorways and major links (including the Harbour Bridge, Harbour Tunnel, Cross City Tunnel and Eastern Distributor). The tolling system is electronic: organise an electronic tag or visitors' pass through any of the following websites: www.roam.com.au, www.roamexpress.com.au, www.tollpay.com.au or www.myetoll.com.au. Note that most car-hire companies can supply e-tags.

TAXI

Metered taxis are easy to flag down in the central city and inner suburbs, except for at changeover times (3pm and 3am). Fares are regulated, so all companies charge the same. Flagfall is $3.60, with a $2.50 'night owl surcharge' after 10pm on a Friday and Saturday until 6am the following morning. The fare thereafter is $2.19 per kilometre, with an additional surcharge of 20% between 10pm and 6am nightly. There's also a $2.50 fee for bookings.

Major operators:

Legion Cabs (☎13 14 51; www.legioncabs.com.au)

Premier Cabs (☎13 10 17; www.premiercabs.com.au)

Taxis Combined (☎133 300; www.taxiscombined.com.au)

WATER TAXI

Water taxis are a fast way to shunt around the harbour (Circular Quay to Watsons Bay in as little as 15 minutes). Companies will quote on any pick-up point within the harbour and the river, including private jetties, islands and other boats. All have a quote generator on their websites. It's much better value for groups than couples.

Water-taxi companies:

Fantasea Yellow Water Taxis (Map p50; ☎1800 326 822; www.yellowwatertaxis.com.au; Cockle Bay Wharf; ⏲7.30am-10pm, prebooking required for service outside these hours)

H2O Maxi Taxis (☎1300 426 829; www.h2owatertaxis.com.au)

Water Taxis Combined (☎02-9555 8888; www.watertaxis.com.au)

Where to Stay

Neighbourhood	Atmosphere
Circular Quay & the Rocks	Big-ticket sights; vibrant nightlife; high-end hotels and restaurants; tourist central.
Sydney Harbour	Everywhere is a pleasant ferry journey from town; can be isolated.
City Centre & Haymarket	Good transport links; lots of sights, bars, fantastic Asian restaurants; can be noisy.
Darling Harbour & Pyrmont	Plenty to see and do; lively nightlife; top-end restaurants; not exactly soulful.
Glebe & Newtown	Bohemian; great coffee; interesting shops; priced for locals; thin on tourist sights.
Surry Hills & Darlinghurst	Sydney's hippest eating and drinking precinct; heart of the gay scene; few actual sights.
Kings Cross & Potts Point	Interesting and idiosyncratic; numerous hostels, bars and clubs; good transport links; sleazy stripclubs and dodgy alleyways.
Paddington & Centennial Park	Leafy and genteel, but not exactly thrilling; bus access to city and beaches; few sights.
Bondi to Coogee	Sand, surf and sexy bods; party bars; slow bus ride to the city.
Manly	Beautiful beaches; community feel; fair weather destination.

Echo Point lookout (p76)

The Blue Mountains

On Sydney's back doorstep, the World Heritage–listed Blue Mountains are a must-see. A dense green canopy gives way to deep valleys, chiselled sandstone outcrops and quaint mountain towns.

Great For...

☑ Don't Miss

Echo Point's clifftop viewing platform, for killer views of the craggy Three Sisters.

Head for the Hills

The Blue Mountains' foothills begin 65km inland from Sydney, rising to an 1100m-high sandstone plateau riddled with valleys eroded into the stone. There are eight connected conservation areas in the region, offering truly fantastic scenery, excellent bushwalks (hikes), Aboriginal engravings, and all the canyons and cliffs you could ask for.

Although it's possible to day-trip from Sydney, consider staying a night (or longer) so you can explore the towns, do at least one bushwalk and eat at some of the excellent restaurants.

Mountain Towns

In order of approach from Sydney, here's a rundown of the main Blue Mountain towns.

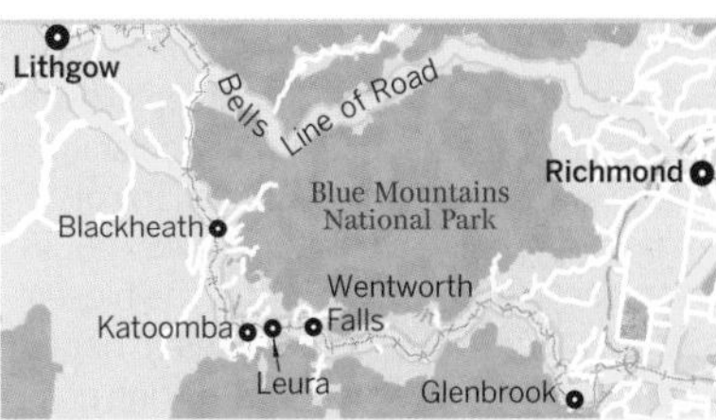

Need to Know

Trains (☎13 15 00; www.sydneytrains.info) run hourly from Sydney's Central Station to Katoomba (two hours). **Blue Mountains Bus** (☎02-4751 1077; www.bmbc.com.au) also links towns.

Take a Break

Katoomba's **Station Bar & Woodfired Pizza** (☎02-4782 4782; www.stationbar.com.au; 287 Bathurst Rd; pizzas $18-26; ⊙noon-midnight; 📶) has good things: craft beer, pizza and live music.

★ Top Tip

The Blue Mountains can get surprisingly chilly, even in summer: bring warm clothes.

Glenbrook

From unassuming Glenbrook you can drive or walk into the lower reaches of Blue Mountains National Park (p77); this is the only part of the park where vehicle entry fees apply ($8). Six kilometres from the park entrance gate is the **Mt Portal Lookout**, with panoramic views into the Glenbrook Gorge, over the Nepean River and back to Sydney. **Red Hands Cave** (www.nationalparks.nsw.gov.au) houses an Aboriginal rock-art gallery: it's an easy 7km walk from **Glenbrook Information Centre** (☎1300 653 408; www.bluemountainscitytourism.com.au; Great Western Hwy; ⊙8.30am-4pm Mon-Sat, to 3pm Sun; 📶).

Wentworth Falls

As you head into Wentworth Falls, you'll get your first real taste of Blue Mountains scenery: views to the south open out across the majestic Jamison Valley. The village itself is pleasant for a short potter along the main street. The **falls** (Falls Rd; 🚊Wentworth Falls) that lend the town its name launch a plume of spray over a 300m drop.

Leura

The Blue Mountains' prettiest town, fashioned around undulating streets, well-tended gardens and sweeping Victorian verandahs. Leura Mall, the tree-lined main street, offers rows of country craft stores and cafes for the daily tourist influx. Southeast of Leura, a sharp, triangular outcrop narrows to the dramatic **Sublime Point** (Sublime Point Rd) lookout with sheer cliffs on each side.

Katoomba

Swirling, otherworldly mists, steep streets lined with art deco buildings, astonishing valley views, and a quirky miscellany of restaurants, buskers, artists, bawdy pubs and classy hotels – Katoomba, the biggest town in the mountains, manages to be bohemian and bourgeois, embracing and distant all at once. The must-see **Echo Point** lookout and **Three Sisters** rock formation are here; **Echo Point Visitors Centre** (☎1300 653 408; www.bluemountainscitytourism.com.au; Echo Point; ⏲9am-5pm) has the local low-down. The natural history exhibits at the **Blue Mountains Cultural Centre** (☎02-4780 5410; www.bluemountainsculturalcentre.com.au; 30 Parke St; adult/child $5/free; ⏲10am-5pm Mon-Fri, to 4pm Sat & Sun) are also worth a look. On the edge of town is the Blue Mountains' most touristy attraction, **Scenic World** (☎02-4780 0200; www.scenicworld.com.au; cnr Violet St & Cliff Dr; adult/child $39/21; ⏲9am-5pm), a cable car offering spectacular views.

Blackheath

The crowds and commercial frenzy fizzle considerably 10km north of Katoomba in neat, petite Blackheath. The town measures up in the scenery stakes, and it makes an excellent base for visiting the Grose and Megalong Valleys. Memorable lookouts around town include **Evans Lookout** (Evans Lookout Rd) and **Govetts Leap Lookout** (Govetts Leap Rd), plus there are trailheads for some top hikes; contact the Blue Mountains Heritage Centre for info.

Hiking the Grand Canyon Walk (p78)

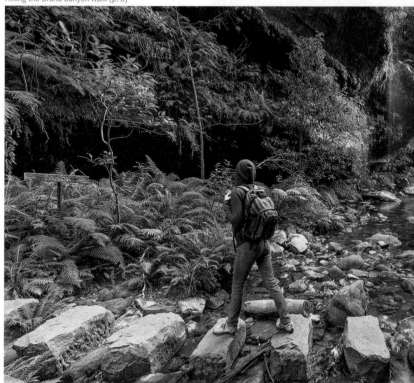

Blackheath is also the gastronomic centre of the region, with some excellent restaurants. For a classy, upbeat dining experience, book a table at **Vesta** (☎02-4787 6899; www.vestablackheath.com.au; 33 Govetts Leap Rd; mains $29-38; ⏰5-10pm Wed-Fri, 12.30-3pm & 5-10pm Sat & Sun, closed Wed summer; 🖉), serving up hearty plates of roasted meats, or **Ashcrofts** (☎02-4787 8297; www.ashcrofts.com; 18 Govetts Leap Rd; mains lunch $20-23, dinner $37-40 ; ⏰6-10pm Thu, 11.30am-2.30pm & 6-10pm Fri, 8am-2.30pm & 6-10pm Sat & Sun), with a short but polished menu of creative flavours.

Did You Know?

The purple haze that gives the Blue Mountains their name comes from a fine mist of oil exuded by eucalyptus trees.

OLGA KASHUBIN/SHUTTERSTOCK ©

Blue Mountains National Park

What is known as the Blue Mountains is actually a sandstone plateau riddled with steep gullies eroded by rivers over thousands of years.

Initially thought to be impenetrable, the mountains were first crossed by European explorers in 1813. On this epic quest, Gregory Blaxland, William Wentworth and William Lawson followed the mountain ridges up over the top; today, their route is pretty much traced by the Great Western Hwy.

More than three million visitors a year visit the scenic lookouts and waterfalls of **Blue Mountains National Park** (www.nationalparks.nsw.gov.au), the most popular and accessible section of the Greater Blue Mountains World Heritage Area. There are bushwalks for everyone, from those with limited fitness to the downright intrepid, lasting from a few minutes to several days.

Bushwalking

For tips on walks to suit your level of experience and fitness, call the National Parks' **Blue Mountains Heritage Centre** (☎02-4787 8877; www.nationalparks.nsw.gov.au; ⏰9am-4.30pm) in Blackheath, or the information centres in Glenbrook (p75) or Katoomba. All three sell a variety of walk pamphlets, maps and books.

As you'd expect in such rugged terrain, there are hazards: walkers get lost, bushfires flare up and there are definitely snakes in the grass. Emergencies are relatively rare, but it pays to get some up-to-date advice from the visitors centres before you propel yourself into the wilderness. The Katoomba police and the national parks and information centres all offer free personal locator beacons and it's strongly suggested you take one with you, especially for longer hikes. Whatever you do, take plenty of water; it can get powerfully hot here, and the steep gradients can dehydrate you fast.

The two most popular bushwalking areas are the Jamison Valley, south of Katoomba, and the Grose Valley, northeast of Katoomba and east of Blackheath. Top choices include the **Golden Stairs Walk** (Glenraphael Dr) in Katoomba and the **Grand Canyon Walk** (Evans Lookout Rd) at Blackheath.

One of the most rewarding long-distance walks is the 45km, three-day **Six Foot Track** from Katoomba along the Megalong Valley to Cox's River and on to the Jenolan Caves. It has camp sites along the way.

Adventure Activities

The Blue Mountains are prime terrain for adventure activities: abseiling, rock climbing, canyoning, mountain biking and guided hiking. The following operators are all in Katoomba.

Blue Mountains Adventure Company Adventure

(02-4782 1271; www.bmac.com.au; 84a Bathurst Rd; abseiling from $150, canyoning $230, bushwalking from $30) Located opposite Katoomba station, this set-up offers abseiling, canyoning, combinations of the two, bushwalking and rock climbing.

High 'n' Wild Australian Adventures Adventure

(02-4782 6224; www.highandwild.com.au; 207 Katoomba St; abseiling $135-225, canyoning $210-260, rock climbing $170) This outfit runs daily tours, offering abseiling, rock climbing, canyoning and various bushwalking and survival courses.

River Deep Mountain High Adventure

(02-4782 6109; www.rdmh.com.au; abseiling $165-230, canyoning $230) A professional outfit rigorous about comfort and safety, these guys offer abseiling, canyoning and a combination of the two. Other options include a range of hiking and mountain-biking tours.

Tours

Blue Mountains Explorer Bus Bus

(1300 300 915; www.explorerbus.com.au; 283 Bathurst Rd; adult/child $44/22; departures 9.45am-4.45pm) Significantly better than its average city equivalents, this is a useful way to get around the most popular Blue Mountains attractions. It offers hop-on, hop-off service on a Katoomba–Leura loop and also has a route taking in Wentworth Falls. Buses leave from Katoomba station every 30 to 60 minutes.

Trolley Tours Bus

(02-4782 7999; www.trolleytours.com.au; 76 Bathurst St; adult/child $25/15) This company runs a hop-on, hop-off bus barely disguised as a trolley, looping around 29 stops in Katoomba and Leura. The same company,

Blue Mountains Botanic Garden Mount Tomah

located opposite Katoomba station, runs buses to the **Jenolan Caves** (☎02-6359 3911; www.jenolancaves.org.au; Jenolan Caves Rd, Jenolan; adult/child from $35/24; ⏰tours 9am-5pm) and various combination packages.

Bells Line of Road

This stretch of road between North Richmond and Lithgow is the most scenic route across the Blue Mountains and is highly recommended if you have the time and your own transport. It's far quieter than the main highway and offers bountiful views.

Bilpin, at the base of the mountains, is known for its apple orchards. The Bilpin Markets are held at the district hall every Saturday from 10am to noon.

Midway between Bilpin and Bell, the **Blue Mountains Botanic Garden Mount Tomah** (☎02-4567 3000; www.rbgsyd.nsw.gov.au; ⏰9am-5.30pm Mon-Fri, 9.30am-5.30pm Sat & Sun) FREE is a cool-climate annexe of Sydney's Royal Botanic Garden where native plants cuddle up to exotic species, including some magnificent rhododendrons.

Worth a Trip

An hour beyond Blackheath are the amazing Jenolan Caves, one of the most extensive, accessible and complex limestone cave systems in the world.

ATTILAVALENTINA/SHUTTERSTOCK ©

Australian Parliament House (p86)

CANBERRA

In this Chapter

Canberra at a Glance...

Canberra is a wonderfully green little city, with a lively and sophisticated dining and bar scene, interesting architecture and a smorgasbord of major institutions to keep even the most avid culture vulture engrossed for days on end.

Canberra was laid out by visionary American architect Walter Burley Griffin and his wife Marion Mahony Griffin following an international design competition. The city features expansive open spaces, broad boulevards and a seamless alignment of built and natural elements... and, of course, the buzz of national politics.

Canberra in Two Days

Begin your Canberra jaunt at the **National Gallery of Australia** (p84). In the afternoon, attend Question Time at **Parliament House** (p86; during sitting weeks), continuing the debate over dinner in the **Civic district** (p89).

Next day, head to the **National Museum of Australia** (p84) then explore the **Australian National Botanic Gardens** (p86). Dine at **Morks** (p90) on the Kingston Foreshore among the city's movers and shakers.

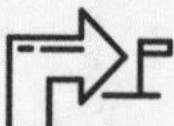

Canberra in Four Days

On day three, check out the faces at the **National Portrait Gallery** (p85), then cycle around impressive **Lake Burley Griffin** (p86). Drinks at the **BentSpoke Brewing Co** (p92) await.

On day four, hit **Lonsdale Street Roasters** (p89) in Braddon, then pay your respects at the haunting **Australian War Memorial** (p85).

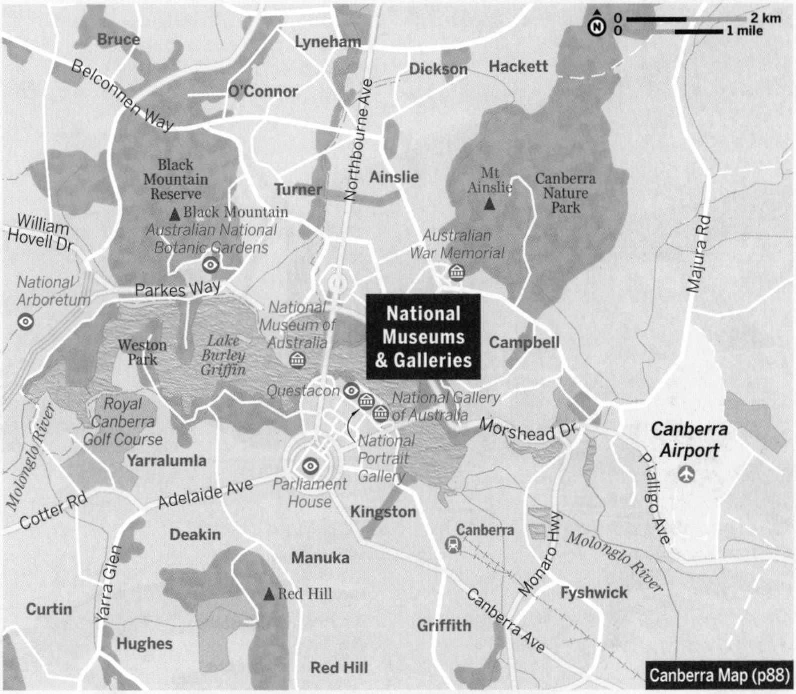

Canberra Map (p88)

Arriving in Canberra

Canberra Airport (p93) It's a 10-minute drive from the airport into the city centre. A taxi costs around $50; Airport Express (p93) shuttles run to the city hourly during the day.

Canberra Railway Station Services from Sydney (four hours) pull into the station in Kingston.

Jolimont Tourist Centre Departure point for interstate buses. It takes five hours to Sydney.

Where to Stay

Canberra is totally geared towards the car: nobody walks anywhere. Wherever you stay, you'll be driving, bussing or cabbing to your daily destinations. Stay in Civic, Kingston or Griffith for eating options; or New Acton, the Kingston Foreshore or Braddon if you're feeling hip. Accommodation gets busy and pricey during parliamentary sitting days (mid-week); rates cool off on weekends.

National Museum of Australia

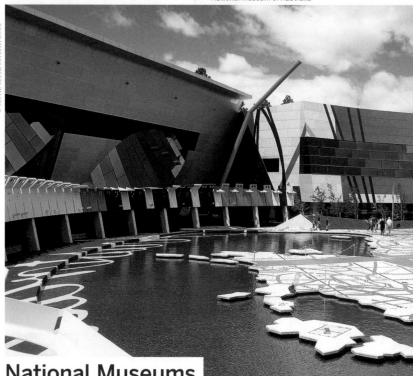

National Museums & Galleries

You don't have to go far in Canberra to find a world-class museum or gallery. The city features some of Australia's best collections of art and artefacts.

Great For...

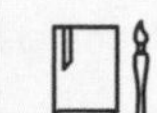

☑ Don't Miss

The National Museum's introductory film, shown in the small rotating Circa Theatre.

National Gallery of Australia Gallery

(☎02-6240 6502; www.nga.gov.au; Parkes Pl, Parkes; costs vary for special exhibitions; ⏱10am-5pm) FREE The nation's extraordinary art collection is showcased in a suitably huge purpose-built gallery within the parliamentary precinct. Almost every big name you could think of from the world of Australian and international art, past and present, is represented. Famous works include one of Monet's *Waterlilies*, several of Sidney Nolan's *Ned Kelly* paintings, Salvador Dalí's *Lobster Telephone*, an Andy Warhol *Elvis* print and a triptych by Francis Bacon.

National Museum of Australia Museum

(☎02-6208 5000; www.nma.gov.au; Lawson Cres, Acton Peninsula; tours adult/child $15/10;

Need to Know

Many museums and galleries here are free; expect admission fees for temporary or special exhibits.

Take a Break

Picnic in Commonwealth Park, outside the National Museum on the sunny lake shore.

Top Tip

Be at the War Memorial for closing time to hear the moving 'Last Post', in honour of the fallen.

9am-5pm) FREE As well as telling Australia's national story, this museum hosts blockbuster touring exhibitions. Don't miss the 12-minute introductory film, shown in the small rotating Circa Theatre before you dig in. The exhibition jam-packed with Aboriginal artefacts is a highlight. However, the disjointed layout of the displays means that the museum didn't quite gel in the way that Canberra's other national cultural institutions do.

National Portrait Gallery Gallery

(02-6102 7000; www.portrait.gov.au; King Edward Tce, Parkes; 10am-5pm) FREE Occupying a flash new purpose-built building, this wonderful gallery tells the story of Australia through its faces – from wax cameos of Indigenous Australians to colonial portraits of the nation's founding families, to Howard Arkley's DayGlo portrait of musician Nick Cave. There is a good cafe for post-exhibition coffee and reflection.

Australian War Memorial Museum

(02-6243 4211; www.awm.gov.au; Treloar Cres, Campbell; 10am-5pm) FREE Canberra's glorious art deco war memorial is a highlight in a city filled with interesting architecture. Built to commemorate 'the war to end all wars', it opened its doors in 1941 when the next world war was already in full swing. Attached to it is a large, exceptionally well designed museum devoted to the nation's military history.

Questacon Museum

(National Science & Technology Centre; 02-6270 2800; www.questacon.edu.au; King Edward Tce, Parkes; adult/child $23/18; 9am-5pm;) This kid-friendly science centre has educational and fun interactive exhibits. Explore the physics of sport, athletics and fun parks; cause tsunamis; and take shelter from cyclones and earthquakes. Exciting science shows, presentations and puppet shows are all included.

SIGHTS

Australian Parliament House Notable Building

(☎02-6277 5399; www.aph.gov.au; ⏰9am-5pm) FREE Opened in 1988, Australia's national parliament building is a graceful and deeply symbolic piece of architecture. The building itself is embedded in the Australian soil, covered with a turf roof and topped by a spindly but soaring 81m-high flagpole. The same detailed thought has been applied to the interior and there's plenty to see inside, whether the politicians are haranguing each other in the chambers or not.

Australian National Botanic Gardens Gardens

(☎02-6250 9588; www.nationalbotanicgardens.gov.au; Clunies Ross St, Acton; ⏰8.30am-5pm) FREE On Black Mountain's lower slopes, these large gardens showcase Australian floral diversity over 35 hectares of cultivated garden and 50 hectares of remnant bushland. Various themed routes are marked out, with the best introduction being the 30- to 45- minute main path, which takes in the eucalypt lawn (70 species are represented), rock garden, rainforest gully and Sydney Region garden. A 3.2km bushland nature trail leads to the garden's higher reaches.

Museum of Australian Democracy Museum

(☎02-6270 8222; www.moadoph.gov.au; Old Parliament House, 18 King George Tce, Parkes; adult/child/family $2/1/5; ⏰9am-5pm) The seat of government from 1927 to 1988, this elegantly proportioned building offers visitors a whiff of the political past. Displays cover Australian prime ministers, the roots of democracy and the history of local protest movements. You can also visit the old Senate and House of Representative chambers, the parliamentary library and the prime minister's office.

Lake Burley Griffin Lake

This ornamental lake was created in 1963 when the 33m-high Scrivener Dam was erected on the Molonglo River. It's lined with important institutions and monuments, including the **National Carillon**

Lake Burley Griffin

WORAWOOT TONG/SHUTTERSTOCK ©

(☎02-6257 1068; www.nationalcapital.gov.au; Aspen Island) and Captain Cook Memorial Water Jet. You can cycle the entire 28km perimeter in two hours or walk it in seven.

National Film & Sound Archive Library

(☎02-6248 2000; www.nfsa.gov.au; McCoy Circuit, Acton; ⊙9am-5pm Mon-Fri) FREE Set in a delightful art deco building (look for the stained-glass platypus in the foyer dome), this archive preserves Australian moving-picture and sound recordings. There's little in the way of displays but there's a cafe and a cute little theatre where documentaries are played.

National Library of Australia Library

(☎02-6262 1111; www.nla.gov.au; Parkes Pl, Parkes; ⊙gallery 10am-5pm) FREE This institution has accumulated more than 10 million items since being established in 1901 and has digitised more than nine billion files. Don't miss the Treasures Gallery, where artefacts such as Captain Cook's *Endeavour* journal and Captain Bligh's list of mutineers are among the regularly refreshed displays; free 30-minute tours are held at 11.30am daily.

National Arboretum Park

(☎02-6207 8484; www.nationalarboretum.act.gov.au; Forest Dr, Weston Creek; ⊙6am-8.30pm Oct-Mar, 7am-5.30pm Apr-Sep) FREE Located on land previously affected by bushfires, Canberra's National Arboretum is an ever-developing showcase of trees from around the world. It is early days for many of the plantings, but it's still worth visiting for the spectacular visitor centre and the excellent views over the city. Regular guided tours are informative, and there is a brilliant adventure playground for kids.

National Capital Exhibition Museum

(☎02-6272 2902; www.nationalcapital.gov.au; Barrine Dr, Commonwealth Park; ⊙9am-5pm) FREE This small but fascinating museum tells the story of how Canberra came to be Australia's capital. Displays include reproductions of the drawings entered in the international competition to design the city, including the exquisite watercolour renderings of the winning design created by Marion Mahony Griffin, the often overlooked wife and creative partner of Walter Burley Griffin.

Cycling Canberra

Canberra has an extensive network of dedicated cycle paths. The Canberra & Region Visitors Centre (p92) stocks the *Lake Burley Griffin Cycle Routes* brochure and the *Walking & Cycling Map* published by Pedal Power ACT (www.pedalpower.org.au). Free-wheelin' good times!

Cycling near Lake Burley Griffin
ANDREW WATSON/GETTY IMAGES ©

TOURS

Balloon Aloft Ballooning

(☎02-6249 8660; www.canberraballoons.com.au; 120 Commonwealth Ave, Yarralumla; adult/child from $330/240) Meet in the foyer of the Hyatt for a flight over Canberra – the ideal way to understand the city's unique design.

Lake Burley Griffin Cruises Cruise

(☎0419 418 846; www.lakecruises.com.au; Barrine Dr, Acton; adult/child $20/9; ⊙mid-Sep–May) Informative one-hour lake cruises.

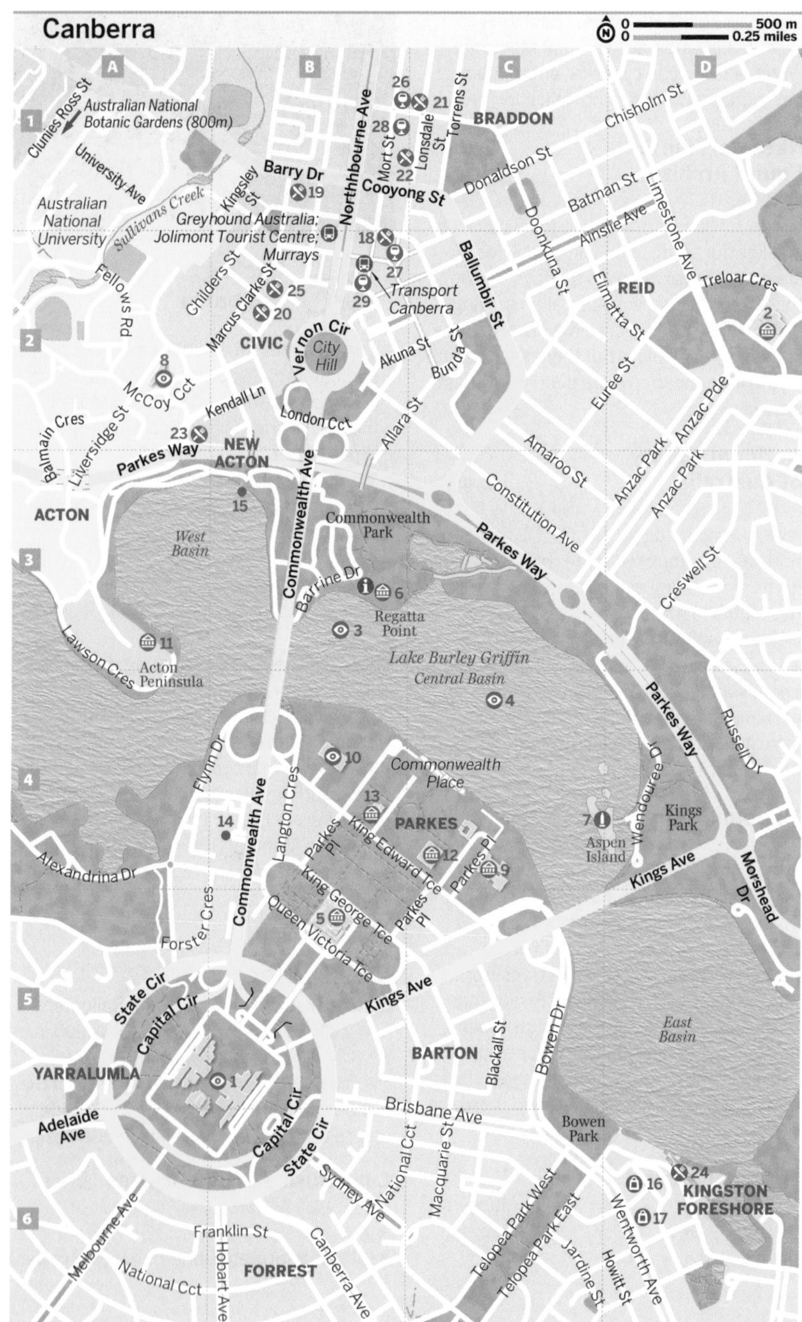

Canberra
0 500 m
0 0.25 miles
A
B
C
D
1
2
3
4
5
6
Australian National Botanic Gardens (800m)
Clunies Ross St
University Ave
Australian National University
Sullivans Creek
Kingsley St
Barry Dr
19
Northbourne Ave
Cooyong St
26
21
28
22
Mort St
Lonsdale St
Torrens St
BRADDON
Chisholm St
Donaldson St
Batman St
Ainslie Ave
Limestone Ave
Doonkuna St
Greyhound Australia; Jolimont Tourist Centre; Murrays
18
27
29
Transport Canberra
Ballumbir St
Elimatta St
REID
Treloar Cres
2
Fellows Rd
Childers St
Marcus Clarke St
25
20
CIVIC
Vernon Cir
City Hill
Akuna St
Bunda St
Euree St
Anzac Pde
8
McCoy Cct
Balmain Cres
Liversidge St
Kendall Ln
London Cct
Allara St
23
Parkes Way
NEW ACTON
Amaroo St
Anzac Park
Constitution Ave
ACTON
15
West Basin
Commonwealth Ave
Commonwealth Park
Parkes Way
Barrine Dr
6
Regatta Point
3
Creswell St
Lawson Cres
11
Acton Peninsula
Lake Burley Griffin
Central Basin
4
Parkes Way
Russell Dr
Flynn Dr
10
Commonwealth Place
Wendouree Dr
Kings Park
Langton Cres
13
14
PARKES
Parkes Pl
King Edward Tce
12
9
7
Aspen Island
Alexandrina Dr
King George Tce
Kings Ave
Morshead Dr
Forster Cres
Queen Victoria Tce
5
State Cir
Capital Cir
Kings Ave
BARTON
Blackall St
Bowen Dr
East Basin
YARRALUMLA
1
Adelaide Ave
Capital Cir
State Cir
Brisbane Ave
Bowen Park
National Cct
Macquarie St
Sydney Ave
24
16
17
KINGSTON FORESHORE
Melbourne Ave
Franklin St
Hobart Ave
FORREST
Canberra Ave
National Cct
Telopea Park West
Telopea Park East
Jardine St
Howitt St
Wentworth Ave

Canberra

Sights

1 Australian Parliament House B5
2 Australian War Memorial D2
3 Captain Cook Memorial Water Jet B3
4 Lake Burley Griffin C4
5 Museum of Australian Democracy B5
6 National Capital Exhibition B3
7 National Carillon C4
8 National Film & Sound Archive A2
9 National Gallery of Australia C4
10 National Library of Australia B4
11 National Museum of Australia A3
12 National Portrait Gallery C4
13 Questacon B4

Activities, Courses & Tours

14 Balloon Aloft B4
15 Lake Burley Griffin Cruises B3

Shopping

16 Canberra Glassworks D6
National Library Bookshop .... (see 10)
17 Old Bus Depot Markets D6

Eating

18 Akiba B2
Brodburger .... (see 16)
19 Courgette B1
20 Cupping Room B2
21 Elk & Pea C1
Lonsdale Street Eatery .... (see 21)
22 Lonsdale Street Roasters B1
23 Monster Kitchen & Bar A2
24 Morks D6
25 Two Before Ten B2

Drinking & Nightlife

26 BentSpoke Brewing Co B1
27 Honky Tonks B2
28 Knightsbridge Penthouse B1
29 Phoenix B2

Entertainment

Palace Electric .... (see 23)

SHOPPING

Old Bus Depot Markets — Market

(02-6295 3331; www.obdm.com.au; 21 Wentworth Ave, Kingston; 10am-4pm Sun) A Sunday institution in Canberra, this large, bustling market has one big hall completely devoted to food and another to crafts.

Canberra Glassworks — Arts & Crafts

(02-6260 7005; www.canberraglassworks.com; 11 Wentworth Ave, Kingston; 10am-4pm Wed-Sun) Call in to this converted Edwardian power station, the young city's oldest public heritage building, to watch glass being blown in the 'hot shop' and to peruse the exquisite results in the adjacent gallery and shop.

National Library Bookshop — Books

(02-6262 1424; http://bookshop.nla.gov.au; Parkes Pl, Parkes; 10am-5pm) Specialises in Australian books.

EATING

Lonsdale Street Roasters — Cafe $

(www.lonsdalestreetroasters.com; 7 Lonsdale St, Braddon; mains $8-12; 6.30am-4pm Mon-Fri, 8am-4pm Sat & Sun) In hip Braddon, this grungy-chic cafe serves up damn fine coffee along with tasty pastries and rolls. There's a bigger **branch** (23 Lonsdale St; mains $15-17; 7am-4pm) just up the road with a large terrace; it has more of an emphasis on eating, but the food's better here at the original.

Two Before Ten — Cafe $

(www.twobeforeten.com.au; 1 Hobart Pl, Civic; mains $11-18; 7am-4pm Mon-Fri, 8am-2pm Sat & Sun) Breaking from the Australian tradition that says good cafes should be bohemian and battered looking, this airy eatery brings a touch of Cape Cod to the centre of a city block. Serves are perhaps a little too fashionably petite but the coffee is excellent.

Malaysian Chapter — Malaysian $$

(02-6251 5670; www.malaysianchapter.com.au; 8 Weedon Close, Belconnen; mains $18-23;

EYEOFPAUL/GETTY IMAGES ©

TRAVELSCAPE IMAGES/ALAMY STOCK PHOTO ©

From left: Poppies in the Australian War Memorial (p85); Glassware display at Canberra Glassworks (p89); Old Bus Depot Markets (p89)

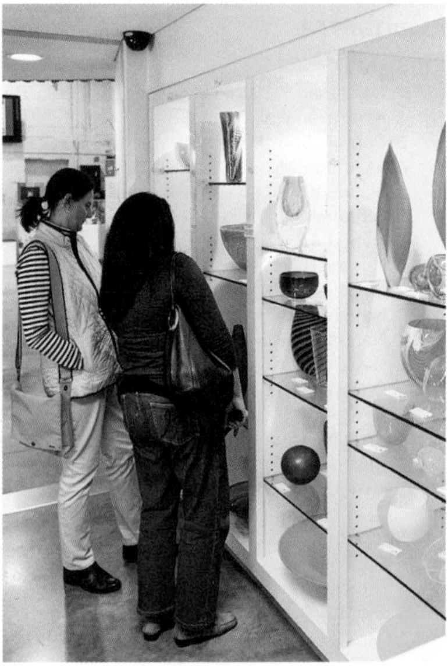

noon-2pm Tue-Fri, 5.30-9pm Mon-Sat;) Fans of authentic Kuala Lumpur hawker cuisine should make the trek around 8km northwest from Civic to this unassuming, family-run spot in the surprisingly large commercial centre of Belconnen. Highlights includes *nasi goreng* (fried rice; served either as a *rendang*, *sambal* or curry), zingy tamarind fish, excellent satay and a cooling sago dessert.

Brodburger Burgers $$

(02-6162 0793; www.brodburger.com.au; Glassworks Bldg, 11 Wentworth Ave, Kingston; burgers $14-21; 11.30am-3pm & 5.30-10pm Tue-Sat, 11.30am-4pm Sun;) Brodburger started as a lakeside caravan takeaway joint. Now it's got a permanent location, but the flame-grilled burgers are as good as ever. Not only is there a good range of meat, fish and vegetarian options, you even get to take your pick from four types of cheese for the cheeseburger.

Elk & Pea Latin American $$

(0436 355 732; www.elkandpea.com.au; 21 Lonsdale St, Braddon; breakfast & lunch $11-25, tacos $8, shared plates $39-45; 7.30am-2.30pm Mon, to 11pm Tue-Sun) Mexican influences pervade the menu and cocktail list of this hip, anytime eatery, which includes spicy eggs for brekkie, burgers and wraps for lunch and Canberra's best tacos for dinner.

Monster Kitchen & Bar Modern Australian $$

(02-6287 6287; www.monsterkitchen.com.au; Hotel Hotel, 25 Edinburgh Ave, New Acton; breakfast $16-19, shared plates $20-35; 6.30am-1am) Concealed in the ubercool Hotel Hotel, Monster is one of Canberra's more versatile eateries. Hotel guests, New Acton trendies and politicians alike check their Instagram feeds over breakfast. Shared plates with a subtle Middle Eastern influence get everyone talking during lunch and dinner. At night it morphs into a bar.

Morks Thai $$

(02-6295 0112; www.morks.com.au; 19 Eastlake Pde, Kingston; mains $24-30; noon-2pm & 6-10pm Tue-Sat, noon-2pm Sun) Our favourite of the restaurants along the Kingston foreshore, Morks offers a contemporary spin on Thai cuisine, with Chinese and Malay elements added to the mix. Ask for a table

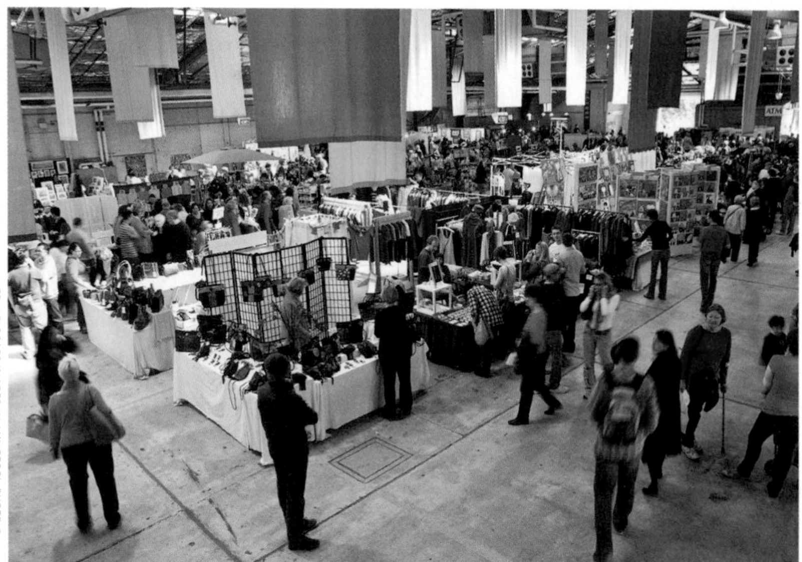
TRAVELSCAPE IMAGES/ALAMY STOCK PHOTO ©

outside to watch the passing promenade, and tuck into multiple serves of the starters; the sweet-potato dumplings in Penang curry are staggeringly good.

Akiba Asian $$

(☎02-6162 0602; www.akiba.com.au; 40 Bunda St, Civic; noodle & rice dishes $12-15, share plates $18-33; ⊙11.30am-midnight Sun-Wed, to 2am Thu-Sat) A high-octane vibe pervades this super-slick pan-Asian eatery, fuelled by a hip young crew that effortlessly splashes together cocktails, dispenses food recommendations and juggles orders without breaking a sweat. A raw bar serves up delectable sashimi, freshly shucked oysters and zingy ceviche.

Cupping Room Cafe $$

(☎02-6257 6412; www.thecuppingroom.com.au; 1 University Ave, Civic; mains $11-24; ⊙7am-4pm; ☑) Queues often form outside this airy corner cafe, drawn by the prospect of Canberra's best coffee and an interesting menu, including vegetarian and vegan options. The seasonal chia pudding is extraordinary, but if you prefer something a little more familiar, the burgers are equally epic.

Aubergine Modern Australian $$$

(☎02-6260 8666; www.aubergine.com.au; 18 Barker St, Griffith; 4-course menu $90; ⊙6-10pm Mon-Sat) You'll need to travel out to the southern suburbs to find Canberra's top-rated restaurant. While the location may be unassuming, the same can't be said for the menu, which is exciting, innovative and seasonally driven. Although only a four-course menu is offered, you can choose between a handful of options for most courses. Service and presentation are assured.

Courgette Modern Australian $$$

(☎02-6247 4042; www.courgette.com.au; 54 Marcus Clarke St, Civic; 3-course lunch $66, 4-course dinner $88; ⊙noon-3pm & 6.30-11pm Mon-Sat) With its crisp white linen, impeccable service and discreet but expensive ambience, Courgette is the kind of place to bring someone you want to impress, like a date or, perhaps, the Finnish ambassador.

Canberra History

In 1901 Australia's separate colonies were federated and became states. The rivalry between Sydney and Melbourne meant neither could become the new nation's capital, so a location between the two cities was carved out of southern New South Wales (NSW) as a compromise. This new city was officially named Canberra in 1913, and replaced Melbourne as the national capital in 1927.

The Ngunnawal people called this place 'Kanberra', believed to mean 'meeting place'. The name was probably derived from huge intertribal gatherings that happened annually when large numbers of Bogong moths appeared in the city.

DRINKING & NIGHTLIFE

BentSpoke Brewing Co Microbrewery

(02-6257 5220; www.bentspokebrewing.com.au; 38 Mort St, Braddon; 11am-midnight) With 16 excellent beers and ciders on tap, BentSpoke is one of Australia's best craft brewers. Sit at the bike-themed bar or relax outside and kick things off with a tasting tray of four beers ($16). Our favourite is the Barley Griffin Ale, subtly tinged with a spicy Belgian yeast.

Honky Tonks Bar

(02-6262 6968; www.drinkhonkytonks.com.au; 17 Garema Pl, Civic; noon-late Mon-Fri, 2pm-late Sat & Sun) Canberra's compadres meet up here to eat tacos, drink margaritas and listen to eclectic sets from the DJ. It's loads of fun.

Knightsbridge Penthouse Cocktail Bar

(02-6262 6221; www.knightsbridgepenthouse.com.au; 34 Mort St, Braddon; 5pm-midnight Tue & Wed, to late Thu-Sat) Kooky, arty and very hip, with good DJs, excellent cocktails and a mellow ambience.

ENTERTAINMENT

Palace Electric Cinema

(02-6222 4900; www.palacecinemas.com.au; 2 Phillip Law St, New Acton) Art-house and independent movies.

Phoenix Pub

(02-6169 5092; www.lovethephoenix.com; 23 East Row, Civic; 5pm-1am Mon-Wed, to 3am Thu-Sat) The studenty Phoenix is a staunch supporter of local music, with bands playing around four nights a week.

INFORMATION

Canberra & Region Visitors Centre (02-6205 0044; www.visitcanberra.com.au; Regatta Point, Barrine Dr, Commonwealth Park; 9am-4pm) Dispenses masses of information, including its own quarterly *Canberra Events* brochure.

Canberra Hospital (02-6244 2222; www.health.act.gov.au; Yamba Dr, Garran; emergency 24hr)

GETTING THERE & AWAY

AIR

Qantas (www.qantas.com) flies to/from Adelaide, Brisbane, Melbourne, Perth and Sydney. **Virgin Australia** (www.virginaustralia.com.au) flies to/from Adelaide, Brisbane, Gold Coast, Melbourne and Sydney. **Tigerair Australia** (www.tigerair.com.au) also heads to Melbourne.

BUS

The interstate bus terminal is at the **Jolimont Tourist Centre** (67 Northbourne Ave, Civic; 5am-10.30pm).

Greyhound Australia (1300 473 946; www.greyhound.com.au) Coaches to Sydney ($42, 3½ hours) and Melbourne ($88, eight hours).

Murrays (13 22 51; www.murrays.com.au; 65 Northbourne Ave; 7am-7pm) Express services to Sydney ($45, 3½ hours).

ALECTRUSLER2015/SHUTTERSTOCK ©

Hot air balloons over Lake Burley Griffin (p86)

CAR & MOTORCYCLE

The Hume Hwy connects Sydney and Melbourne, passing 50km north of Canberra. The Federal Hwy runs north to connect with the Hume near Goulburn.

TRAIN

NSW TrainLink (☎13 22 32; www.nswtrainlink.info) services from Sydney ($56, four hours) pull into Kingston's **Canberra Railway Station** (Wentworth Ave, Kingston) three times daily.

A daily **V/Line** (☎1800 800 007; www.vline.com.au) service combines a train from Melbourne to Albury-Wodonga with a bus to Canberra ($108, nine hours).

GETTING AROUND

TO/FROM THE AIRPORT

Canberra Airport (☎02-6275 2222; www.canberraairport.com.au; 2 Brindabella Circuit) is within the city itself, only 7km southeast of Civic. A taxi to the city centre costs around $50.

Airport Express (☎1300 368 897; www.royalecoach.com.au; one way/return $12/20) runs between the airport and the city roughly hourly during the day. Transport Canberra bus 11 runs between city platform 9 and Brindabella Business Park (next to the airport) at least hourly between 6am and 6pm.

PUBLIC TRANSPORT

The bus network, operated by **Transport Canberra** (☎13 17 10; www.transport.act.gov.au; East Row, Civic; adult/child $4.70/2.30, day pass $9/4.50; information centre 6.30am-10pm Mon-Sat, 8am-7pm Sun), will get you to most places of interest in the city. A smart-card system operates, but if you're only here for a week or so, you're better off paying the driver in cash. The city bus station comprises 11 bus stops along Northbourne Ave, Alinga St, East Row and Mort St.

A new light rail track running north from Civic is scheduled to be completed in late 2018.

TAXI

Cabxpress (☎02-6181 2700; www.cabxpress.com.au)

Canberra Elite Taxis (☎13 22 27; www.canberraelite.com.au)

BYRON BAY

In this Chapter

Byron Bay at a Glance...

The reputation of this famous beach town on the New South Wales north coast precedes it – as they say in Byron, it's got a great vibe! Come to surf epic breaks at dawn, paddle through hazy beach afternoons and sigh at the enchanting sunsets. Come to do reiki, refine your yoga practice, do a raw fast and hang with the fire-twirlers by the beach at sunset. Idle at the town's excellent restaurant tables, then kick on with backpackers, musicians, models, young entrepreneurs, ageing hippies and property developers at one of its beery, shouty pubs. Do it all, then repeat!

Byron Bay in Two Days

Don't muck around: down an excellent cafe breakfast then book a **surf lesson** (p99). Take your pick of excellent dinner options, then hit Byron's bars: everyone seems to end up at **The Rails** (p104).

Next day, ignore your hangover and head for **Cape Byron Lighthouse** (p100) to see the sunrise. A day of alt therapies awaits: yoga, massage, meditation...

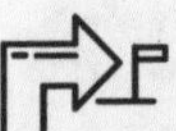

Byron Bay in Four Days

Book a hinterland **day tour** (p100) to check out waterfalls and hippie, smoke-hazed Nimbin. Back in Byron, catch a live band at the **Great Northern** (p104).

Thursday? Don't miss **Byron Farmers' Market** (p100). Otherwise, get a different take on Byron via a kayaking tour in **Cape Byron State Conservation Park** (exhibitionist dolphins guaranteed; p100).

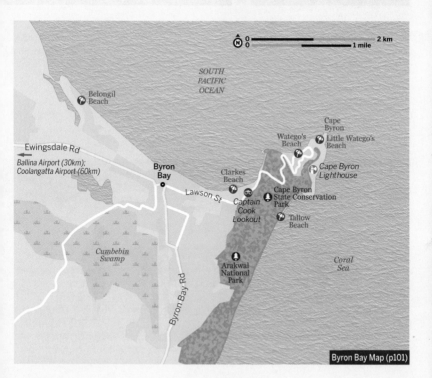

0 2 km
0 1 mile
SOUTH PACIFIC OCEAN
Belongil Beach
Cape Byron
Watego's Beach
Little Watego's Beach
Cape Byron Lighthouse
Ewingsdale Rd
Ballina Airport (30km); Coolangatta Airport (60km)
Byron Bay
Clarkes Beach
Lawson St
Captain Cook Lookout
Cape Byron State Conservation Park
Tallow Beach
Cumbebin Swamp
Arakwal National Park
Coral Sea
Byron Bay Rd

Byron Bay Map (p101)

Arriving in Byron Bay

Byron's train service is no more, so you'll either be arriving here under your own steam (surfing road trip!), rolling into town on a bus, or catching a flight to the nearby Ballina (p105) or Gold Coast Airport (p105). Shuttles service both airports. Qantas flies from Sydney; Jetstar and Virgin also service Melbourne.

Where to Stay

Byron beds are expensive, and the whole town does book out. But if you're in the market for 'barefoot luxury' – relaxed but stylish – you're in luck. Book well in advance for January, during festival times (eg Bluesfest at Easter) and school holidays. If you're not on the edge of 17, avoid Schoolies Week in mid-November.

Surfing in Byron

Learning to surf is an Australian rite of passage – if you feel like joining in, Byron Bay has plenty of good learn-to-surf schools and waves for beginners through to pros.

Great For

☑ Don't Miss

The Ben King Memorial Surf Classic competition in June, running for 40-plus years.

Surf Culture in Australia

Australia has been synonymous with surfing ever since the Beach Boys effused about 'Australia's Narrabeen', one of Sydney's northern beaches, in 'Surfin' USA'. Other surfing hotspots such as Bells Beach, Margaret River, the Pass at Byron Bay, the heavy-breaking Shipstern Bluff in Tasmania and Burleigh Heads on the Gold Coast also resonate with international wave addicts. Iron Man and Surf Lifesaving competitions are also held on beaches around the country, attracting dedicated fans to the sand.

More than a few Australian surfers have attained 'World Champion' status. In the men's competition, legendary surfers include Mark Richards, Tom Carroll, Joel Parkinson and 2013 champ Mick Fanning.

PETE SEAWARD/LONELY PLANET ©

On the women's side, iconic Aussie surfers include Wendy Botha, seven-time champion Layne Beachley, 2014 champ (and six-time winner) Stephanie Gilmore and 2016 winner Tyler Wright.

The Pass

Byron's famous break is the Pass, a long, lusciously peeling right-hander formed by waves refracting around Cape Byron (Australia's most easterly point) and running almost at right angles to the shore. It's surfable even when it's small, but gets mighty crowded when the swell picks up.

It's not really beginners' terrain: cut your teeth over at Main Beach instead.

Need to Know

Surfing apps (eg Magic Seaweed) will help you find the best breaks.

Take a Break

Nurse your sore limbs over an ale at the **Byron Bay Brewing Co** (p104).

★ Top Tip

Belongil Beach, 1km north of Main Beach, is quieter and good for all levels.

Surf Schools

There are plenty of surfing instructors in Byron Bay who can get you safely out into the waves and, with a bit of hard work and natural ability kicking in, have you standing up and barrelling towards the shore after a lesson or two.

Tip: it ain't as easy at it looks!

Surf schools all provide wetsuits and boards. Afterwards, once you've worked up a bit of confidence, most hostels provide free boards to guests, or you can rent all the requisite gear from local surf shops.

Black Dog Surfing Surfing
(☎02-6680 9828; www.blackdogsurfing.com; 11 Byron St; 3½hr lessons $65) Intimate (seven people max) group lessons, including women's and kids' courses. Highly rated.

Soul Surf School Surfing
(☎1800 089 699; www.soulsurfschool.com.au; 4hr lessons $65) Half-day to five-day courses for beginners.

Surfing Byron Bay Surfing
(☎02-6685 7099; www.gosurfingbyronbay.com; 84 Jonson St; 2½hr lessons $60) Surfing lessons for adults and kids, plus a 'surf yoga' combo.

SIGHTS

Cape Byron State Conservation Park State Park
(www.nationalparks.nsw.gov.au/cape-byron-state-conservation-area) Spectacular views reward those who climb up from the **Captain Cook Lookout** (Lighthouse Rd) on the Cape Byron Walking Track. Ribboning around the headland, the track dips and (mostly) soars its way to **Cape Byron Lighthouse** (www.nationalparks.nsw.gov.au; Lighthouse Rd; parking $7; 10am-4pm). Along the way, look out for dolphins (year-round) and migrating whales during their northern (June to July) and southern (September to November) migrations. You're also likely to encounter bold brush turkeys and shyer wallabies. Allow about two hours for the entire 3.7km loop.

Beaches

West of the town centre, wild **Belongil Beach** with its high dunes avoids the worst of the crowds and is clothing optional in parts. At its eastern end is the Wreck, a powerful right-hand surf break.

Immediately in front of town, lifesaver-patrolled **Main Beach** is busy from sunrise to sunset with yoga classes, buskers and fire dancers. As it stretches east it merges into **Clarkes Beach**. The most popular surf break is at the Pass near the eastern headland. Around the rocks is gorgeous **Watego's Beach**, a wide crescent of white sand surrounded by rainforest. A further 400m walk brings you to secluded **Little Watego's** (inaccessible by car) another lovely patch of sand directly under rocky Cape Byron. Tucked under the south side of the Cape (entry via Tallow Beach Rd) is **Cosy Corner** which offers a decent-size wave and sheltered beach when the northerlies are blowing elsewhere.

Tallow Beach is a deserted sandy stretch that extends for 7km south from Cape Byron. This is the place to flee the crowds. **Kings Beach** is a popular gay beach, just off Seven Mile Beach Rd past the Broken Head Holiday Park.

ACTIVITIES

Go Sea Kayaks Kayaking
(0416 222 344; www.goseakayakbyronbay.com.au; adult/child $69/59) Sea-kayak tours in Cape Byron Marine Park led by a team of local surf lifesavers.

Sundive Diving, Snorkelling
(02-6685 7755; www.sundive.com.au; 8/9-11 Byron St; dives from $99, snorkelling tours $70) Two to three expeditions to Julian Rocks daily, plus various courses.

Surf & Bike Hire Cycling
(02-6680 7066; www.byronbaysurfandbikehire.com.au; 31 Lawson St; 9am-5pm) Rents bikes and surfboards (from $10 per day) plus other active gear.

Buddha Gardens Spa
(02-6680 7844; www.buddhagardensdayspa.com.au; 1 Skinners Shoot Rd; 1hr massages from $140; 10am-6pm) Balinese-style day spa with a small courtyard plunge pool for post-treatment relaxation.

TOURS

Mountain Bike Tours Mountain Biking
(0429 122 504; www.mountainbiketours.com.au; half-/full-day tours $79/119) Environmentally aware bike tours into the rainforest and along the coast.

Vision Walks Wildlife
(02-6685 0059; www.visionwalks.com; full-day tours adult/child $125/90) See all manner of creatures in their natural habitat, including nocturnal animals (on the Night Vision Walk) and hippies (on the Hippie Trail Hinterland Tour).

SHOPPING

Byron Farmers' Market Market
(www.byronfarmersmarket.com.au; Butler St Reserve; 8-11am Thu) Both a market and a symbol of the strength of the local

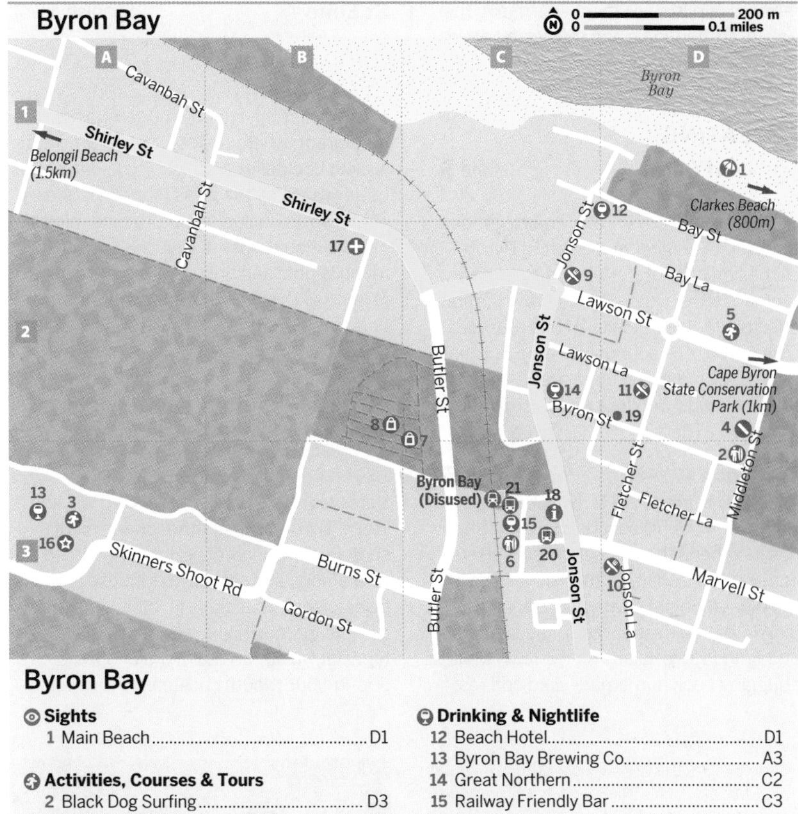

Byron Bay

Sights

1 Main Beach D1

Activities, Courses & Tours

2 Black Dog Surfing D3
3 Buddha Gardens A3
4 Sundive D2
5 Surf & Bike Hire D2
6 Surfing Byron Bay C3

Shopping

7 Byron Community Market C2
8 Byron Farmers' Market B2

Eating

9 Balcony C2
10 Bay Leaf Café D3
11 St Elmo D2

Drinking & Nightlife

12 Beach Hotel D1
13 Byron Bay Brewing Co A3
14 Great Northern C2
15 Railway Friendly Bar C3

Entertainment

16 Pighouse Flicks A3

Information

17 Byron Central Hospital B2
18 Byron Visitor Centre C3

Transport

19 Earth Car Rentals D2
20 Long Distance Bus Stop C3
21 NSW TrainLink C3

community, this weekly market has a wide variety of mainly organic stalls, with fresh produce and all manner of local products. Come early and hang with the locals for great coffee and breakfast, then linger for live music.

Byron Community Market Market

(www.byronmarkets.com.au; Butler St Reserve; 8am-2pm 1st Sun of month) The biggest market in the region, with more than 300 stalls covering several acres. Organic farmers and foodies meet alternative therapists, craftspeople and musicians at this monthly extravaganza.

EATING

Bay Leaf Café Cafe $

(www.facebook.com/bayleafcoffee; 2 Marvell St; mains $14-22; 7am-2pm) You might be tempted to snigger at the raft of Byron clichés on offer at this always-busy cafe (golden lattes, coconut cold brew, kombucha, tousle-haired locals of both sexes, a '70s psych rock soundtrack etc), but that would mean missing out on food and drinks that are made with love and a remarkable attention to detail.

Top Shop Cafe $

(65 Carlyle St; mains $10-14; 6.30am-5pm) High up on the hill east of town, Top Shop has long been the choice of local surfers. Today it's a casually upmarket version of the old-school takeaway, with diners ripping into breakfast burgers, sausage rolls and quinoa kale salads on the lawn while chugging back homemade iced coffees.

St Elmo Spanish $$

(02-6680 7426; www.stelmodining.com; cnr Fletcher St & Lawson Lane; dishes $14.50-28; 5-11pm Mon-Sat, to 10pm Sun) Perch on a stool at this moody modern tapas restaurant, where rock-star bar staff create wicked cocktails or can pour you one of the better wines by the glass found in this part of the world (including natural and minimal intervention drops). The solidly Iberian menu is bold and broad, with traditional favourites mixing it up with contemporary flourishes.

The Roadhouse Modern Australian, Cafe $$

(0403 355 498; www.roadhousebyronbay.com; 6/142 Bangalow Rd; mains $14-29; 6.30am-2.30pm & 6-10pm Tue-Sat, 6.30am-2.30pm Sun & Mon) A short trip out of town will find you at Byron's most atmospheric night spot. Rocking incredible, locally sourced wholefoods and coffee, Roadhouse also transforms into a dimly lit, blues-infused bar late into the night, with more than 500 types of whisky on the menu and fresh, pop-in-your-mouth cocktails.

From left: Wild dolphins; Cape Byron Lighthouse (p100); Buying tomatoes at the Byron Farmers' Market (p100); Balcony restaurant

RUGLIG/SHUTTERSTOCK ©

ANDRII SLONCHAK/SHUTTERSTOCK ©

Balcony Modern European $$

(☎02-6680 9666; www.balcony.com.au; cnr Lawson & Jonson Sts; lunch mains $13.50-25, dinner $24-32; ⏰8am-9pm; 📶) The eponymous architectural feature here wraps around the building and gives you tremendous views of the passing Byron parade (and the ever-busy traffic circle). Decor is an appealing postcolonial pastiche, while the food is a nice mix of solid European-meets-NYC flavours and Med-inflected warm-weather-appropriate salads and snacky things.

Beach Italian $$

(☎1300 583 766; www.beachbyronbay.com.au; Lawson St; mains breakfast $15-22, lunch & dinner $25-33; ⏰7.30am-3pm daily, 5.30-10pm Wed-Sat) The old Byron Beach Cafe has been reborn as single-name superstar Beach and now does triple duty as post-surf coffee and pastry stop, fish-and-chip or egg-and-bacon-roll kiosk, and Byron's best dining-with-a-view option. Lunch and dinner menus in the airy, light dining room are broadly Italian but not slavishly so, with a fresh coastal Australian feel.

John Byron, not Lord Byron

James Cook named Cape Byron, mainland Australia's most easterly point, after renowned navigator John Byron, grandfather of the poet Lord Byron. Later bureaucrats mistakenly planned out streets named after fellow poets such as Jonson, Burns and Shelley.

Rae's Restaurant Seafood $$$

(☎02-6685 5366; www.raesonwategos.com; 8 Marine Pde, Watego's Beach; mains $38-45; ⏰noon-3pm & 6-11.30pm) The sound of the surf perfectly sets off the excellent seafood, poultry and vegetarian dishes at this exclusive little retreat in Watego's. Dishes are simple, clear flavoured and use wonderful local produce. The seafood degustation ($115; or $175 with matched wines) is a super way to while away an afternoon or evening.

GREG ELMS/GETTY IMAGES ©

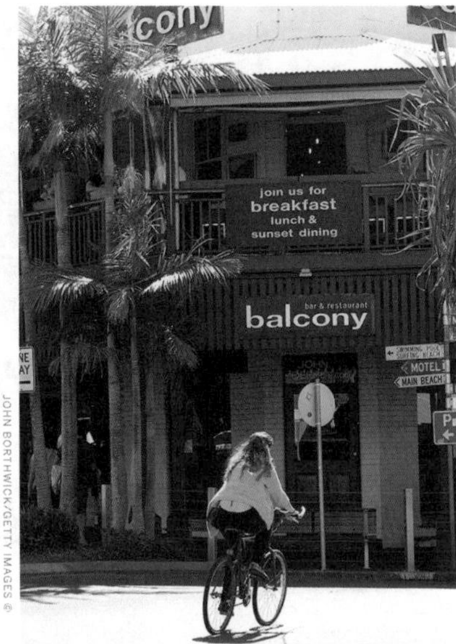

JOHN BORTHWICK/GETTY IMAGES ©

DRINKING & NIGHTLIFE

Treehouse on Belongil Pub
(☎02-6680 9452; www.treehouseonbelongil.com; 25 Childe St; ⊙7.30am-11pm) A home-spun beach bar where wooden decks spill out among the trees, afternoons are for drinking, and live, original music is played all weekend. Most of the food comes from the wood-fired oven.

Byron Bay Brewing Co Brewery
(www.byronbaybrewery.com.au; 1 Skinners Shoot Rd; ⊙11am-midnight) At this old piggery turned booze barn you can drink frosty glasses of house pale lager in a light, louvred space by the brewing vats or outside in the tropical courtyard shaded by a giant fig tree.

Railway Friendly Bar Pub
(The Rails; ☎02-6685 7662; www.therailsbyronbay.com; 86 Jonson St; ⊙11am-late) The Rails' indoor-outdoor mayhem draws everyone from lobster-red British tourists to high-on-life earth mothers and babyboomer tourists. The front beer garden, conducive to long, beery afternoons, has live music. Excellent burgers, with variants including roo, fish and tofu.

Beach Hotel Pub
(www.beachhotel.com.au; cnr Jonson & Bay Sts; ⊙11am-late) Soak up the atmosphere and the views in the iconic beachfront beer garden. Surf movies are screened out the back, and even though the one-time owner, '70s comedy star Strop, has moved on, the original *Crocodile Dundee* hat adorns the bar.

ENTERTAINMENT

Pighouse Flicks Cinema
(☎02-6685 5828; www.pighouseflicks.com.au; 1 Skinners Shoot Rd; tickets adult/child $15/13) Part of the Byron Bay Brewing Co complex, this atmospheric lounge-cinema shows classic reruns and art-house flicks.

Great Northern Pub
(☎02-6685 6454; www.thenorthern.com.au; 35-43 Jonson St; ⊙noon-late) This live-music stalwart is as grungy and boozy as it ever

Main Beach (p100)

was, and plays host to everyone from Billy Bragg to Dizzee Rascal to Dinosaur Jr.

 INFORMATION

Bay Centre Medical (02-6685 6206; www.byronmed.com.au; 6 Lawson St; 8am-5pm Mon-Fri, to noon Sat)

Byron Central Hospital (02-6639 9400; www.ncahs.nsw.gov.au; 54 Ewingsdale Rd; 24hr)

Byron Visitor Centre (02-6680 8558; www.visitbyronbay.com; Old Stationmaster's Cottage, 80 Jonson St; 9am-5pm)

 GETTING THERE & AWAY

AIR

The closest airport is **Ballina** (02-6681 1858; www.ballinabyronairport.com.au; Southern Cross Dr), 30 minutes south, but **Gold Coast Airport** (www.goldcoastairport.com.au; Longa Ave, Bilinga) 40 minutes away in Coolangatta has more services.

Byron Bay Shuttle (www.byronbayshuttle.com.au; adult/child $20/12) and **Xcede** (02-6620 9200; www.byronbay.xcede.com.au) serve both Coolangatta ($37) and Ballina ($18) airports.

BUS

Coaches stop on Jonson St near the tourist office. Operators include **Premier** (13 34 10; www.premierms.com.au), **Greyhound** (1300 473 946; www.greyhound.com.au) and **NSW TrainLink** (13 22 32; www.nswtrainlink.info; Jonson St).

Blanch's (02-6686 2144; www.blanchs.com.au) Regular buses to/from Ballina Byron Gateway Airport ($9.60, one hour).

Underwater Byron

About 3km offshore, Julian Rocks Marine Reserve is a meeting point for cold southerly and warm northerly currents, attracting a profusion of marine species including three types of turtle. You might spot leopard sharks and manta rays in summer, and grey nurse sharks in winter. Superb diving!

Rose Bubble Tip Anemone
AQUARIUSPHOTOGRAPHY/SHUTTERSTOCK ©

Byron Bay Express (www.byronbayexpress.com.au; one way/return $30/55) Five buses a day to/from Gold Coast Airport (1¾ hours).

Byron Easy Bus (02-6685 7447; www.byronbayshuttle.com.au) Minibus service to Ballina Byron Gateway Airport ($20, 40 minutes) and Gold Coast Airport.

 GETTING AROUND

Byron Bay Taxis (02-6685 5008; www.byronbaytaxis.com.au; 24hr)

Earth Car Rentals (02-6685 7472; www.earthcar.com.au; 1 Byron St; from $39.90 per day)

Alexandra Lookout over the Daintree Rainforest (p116)

GREAT BARRIER REEF & THE DAINTREE

In this Chapter

Great Barrier Reef & the Daintree at a Glance...

Tropical, touristy Cairns is unmissable on most travellers' itineraries. Experienced divers and first-time toe-dippers swarm to the steamy city for its easy access to the Great Barrier Reef, while the more party-prone are well served by a barrage of bars and clubs. Further south, the Whitsundays (p129) and Southern Reef Islands are well worth exploring.

The winding road north of Cairns hugs the ludicrously scenic shoreline en route to Port Douglas. North of here, the profuse Daintree Rainforest stretches to Cape Tribulation and beyond, tumbling onto long swaths of white-sand beach.

Great Barrier Reef & the Daintree in Two Days

The 'GBR' and Daintree are VAST: with just two days, do one or the other! For the reef, fly into **Cairns** (p120), explore the esplanade, boardwalk and lagoon and visit Reef Teach ahead of your reef trip the next day. For the Daintree, chill in **Port Douglas** (p124) for a day then day-trip into the jungle.

Great Barrier Reef & the Daintree in Four Days

Four days affords a little flexibility. Either base yourself around the **Southern Reef Islands** (p118) and really get a feel for these tropical climes (Heron Island has some of the world's best diving); or launch into a Cairns–Great Barrier Reef–Port Douglas–Daintree four-day extravaganza.

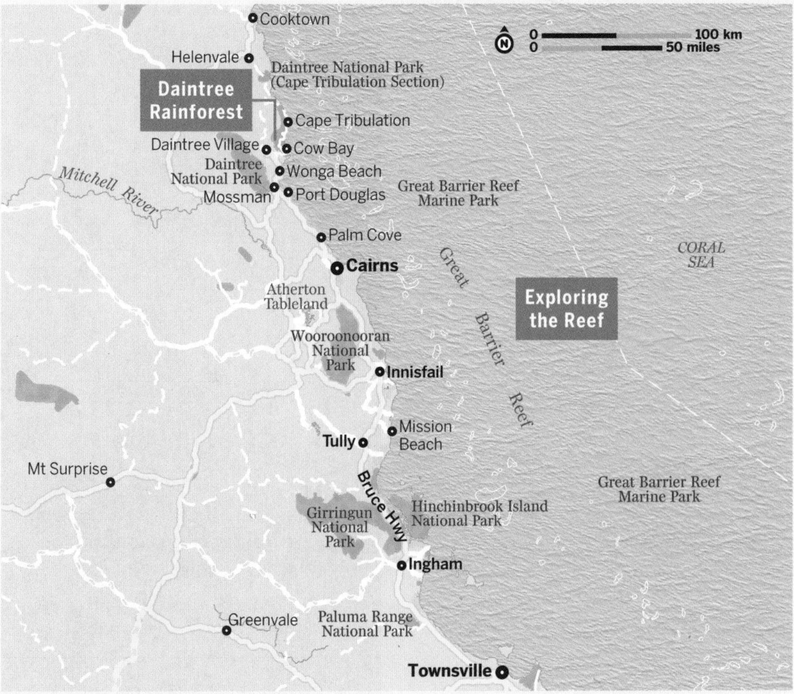

Arriving in Great Barrier Reef & the Daintree

Cairns The main base for exploring the northern reef. Cairns Airport (p123) is 6km north of town: shuttles meet all flights, or a taxi will cost about $30.

Southern Reef Islands Accessible via boat and air connections from Bundaberg, Gladstone and Town of 1770.

Port Douglas An hour's drive north of Cairns; the natural jumping-off point for Daintree adventures.

Where to Stay

Cairns has myriad accommodation for all budgets; Port Douglas too, though businesses here are a little more geared towards the 'luxe' traveller. Most reef island resorts are distinctly high-end, though some (eg Lady Elliot Island) won't break a midrange traveller's bank. Daintree accommodation includes hostels (Cape Tribulation) and jungle B&Bs and lodges around Cape Trib and Cow Bay.

Scuba diving among sea fans and coral

Exploring the Reef

There are many ways to approach this massive undersea wonder: join an organised tour from a gateway town; take a multiday sailing or diving trip; or fly to a remote island.

Great For...

Need to Know

June to November is the best time to visit: not too hot, with good underwater visibility.

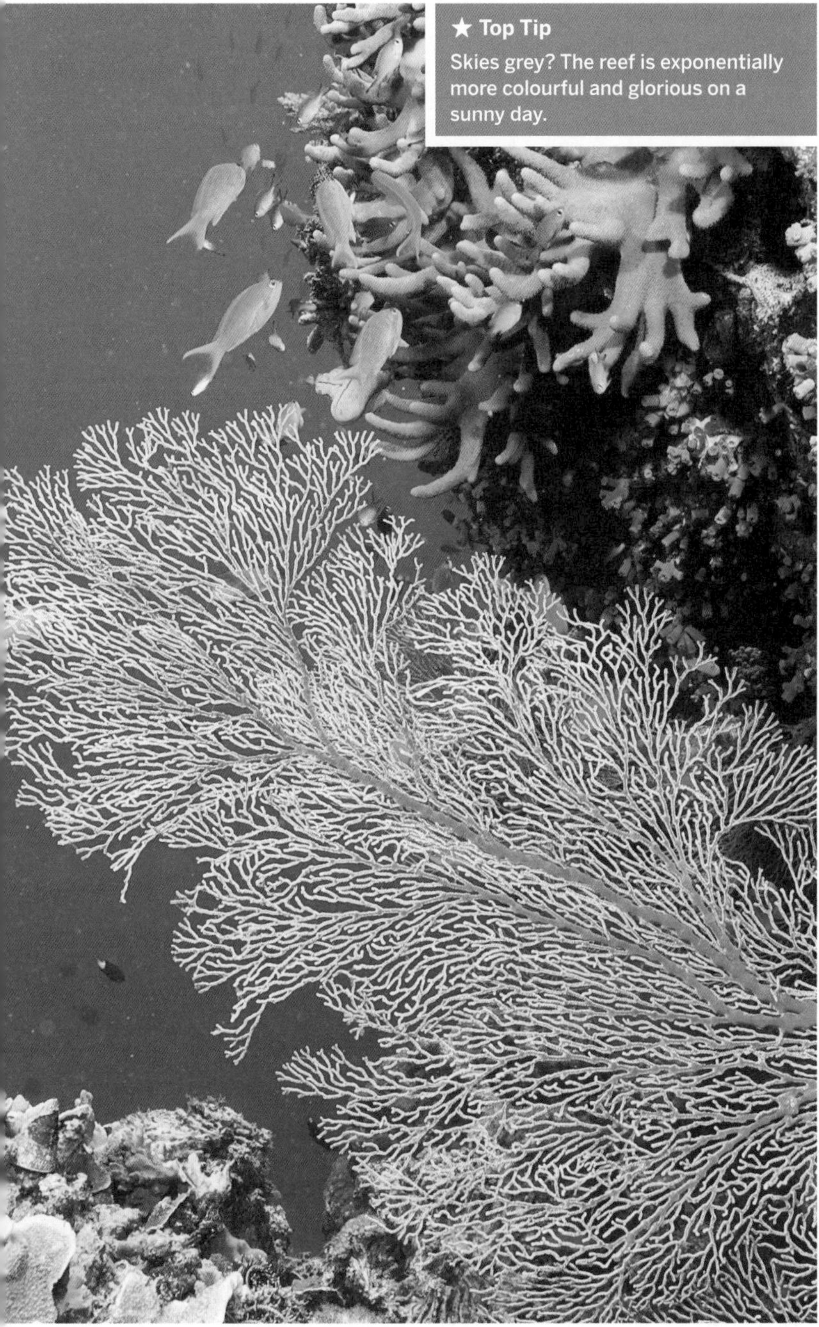

★ **Top Tip**

Skies grey? The reef is exponentially more colourful and glorious on a sunny day.

DEBRA JAMES/SHUTTERSTOCK ©

Picking Your Spot

Given the reef's size, it follows that there are many popular spots from which to access it – but bear in mind that the qualities of individual areas do change over time, depending on the weather, tidal shifts or recent cyclone or coral-bleaching damage.

Mainland Gateways

The major mainland reef access points all offer slightly different experiences or activities. This list is organised from south to north:

- Agnes Water & Town of 1770 (p119)
- Airlie Beach (p134)
- Cairns (p120)
- Port Douglas (p124)

Island Gateways

Rising above the waterline throughout the reef are hundreds of islands and cays, offering instant access to the undersea marvels. Here is a list of some of our favourite islands, travelling from south to north:

- Lady Elliot Island (p118)
- Heron Island (p119)
- Hamilton Island (p138)

Island Resorts

The Great Barrier Reef is home to over a dozen island resorts, offering varying levels of comfort and style. Where to stay depends not only on your budget, but also on what sort of activities you have in mind. Some resorts are small and secluded (and don't allow children), which can be ideal for

Four Mile Beach, Port Douglas (p124)

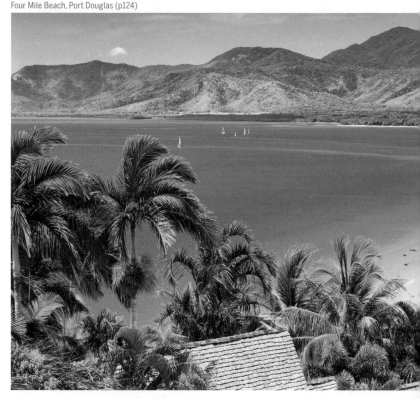

a tropical getaway doing little more than sipping cocktails. If this sounds ideal, try Hayman Island (p139) in the Whitsundays or Orpheus Island. Other resorts have a busier vibe and offer a wide range of activities, from sailing and kayaking to helicopter joy rides, plus restaurants and even some nightlife. If this is more to your liking, try Hamilton Island. You'll find the widest selection of resorts in the Whitsundays.

Boat Excursions

Unless you're staying on a coral-fringed island, you'll need to join a boat excursion to experience the reef's real beauty. Day trips leave from many places along the coast, as well as from island resorts, and typically include the use of snorkelling gear, snacks and a buffet lunch, with scuba diving an optional extra. On some boats, naturalists or marine biologists present talks on the reef's ecology.

Boat trips vary dramatically in passenger numbers, type of vessel and quality – which is reflected in the price – so it's worth getting all the details before committing. When selecting a tour, consider the vessel (motorised catamaran or sailing ship), the number of passengers (from six to 400), what extras are offered and the destination. The outer reefs are usually more pristine. Inner reefs often show signs of damage from humans and coral-eating crown-of-thorns starfish. Coral bleaching is a major issue in far northern sections of the reef. Some operators offer the option of a trip in a glass-bottomed boat or semi-submersible.

Many boats have underwater cameras available for hire, although you'll save money by hiring these on land (or using your own waterproof camera or underwater housing). Some boats also have professional photographers on board who will dive and take high-quality shots of you in action.

★ Top Tip

Remember never to walk on the coral: not only can it cut you badly, it's very fragile. For more responsible practices, see p119.

MARTIN VALIGURSKY/SHUTTERSTOCK ©

Diving & Snorkelling on the Reef

Much of the diving and snorkelling on the reef is boat-based, although there are some excellent reefs accessible by walking straight off the beach of some islands. Free use of snorkelling gear is usually part of any day cruise to the reef – you can typically fit in around three hours of underwater wandering. Overnight or live-aboard trips obviously provide a more in-depth experience and greater coverage of the reefs.

If you don't have a diving certificate, many operators offer the option of an introductory dive, where an experienced diver conducts an underwater tour. A lesson in

safety and procedure is given beforehand and you don't require a five-day Professional Association of Diving Instructors (PADI) course or a 'buddy'.

Top Reef Dive Spots

The Great Barrier Reef is home to some of the world's best diving sites. Here are a few of our favourite spots to get you started:

SS Yongala A sunken shipwreck that has been home to a vivid marine community for more than 90 years.

Cod Hole Go nose-to-nose with a potato cod.

Heron Island Join a crowd of colourful fish straight off the beach.

Lady Elliot Island With 19 highly regarded dive sites.

Wheeler Reef Massive variety of marine life, plus a great spot for night dives.

Top Snorkelling Sites

Some non-divers may wonder if it's really worth making the trip out to the Great Barrier Reef 'just to snorkel'. The answer is a resounding 'Yes!'. Much of the rich, colourful coral lies just underneath the surface (as coral needs bright sunlight to flourish) and is easily accessible. Here's a round-up of what we think are the top snorkelling sites:

Fitzroy Reef Lagoon (Town of 1770)

Heron Island (Capricorn Coast)

Great Keppel Island (Capricorn Coast)

Lady Elliot Island (Capricorn Coast)

Lady Musgrave Island (Capricorn Coast)

Lizard Island (Cairns)

Michaelmas Reef (Cairns)

Hastings Reef (Cairns)

Norman Reef (Cairns)

Saxon Reef (Cairns)

Green Island (Cairns)

Trips from Cairns

Reef trips generally include transport, lunch, stinger-suits and snorkelling gear. When choosing a tour, consider the vessel type, its capacity, inclusions and destination: outer reefs are more pristine but further afield; inner reefs can be patchy and show signs of decay. Some prefer smaller, less-crowded vessels, while others go for the wide range of inclusions bigger boats promise.

Vendors with their own pontoon offer all-round value: pontoons are a great way for families to experience the reef – those who aren't keen on getting in the water can enjoy the pontoon's facilities, or a trip in a glass-bottomed boat or semi-submersible.

Almost all boats depart from the Marlin Wharf (with check-in and booking facilities

Clownfish

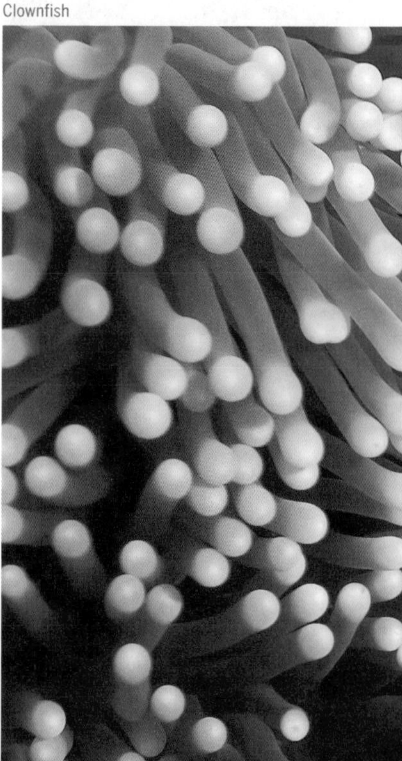

located inside the Reef Fleet Terminal) around 8am, returning around 6pm. Smaller operators may check-in boat-side at their berth on the wharf itself; check with your operator. Operators include the following:

Tusa Dive (07-4047 9100; www.tusadive.com; cnr Shields St & Esplanade; adult/child day trips from $205/130) A maximum of 60 passengers aboard the custom-designed reef vessel (the T6), a roving outer-reef permit and a high staff-to-passenger ratio make this operator an excellent choice for day trips.

Reef Magic (07-4031 1588; www.reefmagiccruises.com; Reef Fleet Terminal; adult/child/family day trips from $210/105/525) A long-time family favourite, Reef Magic's high-speed cat sails to its all-weather Marine World pontoon moored on the edge of the outer reef. If you're water shy, try a glass-bottomed boat ride, chat with the marine biologist or have a massage!

Great Adventures (07-4044 9944; www.greatadventures.com.au; Reef Fleet Terminal; adult/child/family day trips from $230.50/122.50/590) Great Adventures runs trips to Green Island and the outer Great Barrier Reef aboard its fast catamaran. Diving add-ons, and glass-bottomed boat, semi-submersible and Scuba Doo underwater scooter tours are also available.

Did You Know?

The Great Barrier Reef is approximately 8000 years old and is around the size of Germany.

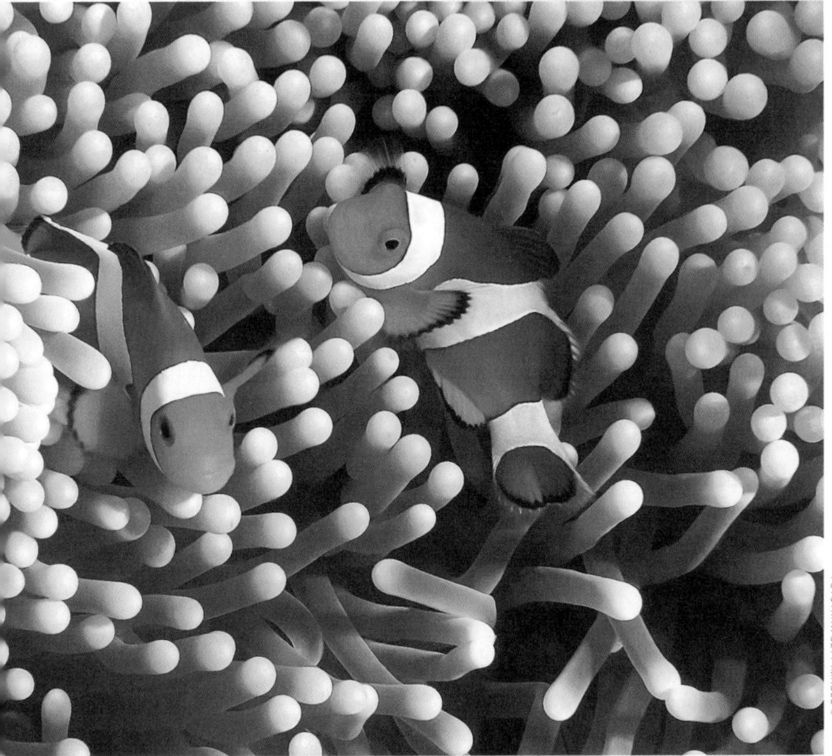

FOTOTRAV/GETTY IMAGES ©

Fan palms

Daintree Rainforest

The impossibly lush Daintree represents many things: World Heritage–listed rainforest, a river, a reef, laid-back villages and the home of its traditional custodians, the Kuku Yalanji people.

Great For...

☑ Don't Miss

A long beach-combing amble along Cape Tribulation Beach or Myall Beach at Cape Trib.

An Amazing Rainforest

Upon entering the forest, you'll be enveloped by a cacophony of birdsong, frog croaking and the buzz of insects. Continue exploring the area via wildlife-spotting night tours, mountain treks, interpretive boardwalks, canopy walks, self-guided walking trails, 4WD trips, horse riding, kayaking, croc-spotting cruises, tropical-fruit orchard tours and tastings... Whew! If you're lucky, you might even spot a cassowary.

History, Controversy & Control

The greater Daintree Rainforest is protected as part of Daintree National Park, but this protection is not without controversy. In 1983, despite conservationist blockades, what's now the Bloomfield Track was bulldozed through lowland rainforest from Cape Tribulation to the Bloomfield River.

Cassowary

MILOSZ MASLANKA/SHUTTERSTOCK ©

Ensuing publicity led to the federal government nominating Queensland's wet tropical rainforests for World Heritage listing, generating state government and timber industry opposition. In 1988 the area was inscribed on the World Heritage List and commercial logging here was banned.

Unesco World Heritage listing (www.whc.unesco.org) doesn't affect ownership rights or control. Since the 1990s the Queensland government and conservation agencies have attempted to buy back and rehabilitate freehold properties in the area, adding them to the Daintree National Park. Sealing the road to Cape Tribulation in 2002 triggered the buy-back of even more land, which, coupled with development controls, now bears the fruits of forest regeneration. Check out Rainforest Rescue (www.rainforestrescue.org.au) for more information.

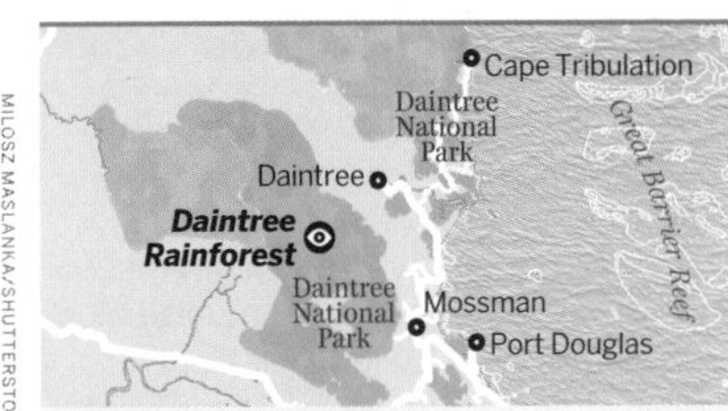

Need to Know

www.daintreerainforest.com

Take a Break

Mason's Store & Cafe (p127) in Cape Tribulation is a one-stop-shop for food, booze and info.

★ Top Tip

The water of the Daintree River looks inviting: the resident saltwater crocodiles agree.

Daintree Tours

Cape Tribulation Wilderness Cruises — Boating

(☎0457 731 000; www.capetribcruises.com; Cape Tribulation Rd; adult/child from $30/22) This is the only tour boat permitted in the Cape Trib section of the Daintree National Park, cruising Cooper Creek in search of crocs. Book ahead.

Cooper Creek Wilderness — Walking

(☎07-4098 9126; www.coopercreek.com.au; 2333 Cape Tribulation Rd; guided walks $60-170) Book ahead for expert guided rainforest walks that include a dip in Cooper Creek. A variety of itineraries are available.

Tony's Tropical Tours — Tours

(☎07-4099 3230; www.tropicaltours.com.au; day tours adult/child $185/160) This luxury, small-group (eight to 10 passengers) tour operator specialises in trips to out-of-the-way sections of the Mossman Gorge and Daintree Rainforest.

Southern Reef Islands

While much fuss is made about the Great Barrier Reef's northern splendour, the Southern Reef Islands are the place of 'castaway' dreams: tiny coral atolls fringed with sugary white sand and turquoise-blue seas, and hardly anyone within flipper-flapping reach. From beautiful Lady Elliot Island, 80km northeast of Bundaberg, secluded and uninhabited coral reefs and atolls dot the ocean for about 140km up to Tryon Island. Access is from Town of 1770 and Gladstone.

Lady Elliot Island

Set on the southern rim of the Great Barrier Reef, Lady Elliot is a 40-hectare vegetated coral cay populated with nesting sea turtles and an impressive number of seabirds. It's considered to have the best snorkelling in the southern Great Barrier Reef and the diving is good too.

Lady Elliot Island is not a national park, and camping is not allowed; your only option is the low-key **Lady Elliot Island Eco Resort** (☎1800 072 200; www.ladyelliot.com.au; r $175-420, child $95).

The only way to reach the island is in a light aircraft. Resort guests are flown in from Bundaberg, the Gold Coast and Hervey Bay. The resort also manages fantastic, great-value day trips for around $365, including a scenic flight, a snorkelling tour and lunch.

Lady Musgrave Island

Wannabe castaways look no further. This tiny, 15-hectare cay, 100km northeast of Bundaberg, sits on the western rim of a stunning, turquoise-blue reef lagoon renowned for its safe swimming, snorkelling and diving. A squeaky, white-sand beach fringes a dense canopy of pisonia forest brimming with roosting bird life, including terns, shearwaters and white-capped noddies. Birds nest from October to April while green turtles nest from November to February.

Day trips ($205) to Lady Musgrave depart from Bundaberg as part of the **Lady Musgrave Experience** (☎0427 009 922;

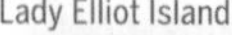
Lady Elliot Island

JANELLE LUGGE/SHUTTERSTOCK ©

www.ladymusgraveexperience.com.au; Bundaberg Port Marina, 15-17 Marina Drive Burnett Heads; adult/child $205/$105).

Heron Island

Part of the smaller Capricornia Cays group, Heron Island is ranked among the finest scuba-diving spots in the world, particularly in terms of ease of access. Visitors to Heron generally know what they are coming for – underwater paradise – but the island's rugged beauty is reason enough to stay above the surface. There's **Heron Island Resort** (☎1300 863 248; www.heronisland.com; d/ste from $330/572) and a research station on the northeastern third of the island; the remainder is national park.

The **Heron Islander** (☎1800 837 168; www.heronisland.com; adult/child one-way $62/31) departs Gladstone daily at 2pm (2½ hours).

For a more glamorous approach, take a **seaplane** (☎1300 863 248; www.heronisland.com; $338 one-way).

 GETTING THERE & AWAY

Depending on their remoteness, the Southern Reef Islands are accessible from mainland by boat (from Town of 1770) or plane or helicopter (from Bundaberg, Gladstone or Hervey Bay).

 GETTING AROUND

Once on the islands, boats organised by the resorts or local operators are the only means of transport.

Agnes Water & Town of 1770

The tiny settlement of Agnes Water has the east coast's most northerly surf beach, while the even tinier Town of 1770 (little more than a marina!) marks Captain Cook's first landing in the state (you guessed it, in 1770), and is great for kayaking and stand-up paddleboarding.

ANTHONY BRITTEN/500PX ©

Looking After the Reef

The Great Barrier Reef is incredibly fragile: it's worth taking some time to educate yourself on responsible practices to minimise the impact of your visit.

- It is an offence to damage or remove coral in the marine park.
- If you touch or walk on coral you'll damage it (and probably get some nasty cuts).
- Don't touch or harass marine animals, and don't enter the water near a dugong.
- If you have a boat, be aware of the rules in relation to anchoring around the reef, including 'no anchoring areas' to avoid coral damage.
- If you're diving, check that you are weighted correctly before entering the water and keep your buoyancy control well away from the reef. Ensure that equipment such as secondary regulators and gauges aren't dragging over the reef.
- Hire a wetsuit or a 'rashie' rather than slathering on sunscreen, which can damage the reef.
- Watch where your fins are – try not to stir up sediment or disturb coral.
- Note that there are limits on the amount and types of shells that you can collect.

Kuranda Scenic Railway

Winding 34km from Cairns to Kuranda through picturesque mountains, the track used by the **Kuranda Scenic Railway** (07-4036 9333; www.ksr.com.au; adult/child one-way from $50/25, return from $76/38) was completed in 1891: workers dug tunnels by hand, battling sickness, steep terrain and venomous creatures. The two-hour pleasure trip includes seating in heritage-style carriages, audio commentary, souvenir trip guide and a stop at the Barron Falls viewing platform.

Trains depart **Cairns Central Railway Station** (Bunda St) at 8.30am and 9.30am daily, returning from Kuranda station at 2pm and 3.30pm.

Kuranda Scenic Railway and **Skyrail Rainforest Cableway** (07-4038 5555; www.skyrail.com.au; cnr Cook Hwy & Cairns Western Arterial Rd, Smithfield; adult/child one-way from $50/25, return $75/37.50; 9am-5.15pm) offer combination tickets (adult/child from $109.50/54.75): take the railway up, the cableway back down.

Skyrail Rainforest Cableway
CHAMELEONSEYE/SHUTTERSTOCK ©

ACTIVITIES

1770 Liquid Adventures Kayaking
(0428 956 630; www.1770liquidadventures.com.au) Paddle off on a spectacular twilight kayak tour. For $55 you ride the waves off 1770, before retiring to the beach for drinks and snacks as the sun sets – keep an eye out for dolphins. You can also rent kayaks (from $20/30 per hour/two hours). Family tours also available.

EATING

Getaway Garden Café Modern Australian $$
(07-4974 9323; 303 Bicentennial Dr, Agnes Water; breakfast $7-19, lunch $10-22, dinner $20-25; 8am-4pm Sun-Thu, & 5.30pm-late Wed & Sun) The region's most revered eatery continues to impress due to its culinary simplicity using only local ingredients, impeccable family-oriented service and natural, waterside setting. Breakfasts are healthy and accompanied by fine coffee and juices. Lunch features pizza, fish and burgers. Book for lamb spit roasts on Wednesday and Sunday nights.

INFORMATION

Agnes Water Visitors Centre (07-4902 1533; 71 Springs Rd, Town of 1770; 9am-5pm Mon-Fri, to 4pm Sat & Sun) Staffed by above-and-beyond volunteers who even leave out information and brochures when it's closed, just in case a lost soul blows into town.

GETTING THERE & AWAY

A handful of **Greyhound** (1300 473 946; www.greyhound.com.au) buses detour off the Bruce Hwy to Agnes Water; daily services include Cairns ($210, 21 hours). **Premier Motor Service** (13 34 10; www.premierms.com.au) also goes in and out of town.

Cairns

Cairns (pronounced by many as 'Cans' – but we prefer the phonetic version) has come a long way since its beginnings as a boggy swamp and rollicking goldfields port. Heaving under the weight of countless resorts, tour agencies, souvenir shops and a million reminders of its proximity to the Great Barrier Reef, Cairns is unabashedly geared towards tourism.

Cairns is awash with bars, clubs, eateries and cafes suiting all budgets. There's no beach in town, but the magnificent Esplanade Lagoon more than makes up for it; otherwise, the northern beaches are but a local bus ride or short drive away.

SIGHTS & ACTIVITIES

Cairns Esplanade, Boardwalk & Lagoon Waterfront

(www.cairns.qld.gov.au/esplanade; lagoon 6am-9pm Thu-Tue, noon-9pm Wed;) FREE Sunseekers and fun-lovers flock to Cairns Esplanade's spectacular **swimming lagoon** on the city's reclaimed foreshore. The artificial, sandy-edged, 4800-sq-metre saltwater pool is lifeguard patrolled and illuminated nightly. The adjacent 3km foreshore **boardwalk** has picnic areas, birdwatching vantage points, free barbecues and fitness equipment.

Reef Teach Cultural Centre

(07-4031 7794; www.reefteach.com.au; 2nd fl, Mainstreet Arcade, 85 Lake St; adult/child/family $23/14/60; lectures 6.30-8.30pm Tue-Sat) Take your knowledge to new depths at this fun, informative centre, where marine experts explain how to identify specific species of fish and coral, and how to approach the reef respectfully.

Tjapukai Aboriginal Cultural Park Cultural Centre

(07-4042 9999; www.tjapukai.com.au; Cairns Western Arterial Rd, Caravonica; adult/child/family $62/42/166; 9am-5pm) Managed by the area's original custodians, this award-winning cultural extravaganza tells the story of creation using giant holograms and actors. There's a dance theatre, a gallery, boomerang- and spear-throwing demonstrations, turtle-spotting canoe rides and dinner-and-show packages (adult/child/family $123/75/321).

SHOPPING

Rusty's Markets Market

(07-4040 2705; www.rustysmarkets.com.au; 57-89 Grafton St; 5am-6pm Fri & Sat, to 3pm Sun) No weekend in Cairns is complete without a visit to this busy and vibrant multicultural market. Weave (and taste) your

'The Woven Fish' by Brian Robinson, Cairns Esplanade swimming lagoon

From left: Birdwing butterfly; Actor performing at the Tjapukai Aboriginal Cultural Park (p121); Cairns Marlin Marina

way through piles of seasonal tropical fruits, veggies and herbs, plus farm-fresh honey, locally grown flowers, excellent coffees, curries, cold drinks, antiques and more.

EATING

Prawn Star Seafood $$

(☎0456 421 172; www.facebook.com/prawnstarcairns; E-Finger, Berth 31, Marlin Marina; seafood from $20; ⏰10am-8pm) Trawler restaurant Prawn Star is tropical dining perfection: clamber aboard and fill yourself with prawns, mud crabs, oysters and whatever else was caught that day, while taking in equally delicious harbour views. It's a small boat, so seating is limited; get there early.

Spicy Bite Indian, Fusion $$

(☎07-4041 3700; www.spicybitecairns.com; cnr Shields St & Esplanade; mains $15.50-35; ⏰5-10pm; 🌶) Cairns has plenty of good Indian restaurants, but none are quite as innovative as this unassuming place, where fusion food has been turned into a write-home-about-it experience: where else on earth could you try crocodile masala or kangaroo tikka?

Ochre Modern Australian $$$

(☎07-4051 0100; www.ochrerestaurant.com.au; Marlin Pde; mains $28-40; ⏰11.30am-2.30pm & 5.30-9.30pm) The menu at this innovative waterfront restaurant utilises native Aussie fauna (such as croc with native pepper, or roo with quandong-chilli glaze) and flora (try wattle-seed damper loaf or Davidson plum mousse). It also cooks Tablelands steaks to perfection.

DRINKING & NIGHTLIFE

Jack Pub

(☎07-4051 2490; www.thejack.com.au; cnr Spence & Sheridan Sts; ⏰10am-late) The Jack is a kick-arse pub by any standards, housed in an unmissable heritage Queenslander with an enormous shaded beer garden. There are nightly events, including live music and DJs, killer pub grub, and an adjacent hostel (dorm from $26) for those who just can't tear themselves away.

Three Wolves Bar

(☎07-4031 8040; www.threewolves.com.au; Red Brick Laneway, 32 Abbott St; ⏲4pm-midnight Thu-Sat & Mon, 2-10pm Sun) Intimate, understated and bang-on-trend (think Edison bulbs, copper mugs and mixologists in old-timey barkeep aprons), this new laneway bar has delivered a very welcome dash of Melbourne to Cairns. It's got an excellent selection of speciality spirits, cocktails and beers, plus a bar menu including hip faves like pulled-pork tortillas, sliders and New York–style hot dogs.

INFORMATION

Cairns & Tropical North Visitor Information Centre (☎07-4051 3588; www.tropicalnorthqueensland.org.au; 51 Esplanade; ⏲8.30am-6pm Mon-Fri, 10am-6pm Sat & Sun) This is the only government-run visitor information centre in town offering impartial advice. Friendly staff can help with tour bookings.

Cairns 24 Hour Medical Centre (☎07-4052 1119; cnr Grafton & Florence Sts; ⏲24hr) Centrally located medical centre open 24 hours; it also does dive medicals.

GETTING THERE & AWAY

AIR

Qantas (☎13 13 13; www.qantas.com.au) , **Virgin Australia** (☎13 67 89; www.virginaustralia.com) and **Jetstar** (☎13 15 38; www.jetstar.com.au), (and a handful of international carriers, arrive and depart **Cairns Airport** (☎07-4080 6703; www.cairnsairport.com; Airport Ave), located approximately 6km from the city centre, with direct services to most Australian capitals.

BUS

Long-distance buses arrive at and depart from the **Interstate Coach Terminal** (Reef Fleet Terminal). The two main operators are **Greyhound Australia** (☎1300 473 946; www.greyhound.com.au) and **Premier Motor Service** (☎13 34 10; www.premierms.com.au). **Sun Palm** (☎07-4087 2900; www.sunpalmtransport.com.au) runs to Port Douglas.

CAR & MOTORCYCLE

Major car-rental companies have downtown and airport branches.

TRAIN

Queensland Rail (☎1300 131 722; www.queenslandrailtravel.com.au) runs the state-of-the-art Spirit of Queensland train – with both economy seating (from $222) and RailBed class (from $389) – on its scenic, 24-hour run between Brisbane and Cairns.

GETTING AROUND

TO/FROM THE AIRPORT

Many hotels and hostels offer courtesy pick-up. **Sun Palm** (☎07-4087 2900; www.sunpalmtransport.com.au) can shuttle you door-to-door (adult/child $15/7.50), or book **Cairns Airport Shuttle** (☎0432 488 783; www.cairnsairportshuttle.com.au) for $15. Taxis to the city centre are around $25 (plus $4 airport surcharge).

BUS

Sunbus (☎07-4057 7411; www.sunbus.com.au/cairns; single/daily/weekly ticket from $2.40/4.80/19.20) runs regular services in and around Cairns from the Cairns Transit Mall.

TAXI

Cairns Taxis (☎13 10 08; www.cairnstaxis.com.au)

Port Douglas

From its early days as a fishing village, Port Douglas has grown into a sophisticated and upmarket resort town that's quite a contrast to Cairns' hectic tourist scene. With the outer Great Barrier Reef less than an hour offshore, the Daintree Rainforest practically in the backyard, and more resorts than you can poke a snorkel at, a growing number of travellers choose Port Douglas as their Far North base.

SIGHTS

Wildlife Habitat Port Douglas Zoo

(☎07-4099 3235; www.wildlifehabitat.com.au; Port Douglas Rd; adult/child/family $34/17/85; 🕗8am-5pm) This sanctuary endeavours to keep and showcase native animals in enclosures that mimic their natural environment,

Mossman Gorge

while allowing you to get up close to koalas, kangaroos, crocs, cassowaries and more.

 ACTIVITIES

Wind Swell Water Sports

(☎0427 498 042; www.windswell.com.au; Barrier St; lessons from $50) Kitesurfing and stand-up paddleboarding (SUP) for everyone from beginners to high flyers. Kitesurfing lessons and SUP tours from the beach start at $50, but there are plenty of advanced options. Find them in action at the southern end of **Four Mile Beach**.

 TOURS

Quicksilver Cruise

(☎07-4087 2100; www.quicksilver-cruises.com; Reef Marina; adult/child/family $238/119/535) Major operator with fast cruises to its own pontoon on Agincourt Reef. Try an 'ocean walk' helmet dive ($166) on a submerged platform or snorkelling with a marine biologist (from $60).

Reef Sprinter Snorkelling

(☎07-4099 6127; www.reefsprinter.com.au; Shop 3, Reef Marina; adult/child from $130/110) The fastest way to the reef, this 2¼-hour snorkelling trip gets to the Low Isles in just 15 minutes for one to 1½ hours in the water. Half-day outer reef trips are also available (from $200).

 SHOPPING

Port Douglas Markets Market

(Anzac Park, Macrossan St; ⏲8am-2pm Sun) These Sunday markets feature handmade crafts and jewellery, local tropical fruits and fresh produce.

 EATING

On the Inlet Seafood $$

(☎07-4099 5255; www.ontheinlet.com.au; 3 Inlet St; mains $26-42; ⏲noon-11.30pm) You'll feel like you're floating over Dickson Inlet here, with tables spread out along a huge deck from where you can await the 5pm arrival of George the 250kg groper, who comes to feed most days. Take up the bucket-of-prawns-and-a-drink deal ($18 from 3.30pm to 5.30pm) and watch the reef boats come in.

Flames of the Forest Modern Australian $$$

(☎07-4099 3144; www.flamesoftheforest.com.au; Mowbray River Rd; dinner with show, drinks & transfers from $219; ⏲Tue, Thu & Sat) This unique experience goes way beyond the traditional concept of 'dinner and a show', with diners escorted deep into the rainforest for a truly immersive night of theatre, culture and gourmet cuisine. Transport provided from Port Douglas or Cairns (no self-drive). Bookings essential.

Harrisons Restaurant Modern Australian $$$

(☎07-4099 4011; www.harrisonsrestaurant.com.au; 22 Wharf St; lunch $19-26, dinner mains from $38; ⏲noon-2pm & 5-10pm) Marco Pierre White–trained chef/owner Spencer Patrick whips up culinary gems that stand toe-to-toe with Australia's best. Fresh locally sourced produce is turned into dishes such as smoked duck breast and tamarind beef cheeks.

Mossman Gorge

In the southeast corner of Daintree National Park, 5km west of Mossman town (itself 20km north of Port Douglas), Mossman Gorge forms part of the traditional lands of the Kuku Yalanji people. The gorge is a boulder-strewn valley where sparkling water washes over ancient rocks. It's 3km by road from the **visitor centre** (☎07-4099 7000; www.mossmangorge.com.au; ⏲8am-6pm) to a viewpoint and refreshing swimming hole – take care as the currents can be swift. Walk the 3km or take the shuttle (adult/child return $9.10/4.55, every 15 minutes).

Daintree Village

For wildlife lovers and birdwatchers, it's well worth taking the 20km each-way detour from the Mossman-Daintree Rd to tiny Daintree Village, set on a plateau of farmland on the Upper Daintree River. Croc-spotting cruises are the main event.

Try long-running **Crocodile Express** (07-4098 6120; www.crocodileexpress.com; 1hr cruises adult/child/family $28/14/65; cruises 8.30am), **Daintree River Wild Watch** (0447 734 933; www.daintreeriverwildwatch.com.au; 2hr cruises adult/child $60/35), which has informative sunrise birdwatching cruises and sunset photography nature cruises, or **Daintree River Cruise Centre** (07-4098 6115; www.daintreerivercruisecentre.com.au; 2914 Mossman-Daintree Rd; adult/child $28/14; 9.30am-4pm).

Crocodile
RICHARD HORTON/SHUTTERSTOCK ©

DRINKING & NIGHTLIFE

Hemingway's Microbrewery
(07-4099 6663; www.hemingwaysbrewery.com; Reef Marina, 44 Wharf St) Port Douglas deserves its own brewery and Hemingway's makes the most of a fabulous location on the Reef Marina with a broad deck, a long bar and Dickson Inlet views. There are currently six brews on tap, including Hard Yards dark lager and Pitchfork Betty's pale ale. Naturally, food is available, but this is one for the beer connoisseurs.

ENTERTAINMENT

Moonlight Cinema Cinema
(www.moonlight.com.au/port-douglas; QT Resort, 87-109 Port Douglas Rd; adult/child $17.50/13; Thu-Sun Jun-Oct) Bring a picnic or hire a bean bag for outdoor twilight movie screenings on the lawn at QT Resort. Check the website for film schedules.

INFORMATION

Port Douglas Tourist Information Centre
(07-4099 5599; www.infoportdouglas.com.au; 23 Macrossan St; 8am-6.30pm) Not a government tourist office but a reliable private booking agency; pick up brochures here and book tours.

GETTING THERE & AROUND

Port Douglas Bus (070-4099 5665; www.portdouglasbus.com.au) and **Sun Palm** (07-4087 2900; www.sunpalmtransport.com.au; adult/child $35/17.50) operate daily between Port Douglas, Cairns and the airport.

Coral Reef Coaches (07-4098 2800; www.coralreefcoaches.com.au) runs shuttle buses around town and regular services between Port Douglas, Mossman and Cairns.

The Daintree

Part of the Wet Tropics World Heritage Area, the spectacular region from the Daintree River north to Cape Tribulation features ancient rainforest, sandy beaches and rugged mountains. North of the Daintree River, electricity is supplied by generators or, increasingly, solar power. Shops and services are limited, and mobile-phone reception is patchy at best. The **Daintree River Ferry** (www.douglas.qld.gov.au/community/daintree-ferry; one-way/return car $14/26, motorcycle $5/10, pedestrian & bicycle $1/2; 6am-midnight) carries wanderers and their wheels across the river every 15 minutes or so.

Cow Bay & Around

Tiny Cow Bay is the first community you reach after the Daintree ferry crossing.

Cow Bay Beach, at the end of Buchanan Creek Rd, rivals any coastal paradise.

SIGHTS

Daintree Discovery Centre — Nature Reserve

(07-4098 9171; www.discoverthedaintree.com; Tulip Oak Rd; adult/child/family $32/16/78; 8.30am-5pm) This award-winning attraction's **aerial walkway**, which includes a 23m tower used to study carbon levels, takes you high into the forest canopy. A theatre screens films on cassowaries, crocodiles, conservation and climate change.

EATING

Daintree Ice Cream Company — Ice Cream $

(07-4098 9114; www.daintreeicecream.com.au; Lot 100, Cape Tribulation Rd; ice creams $6.50; 11am-5pm) We dare you to drive past this all-natural ice-cream producer with a palette of flavours that changes daily. You might get macadamia, black sapote and wattleseed – they're all delicious.

Cape Tribulation

Cape Trib is at the end of the winding sealed road from the Daintree River and, with its magnificent beaches – **Myall** and **Cape Tribulation** – laid-back vibe, backpacker bars, rainforest walks and compact village, it's a little slice of paradise.

TOURS

Ocean Safari — Tours

(07-4098 0006; www.oceansafari.com.au; Cape Tribulation Rd; adult/child/family $139/89/415; 8am & noon) Ocean Safari leads small groups (25 people maximum) on morning and afternoon snorkelling cruises to the Great Barrier Reef, just half an hour offshore.

Jungle Surfing Canopy Tours — Outdoors

(07-4098 0043; www.junglesurfing.com.au; ziplines $95, night walks $45, combo $130; 7.45am-3.30pm, night walks 7.30pm) Get right up into the rainforest on an exhilarating two-hour flying-fox (zipline) surf through the canopy. Guided night walks follow biologist-guides who shed light on the dark jungle.

Paddle Trek Kayak Tours — Kayaking

(07-4098 1950; www.capetribpaddletrek.com.au; Lot 7, Rykers Rd; half-day guided trips $75-85) Morning (2½-hour) and afternoon (3½-hour) guided sea-kayaking trips.

EATING

Mason's Store & Cafe — Cafe $$

(07-4098 0016; 3781 Cape Tribulation Rd; mains $9-18, tasting plates from $29; 10am-4pm) Everyone calls into Mason's for tourist info, the liquor store, or to dine out on exotic meats. Pride of place on the menu at this laid-back alfresco cafe goes to the croc burger, but you can also try camel, emu and kangaroo in burgers or tasting plates. A short walk away is a crystal-clear, croc-free swimming hole ($1).

GETTING THERE & AWAY

Trans North (07-4095 8644; www.transnorthbus.com.au) runs services from Cairns to Cape Tribulation three times a week. The road to Cape Tribulation is sealed so it's suitable for any hire vehicle.

THE WHITSUNDAYS

In this Chapter

The Whitsundays at a Glance...

Seen from above, the Whitsundays archipelago resembles an organism under a microscope: indigo, aqua, yellow and bottle-green blobs are mesmerising. Sheltered by the Great Barrier Reef, these waters are perfect for sailing – any of the 74 islands will hypnotise on approach and leave you giddy with good fortune.

Five islands here have resorts, but most are uninhabited. Whitehaven Beach is the finest beach in the Whitsundays and, many claim, the world. Airlie Beach, on the mainland, is the major gateway to the islands, where you can book myriad tours and activities, or just party.

The Whitsundays in Two Days

Get your bearings (then forget where you put them) in **Airlie Beach** (p134), one of Queensland's great party towns. Shake off your efforts the next day with a day trip out to see the sea – perhaps to **Daydream Island** (p137), where hair-of-the-dog bars entice. Alternatively, **Ocean Rafting** (p135) runs excellent high-speed day trips to Whitehaven Beach.

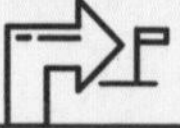

The Whitsundays in Four Days

With four days to play with, book yourself onto a longer sailing jaunt, perhaps a two-nighter taking in **Whitsunday Island** (p138), **Whitehaven Beach** (p138) and **Hook Island** (p138) with lots of snorkelling and wildlife spotting. Or just check yourself into the flashy **Hayman Island Resort** (p139) and chill to the absolute max.

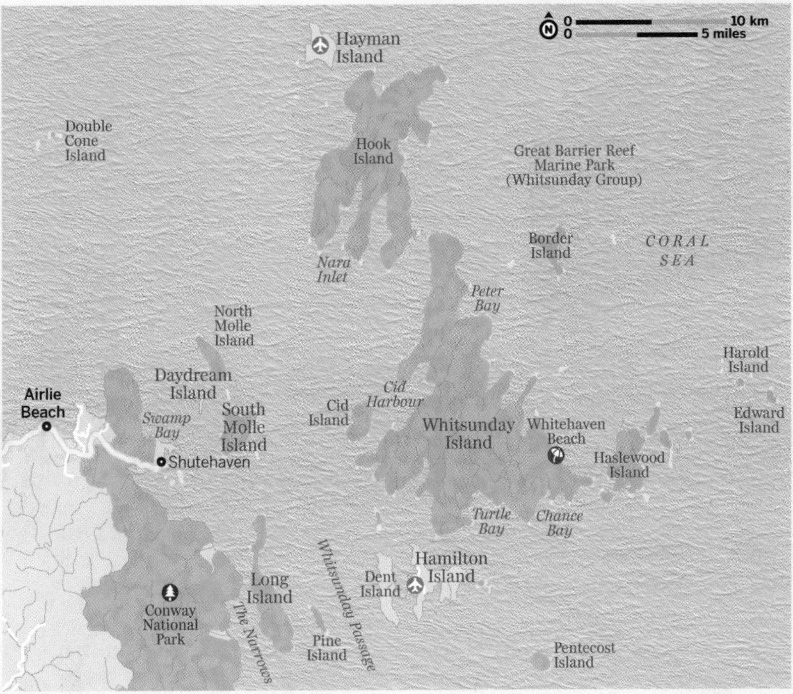

Arriving in the Whitsundays

The two main entry points for the Whitsundays are Airlie Beach, on the mainland, and the resort island of Hamilton Island, which has a major domestic airport, with connections to Sydney, Melbourne, Brisbane and Cairns. Airlie Beach is on Queensland's major coastal bus route between Brisbane and Cairns.

Where to Stay

Airlie Beach is a backpacker haven, but hostel standards vary wildly. There is also a remarkable variety of midrange accommodation here, particularly suitable for families. For a more top-end experience, head to the swish island resort of your choice: Hamilton, Daydream and Hayman islands top the list. You can also camp on some islands: see www.npsr.qld.gov.au.

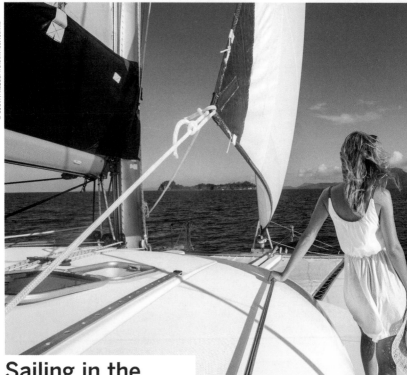

Sailing in the Whitsundays

The Whitsundays are the place to skim across fantasy-blue waters on a tropical breeze. Most sailing trips offer snorkelling on colourful fringing reefs; diving and other activities are often optional extras.

Great For

☑ **Don't Miss**

The staggeringly photogenic Whitehaven Beach, often acclaimed as Australia's finest.

Day Trip or Overnighter?

Other than super-fast boat trips run by the likes of **Ocean Rafting** (☎07-4946 6848; www.oceanrafting.com.au; Abel Point Marina, Airlie Beach; adult/child/family $149/96/446) and Big Fury (p135), most yachts can't reach Whitehaven Beach on day trips from Airlie. Instead, they usually go to the lovely Langford Reef and Hayman Island; check before you book.

Most overnight sailing packages are for three days and two nights, or two days and two nights – plenty of time to see the best bits of the archipelago.

Crewing

In return for a free bunk, meals and a sailing adventure, crewing will see you hoisting the

mainsail and cleaning the head. Look for 'Crew Wanted' signs around the marina, at restaurants and hotels. Your experience will depend on the vessel, skipper, other crew members (if any) and your own attitude. Be sure to let someone know where you're going, with whom and for how long.

Top Sailing Experiences

Derwent Hunter Boating
(☎1800 334 773; www.tallshipadventures.com.au; day trips $195) A deservedly popular sailing safari on a beautiful timber gaff-rigged schooner. A good option for couples and those more keen on wildlife than the wild life.

Need to Know

Sailing here is best between August and October (mild weather, calm seas).

Take a Break

Daydream Island Resort (p138) has a clutch of bars and restaurants open to nonresidents.

★ Top Tip

If you're aboard a smaller boat without a bar, you can usually BYO bottle(s) along.

Illusions Boating
(☎0455 142 021; www.illusion.net.au; day tours $125) A 12m catamaran that offers the least expensive, yet consistently good, sailing tours to the islands.

Prima Sailing Boating
(☎0447 377 150; www.primasailing.com.au; 2-day, 2-night tours from $390) Fun tours with a 12-person maximum. Ideal for couples chasing style and substance.

Booking Your Boat

If you're flexible with dates, last-minute stand-by rates can considerably reduce costs. Many travellers hang out in Airlie for a few days for this exact purpose (just don't blow your savings in the pub!).

Book your boat via one of the many booking agencies in Airlie Beach, including:

Whitsundays Central Reservation Centre (☎1800 677 119; www.airliebeach.com; 259 Shute Harbour Rd)

Whitsunday Sailing Adventures (☎07-4946 4999; www.whitsundayssailingadventures.com.au; The Esplanade)

Explore Whitsundays (☎07-4946 5782; www.explorewhitsundays.com; 4 The Esplanade; 2-day, 1-night trips from $359)

Airlie Beach

Aside from being the obvious departure point for most trips to the unparalleled Whitsunday Islands, Airlie has long been a destination par excellence on the east coast road-trip party trail. Its multiple hostels and massive beer gardens sit opposite a lawn-surrounded swimming lagoon where nothing much happens but the passing of carefree youth.

Those looking to avoid the party scene – families especially – will have no trouble finding quieter lodgings near town. And it's possible to enjoy nautical activities close to shore, as well as excursions into Conway National Park, without the hassle of full-day trips and overnight yachts.

ACTIVITIES

Salty Dog Sea Kayaking Kayaking
(☎07-4946 1388; www.saltydog.com.au; Shute Harbour; half-/full-day trips $80/130) Offers guided full-day tours and kayak rental (per half-/full day $50/80), plus longer kayak/camping missions (the six-day challenge costs $1650). It's a charming and healthy way to see the islands.

Lagoon Swimming
(Shute Harbour Rd) FREE Take a dip year-round in the stinger-croc-and-tropical-nasties-free lagoon in the centre of town.

Skydive Airlie Beach Skydiving
(☎07-4946 9115; www.skydive.com.au/airlie-beach; skydives from $199) Jump out of a plane from 6000, 8000 or 14,000ft and land in front of the cafe set on Airlie Beach. Fabulous group and there is not a more beautiful view in the world for a death-defying plummet.

TOURS

Cruise Whitsundays Cruise
(☎07-4846 70602; www.cruisewhitsundays.com; Shingley Dr, Abel Point Marina; full-day cruises from $99) As well as operating a ferry to the Whitsunday Islands, Cruise Whitsundays offers trips to Hardy Reef, Whitehaven Beach and islands including Daydream and Long. Or grab a daily Island Hopper pass

Airlie Beach

TANYA PUNTTI/SHUTTERSTOCK ©

(adult/child $125/65) and make your own itinerary. It also operates a popular day trip aboard the *Camira* ($195).

Red Cat Adventures Boating
(☎1300 653 100, 07-4940 2000; www.redcatadventures.com.au) Excellent family-owned operation with three distinct crafts and tours. Our pick is the Ride to Paradise ($569), a two-night adventure to a 'secret' resort, as well as many highlights of the Whitsundays.

Just Tuk'n Around Guided Tour
(www.justtuknaround.com.au; tours per person $30) Fun and informative 30-minute tours around the 'secrets' of Airlie Beach reveal more than you'd think possible in a small coastal town.

Air Whitsunday Scenic Flights
(☎07-4946 9111; www.airwhitsunday.com.au; Terminal 1, Whitsunday Airport) Offers a range of tours, including day trips to Whitehaven ($255) and scenic-flight-plus-snorkelling tours of the Great Barrier Reef ($375).

Ecojet Safari Tours
(☎07-4948 2653; tours per person $195) Explore the islands, mangroves and marine life of the northern Whitsundays on these three-hour, small-group jet-ski safaris (two people per jet ski).

High-Speed Boat Trips from Airlie Beach

Ocean Rafting (☎07-4946 6848; www.oceanrafting.com.au; adult/child/family from $134/87/399) Visit the 'wild' side of the islands in a very fast, big yellow speedboat. Swim at Whitehaven Beach, regain your land legs with a guided national park walk, or snorkel the reef at Mantaray Bay and Border Island.

Big Fury (☎07-4948 2201; www.magicwhitsundays.com; adult/child/family $130/70/350) Speed out to Whitehaven Beach on an open-air sports boat, and follow up with lunch and snorkelling at a secluded reef nearby. Great value and bookable through Airlie Beach travel agencies.

Pioneer Jet Whitsundays (☎1800 335 975; www.pioneerjet.com.au; Abel Point Marina; adult/child $69/49) The Ultimate Bay Blast is a thunderous 30-minute spin in a jet boat. Fun and informative guides round off the experience. Expect to get very wet.

EATING

Harry's Corner Cafe $
(☎07-4946 7459; 273 Shute Harbour Rd; mains $7-18; ⏲7am-3pm) Locals are wild about Harry's, which serves quaint European tea sets, Danish sandwiches, filled bagels and good-sized salads. The all-day breakfasts are a must for a hangover.

Mr Bones Pizza $$
(☎0413 017 331; Lagoon Plaza, 263 Shute Harbour Rd; shared plates $12-17, pizzas $15-23; ⏲9am-9pm Tue-Sat) Carefully curated play lists and creative thin-based pizzas have made Mr Bones the coolest place to eat in Airlie since it opened six years ago. Overlooking the lagoon, the small, sunny restaurant also has an extensive 'not pizzas' menu of appetisers to play around with. Service is upbeat and interested. Great coffee, too.

Fish D'vine Seafood $$
(☎07-4948 0088; 303 Shute Harbour Rd; mains $17-33; ⏲5pm-late) Pirates were definitely onto something: this fish-and-rum bar is shiploads of fun, serving up all things nibbly from Neptune's realm and lashings and lashings of rum (more than 200 kinds of the stuff). Yo-ho-ho! Sport eaters can take on the 'Seafood Indulgence', a mountain of shells and claws for a whopping $149.

Airlie Beach Treehouse Modern Australian $$
(☎07-4946 5550; www.airlietreehouse.com; 6/263-265 Shute Harbour Rd; mains $18-36;

RICHARD CUMMINS/GETTY IMAGES ©

From left: Lagoon, Airlie Beach (p134); Marina, Hamilton Island (p138); Helicopter view of Hill Inlet and Whitehaven Beach (p138)

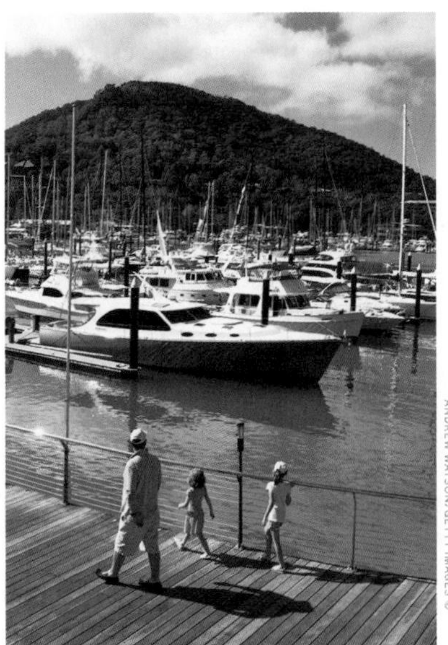
ANDREW WATSON/GETTY IMAGES ©

⌚8.30am-9.30pm) This new restaurant by the lagoon is making ripples for its uncomplicated service and quality food in a shady setting.

Denman Cellars Beer Cafe Tapas **$$**
(☎07-4948 1333; Shop 15, 33 Port Dr; tapas $10, mains $18-38; ⌚11am-10pm Mon-Fri, 8am-11pm Sat & Sun) Regular live music and a convivial mood are found in this tapas bar that stocks more boutique beers than the rest of the town combined (700 brews!). The food – such as a shared seafood platter ($57), and 'beer bites' such as zucchini balls ($14) and duck pancakes ($17) – is decent. Larger meals are available.

DRINKING & NIGHTLIFE

Mama Africa Club
(263 Shute Harbour Rd; ⌚9pm-5am) Mama's is a jumping African-style safari nightclub throbbing with a beat that both hunter and prey find hard to resist. Themed nights and all kinds of promotions aimed at the backpacker party set ensure spontaneous all-nighters any day of the week.

Just Wine & Cheese Wine Bar
(Shop 8, 33 Port Dr; wines by the glass $7-18; ⌚3-10pm) Run by two astute wine aficionados, this glamorous bottle shop–bar serves fine examples of what it promises, with a view of the Port of Airlie marina.

GETTING THERE & AWAY

AIR

The closest major airports are Whitsunday Coast (Proserpine) and Hamilton Island.

BOAT

Transfers between the **Port of Airlie** (www.portofairlie.com.au) and Hamilton, Daydream and Long islands are provided by Cruise Whitsundays (p134).

BUS

Greyhound (☎1300 473 946; www.greyhound.com.au) and **Premier Motor Service** (☎13 34 10; www.premierms.com.au) buses detour off the Bruce Hwy to Airlie Beach.

Whitsunday Transit (☎07-4946 1800; www.whitsundaytransit.com.au) connects Proserpine

(Whitsunday Airport), Cannonvale, Abel Point, Airlie Beach and Shute Harbour.

Long Island

Long Island has secluded, pretty white beaches and lots of adorable, wild rock wallabies. The beaches here are among the best in the Whitsundays, and there are 13km of walking tracks with some fine lookouts. Long Island has seen its two major resorts close down in recent years. The new **Palm Bay Resort** (☎1300 655 126; www.palmbayresort.com.au; villas/bures/bungalows from $229/249/329) has filled a void at the high end, while campers are adequately served at **Long Island National Park Camp Site** (www.nprsr.qld.gov.au; sites per person/family $6.15/24.60).

The **NPSR office** (☎13 74 68; www.npsr.qld.gov.au; cnr Shute Harbour & Mandalay Rds; 9am-4.30pm Mon-Fri) in Airlie Beach can offer advice on getting to the island. Alternatively, you can talk to **Scamper** (☎07-4946 6285; www.whitsundaycamping.com.au).

Cruise Whitsundays (☎07-4946 4662; www.cruisewhitsundays.com) connects Palm Bay Resort to the Port of Airlie by frequent daily services.

South Molle Island

The largest of the Molle group of islands at 4 sq km, South Molle is virtually joined to Mid and North Molle Islands. Apart from the private residence area and golf course at Bauer Bay in the north, the island is all national park and is criss-crossed by 15km of walking tracks, with some superb lookout points. If you want to stay the night, you can either camp or stay at **Adventure Island Resort** (☎1800 466 444; 2 nights/3 days Sail and Stay package $379;).

Island Transfers (☎0488 022 868) can arrange quick and easy transport to South Molle. Otherwise, contact Adventure Island Resort or Scamper.

Daydream Island

Daydream Island is the closest resort to the mainland and perfectly located to attract the tourist hordes. Recently sold to a new investment group who plan to make it a 'luxury' destination, it will likely retain its popularity as a day-trip destination and is suitable for everybody, especially busy families, or travellers with little time to explore the 'real' Whitsundays.

Daydream Island Resort & Spa (1800 075 040; www.daydreamisland.com; d from $245;) has a monopoly on the accommodation on the island. You might expect some shoddy efforts from the Daydream team, but they know their clientele – families with kids, cautious international travellers and time-poor holiday-makers – and understand the buzz generated by the location alone. Rooms are reasonably priced and many face out to the glorious Coral Sea.

Cruise Whitsundays (07-4946 4662; www.cruisewhitsundays.com; one-way adult/child $40/27) connects Daydream Island to Abel Point Marina in Airlie Beach and Shute Harbour with frequent daily services.

Hook Island

The 53-sq-km Hook Island, the second-largest island in the Whitsundays group, is predominantly national park and rises to 450m at Hook Peak. There are a number of good beaches dotted around the island, and some of the region's best diving and snorkelling locations. If you want to stay the night, the only option here is **camping** (www.npsr.qld.gov.au; sites per person/family $6.15/24.60). Brilliant!

Transfers are arranged when you book your accommodation. Otherwise, **Scamper** (07-4946 6285; www.whitsundaycamping.com.au) can organise drop-offs to the camping grounds.

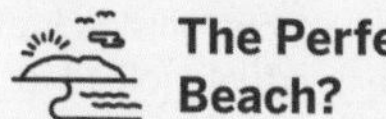

The Perfect Beach?

Whitehaven Beach, on Whitsunday Island, is a pristine 7km-long stretch of blinding sand (at 98% pure silica, said sand is some of the whitest in the world), bounded by lush tropical vegetation and a brilliant blue sea. From Hill Inlet at the northern end of the beach, the swirling pattern of dazzling sand through the turquoise and aquamarine water paints a magical picture. There's excellent snorkelling from its southern end.

Camping is the only sleeping option on the island. The NPSR office (p137) in Airlie Beach issues permits and can advise on transport. Alternatively, take a boat tour or contact Scamper.

Hamilton Island

Welcome to a little slice of resort paradise where the paved roads are plied by golf buggies, steep, rocky hills are criss-crossed by walking trails blessed with magnificent sea views, and the white beaches are buzzing with water-sports action. Though it's not everyone's idea of a perfect getaway, it's hard not to be impressed by the selection of high-end accommodation (resorts, hotels, cabins), restaurants, bars and activities – if you've got the cash, there's something for everyone. Our pick is **Qualia** (1300 780 959; www.qualia.com.au; d from $1100;), an ultraluxe resort set on 12 secluded hectares, with modern villas materialising like heavenly tree houses in the leafy hillside.

ACTIVITIES

From **Catseye Beach**, in front of the resort area, you can hire stand-up paddleboards, kayaks, windsurfers, catamarans, jet skis and other equipment, and go parasailing or waterskiing. Nonmotorised equipment costs around $12 for half-hour rental, $20 for an hour.

A few shops by the harbour organise dives and certificate courses, and just about everyone is ready to sign you up for a variety of cruises to other islands and the outer reef.

If you only have time for one walk, make it the clamber up to **Passage Peak** (239m) on the northeastern corner of the island.

 EATING

The main resort complex has a number of restaurants. The marina also offers plenty of choices including a good **bakery-deli** (Front St; sandwiches from $9; ⏲7am-4pm), a **fish 'n' chip shop** (Front St; fish & chips $11.50; ⏲10am-9pm Sun-Thu, 11.30am-9pm Fri & Sat), a **tavern** (☎07-4946 8839; Marina Village; mains from $17.50; ⏲11am-midnight), and a general store for self-caterers.

 GETTING THERE & AWAY

AIR

Hamilton Island Airport is the main arrival centre for the Whitsundays, and is serviced by **Qantas** (☎13 13 13; www.qantas.com.au), **Jetstar** (☎13 15 38; www.jetstar.com.au) and **Virgin** (☎13 67 89; www.virginaustralia.com.au).

BOAT

Cruise Whitsundays (☎07-4946 4662; www.cruisewhitsundays.com) connects Hamilton Island Airport and the marina with the Port of Airlie in Airlie Beach ($48).

Hayman Island

The most northern of the Whitsunday group, little Hayman is just 4 sq km in area and rises to 250m above sea level. It has forested hills, valleys and beaches, and a luxury five-star resort.

An avenue of stately date palms leads to the main entrance of the gorgeous **One&Only Hayman Island Resort** (☎07-4940 1838; www.hayman.com.au; r incl breakfast $730-12,300; ❄@📶🏊). It's one of the most gilded playgrounds on the Great Barrier Reef with a hectare of swimming pools, landscaped gardens and grounds, and exclusive boutiques.

Resort guests must first fly to Hamilton Island Airport before being escorted to Hayman's fleet of luxury cruisers for a pampered transfer to the resort.

 Top Five Beaches

There are plenty of secluded, postcard-perfect, sandy bays in this tropical paradise. The following are reasonably accessible for most tour companies:

Whitehaven Beach (p138) With azure-blue waters lapping the pure-white, silica sand, Whitehaven on Whitsunday Island is absolutely stunning.

Chalkies Beach Opposite Whitehaven Beach, on Haslewood Island, this is another idyllic, white-sanded beach.

Langford Island At high tide, Langford is a thin strip of sand on the rim of a ludicrously picturesque coral-filled turquoise lagoon.

Butterfly Bay On the northern side of Hook Island is this protected bay, which flutters with butterfly song each winter.

Catseye Beach Catseye Beach on Hamilton Island is a busy-ish spot, but you can rent kayaks and buy a drink!

Catseye Beach
DARREN TIERNEY/SHUTTERSTOCK ©

View of the city skyline and Flinders Street Station (p152) from Federation Square (p144

MELBOURNE

In this Chapter

Melbourne at a Glance...

Stylish, arty Melbourne is dynamic, sports-mad and cosmopolitan. Its stately architecture and multicultural make-up reflect the city's history; edgy street art, top museums and sticky-carpeted band venues point to its present-day personality.

The city's character is defined by its collection of inner-city neighbourhoods. Despite a long-standing north–south divide (flashy St Kilda vs hipster Fitzroy), there's a coolness about its bars, cafes, restaurants, festivals and inhabitants that transcends the borders. The city centre has meanwhile reinvented itself, with chic eateries and rooftop bars opening in former industrial buildings.

Melbourne in Two Days

Check out the galleries at **Federation Square** (p144), then join **Melbourne by Foot** (p156) to see the city's streetscapes or just chill in a **rooftop bar** (p161). On day two, stroll along **Birrarung Marr** (p152) and into the **Royal Botanic Gardens** (p153), then shop your way to the Queen Victoria Market (p146). Head to **St Kilda** for an afternoon stroll along the foreshore and catch a band at the **Prince Bandroom** (p161) in the evening.

Melbourne in Four Days

Visit the **Melbourne Museum** (p153), then revive with coffee on bohemian Brunswick St, Fitzroy. Back in the CBD, check out the street art in **Hosier Lane** (p153), explore **Chinatown** (p152) and see Ned Kelly's armour at the State Library. On day four, catch a footy game or take a tour at the **MCG** (p148). Wind up with dinner on Smith St, Collingwood, then head to the **Tote** (p162) for more live tunes.

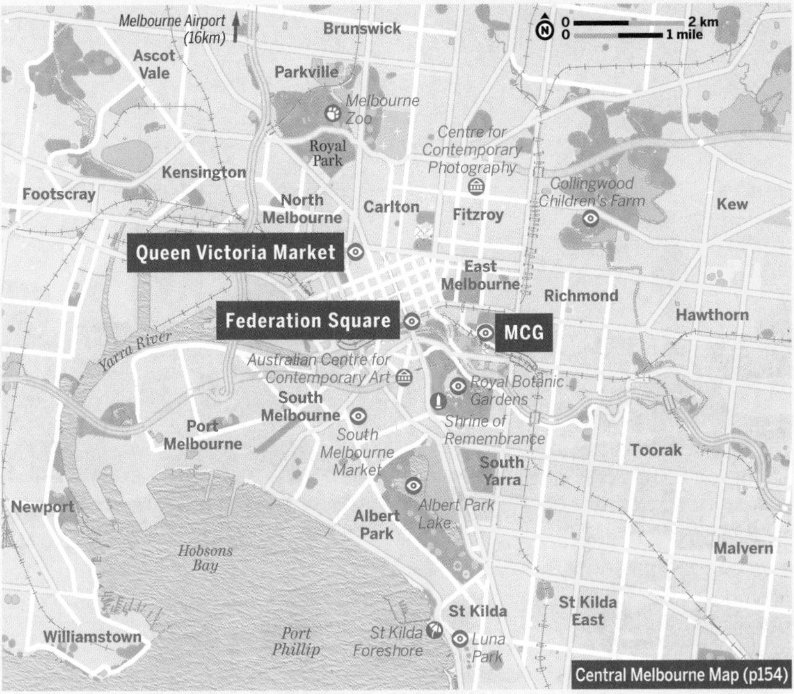

Arriving in Melbourne

Melbourne Airport Most travellers arrive at this airport, 22km north of the city; you can get into the city centre via Skybus ($18) shuttle and taxi (around $65).

Southern Cross Station Interstate trains and buses arrive at this station in the CBD.

Station Pier The *Spirit of Tasmania* (p163) vehicle ferry docks in Port Melbourne.

Where to Stay

Carlton and Fitzroy, north of the CBD, have lots of midrange accommodation, plus great drinking and eating. Central Melbourne is studded with apartments, swish hotels and budget hostels. Down on the bay, raffish St Kilda has both budget and boutique options; while East Melbourne is somewhat refined and removed from the hubbub.

For more information on where to stay see p165.

Federation Square

It's taken a while, but Melburnians are finally embracing 'Fed Square' as their own – somewhere to celebrate, protest, watch the big game or hang out in deckchairs.

Great For...

☑ Don't Miss

The buzz when major sporting events flicker across the giant screen.

The Heart of the City

Occupying a prominent city block, Federation Square is far from square: its undulating and patterned forecourt is paved with 460,000 hand-laid cobblestones from the Kimberley region in Western Australia, with sight lines to important Melbourne landmarks. Its buildings are clad in a fractal-patterned reptilian skin.

Within the square are some cultural heavyweight sights, restaurants, bars, and at the square's street junction is the subterranean Melbourne Visitor Centre (p162). There are always free public events going on here, particularly on weekends.

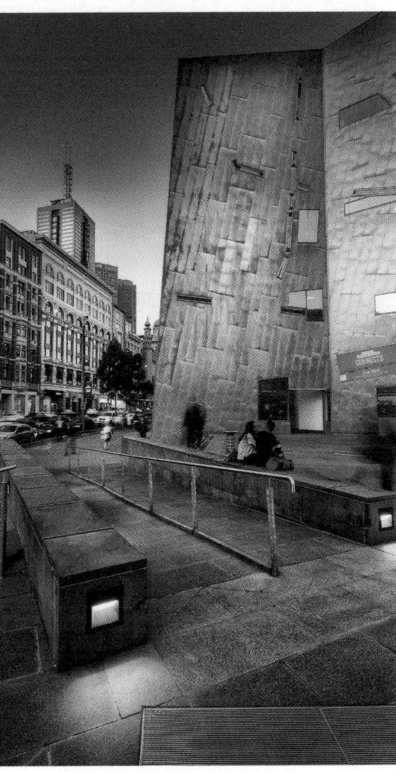
STONEOGRAPHY/GETTY IMAGES ©

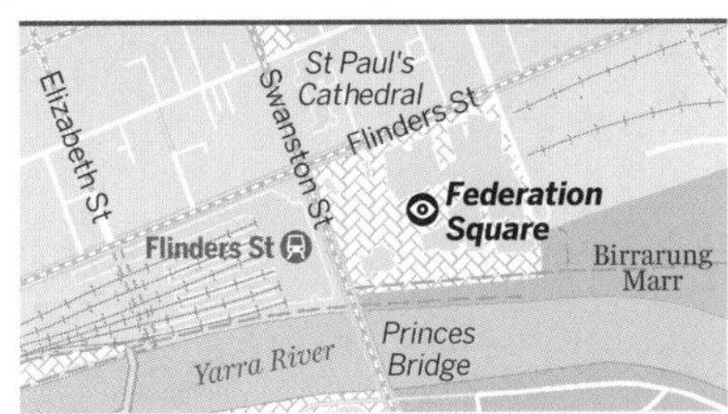

Need to Know

www.fedsquare.com; cnr Flinders & Swanston Sts; 📶; 🚆Flinders St

Take a Break

MoVida (p157), the genre-defining Melbourne Spanish restaurant, is just over Flinders St.

★ Top Tip

Free tours depart 11am Monday to Saturday; spaces are limited, so arrive 15 minutes early.

Big-Ticket Sights

Ian Potter Centre: NGV Australia — Gallery

(☎03-8620 2222; www.ngv.vic.gov.au; 🕙10am-5pm) **FREE** The National Gallery of Victoria's impressive Fed Sq offshoot was set up to showcase its extraordinary collection of Australian works. Set over three levels, it's a mix of permanent (free) and temporary (ticketed) exhibitions, comprising paintings, decorative arts, photography, prints, sculpture and fashion. Free tours are conducted daily at 11am, noon, 1pm and 2pm.

Australian Centre for the Moving Image — Museum

(ACMI; ☎03-8663 2200; www.acmi.net.au; 🕙10am-5pm; 📶) **FREE** Managing to educate, enthral and entertain in equal parts, ACMI is a visual feast that pays homage to Australian cinema and TV, offering an insight into the modern-day Australian psyche perhaps as no other museum can. Its screens don't discriminate against age, with TV shows, games and movies on call, making it a great place to spend a day watching TV and not feel guilty about it. Free tours are conducted daily at 11am and 2.30pm.

Koorie Heritage Trust — Cultural Centre

(☎03-8662 6300; www.koorieheritagetrust.com; Yarra Bldg; tours adult/child $33/17; 🕙10am-5pm) **FREE** Devoted to southeastern Aboriginal culture, this centre houses interesting artefacts and oral history. There's a shop and gallery downstairs, while upstairs carefully preserved significant objects can be viewed in display cases and drawers. It also runs hour-long tours along the Yarra during summer, evoking the history and memories that lie beneath the modern city (book online).

Queen Victoria Market

With more than 600 traders, the effervescent Queen Vic Market is the largest open-air market in the southern hemisphere and attracts thousands of shoppers.

Great For...

☑ **Don't Miss**

Stallholders spruiking discounted meat and seafood (still perfectly fresh) just before closing time.

Food, Glorious Food

This is where Melburnians sniff out fresh produce among the booming cries of spruiking fishmongers and fruit-and-veg vendors. The wonderful deli hall (with art deco features) is lined with everything from soft cheeses, wines and Polish sausages to Greek dips, truffle oil and kangaroo biltong.

The market has been here for more than 130 years; before that, from 1837 to 1854, it was the old Melbourne Cemetery (remarkably, around 9000 bodies remain buried here, from underneath Shed F to the car park leading to Franklin St). There's a small memorial on the corner of Queen and Therry Sts.

As well as the deli hall, make sure you check out the food court, the shops on Elizabeth and Victoria Sts, and the latest addition to the market, String Bean Alley,

Shopping in the deli hall

TRAVELGAME/GETTY IMAGES ©

Need to Know

www.qvm.com.au; 513 Elizabeth St; 6am-2pm Tue & Thu, to 5pm Fri, to 3pm Sat, 9am-4pm Sun; Flagstaff

Take a Break

The market's outpost of the **Padre Coffee Empire** (www.padrecoffee.com.au; L Shed, String Bean Alley; 7am-3pm Fri-Sun) is the perfect pit stop.

★ Top Tip

Various market tours transpire, including heritage, cultural and foodie tours; check the website.

a series of shipping containers housing artisans and traders (open Friday, Saturday and Sunday).

Join the thronging locals and snatch up some classic Vic Market treats:

- A bratwurst from the Bratwurst Stall (with German mustard and sauerkraut).
- Terrine from the French Shop (with French butter and cornichons).
- African hot-smoked blue-eye cutlets from Tribal Tastes (or biltong, or *shitto* – Ghanaian smoked fish and chilli sauce).
- Superb 'wedding sausage', ham, brawn or bacon from the Polish deli (and perhaps a Polish doughnut).
- A perfectly blended *ras el hanout* from Gewürzhaus.

What's On

Saturday morning is particularly buzzing, with marketgoers breakfasting to the sounds and shows of buskers. Clothing and knickknack stalls dominate on Sunday; they're big on variety, but don't come looking for style. (If you're in the market for sheepskin moccasins or cheap T-shirts, you'll be in luck.)

On Wednesday evenings from mid-November to the end of February, the Summer Night Market takes over. It's a lively social event featuring hawker-style food stalls, bars, and music and dance performances. There's also a Winter Night Market each Wednesday evening from June to August.

Major restoration and redevelopment works are planned: by late 2017 the fruit-and-veg traders should have moved into a striking new glass pavilion on Queen St.

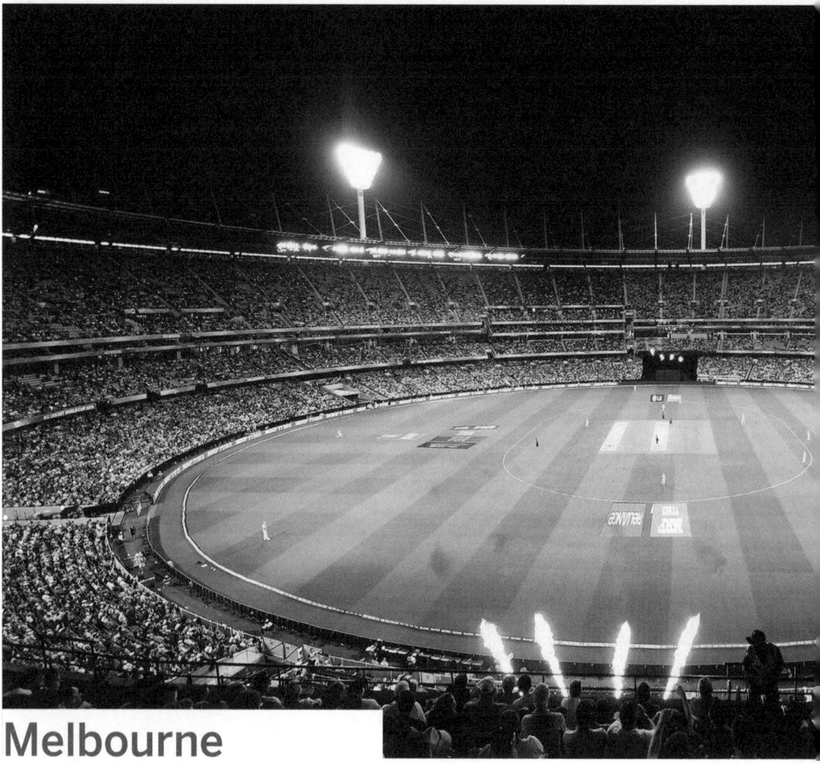

Melbourne Cricket Ground

With a capacity of 100,000 people, the MCG is one of the world's great sports venues, hosting cricket in the summer, and AFL footy in the winter. Hallowed ground!

Great For...

☑ Don't Miss

The Indigenous Round in the AFL – a celebration of Aboriginal footballers' sublime skills.

History

In 1858 the first game of Aussie Rules football was played where the MCG and its car parks now stand, and in 1877 it was the venue for the first Test cricket match between Australia and England. The MCG was the central stadium for the 1956 Melbourne Olympics and the 2006 Commonwealth Games. It was also used as army barracks during WWII.

MCG Dreaming

Where did Australian Rules football come from? There's plenty of evidence to suggest that Aboriginal men and women played a form of football (called 'marngrook') prior to white settlement. Did they play it at the MCG site pre-settlement? The MCG has two scar trees from which bark was

Need to Know

MCG; 03-9657 8888; www.mcg.org.au; Brunton Ave, East Melbourne; tours adult/child/family $23/12/55, incl museum $32/16/70; tours 10am-3pm; Jolimont

Take a Break

Richmond Hill Cafe & Larder (03-9421 2808; www.rhcl.com.au; 48-50 Bridge Rd, Richmond; lunch $12-27; 7am-5pm; 48, 75) is a 10-minute walk away.

Top Tip

Never try to drive to 'the G' on a big match day: you'll surely regret it.

removed by Aboriginal people to make canoes. These reminders make it clear that Melbourne's footy fans (and perhaps players) were not the first to gather at the site of the MCG.

Visiting 'the G'

Make it to a game if you can (highly recommended). Otherwise, non-match-day tours take you through the stands, media and coaches' areas, change rooms and out onto the ground.

Sports fans can also visit the **National Sports Museum** (03-9657 8879; www.nsm.org.au; Gate 3; adult/child/family $23/12/55; 10am-5pm) in the bowels of the ground, focusing on Australia's favourite sports and historic sporting moments. Kids will love the interactive section where they can test their footy, cricket or netball skills. There's even a hologram of cricketer Shane Warne.

Objects on display include the handwritten rules of Australian Rules football from 1859; a collection of baggy green caps worn by Australian cricket legends (including Don Bradman); olive branches awarded to Edwin Flack, Australia's first Olympic medallist (1886); various Olympic medals; and sprinter Cathy Freeman's famous Sydney Olympics swift suit.

MCG Events

AFL Grand Final Sports

(www.afl.com.au; Sep) Grand Final tickets are next to impossible to procure. But pubs across the city buzz with finals fever.

Boxing Day Test Sports

(www.mcg.org.au; 26 Dec) Boxing Day is day one of Melbourne's hugely popular annual Test cricket match.

Arcades & Lanes

Central Melbourne is a warren of 19th-century arcades and gritty-turned-hip cobbled bluestone lanes featuring street art, basement restaurants, boutiques and bars.

Start Campbell Arcade

Distance 3km

Duration 2½ hours

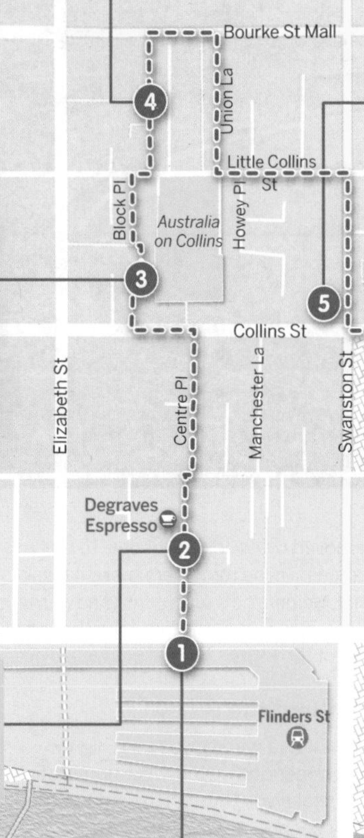

4 Across Little Collins St, head into **Royal Arcade** (www.royalarcade.com.au; 335 Bourke St Mall) to see the 1892 Gaunt's Clock striking the hour.

3 Cross Collins St and enter the gorgeous **Block Arcade** (☎03-9654 5244; www.theblock.com.au; 282 Collins St), dating to 1891 and featuring etched-glass ceilings and mosaic floors.

2 Head upstairs to graffiti-spangled **Degraves St** then cross Flinders Lane to cafe-filled Centre Place.

1 Start off underground at the art deco **Campbell Arcade**, built for the '56 Olympics and now home to indie stores.

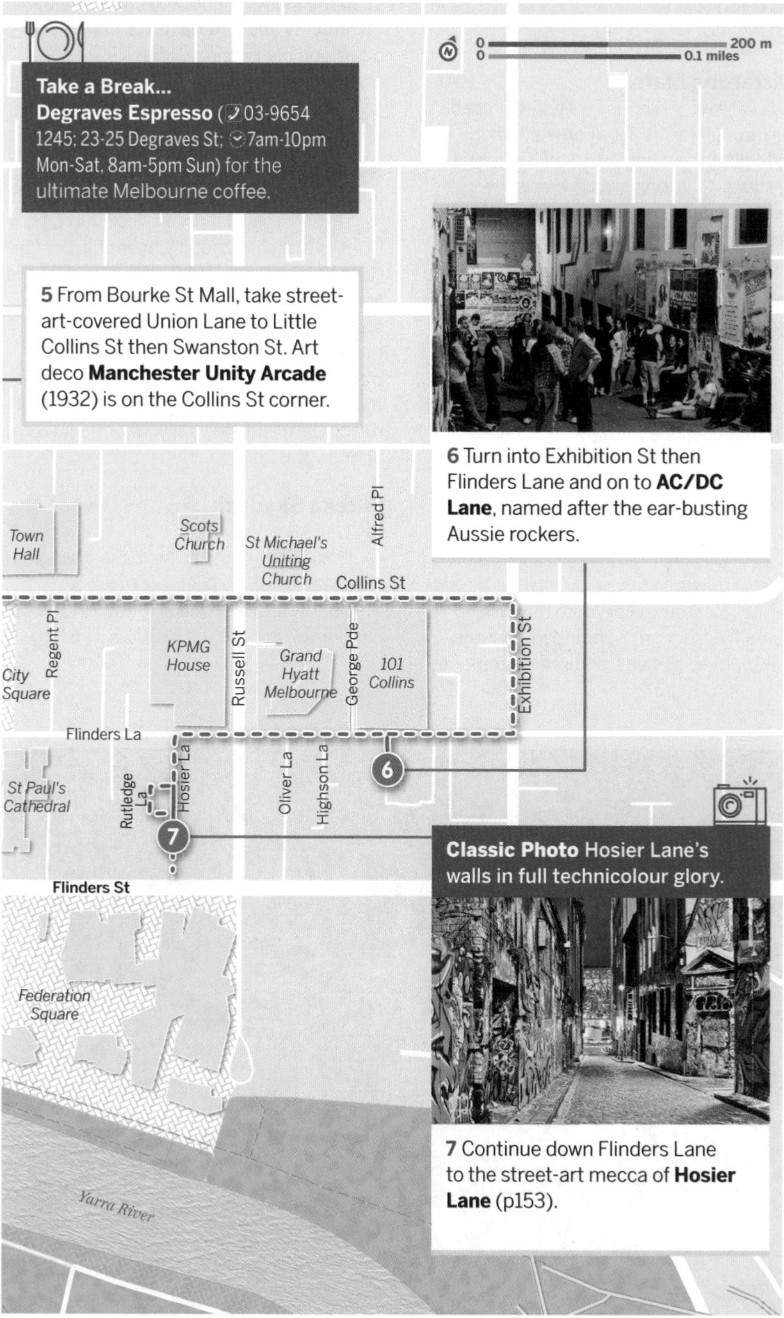

Take a Break...
Degraves Espresso (☎03-9654 1245; 23-25 Degraves St; ⏰7am-10pm Mon-Sat, 8am-5pm Sun) for the ultimate Melbourne coffee.

5 From Bourke St Mall, take street-art-covered Union Lane to Little Collins St then Swanston St. Art deco **Manchester Unity Arcade** (1932) is on the Collins St corner.

6 Turn into Exhibition St then Flinders Lane and on to **AC/DC Lane**, named after the ear-busting Aussie rockers.

0 200 m
0 0.1 miles

Town Hall
Scots Church
St Michael's Uniting Church
Alfred Pl
Collins St
Regent Pl
City Square
KPMG House
Russell St
Grand Hyatt Melbourne
George Pde
101 Collins
Exhibition St
Flinders La
St Paul's Cathedral
Rutledge La
Hosier La
Oliver La
Highson La
Flinders St
Federation Square
Yarra River

Classic Photo Hosier Lane's walls in full technicolour glory.

7 Continue down Flinders Lane to the street-art mecca of **Hosier Lane** (p153).

SIGHTS

Central Melbourne

Birrarung Marr Park

(Batman Ave; 🚊Flinders St) Multi-terraced Birrarung Marr is a welcome addition to Melbourne's patchwork of parks and gardens, featuring grassy knolls, river promenades, thoughtful planting of indigenous flora and great viewpoints of the city and the river.

Flinders Street Station Historic Building

(cnr Flinders & Swanston Sts; 📶; 🚊Flinders St) If ever there were a true symbol of the city, Flinders St Station would have to be it. Stretching along the Yarra, it's a beautiful neoclassical building (1854) topped with a striking octagonal dome.

Chinatown Area

(www.chinatownmelbourne.com.au; Little Bourke St, btwn Swanston & Exhibition Sts; 🚊Melbourne Central, Parliament) For more than 150 years this section of central Melbourne, now flanked by five traditional arches, has been the focal point for the city's Chinese community and it remains a vibrant neighbourhood of historic buildings filled with Chinese (and other Asian) restaurants.

Southbank

NGV International Gallery

(☎03-8662 1555; www.ngv.vic.gov.au; 180 St Kilda Rd; ⊙10am-5pm; 📶; 🚊Flinders St) FREE Housed in a vast, brutally beautiful, bunker-like building, the international branch of the National Gallery of Victoria has an expansive collection that runs the gamut from the ancient to the bleeding edge. Regular blockbuster exhibitions (prices vary) draw the crowds. Free 45-minute highlights tours run at 11am and 1pm daily; hour-long tours at noon and 2pm.

Eureka Skydeck Viewpoint

(☎03-9693 8888; www.eurekaskydeck.com.au; 7 Riverside Quay; adult/child $20/12, Edge extra $12/8; ⊙10am-10pm; 🚊Flinders St) Melbourne's tallest building, the 297m-high Eureka Tower was built in 2006. The Edge –

Flinders Street Station

a slightly sadistic glass cube – cantilevers you out of the building.

Fitzroy & Around

Collingwood Children's Farm Farm

(www.farm.org.au; 18 St Heliers St, Abbotsford; adult/child/family $10/5/20; 9.15am-4.30pm; 200, 207, Victoria Park) The inner city melts away at this rustic riverside retreat that's beloved not just by children. There's a range of frolicking farm animals that kids can help feed, as well as cow milking and guinea-pig cuddles!

Carlton & Around

Melbourne Museum Museum

(13 11 02; www.museumvictoria.com.au; 11 Nicholson St, Carlton; adult $14, child & student free, exhibitions extra; 10am-5pm; Tourist Shuttle, City Circle, 86, 96, Parliament) This museum provides a grand sweep of Victoria's natural and cultural histories, incorporating dinosaur fossils, giant-squid specimens, a taxidermy hall, a 3D volcano and an open-air forest atrium of Victorian flora. There's also an IMAX cinema.

Royal Exhibition Building Historic Building

(13 11 02; www.museumvictoria.com.au/reb; 9 Nicholson St, Carlton; tours adult/child $10/7; Tourist Shuttle, City Circle, 86, 96, Parliament) Built for the 1880 International Exhibition, and winning Unesco World Heritage status in 2004, this beautiful Victorian edifice symbolises the glory days of the Industrial Revolution. Tours leave from Melbourne Museum (opposite) at 2pm.

Melbourne Zoo Zoo

(1300 966 784; www.zoo.org.au; Elliott Ave, Parkville; adult/child $33/17, child weekends & holidays free; 8am-5pm; Royal Park) Established in 1861, this compact zoo is the oldest in Australia and the third-oldest in the world. It continues to innovate, recently becoming the world's first carbon-neutral zoo.

Street Art Hot Spots

Hosier Lane (Flinders St) Melbourne's most celebrated laneway for street art, Hosier Lane's cobbled length draws camera-wielding crowds snapping edgy graffiti, stencils and art installations. Pieces change almost daily (not even a Banksy is safe here). Be sure to see Rutledge Lane (which horseshoes around Hosier), too.

Blender Lane (03-9328 5556; www.theblenderstudios.com; 110 Franklin St; Melbourne Central) This unsigned laneway, located off Franklin St, features some of Melbourne's best street art, showcasing the work of the underground artists from the Blender Studios warehouse next door. It also runs the highly recommended **Melbourne Street Tours** (03-9328 5556; www.melbournestreettours.com; tours $69; city centre 1.30pm Tue, Thu & Sat, Fitzroy 11am Sat).

Hosier Lane
MELANIE CONROY/500PX ©

South Yarra

Royal Botanic Gardens Gardens

(www.rbg.vic.gov.au; Birdwood Ave; 7.30am-sunset; Tourist Shuttle, 1, 3, 5, 6, 16, 64, 67, 72) FREE Drawing over 1.5 million visitors annually, Melbourne's Royal Botanic Gardens is considered one of the finest examples of Victorian-era landscaping in the world. You will find a global selection of plantings and endemic Australian flora.

Central Melbourne

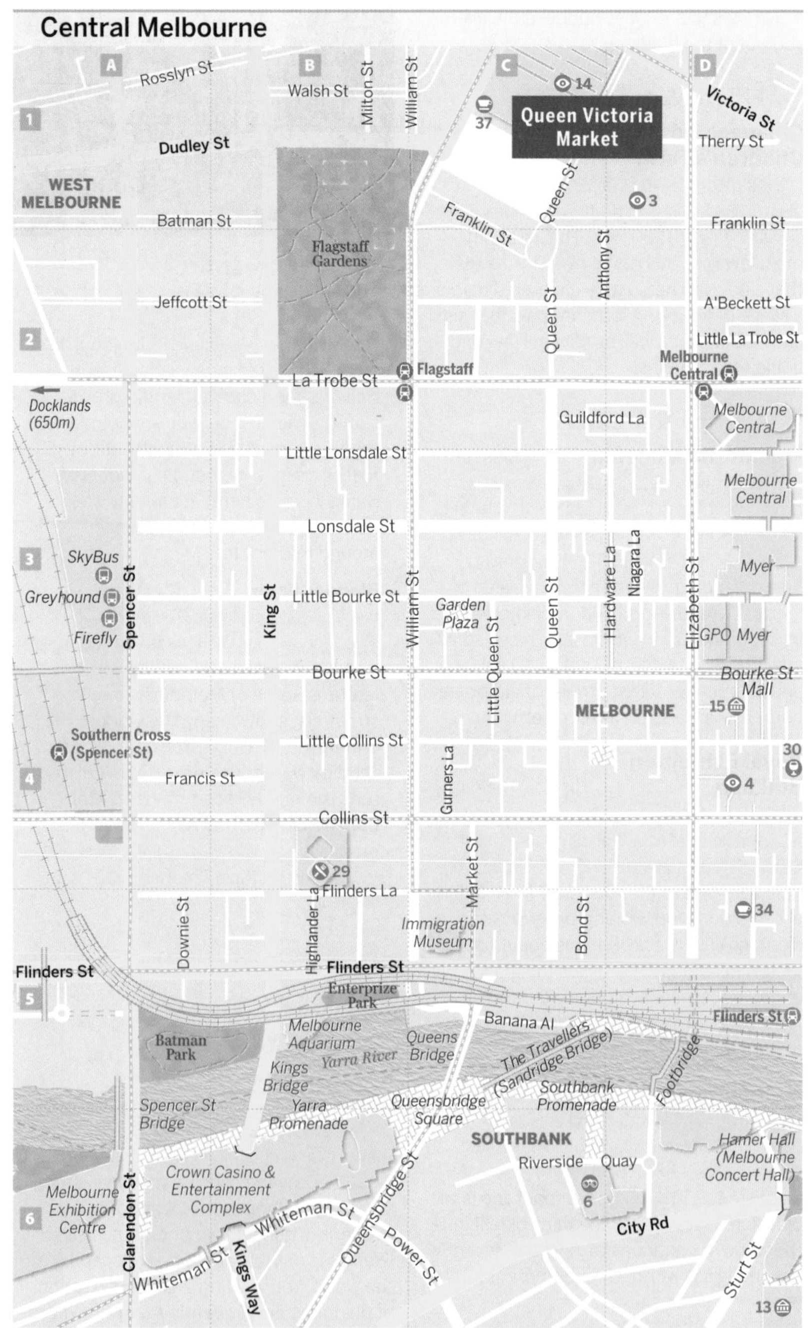
A
B
C
D
1
2
3
4
5
6
Rosslyn St
Walsh St
Milton St
William St
14
37
Queen Victoria Market
Victoria St
Therry St
Dudley St
WEST MELBOURNE
Batman St
Queen St
3
Franklin St
Franklin St
Flagstaff Gardens
Anthony St
Jeffcott St
Queen St
A'Beckett St
Little La Trobe St
Melbourne Central
Flagstaff
La Trobe St
Docklands (650m)
Guildford La
Melbourne Central
Little Lonsdale St
Melbourne Central
Lonsdale St
SkyBus
Greyhound
Firefly
Spencer St
King St
Little Bourke St
William St
Garden Plaza
Queen St
Hardware La
Niagara La
Elizabeth St
Myer
GPO Myer
Little Queen St
Bourke St
Bourke St Mall
MELBOURNE
15
Southern Cross (Spencer St)
Little Collins St
Gurners La
30
Francis St
4
Collins St
Market St
29
Flinders La
Highlander La
Downie St
Immigration Museum
Bond St
34
Flinders St
Flinders St
Enterprize Park
Banana Al
Flinders St
Batman Park
Melbourne Aquarium
Queens Bridge
The Travellers (Sandridge Bridge)
Kings Bridge
Yarra River
Footbridge
Spencer St Bridge
Yarra Promenade
Queensbridge Square
Southbank Promenade
SOUTHBANK
Hamer Hall (Melbourne Concert Hall)
Riverside
Quay
Crown Casino & Entertainment Complex
Queensbridge St
6
Melbourne Exhibition Centre
Clarendon St
Whiteman St
City Rd
Whiteman St
Kings Way
Power St
Queensbridge St
Sturt St
13

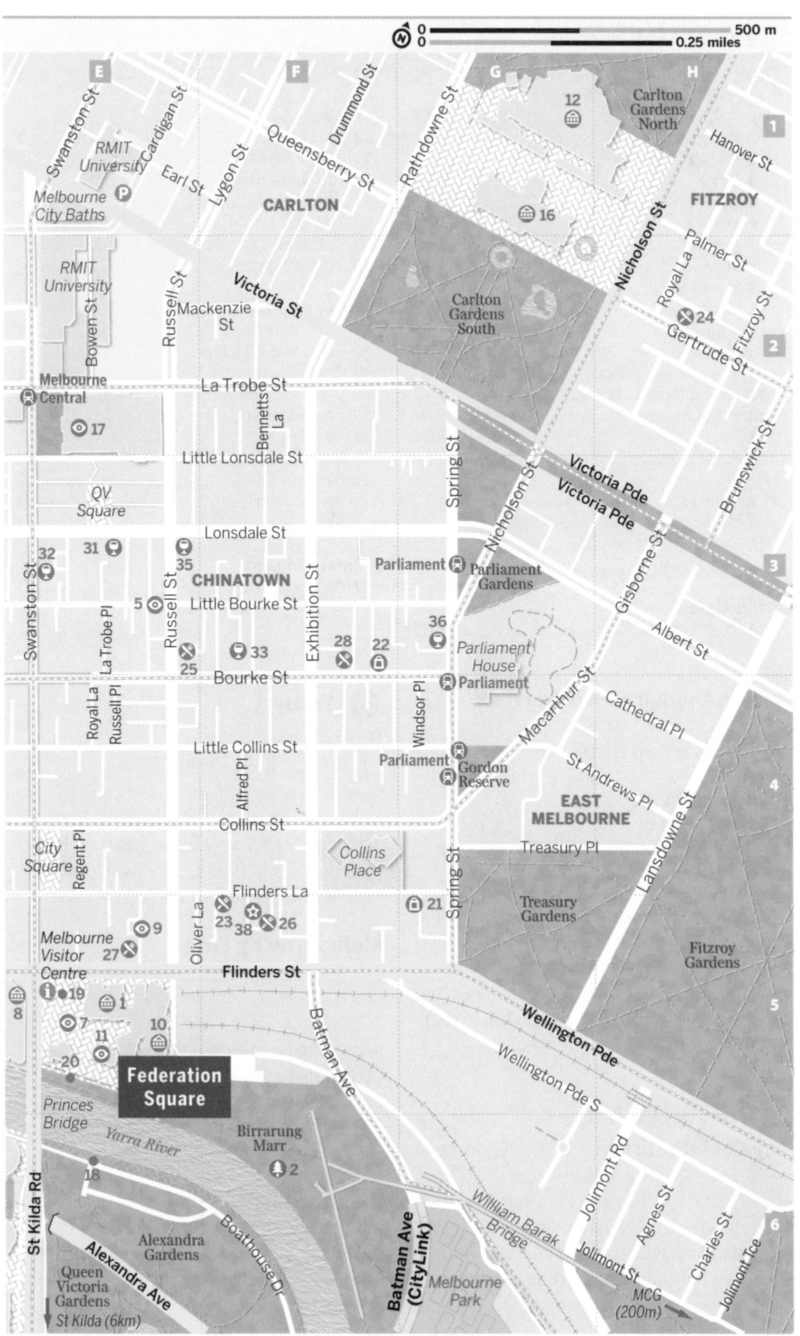
0
500 m
0
0.25 miles
E
F
G
H
1
2
3
4
5
6
Swanston St
Cardigan St
RMIT University
Melbourne City Baths
Earl St
Lygon St
Queensberry St
Drummond St
Rathdowne St
CARLTON
12
Carlton Gardens North
Hanover St
FITZROY
16
Nicholson St
Palmer St
Royal La
Fitzroy St
24
Gertrude St
Carlton Gardens South
Victoria St
Russell St
Mackenzie St
Bowen St
La Trobe St
Melbourne Central
Bennetts La
17
Little Lonsdale St
Spring St
Victoria Pde
Brunswick St
QV Square
Lonsdale St
32
31
35
CHINATOWN
Parliament
Parliament Gardens
Gisborne St
5
Little Bourke St
Exhibition St
36
Albert St
La Trobe Pl
33
28
22
25
Bourke St
Parliament House
Macarthur St
Cathedral Pl
Royal La
Russell Pl
Windsor Pl
Little Collins St
Alfred Pl
Gordon Reserve
St Andrews Pl
EAST MELBOURNE
Collins St
Lansdowne St
City Square
Regent Pl
Collins Place
Treasury Pl
Treasury Gardens
Flinders La
23
38
26
21
Oliver La
Melbourne Visitor Centre
9
27
Fitzroy Gardens
Flinders St
19
8
1
7
10
11
Batman Ave
Wellington Pde
20
Federation Square
Wellington Pde S
Princes Bridge
Yarra River
Birrarung Marr
2
18
Jolimont Rd
St Kilda Rd
William Barak Bridge
Agnes St
Charles St
Boathouse Dr
Alexandra Gardens
Jolimont St
Jolimont Tce
Alexandra Ave
Queen Victoria Gardens
Batman Ave (CityLink)
Melbourne Park
MCG (200m)
St Kilda (6km)

Central Melbourne

Sights
1 Australian Centre for the Moving Image ... E5
2 Birrarung Marr ... F6
3 Blender Lane ... D1
4 Block Arcade ... D4
5 Chinatown ... E3
6 Eureka Skydeck ... C6
7 Federation Square ... E5
8 Flinders Street Station ... E5
9 Hosier Lane ... E5
10 Ian Potter Centre: NGV Australia ... E5
11 Koorie Heritage Trust ... E5
12 Melbourne Museum ... G1
13 Queen Victoria Market ... C1
14 Royal Arcade ... D4
15 Royal Exhibition Building ... G1
16 State Library of Victoria ... E2

Activities, Courses & Tours
17 Kayak Melbourne ... E6
18 Melbourne By Foot ... E5
19 Rentabike ... E5

Shopping
20 Craft Victoria ... G5
21 Melbournalia ... F3

Eating
22 Chin Chin ... F5
23 Cutler & Co ... H2
24 Hakata Gensuke ... E3
25 Lee Ho Fook ... F5
26 MoVida ... E5
27 Pellegrini's Espresso Bar ... F3
28 Vue de Monde ... B4

Drinking & Nightlife
29 Bar Americano ... D4
30 Boilermaker House ... E3
31 Cookie ... E3
32 Croft Institute ... F3
33 Degraves Espresso ... D5
34 Heartbreaker ... E3
35 Melbourne Supper Club ... G3
36 Padre Coffee ... C1
Rooftop Bar ... (see 31)
Siglo ... (see 35)

Entertainment
37 Cherry ... F5

Book an **Aboriginal Heritage Walk** (03-9252 2429; www.rbg.vic.gov.au; adult/child $31/12; 11am Sun-Fri).

St Kilda

Luna Park Amusement Park
(03-9525 5033; www.lunapark.com.au; 18 Lower Esplanade; adult/child single ride $11/10, unlimited rides $50/40; hours vary; 3, 16, 96) Luna Park opened in 1912 and still has the feel of an old-style amusement park. Don't miss the heritage-listed 'scenic railway' (the oldest operating roller coaster in the world) and the beautifully baroque carousel.

ACTIVITIES

Kayak Melbourne Kayaking
(0418 106 427; www.kayakmelbourne.com.au; Alexandra Gardens, Boathouse Dr, Southbank; tours $82-110; 11, 48) Ninety-minute City Sights tours paddle past Southbank to Docklands, while two-hour River to Sky tours include entry to the Eureka Skydeck (p152).

TOURS

Rentabike Cycling
(0417 339 203; www.rentabike.net.au; Federation Wharf; rental per hour/day $15/40, 4hr tours incl lunch adult/child $110/79; 10am-5pm; Flinders St) Rents bikes and runs Real Melbourne Bike Tours, offering a local's insight into the city, with a foodie focus.

Melbourne by Foot Walking
(1300 311 081; www.melbournebyfoot.com; departs Federation Sq; tours $40; 1pm; Flinders St) Take a few hours out and experience a mellow, informative three-hour walking tour that covers laneway art, politics, Melbourne's history and diversity. There's also a Beer Lovers tour ($85).

Melbourne Visitor Shuttle Bus
(https://whatson.melbourne.vic.gov.au; 2 days $10; 9.30am-3.45pm) Hop-on, hop-off bus tour with an audio commentary, stopping at 13 of Melbourne's main sights on a 90-minute loop.

SHOPPING

Readings Books
(www.readings.com.au; 309 Lygon St, Carlton; 9am-11pm Mon-Sat, 10am-9pm Sun; Tourist Shuttle, 1, 6) A potter around this defiantly prosperous indie bookshop can occupy an entire afternoon if you're so inclined. There's a dangerously loaded (and good-value) specials table and switched-on, helpful staff.

Polyester Records Music
(03-9419 5137; www.polyesterrecords.com; 387 Brunswick St, Fitzroy; 10am-8pm Mon-Thu & Sat, to 9pm Fri, 11am-6pm Sun; 11) This popular record store has been selling Melburnians independent music from around the world for decades, and it also has a great range of local stuff.

Craft Victoria Arts & Crafts
(03-9650 7775; www.craft.org.au; 31 Flinders Lane; 11am-6pm Mon-Sat; Parliament) This retail arm of Craft Victoria showcases handmade goods, mainly by Victorian artists and artisans: jewellery, textiles, accessories, glass and ceramics.

Crumpler Fashion & Accessories
(03-9417 5338; www.crumpler.com; 87 Smith St, Fitzroy; 10am-6pm Mon-Sat, to 5pm Sun; 86) Crumpler's bike-courier bags are what started it all. The brand's durable, practical designs now extend to bags for cameras, laptops and iPads. The original messenger bags start at around $150.

Melbournalia Gifts & Souvenirs
(03-9663 3751; www.melbournalia.com.au; 50 Bourke St; 10am-7pm; Parliament) This is the place to stock up on interesting souvenirs by more than 100 local designers – prints featuring city icons, crazy socks and great books on Melbourne.

St Kilda Esplanade Market Market
(www.stkildaesplanademarket.com.au; Esplanade, St Kilda; 10am-4pm Sun May-Sep, to 5pm Oct-Apr; 3, 12, 16, 96) Fancy a Sunday stroll shopping by the seaside? Well, here's the place, with a kilometre of trestle tables joined end to end.

EATING

Central Melbourne

Hakata Gensuke Ramen $
(03-9663 6342; www.gensuke.com.au; 168 Russell St; mains $13-14; 11.30am-2.45pm & 5-9.30pm Mon-Fri, noon-9.30pm Sat & Sun; Parliament) Gensuke is one of those places that only does one thing and does it extraordinarily well. In this case it's *tonkotsu* (pork broth) ramen. Choose from three types (signature, sesame-infused 'black' or spicy 'god fire').

Chin Chin Southeast Asian $$
(03-8663 2000; www.chinchinrestaurant.com.au; 125 Flinders Lane; mains $20-39; 11am-late; Flinders St) Insanely popular, and for good reason, chic Chin Chin serves delicious Southeast Asian hawker-style food designed as shared plates. It's housed in a glammed-up old warehouse with a real New York feel, and while there are no bookings, you can wait at Go Go Bar downstairs.

Pellegrini's Espresso Bar Italian $$
(03-9662 1885; 66 Bourke St; mains $18; 8am-11pm Mon-Sat, noon-8pm Sun; Parliament) The Italian equivalent of a classic '50s diner, locally famous Pellegrini's has remained genuinely unchanged for decades. There's no menu with prices; the staff will tell you what's available. Expect classic Italian comfort food: lasagne, spaghetti bolognese and big slabs of cake.

MoVida Tapas $$
(03-9663 3038; www.movida.com.au; 1 Hosier Lane; tapas $4-8, raciones $16-34; noon-late; Flinders St) MoVida's location in much-graffitied Hosier Lane is about as Melbourne as it gets. Line up by the bar, cluster around little window tables or, if you've booked, take a seat in the dining area for fantastic Spanish tapas and *raciones*.

Lee Ho Fook Chinese $$$

(☎03-9077 6261; www.leehofook.com.au; 11-15 Duckboard Pl; mains $32-42; ⏰noon-2.30pm & 6-11pm Mon-Fri, 6-11pm Sat & Sun; 🚉Parliament) Occupying an old brick warehouse down a fabulously skungy laneway, Lee Ho Fook is the epitome of modern Chinese culinary wizardry. The kitchen packs an extraordinary amount of flavour into signature dishes such as crispy eggplant with red vinegar, chicken crackling, liquorice wagyu beef, and crab and scallop rice with home-made XO sauce. The service is terrific too.

Vue de Monde Modern Australian $$$

(☎03-9691 3888; www.vuedemonde.com.au; 55th fl, Rialto, 525 Collins St; set menu $230-275; ⏰6-11pm Mon-Wed, noon-2pm & 6-11pm Thu-Sun; 🚉Southern Cross) Surveying the world from the old observation deck of the Rialto tower, Melbourne's favoured spot for occasion dining has views to match its storied reputation. Visionary chef Shannon Bennett, when he's not mentoring on *MasterChef*, produces sophisticated set menus showcasing the very best Australian ingredients. Book months ahead.

Fitzroy

Industry Beans Cafe $

(☎03-9417 1034; www.industrybeans.com; 3/62 Rose St; ⏰7am-4pm Mon-Fri, 8am-4pm Sat & Sun; 📶; 🚋96, 11) It's all about coffee chemistry at this warehouse cafe tucked in a Fitzroy side street. The coffee guide takes you through the speciality styles on offer (roasted on-site), from Aeropress and pourover to cold drip and espresso, and helpful staff take the pressure off deciding.

Lune Croissanterie Bakery $

(www.lunecroissanterie.com; 119 Rose St; pastries $5.50-12.50; ⏰7.30am-3pm Mon, Thu & Fri, from 8am Sat & Sun; 🚋11) Some of the best pastries you'll ever taste – from the lemon-curd cruffin to a classic almond croissant. In the centre of this warehouse space sits a climate-controlled glass cube, the Lune Lab, where the magic happens.

Melbourne Museum (p153)

Cutler & Co Modern Australian $$$
(☎03-9419 4888; www.cutlerandco.com.au; 55 Gertrude St; mains $36-48; ⏰6pm-late Tue-Sun, lunch from noon Sun; 🚋86) Hyped for all the right reasons, this is Andrew McConnell's flagship Melbourne restaurant. The menu strives to incorporate the best seasonal produce across the à la carte offering, the degustation menu (from $150), and the casual Sunday lunch designed for sharing.

Carlton & Around

Seven Seeds Cafe $
(☎03-9347 8664; www.sevenseeds.com.au; 114 Berkeley St; ⏰7am-5pm Mon-Sat, 8am-5pm Sun; 🚋19, 59) The most spacious location in the Seven Seeds coffee empire, this rather out-of-the-way warehouse cafe has plenty of room to store your bike and sip a splendid coffee.

D.O.C. Espresso Italian $$
(☎03-9347 8482; www.docgroup.net; 326 Lygon St, Carlton; mains $12-20; ⏰7.30am-late Mon-Sat, 8am-late Sun; 🚌Tourist Shuttle, 🚋1, 6) Run by third-generation Italian Australians, authentic D.O.C. has breathed new life into Lygon St. The espresso bar features home-made pasta specials, Italian microbrewery beers and *aperitivo* time (4pm to 7pm).

Rumi Middle Eastern $$
(☎03-9388 8255; www.rumirestaurant.com.au; 116 Lygon St, East Brunswick; dishes $13-28; ⏰6-10pm; 🚋1, 6) A fabulously well-considered place that serves up a mix of traditional Lebanese cooking and contemporary interpretations of old Persian dishes. The *sigara boregi* (cheese and pine-nut pastries) are a local institution.

St Kilda & Around

Newmarket Hotel American $$
(☎03-9537 1777; www.newmarketstkilda.com.au; 34 Inkerman St, St Kilda; sharing plates from $13; ⏰noon-3pm & 6-10.30pm; 🚋3, 16, 67) This historic pub channels the California–Mexico border with tasty dishes like tacos, smoked-chicken quesadillas and scallop ceviche with salt-water cream and chilli. There's a top-shelf bar to boot.

Gay & Lesbian Melbourne

These days, Melbourne's gay and lesbian community is well and truly integrated into the general populace. Highlights include: **Midsumma Festival** (www.midsumma.org.au; ⏰Jan/Feb), a diverse program of more than 100 cultural, community and sporting events, and **Melbourne Queer Film Festival** (www.melbournequeerfilm.com.au; ⏰Mar), Australia's largest gay film festival.

Gay and lesbian community radio station JOY 94.9 FM (www.joy.org.au) is another important resource for visitors and locals.

On the drinking front, gay guys will feel particularly welcome at the **Peel Hotel** (☎03-9419 4762; www.thepeel.com.au; 113 Wellington St, Collingwood; ⏰11pm-5am Thu, to 7am Fri & Sat; 🚋86), **Sircuit** (www.sircuit.com.au; 103 Smith St, Fitzroy; ⏰7.30pm-late Wed-Sun; 🚋86) and **Laird** (☎03-9417 2832; www.lairdhotel.com; 149 Gipps St, Abbotsford; ⏰5pm-late Mon-Sat, from 4pm Sun; 🚉Collingwood).

Stokehouse Seafood $$$
(☎03-9525 5555; www.stokehouse.com.au; 30 Jacka Blvd, St Kilda; mains $36-42; ⏰noon-3pm & 6pm-late; 🚋3a, 16, 96) Contemporary architecture and floor-to-ceiling bay views set the right tone for fresh, modern, seafood-centric dishes, not to mention a stuff-of-legend bombe Alaska. One of Melbourne's hottest restaurants: book ahead.

Attica Modern Australian $$$
(☎03-9530 0111; www.attica.com.au; 74 Glen Eira Rd, Ripponlea; tasting menu $250; ⏰6pm-late Tue-Sat; 🚋67, 🚉Ripponlea) The only Australian restaurant on the San Pellegrino World's Top 50 Restaurants list, Attica is home to prodigious Kiwi import Ben Shewry and his extraordinary creations.

Native ingredients shine in dishes like bunya bunya with salted red kangaroo, or bush-currant granité with lemon aspen and rosella flower. Reservations accepted three months ahead, on the first Wednesday of each month at 9am.

DRINKING & NIGHTLIFE

Central Melbourne

Croft Institute Bar

(www.thecroftinstitute.com.au; 21 Croft Alley; ⏲5pm-midnight Mon-Thu, 5pm-3am Fri, 8pm-3am Sat; 86, 96) Hidden in a graffitied laneway off a laneway, the slightly creepy Croft is a laboratory-themed bar downstairs, while upstairs at weekends the 1950s-themed gymnasium opens as a club. There's a $5 cover charge for DJs Friday and Saturday nights.

Heartbreaker Bar

(☎03-9041 0856; www.heartbreakerbar.com.au; 234a Russell St; ⏲5pm-3am Mon-Sat, to 11pm Sun; Melbourne Central) Black walls, red lights, skeleton handles on the beer taps, random taxidermy, craft beer, a big selection of bourbon, rock and punk on the sound system, and tough-looking sweethearts behind the bar – all the prerequisites, in fact, for a hard-rocking good time.

Bar Americano Cocktail Bar

(www.baramericano.com.au; 20 Presgrave Pl; ⏲5pm-1am Mon-Sat; Flinders St) A hideaway bar in a lane off Howey Pl, Bar Americano is a teensy standing-room-only affair with black-and-white chequered floors complemented by classic 'do not spit' subway-tiled walls and a subtle air of speakeasy.

Cookie Bar

(☎03-9663 7660; www.cookie.net.au; 1st fl, Curtin House, 252 Swanston St; ⏲noon-3am; Melbourne Central) Part bar, part Thai restaurant, this kooky-cool venue with grand bones is one of the more enduring rites of passage of the Melbourne night. The bar is unbelievably well stocked with fine whiskies, wines, and plenty of craft beers among the more than 200 brews on offer.

Pellegrini's Espresso Bar (p157)

NILS VERSEMAN/SHUTTERSTOCK ©

Boilermaker House Bar

(www.boilermakerhouse.com.au; 209-211 Lonsdale St; 4pm-3am; Melbourne Central) A real surprise on busy, workaday Lonsdale St, this dimly lit haven of urbanity has a phenomenal 850 whiskies on its list, along with 12 craft beers on tap and a further 40 by the bottle. Snack on cheese, charcuterie and jalapeño poppers as you make your way through them.

Fitzroy

Black Pearl Cocktail Bar

(03-9417 0455; www.blackpearlbar.com.au; 304 Brunswick St; 5pm-3am, Attic Bar 7pm-2am Thu-Sat; 11) Low lighting, leather banquettes and candles set the mood downstairs: prop at the bar to study the extensive cocktail list or let the expert bartenders concoct something to your taste. Upstairs is the table-service Attic Bar; book ahead.

Napier Hotel Pub

(03-9419 4240; www.thenapierhotel.com; 210 Napier St; 3-11pm Mon-Thu, noon-1am Fri, noon-11pm Sat, 1-11pm Sun; 86, 11) The Napier has stood on this corner for over a century; many pots have been pulled as the face of the neighbourhood changed, as demonstrated by the memorabilia of the sadly departed Fitzroy footy team.

Carlton

Jimmy Watson's Wine Bar

(03-9347 3985; www.jimmywatsons.com.au; 333 Lygon St; wine bar 11am-11pm, Wolf's Lair rooftop 4-11pm; Tourist Shuttle, 1, 6) Keep it tidy at Watson's wine bar with something nice by the glass, settle in the leafy courtyard, or head up to the Wolf's Lair rooftop for cocktails with a view.

St Kilda

Bar Di Stasio Wine Bar

(03-9525 3999; www.distasio.com.au; 31 Fitzroy St; 11.30am-midnight; 3, 12, 16, 96) Within Pompidou-style scaffolding lies this buzzing, grown-up bar, dominated by a floor-to-ceiling mural of Caravaggio's *Flagellation of Christ*. Behind the deep marble bar, waiters mix perfect Campari *spritzes*. Book: the place is extremely popular.

Rooftop Drinking

If you like your brew with a view, swing up to these excellent Melbourne rooftop bars.

Siglo (03-9654 6631; www.siglobar.com.au; 2nd fl, 161 Spring St; 5pm-3am; Parliament) Siglo's sought-after terrace comes with Parisian flair, wafting cigar smoke and serious drinks. Mull over a classic cocktail, snack on upper-crust morsels and admire the vista over Parliament. Entry is via the similarly unsigned **Melbourne Supper Club** (03-9654 6300; www.melbournesupperclub.com.au; 1st fl, 161 Spring St; 5pm-4am Sun-Thu, to 6am Fri & Sat; Parliament).

Naked for Satan (03-9416 2238; www.nakedforsatan.com.au; 285 Brunswick St, Fitzroy; noon-midnight Sun-Thu, to 1am Fri & Sat; 11) Vibrant and loud, this place packs a punch with its popular *pintxos* (Basque tapas; $1 to $2), huge range of beverages, and unbeatable roof terrace (Naked in the Sky) with wraparound balcony.

Rooftop Bar (03-9654 5394; www.rooftopcinema.com.au; 6th fl, Curtin House, 252 Swanston St; noon-1am; Melbourne Central) This bar sits at dizzying heights atop happening Curtin House. In summer it transforms into an outdoor cinema with striped deckchairs and a calendar of new and classic favourite flicks.

ENTERTAINMENT

Prince Bandroom Live Music

(03-9536 1168; www.princebandroom.com.au; 29 Fitzroy St, St Kilda; 12, 16, 96) The Prince is a legendary St Kilda venue, with a solid line-up of local and international acts spanning hip-hop, dance, rock and indie.

The Tote Live Music
(03-9419 5320; www.thetotehotel.com; cnr Johnston & Wellington Sts, Collingwood; 4pm-late Wed-Sun; 86) One of Melbourne's most iconic live-music venues, this divey Collingwood pub has a great roster of local and international punk and hardcore bands, and one of the best jukeboxes in the universe.

Cherry Live Music
(www.cherrybar.com.au; AC/DC Lane; 6pm-late Mon-Sat, 2pm-late Sun; Flinders St) There's often a queue at Cherry, but once you're inside a welcoming, slightly anarchic spirit prevails. Live music and DJs play seven nights a week, and there's a long-standing soul night on Thursday.

Cinema Nova Cinema
(03-9347 5331; www.cinemanova.com.au; 380 Lygon St, Carlton; Tourist Shuttle, 1, 6) See the latest in art-house, docos and foreign films at this locals' favourite. Cheap Monday screenings ($7 before 4pm, $9 after 4pm).

Melbourne Theatre Company Theatre
(MTC; 03-8688 0800; www.mtc.com.au; 140 Southbank Blvd, Southbank; 1) Melbourne's major theatrical company stages around a dozen productions each year, ranging from contemporary (including many new Australian works) to Shakespeare and other classics.

INFORMATION

Melbourne Visitor Centre (03-9658 9658; https://whatson.melbourne.vic.gov.au; Federation Sq; 9am-6pm; ; Flinders St) Comprehensive information on Melbourne and regional Victoria.

Royal Melbourne Hospital (03-9342 7000; www.thermh.org.au; 300 Grattan St, Parkville; 19, 55, 59) Public hospital with an emergency department.

FEDERATION BELLS IN BIRRARUNG MARR, DESIGNED BY ANTON HASELL & NEIL MCLACHLAN
SUNFLOWEREY/SHUTTERSTOCK ©

GETTING THERE & AWAY

AIR

Melbourne Airport (www.melbourneairport.com.au; Departure Rd, Tullamarine) is the city's only international and main domestic airport, 22km northwest of the city centre. The main domestic airlines are **Qantas** (13 11 31; www.qantas.com), **Jetstar** (131 538; www.jetstar.com), **Virgin Australia** (13 67 89; www.virginaustralia.com) and **Tigerair** (1300 174 266; www.tigerair.com).

BOAT

Spirit of Tasmania (1800 634 906, 03-6419 9320; www.spiritoftasmania.com.au; Station Pier, Port Melbourne; adult/car one-way from $99/188) *Spirit of Tasmania* crosses Bass Strait from Melbourne to Devonport, Tasmania, at least nightly; there are also day sailings during peak seasons. Around 10 hours.

BUS

From the main long-distance bus terminus in Southern Cross Station, services run to all Australian capitals except Hobart and Perth. The key operators:

Firefly (1300 730 740; www.fireflyexpress.com.au)

Greyhound (1300 473 946; www.greyhound.com.au)

V/Line (1800 800 007; www.vline.com.au)

TRAIN

Southern Cross Station is the terminus for intercity and interstate trains.

Great Southern Rail (1800 703 357; www.greatsouthernrail.com.au) Runs the Overland between Melbourne and Adelaide ($149, 10½ hours, twice weekly).

NSW TrainLink (13 22 32; www.nswtrainlink.info) Twice-daily services to/from Sydney ($92, 11½ hours).

V/Line (1800 800 007; www.vline.com.au) Operates the Victorian train network, including direct services to Geelong ($9, one hour) with bus connections to the Great Ocean Road.

GETTING AROUND

TO/FROM THE AIRPORT

There are no direct trains or trams to Melbourne Airport. Taxis charge around $65 for the trip to

★ Top Five For Kids

Australian Centre for the Moving Image (p145)

Melbourne Zoo (p153)

National Sports Museum (p149)

Melbourne Museum (p153)

Collingwood Children's Farm (p153)

From left: Birrarung Marr park (p152) featuring the Federation Bells; Royal Exhibition Building (p153); Entrance to Luna Park (p156)

Yarra Valley Wineries

The lush Yarra Valley, about an hour northeast of Melbourne, has more than 80 wineries and 50 cellar doors scattered around its rolling hills. Cool-climate chardonnay and pinot noir are why you're here. The pick of the bunch:

Domain Chandon (03-9738 9200; www.chandon.com; 727 Maroondah Hwy, Coldstream; 10.30am-4.30pm) This slick operation is worth a visit for the free guided tours (11am, 1pm and 3pm).

Oakridge (03-9738 9900; www.oakridgewines.com.au; 864 Maroondah Hwy, Coldstream; 10am-5pm) Awesome vineyard views and a chic restaurant.

Yering Station (03-9730 0100; www.yering.com; 38 Melba Hwy, Yering; 10am-5pm) Taste wines in the original 1859 winery. Modern fine-dining restaurant, too.

Hot air ballooning over Domain Chandon vineyard
JULIET COOMBE/GETTY IMAGES ©

Melbourne's CBD, or you can catch the **SkyBus** (1300 759 287; www.skybus.com.au; Southern Cross Station, 99 Spencer St; adult/child $18/9; Southern Cross), a 25-minute express service to/from Southern Cross Station.

BICYCLE

Melbourne Bike Share (1300 711 590; www.melbournebikeshare.com.au; subscription day/week $3/8) An automated, self-service bike-share system with 52 bright-blue stations scattered around the city, central suburbs and St Kilda. The first half-hour is free once you pay for your subscription.

BUS

Melbourne has an extensive bus network. Most routes operate from about 5.30am until about 11.30pm. You'll need a myki card to use the buses; see PTV **PTV** (Public Transport Victoria; 1800 800 007; www.ptv.vic.gov.au) for more information.

CAR & MOTORCYCLE

CAR HIRE

All the main international car- and campervan-hire players have offices at Melbourne Airport and in the city or inner suburbs.

TOLL ROADS

Drivers and motorcyclists will need to purchase a Melbourne Pass ($5.50 start-up fee, plus tolls and a 75c vehicle-matching fee per trip) if they're planning on using one of the two toll roads: **CityLink** (13 26 29; www.citylink.com.au), from Melbourne Airport to the city and eastern suburbs, or **EastLink** (03-9955 1400; www.eastlink.com.au), from Ringwood to Frankston. Pay online or via phone (within three days of using the toll road to avoid a fine).

TAXI

Melbourne's taxis are metered and require an estimated prepaid fare when hailed between 10pm and 5am. Toll charges are added to fares. Two of the largest taxi companies are **Silver Top** (131 008; www.silvertop.com.au) and **13 Cabs** (13 22 27; www.13cabs.com.au). **Uber** (www.uber.com) also operates in Melbourne.

TRAIN

Flinders St Station is the main city hub for Melbourne's 17 train lines, which run from around 5am to around 11.30pm daily. Payment is via myki card; see **PTV** (Public Transport Victoria; 1800 800 007; www.ptv.vic.gov.au).

TRAM

Melbourne's extensive tram network covers the city, trams running roughly every 10 minutes Monday to Friday, every 15 minutes on Saturday and every 20 minutes on Sunday.

The entire city centre is a free tram zone. Beyond this, pay with a myki card. See the PTV website for more details.

Where to Stay

While you'll have no trouble finding a place to stay that suits your taste and budget, for a city that's big on style Melbourne has only a handful of small, atmospheric hotels. Prices peak for major sporting events and over the summer.

Neighbourhood	Atmosphere
Carlton	Midrange places aimed at the university and hospital crowd.
Central Melbourne	Lots of places across all price ranges; in the heart of the action.
East Melbourne	Takes you out of the action; walking distance from the city; ready access to the MCG.
Fitzroy	Vibrant area; plenty of attractions; a walk away from the city.
St Kilda	A budget traveller enclave but there are some stylish options a short walk from the beach.

Twelve Apostles (p170)

GREAT OCEAN ROAD

In this Chapter

Great Ocean Road at a Glance...

The Great Ocean Road is an epic Australian road trip and a rite-of-passage experience for surfers. The drive takes travellers past world-class beach breaks, through pockets of rainforest and becalmed seaside towns, and under koala-filled tree canopies. Along the way are sheer limestone cliffs, dairy farms and heathlands, with the crashing waves of the Southern Ocean an ever-present soundtrack.

Day-tripping tourists from Melbourne rush in and out in less than 12 hours, but in a perfect world (and along this stretch of coast, it seems that way), you'd spend at least a week here.

The Great Ocean Road in Two Days

The Great Ocean Road officially begins at **Torquay** (p172). A slight detour takes you to famous **Bells Beach** (p172), the powerful point break that is part of international surfing folklore.

Take a **surf lesson** (p173) in Anglesea, stop for a night in stylish **Lorne** (p173), then continue west to **Apollo Bay** (p175), a tight-knit community of fisherfolk, artists, musicians and seachangers.

The Great Ocean Road in Four Days

Go koala spotting around **Cape Otway** (p176), then continue west to **Port Campbell National Park** (p176), home to the much-photographed **Twelve Apostles** (p170). Count them from the clifftops, then roll into **Port Campbell** (p176) itself for a night.

Further west is endearing maritime **Port Fairy** (p177), home of Australia's best folk festival and your final destination along the Great Ocean Road.

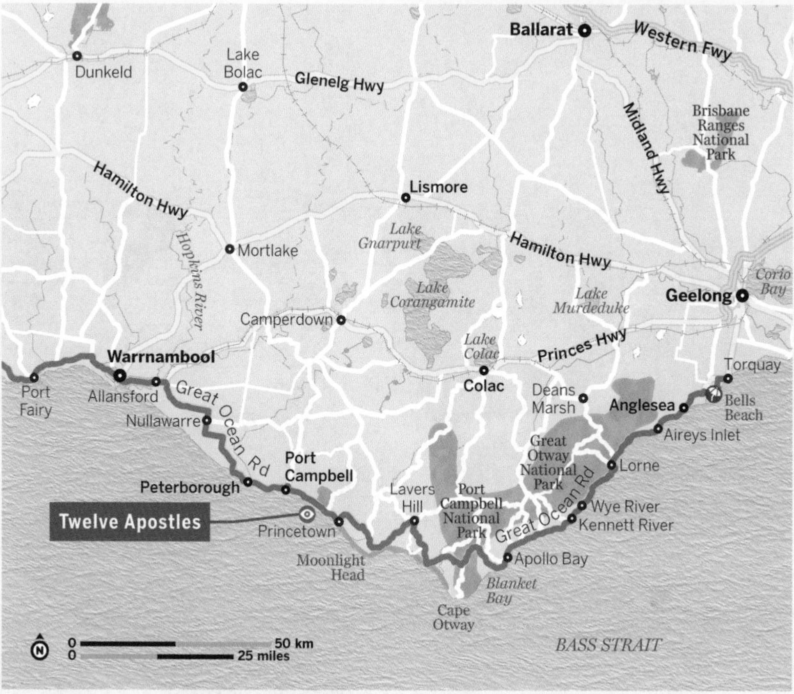

Arriving at the Great Ocean Road

Public transport can get you here (train from Melbourne to Geelong, then the bus), but to best explore this gorgeous coastline, bring your own wheels. If you're in a rush, bypass Geelong and take the Princes Hwy via Colac directly to the Twelve Apostles...but the lure here is in the slow-and-scenic coastal route.

Where to Stay

Historic hotels, lighthouse cottages and boutique beach houses are just some of the memorable places to stay along the Great Ocean Road. Most towns have a hostel, as well as caravan parks.

Things book out solidly come the summer holidays, Easter and long weekends, so reserve well ahead if visiting during peak periods.

ASHLEY WHITWORTH/SHUTTERSTOCK ©

Twelve Apostles

The Great Ocean Road's iconic sight, the Twelve Apostles rock stacks rise spectacularly from the ocean, seemingly abandoned to the sea by the retreating headland.

Great For

☑ Don't Miss

Snaring the classic Twelve Apostles photo from atop the cliffs.

The Approach

East of the Otways, the Great Ocean Road levels out and enters narrow, flat scrubby escarpment lands that fall away to sheer, 70m-high cliffs along the coast between Princetown and Peterborough – a distinct change of scene. This is Port Campbell National Park, home to the Twelve Apostles, and the most famous and most photographed stretch of the Great Ocean Road.

How Many Apostles?

The Twelve Apostles are not 12 in number and, from all records, never have been. From the viewing platform you can clearly count seven Apostles, but maybe some obscure others? We consulted widely with

Parks Victoria officers, tourist-office staff and even the cleaner at the lookout, but it's still not clear. Locals tend to say 'It depends where you look from', which really is true.

The Apostles are called 'stacks' in geologic parlance, and the rock formations were originally called the 'Sow and Piglets'. Someone in the 1960s (nobody can recall who) thought they might attract some tourists with a more venerable name, so they were renamed 'the Apostles'. Since apostles tend to come by the dozen, the number 12 was added sometime later. The two stacks on the eastern (Otway) side of the viewing platform are not technically Apostles – they're Gog and Magog.

Need to Know

The Apostles are 15km from Port Campbell. Unless you're taking a tour, driving here is your best option.

Take a Break

The **Twelve Apostles Visitor Centre Kiosk** (10am-5pm Sun-Fri, to 5.30pm Sat) serves sandwiches and fast food.

★ Top Tip

Visit at sunset: optimum photographic conditions, no tour-bus crowds and little penguins returning ashore.

The soft limestone cliffs are dynamic and changeable, with constant erosion from the unceasing waves – one 70m-high stack collapsed into the sea in 2005 and the Island Archway lost its archway in 2009.

Guided Tours

12 Apostles Helicopters Scenic Flights

(03-5598 8283; www.12apostleshelicopters.com.au; 15min flights $145) For the undisputed best views, head up into the skies for a chopper tour of the Twelve Apostles and surrounding sights. They're based at Twelve Apostles Visitor Centre.

Port Campbell Touring Company Tours

(03-5598 6424, 0447 986 423; www.portcampbelltouring.com.au; half-day tours per person from $120, walks from $85) Runs walking tours to visit the famous sites in the region, plus all the food and wine stops too.

Go West Tours Bus

(03-9485 5290; www.gowest.com.au; tours $130) Melbourne-based company offering full-day tours taking in Bells Beach, koalas in the Otways, the Twelve Apostles and around, returning back to Melbourne.

Harrd Yakka

The first sections of the Great Ocean Road were constructed by hand (using picks, shovels and crowbars) by returned WWI soldiers. Work began in September 1919 and the road between Anglesea and Apollo Bay was completed in 1932.

Torquay

In the 1960s and '70s, Torquay was just another sleepy seaside town. Back then surfing in Australia was a decidedly counter-cultural pursuit, and its devotees were crusty hippie drop-outs living in clapped-out Kombis, smoking pot and making off with your daughters. Since then surfing has become unabashedly mainstream, a huge transglobal business. The town's proximity to world-famous Bells Beach and status as home of two iconic surf brands – Ripcurl and Quiksilver, both initially wetsuit makers – ensures Torquay is the undisputed capital of Australian surfing.

SIGHTS & ACTIVITIES

Bells Beach Beach

(Great Ocean Rd) The powerful point break at Bells Beach is part of international surfing folklore and is the site of world championship **surfing contests** (www.aspworldtour.com; Easter) held every Easter since 1973. When the long right hander is working, it's one of the longest rides in the country, but it's a wave for experienced surfers only.

Australian National Surfing Museum Museum

(03-5261 4606; www.surfworld.com.au; Surf City Plaza, 77 Beach Rd; adult/child/family $12/8/25; 9am-5pm) The perfect starting point for those embarking on a surfing safari is this well-curated museum that pays homage to Australian surfing. Here you'll see Simon Anderson's ground-breaking 1981 thruster, Mark Richard's awesome airbrushed board art collection and, most notably, Australia's Surfing Hall of Fame.

EATING

Bomboras Kiosk Cafe $$

(www.bomboras.com.au; 48 The Esplanade, Fisherman's Beach; meals $5-22; 7.30am-5pm) Right on the sand, this is just the place for hungry beachgoers to recharge with homemade sausage rolls, cakes, salads, milkshakes or locally roasted coffee. During the summer they open the rooftop bar with local brews, ciders, DJs and prime ocean views.

INFORMATION

Torquay Visitor Information Centre (www.greatoceanroad.org; Surf City Plaza, Beach Rd; 9am-5pm) Has a well-resourced tourist office next to the Australian National Surfing Museum, which makes a good starting point along the Great Ocean Road to fine tune your itinerary.

GETTING THERE & AWAY

McHarry's Buslines (03-5223 2111; www.mcharrys.com.au) runs buses hourly from 9am to 8pm (around 5pm weekends) from Geelong to Torquay ($3.60, 30 minutes).

If you're driving, Torquay is 15 minutes south of Geelong on the B100.

Anglesea

Mix sheer orange cliffs falling into the ocean with hilly, tree-filled 'burbs and a population that booms in summer and you've got Anglesea, where sharing fish and chips with seagulls by the Anglesea River is a decades-long family tradition for many.

ACTIVITIES

Go Ride a Wave Surfing
(☎03-5263 2111, 1300 132 441; www.goridea wave.com.au; 143b Great Ocean Rd; 2hr lessons adult/child from $69/59, 2hr board hire from $25; ⏰9am-5pm) Long-established surf school that runs lessons and hires out boards, SUPs and kayaks.

EATING

Captain Moonlite Modern Australian **$$**
(☎03-5263 2454; www.captainmoonlite.com.au; 100 Great Ocean Rd; mains from $25; ⏰8am-10pm Fri-Sun, 8am-4pm Mon, 5-10pm Thu) With unbeatable views over the beach, Captain Moonlite mixes unpretentious decor with a quality, highly seasonal menu, which it describes as 'coastal European'. Expect tasty breakfasts such as ocean trout and soft-boiled egg on rye, mezze-style plates and mains such as slow-roasted lamb and fresh seafood.

INFORMATION

Anglesea Visitor Information Centre (www.visitgreatoceanroad.org.au; Great Ocean Rd; ⏰9am-5pm; 📶) On the Anglesea River, this information centre has a heap of brochures for the area, including walks in the surrounding national park.

GETTING THERE & AWAY

V/Line (☎1800 800 007; www.vline.com.au; Gordon Ave, Geelong Train Station) has services linking Anglesea with Geelong and the Great Ocean Road.

The Geelong bypass has reduced the time it takes to drive from Melbourne to Anglesea to around 75 minutes.

Lorne

One of the Great Ocean Road's original resort towns, Lorne may be a tad over-developed these days but it still retains all the charms that have lured visitors here since the 19th century. Beyond its main

Australian National Surfing Museum, Torquay

From left: Wild short-beaked echidna; Sleeping koala; Bells Beach (p172)

strip it has an incredible natural beauty: tall old gum trees line its hilly streets, and Loutit Bay gleams irresistibly.

SIGHTS & ACTIVITIES

Qdos Art Gallery Gallery

(03-5289 1989; www.qdosarts.com; 35 Allenvale Rd; 9am-5pm Thu-Mon, daily Jan) FREE Amid the lush forest that backs on to Lorne, Qdos always has something interesting showing at its contemporary gallery, to go with its open-air sculpture garden. There's also a lovely little cafe doing wood-fired pizzas.

EATING

Lorne Beach Pavilion Modern Australian **$$**

(03-5289 2882; www.lornebeachpavilion.com.au; 81 Mountjoy Pde; breakfast $9-23, mains $19-45; 9am-5pm Mon-Thu, 9am-9pm Fri, 8am-9pm Sat & Sun) With its unbeatable location on the foreshore, life here is literally a beach, especially with a cold drink in hand. Cafe-style breakfasts and lunches hit the spot, while a more upmarket Modern Australian menu of seafood and rib-eye steaks is on for dinner. Come at happy hour for $7 pints, or otherwise swing by at sunset for a bottle of prosecco.

INFORMATION

Lorne Visitor Centre (03-5289 1152, 1300 891 152; www.lovelorne.com.au; 15 Mountjoy Pde; 9am-5pm;) Stacks of information (including heaps of ideas for walks in the area), helpful staff, fishing licences, bus tickets and accommodation referrals.

GETTING THERE & AWAY

V/Line buses arrive daily from Geelong ($11.60, 1½ hours) en route to Apollo Bay ($5, from one hour). Alternatively, Lorne is a two-hour drive from Melbourne.

BENNYMARTY/GETTY IMAGES ©

Apollo Bay

One of the larger towns along the Great Ocean Road, Apollo Bay has a tight-knit community of fisherfolk, artists, musicians and seachangers. Rolling hills provide a postcard backdrop to the town, while broad, white-sand beaches dominate the foreground.

It has some of the best restaurants along the coast and several lively pubs.

SIGHTS & ACTIVITIES

Apollo Bay Surf & Kayak Adventure

(☎0405 495 909; www.apollobaysurfkayak.com.au; 157-159 Great Ocean Rd; 2hr kayak tours $70, 2hr surf lessons adult/child $65/60) Head out to an Australian fur seal colony in a double kayak. Tours (with full instructions for beginners) depart from Marengo Beach (to the south of the town centre).

Also offers surf and SUP lessons, plus boards and mountain bikes (half-day $30) for hire.

EATING

Chris's Beacon Point Restaurant Greek $$$

(☎03-5237 6411; www.chriss.com.au; 280 Skenes Creek Rd; mains from $34; ⏰6pm-late daily, plus noon-2pm Sat & Sun; 📶) Feast on memorable ocean views, deliciously fresh seafood and Greek-influenced dishes at Chris's hilltop fine-dining sanctuary among the treetops. Reservations recommended.

INFORMATION

Great Ocean Road Visitor Centre (☎1300 689 297; www.visitapollobay.com; 100 Great Ocean Rd; ⏰9am-5pm; 📶) Modern and professional tourist office with a heap of info for the area, and an 'eco-centre' with displays. It has free wi-fi and can book bus tickets, too.

GETTING THERE & AWAY

Driving to Apollo Bay along the Great Ocean Road from Melbourne is a 4½-hour drive. Alternatively, catch a train to Geelong then transfer to a connecting bus ($27.20, 3½ hours).

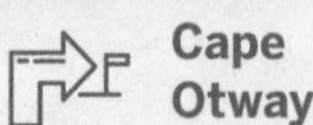

Cape Otway

Cape Otway is the second-most-southerly point of mainland Australia (after Wilsons Promontory) and one of the wettest parts of the state. This coastline is particularly beautiful, rugged and historically treacherous for passing ships. The turn-off for Lighthouse Rd, which leads 12km down to 1848 **Cape Otway Lightstation** (03-5237 9240; www.lightstation.com; Lighthouse Rd; adult/child/family $19.50/7.50/49.50; 9am-5pm), is 21km from Apollo Bay. It's a beautiful forested road with towering trees, which are home to a sizeable population of koalas.

Cape Otway Lightstation

MARCELLA MIRIELLO/SHUTTERSTOCK ©

Port Campbell & Port Campbell National Park

This small, windswept town is poised on a dramatic, natural bay, eroded from the surrounding limestone cliffs, and almost perfectly rectangular in shape. It's a friendly place with some great bargain accommodation options, and makes an ideal spot for debriefing after the Twelve Apostles (p170) within Port Campbell National Park, 12km from the town.

SIGHTS

Loch Ard Gorge Beach

Close to the Twelve Apostles, Loch Ard Gorge is where the Shipwreck Coast's most famous and haunting tale unfolded when, in 1878, two young survivors of the wrecked iron clipper *Loch Ard* made it to shore. There are several walks in the area taking you down to the cave where they took shelter, plus a cemetery and rugged beach.

EATING

Forage on the Foreshore Cafe $$

(03-5598 6202; 32 Cairns St; mains from $14; 9am-5pm;) In the old post office is this seafront cottage cafe with wooden floorboards, art on the walls, an open fireplace and a vintage record player spinning vinyl. There's an all-day breakfast menu, burgers and curries for lunch, and items featuring fresh crayfish and abalone.

INFORMATION

Port Campbell Visitor Centre (1300 137 255; www.visit12apostles.com.au; 26 Morris St; 9am-5pm) Stacks of regional and accommodation information and interesting relics from various shipwrecks – the anchor from the *Loch Ard* is out the front.

GETTING THERE & AWAY

V/Line buses leave Geelong and travel through to Port Campbell ($32, five hours), but you'll need to transfer to a different bus in Apollo Bay ($11.20, two hours 15 minutes).

West of Port Campbell

The Great Ocean Road continues west of Port Campbell passing more rock stacks. The next one is the Arch, offshore from Point Hesse. Nearby is London Bridge (fallen down!) and the Grotto. The Bay of Islands is 8km west of tiny Peterborough. A short walk from the car park takes you to magnificent lookout points.

RACHEL LEWIS/GETTY IMAGES ©

Port Fairy harbour

The Great Ocean Road ends near here where it meets the Princes Hwy, which continues through the traditional lands of the Gunditjmara people into South Australia.

Port Fairy

Settled in 1833 as a whaling and sealing station, Port Fairy – 20 minutes west of Warrnambool – retains its historic 19th-century charm with a relaxed, salty feel, heritage bluestone and sandstone buildings, whitewashed cottages, colourful fishing boats and wide, tree-lined streets.

Australia's premier folk-music festival, **Port Fairy Folk Festival** (www.portfairyfolkfestival.com; tickets $250-300; Mar) is held on the Labour Day long weekend in early March. Book accommodation early.

Port Fairy Visitor Centre (03-5568 2682; www.portfairyaustralia.com.au; Bank St; 9am-5pm;) provides the usual swathe of brochures, including the *Maritime & Shipwreck Heritage Walk*. Architecture buffs will want to buy a copy of *Historic Buildings of Port Fairy*. Buy V/Line tickets here too, or hire a bike (half-/full day $15/25).

kunanyi/Mt Wellington (p188)

HOBART

In this Chapter

Hobart at a Glance...

No doubt about it, Hobart's future is looking rosy. Tourism is booming and the old town is brimming with new-found self-confidence.

Riding high above the city is kunanyi/Mt Wellington, a rugged monolith seemingly made for mountain biking and bushwalking. Down on the waterfront, the Salamanca Place cafes, bars and restaurants showcase the best of Tassie produce. There's more great eating and boozing along Elizabeth St in bohemian North Hobart. And don't miss Battery Point, Hobart's first neighbourhood, which oozes historic charm.

Hobart in Two Days

Get your head into history mode with an amble around **Battery Point** (p188). Afterwards, wander down Kelly's Steps to **Salamanca Place** (p184) and check out the craft shops, restaurants and chug a few ales. On day two, catch the ferry to **MONA** (p182), with dinner and some live music afterwards in **North Hobart** (p189).

Hobart in Four Days

Blow out the cobwebs with a mountain-bike ride on the **Mt Wellington Descent** (p191). In the foothills of the mountain is the legendary **Cascade Brewery** (p189): take a tour and sip a few, before dinner back on the waterfront. On day four, hit the museums: top of your list are the **Tasmanian Museum & Art Gallery** (p188) and **Mawson's Huts Replica Museum** (p189).

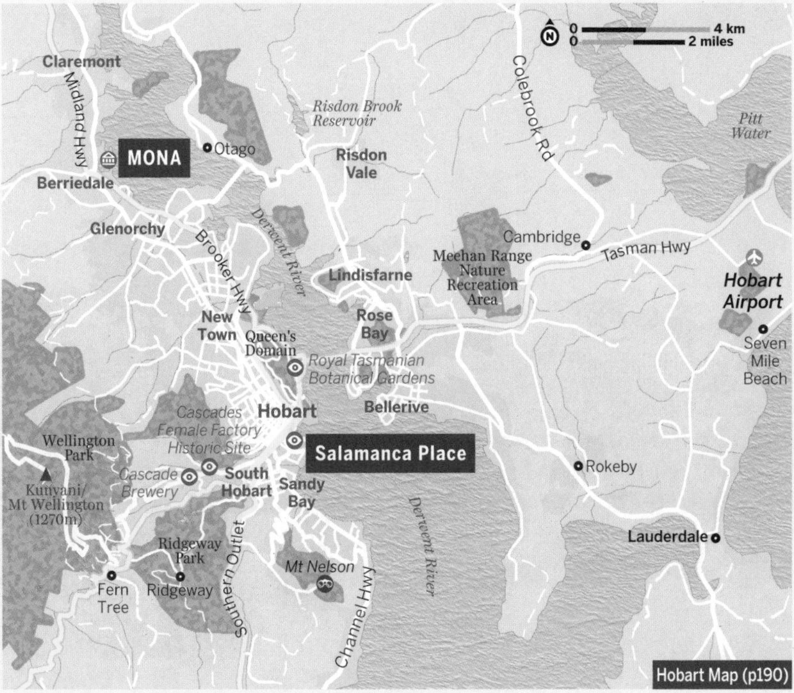

Hobart Map (p190)

Arriving in Hobart

Hobart Airport (p197) The airport is at Cambridge, 19km east of the city. Many visitors to Hobart rent a car: rental desks proliferate in the airport terminal. There's no public transport to the airport, so grab a cab ($50, 20 minutes) or pre-book a seat on a shuttle bus (adult/child $19/14).

Where to Stay

The pumping-est areas to stay in Hobart are the waterfront and Salamanca Place (apartments and boutique hotels aplenty), though prices here are usually sky-high and vacancy rates low. If you're visiting in January, book as far in advance as humanly possible. The CBD has less atmosphere, but most of the backpacker hostels, pubs with accommodation and midrange hotels are here.

MONA

No matter what your expectations are – arresting architecture, exquisite artefacts, confronting installations, quirky festivals or fab food and wine – MONA delivers.

Great For...

☑ **Don't Miss**

bit.fall: Julius Popp's two-storey installation dripping random phrases from news websites.

The MONA Effect

Twelve kilometres north of Hobart's city centre, occupying a saucepan-shaped peninsula jutting into the Derwent River, MONA is so darn popular it's almost single-handedly dragged Hobart onto the world stage. The so-called 'MONA effect' has elevated the city's hospitality and business standards in kind. The brainchild of Hobart philanthropist and eccentric gambling millionaire David Walsh, $75-million MONA is arrayed across three underground levels abutting sheer rock faces. Described by Walsh as 'a subversive adult Disneyland', the museum features ancient antiquities showcased next to contemporary works: the experience is sexy, provocative, disturbing and deeply engaging.

Need to Know

Museum of Old & New Art; ☎03-6277 9900; www.mona.net.au; 655 Main Rd, Berriedale; adult/child $25/free, Tasmanian residents free; ⏰10am-6pm daily Jan, 10am-6pm Wed-Mon Feb-Apr & Dec, 10am-5pm Wed-Mon May-Nov

Take a Break

Outstanding **Source** (☎03-6277 9904; mains $22-38; ⏰7.30-10am & noon-2pm Mon, Wed, Thu & Sun, 7.30-10am, noon-2pm & 6pm-late Fri & Sat) restaurant is on-site.

★ Top Tip

Catch the ferry here, sitting in the 'Posh Pit' (champagne and canapes!).

Monanism

'Monanism' is the name given to the broad collection of art here, numbering upwards of 1900 pieces. Some works are so big and/or important that the museum was designed around them, including *Snake*, a 46m-long array of images exploring the connections between myth and modernity; and the *Chamber of Pausiris*, containing the coffin and mummy of a 2000-year-old Egyptian. Other must-sees include the room dedicated solely to the worship of Madonna; the fabulous programmed waterfall *bit.fall;* and every kid's favourite, the impressive poo machine *Cloaca Professional*, which recreates (with alarmingly accurate waste products) the human digestive system.

Moorilla

As well as the gallery, MONA is home to the cellar door for **Moorilla** (☎03-6277 9960; www.moorilla.com.au; tastings/tours $10/15, redeemable with purchase; ⏰tastings 9.30am-5pm Mon-Wed, tours 3.30pm Wed-Mon), a winery established here in the 1950s; duck in for a wine or a beer tasting.

Festivals at MONA

MONA FOMA Art, Music

(MOFO; www.mofo.net.au; ⏰Jan) Acronyms ahoy! On the grounds of MONA, the wonderfully eclectic Festival of Music & Arts features a high-profile 'Eminent Artist in Residence' (EAR) every year. Stirring stuff.

Dark MOFO Art, Music

(www.darkmofo.net.au; ⏰Jun) Dark MOFO broods in the half-light of June's winter solstice. Expect live music, installations, readings, film noir, bonfires, red wine and midnight feasts, all mainlining Tasmania's gothic blood flow.

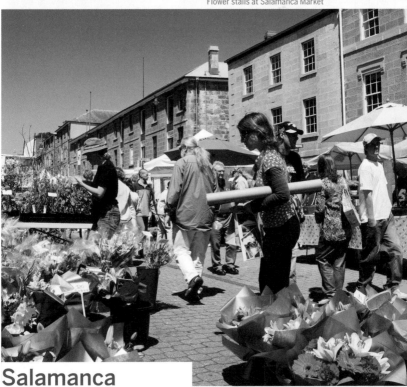

Flower stalls at Salamanca Market

Salamanca Place

A gorgeous row of 1830s stone warehouses, Salamanca Place hosts myriad restaurants, cafes, bars and shops, and Saturday's unmissable Salamanca Market.

Great For...

☑ Don't Miss

Behind Salamanca Place is Salamanca Square, a former quarry lined with cafes, bars and shops.

Eating & Drinking

Interesting fact for the day: Salamanca Place takes its name from the Spanish province of Salamanca, where the Duke of Wellington claimed victory in the Battle of Salamanca in 1812. Something to discuss over a meal or an evening drink, perhaps – eating and drinking being the prime reasons you're here! So popular is the Salamanca scene that the Hobart City Council recently widened the footpath in front of the warehouses, to allow restaurants and bars more space for street-side tables and chairs. Wander along and see what grabs you.

Salamanca Market

What started out as a couple of hippies selling raspberries in 1972 has evolved

Local crafts at Salamanca Market

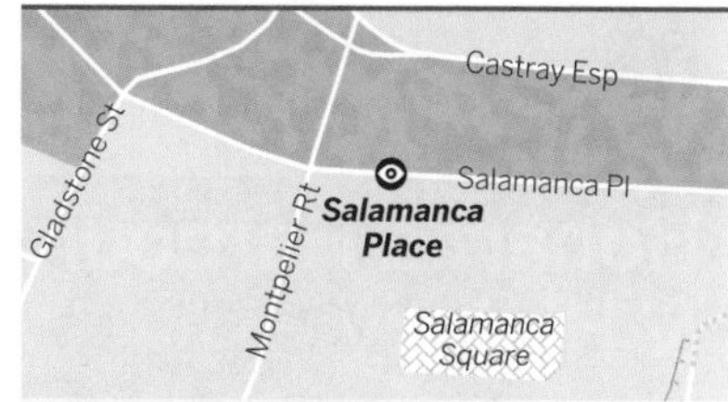

Need to Know

www.salamanca.com.au

Take a Break

Keep **Retro Cafe** (p193) at the top of your Salamanca Place cafe list.

★ Top Tip

Salamanca Place is closed to traffic on market days, and parking anywhere nearby is hell. Walk instead!

into a kilometre-long frenzy of food and commerce that consumes *all* of Salamanca Place every Saturday morning. With thousands of people here every week, **Salamanca Market** (03-6238 2843; www.salamanca.com.au; 8am-3pm Sat) is something to behold: make a slow-shuffling circuit down one side of the stalls then back down the other. The cafes overflow, the buskers are in fine voice and (even in winter) the vibe is downright convivial.

Salamanca Arts Centre

As with many of Tasmania's architectural relics, the Salamanca Place warehouses only survived the 20th century because no-one here had the money to knock them down. Thank goodness! Indeed, these chunky stone walls would take some shifting: step into the **Salamanca Arts Centre** (SAC; 03-6234 8414; www.salarts.org.au; 77 Salamanca Pl; shops & galleries 9am-5pm) for a close-up look...oh, and to check out the dozens of artists' studios, retail spaces, performance venues, cafes and galleries that comprise this progressive art co-op, running since 1975.

Friday Night Fandango

Some of Hobart's best live tunes get an airing every Friday night at the **Salamanca Arts Centre Courtyard** (www.salarts.org.au/rektango; 5.30-7.30pm Fri), just off Woobys Lane. It's a free community event that started in about 2000, with the adopted name 'Rektango', borrowed from a band that sometimes graces the stage. Acts vary from month to month – expect anything from African beats to rockabilly, folk and gypsy-Latino. Drinks essential (sangria in summer, mulled wine in winter); dancing near-essential.

Hobart's Harbour & History

Catch Hobart's historic vibe with a walk from the city centre, through historic Battery Point and down to Salamanca Place on the waterfront.

Start Franklin Square

Distance 3km

Duration Three hours

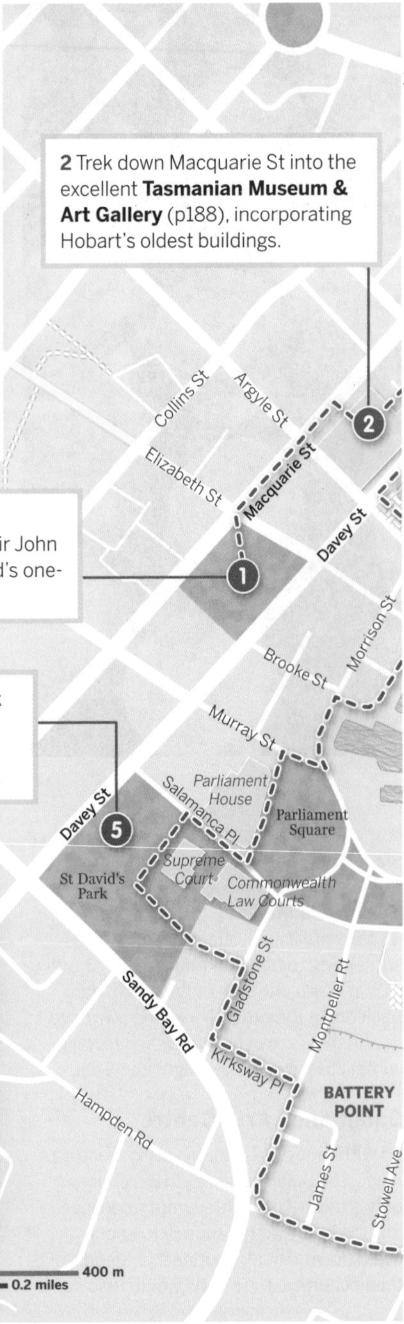

2 Trek down Macquarie St into the excellent **Tasmanian Museum & Art Gallery** (p188), incorporating Hobart's oldest buildings.

1 Launch your expedition at **Franklin Sq**, named after Sir John Franklin, Van Diemen's Land's one-time lieutenant-governor.

5 Skirt around Constitution Dock and the broad Sullivans Cove waterfront to **St David's Park**, Hobart Town's original cemetery.

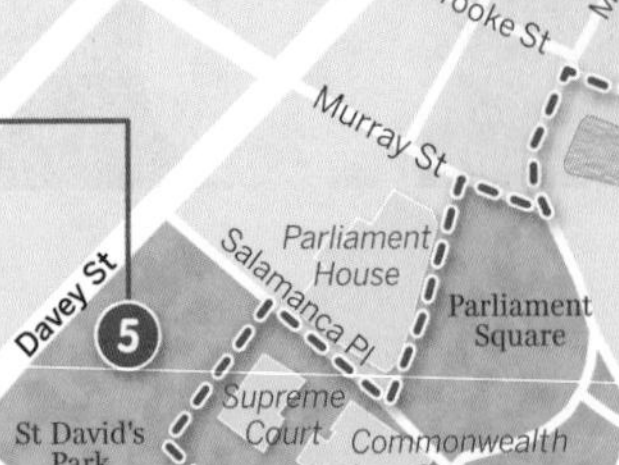

Classic Photo Arthur Circus is an improbably quaint roundabout lined with Georgian cottages.

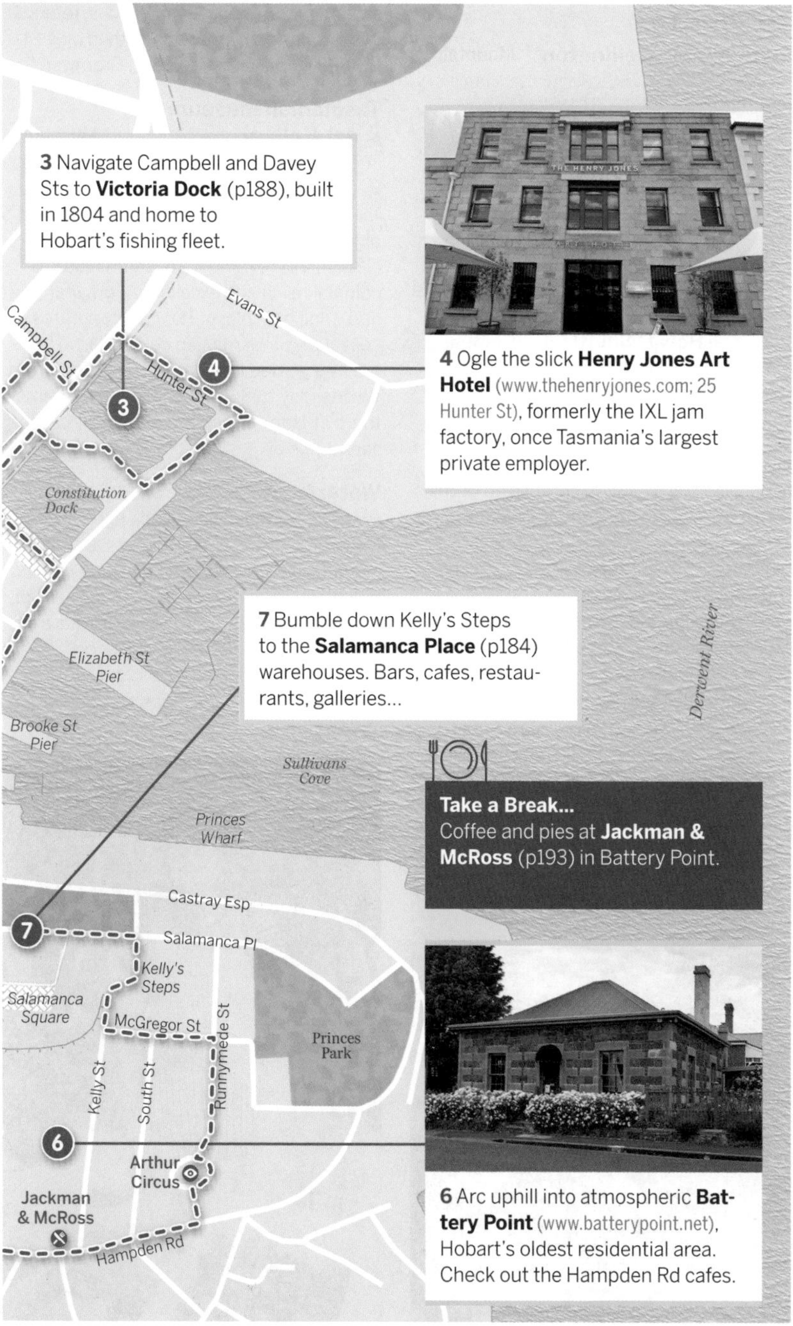

3 Navigate Campbell and Davey Sts to **Victoria Dock** (p188), built in 1804 and home to Hobart's fishing fleet.

4 Ogle the slick **Henry Jones Art Hotel** (www.thehenryjones.com; 25 Hunter St), formerly the IXL jam factory, once Tasmania's largest private employer.

7 Bumble down Kelly's Steps to the **Salamanca Place** (p184) warehouses. Bars, cafes, restaurants, galleries…

Take a Break...
Coffee and pies at **Jackman & McRoss** (p193) in Battery Point.

6 Arc uphill into atmospheric **Battery Point** (www.batterypoint.net), Hobart's oldest residential area. Check out the Hampden Rd cafes.

SIGHTS

kunanyi/Mt Wellington Mountain

(☎03-6238 4222; www.wellingtonpark.org.au; Pinnacle Rd, via Fern Tree) Cloaked in winter snow, kunanyi/Mt Wellington (1271m) towers over Hobart like a benevolent overlord. The citizens find reassurance in its constant, solid presence, while outdoorsy types find the space to hike and bike on its leafy flanks. And the view from the top is unbelievable! You can drive all the way to the summit on a sealed road; alternatively, the **Hobart Shuttle Bus Company** (☎0408 341 804; www.hobartshuttlebus.com; transfers & tours per adult/child from $30/20) runs daily two-hour tours to the summit.

Battery Point Historic Site

(www.batterypoint.net) An empty rum bottle's throw from the waterfront, the old maritime village of Battery Point is a tight nest of lanes and 19th-century cottages, packed together like shanghaied landlubbers in a ship's belly. Spend an afternoon exploring: stumble up Kelly's Steps from Salamanca Place and dogleg into South St, where the red lights once burned night and day. Spin around picturesque Arthur Circus, refuel in the cafes on Hampden Rd, then ogle St George's Anglican Church on Cromwell St.

Tasmanian Museum & Art Gallery Museum

(TMAG; ☎03-6165 7000; www.tmag.tas.gov.au; Dunn Pl; ⏰10am-4pm daily Jan-Mar, 10am-4pm Tue-Sun Apr-Dec) FREE Incorporating Hobart's oldest building, the Commissariat Store (1808), this revamped museum features colonial relics and excellent Aboriginal and wildlife displays. The gallery curates a collection of Tasmanian colonial art. There are free guided tours at 1pm and 2pm from Wednesday to Sunday, plus special themed tours at 11am: check the website or call to see what's on.

Waterfront Area

(off Davey St) Hobartians flock to the city's waterfront like seagulls to chips. Centred on Victoria Dock (a working fishing harbour) and Constitution Dock (chock-full of floating takeaway-seafood punts), it's a brilliant place to explore. The obligatory Hobart experience is to sit in the sun, munch some fish and chips and watch the

From left: Shelter on the summit of Mt Wellington; Salamanca Market (p184); Cascade Brewery; Tasmanian Devil

BOYLOSO/SHUTTERSTOCK ©

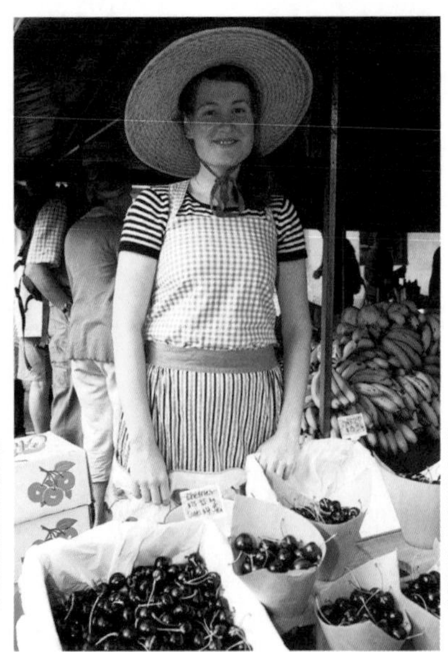

JULIAN LOVE/GETTY IMAGES ©

harbour hubbub. If you'd prefer something with a knife and fork, there are some superb restaurants here, too – head for Elizabeth St Pier.

Cascade Brewery Brewery
(☎03 6212 7800; www.cascadebrewery.com.au; 140 Cascade Rd, South Hobart; brewery tours adult/child 16-18yr $30/15, Cascade Story tour adult/child $15/5; ⏲tours daily) Standing in startling, gothic isolation next to the clean-running Hobart Rivulet, Cascade is Australia's oldest brewery (1832) and is still pumping out superb beers. Ninety-minute tours involve plenty of history, with tastings at the end. Bookings essential.

Cascades Female Factory Historic Site Historic Site
(☎03-6233 6656; www.femalefactory.org.au; 16 Degraves St, South Hobart; adult/child/family $5/5/15, tour $15/10/40, 'Her Story' dramatisation $20/12.50/60; ⏲9.30am-4pm, tours hourly 10am-3pm, except noon, 'Her Story' dramatisation 11am) Enshrined by Unesco as a World Heritage historic site, this was where Hobart's female convicts were incarcerated and put to work. Explore the site under your own steam, or book a guided tour or excellent 'Her Story' dramatisation to best understand the site, which looked very different back in the early 1800s.

North Hobart Neighbourhood
Hobart at its most bohemian and multicultural, the Elizabeth St strip in North Hobart (or 'NoHo' to those with a sense of humour) is lined with dozens of cafes, restaurants, bars and pubs – enough to keep you coming back meal after meal after meal... Must-do Hobart!

Mawson's Huts Replica Museum Museum
(☎1300 551 422, 03-6231 1518; www.mawsons-huts-replica.org.au; cnr Morrison & Argyle Sts; adult/child/family $12/4/28; ⏲9am-6pm Oct-Apr, 10am-5pm May-Sep) This excellent waterfront installation is an exact model of one of the huts in which Sir Douglas Mawson hunkered down on his 1911–14 Australasian Antarctic Expedition, which set sail from Hobart. Inside it is 100% authentic, right down to the matches, the stove and the bunks.

DARYL ARIAWAN/SHUTTERSTOCK ©

ROB D/SHUTTERSTOCK ©

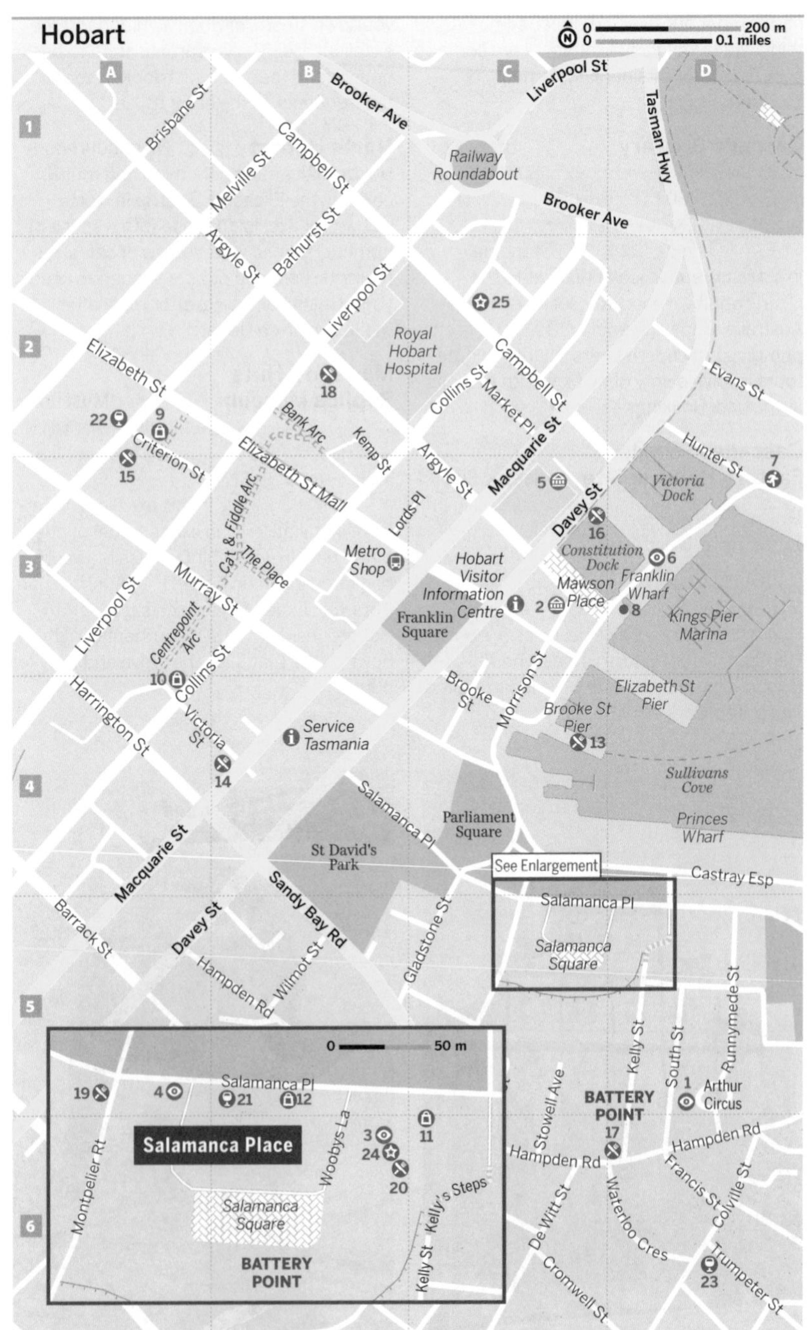
Hobart
0 200 m
0 0.1 miles
A
B
C
D
1
2
3
4
5
6
Brisbane St
Melville St
Campbell St
Brooker Ave
Liverpool St
Tasman Hwy
Railway Roundabout
Brooker Ave
Argyle St
Bathurst St
Liverpool St
25
Royal Hobart Hospital
Elizabeth St
18
Collins St
Market Pl
Campbell St
Macquarie St
Evans St
22
9
Criterion St
15
Bank Arc
Kemp St
Elizabeth St Mall
Argyle St
Lords Pl
5
Davey St
16
Hunter St
7
Victoria Dock
Cat & Fiddle Arc
The Place
Metro Shop
Hobart Visitor Information Centre
Constitution Dock
6
Franklin Wharf
Mawson Place
2
8
Kings Pier Marina
Murray St
Liverpool St
Centrepoint Arc
Franklin Square
10
Collins St
Harrington St
Victoria St
Brooke St
Morrison St
Elizabeth St Pier
Brooke St Pier
13
Service Tasmania
14
Sullivans Cove
Salamanca Pl
Parliament Square
Princes Wharf
Macquarie St
St David's Park
See Enlargement
Castray Esp
Salamanca Pl
Salamanca Square
Barrack St
Davey St
Sandy Bay Rd
Gladstone St
Hampden Rd
Wilmot St
Runnymede St
Kelly St
South St
0 50 m
19
4
Salamanca Pl
21
12
Salamanca Place
Montpelier Rt
Woobys La
3
24
20
11
Kelly's Steps
Salamanca Square
BATTERY POINT
Kelly St
Stowell Ave
BATTERY POINT
1
Arthur Circus
17
Hampden Rd
Hampden Rd
De Witt St
Waterloo Cres
Francis St
Colville St
Cromwell St
23
Trumpeter St

Hobart

Sights

1 Battery Point ... D5
2 Mawson's Huts Replica Museum ... C3
3 Salamanca Arts Centre ... B6
4 Salamanca Place ... A5
5 Tasmanian Museum & Art Gallery ... C3
6 Waterfront ... D3

Activities, Courses & Tours

7 Hobart Bike Hire ... D3
8 Pennicott Wilderness Journeys ... D3

Shopping

9 Cool Wine ... A2
10 Fullers Bookshop ... A4
11 Handmark Gallery ... C6
12 Salamanca Market ... B5

Eating

13 Aloft ... C4
14 Astor Grill ... B4
15 Farm Gate Market ... A3
16 Flippers ... C3
17 Jackman & McRoss ... D6
18 Pilgrim Coffee ... B2
19 Retro Cafe ... A5
20 Tricycle Cafe & Bar ... B6

Drinking & Nightlife

Glass House ... (see 13)
21 Jack Greene ... B5
22 New Sydney Hotel ... A2
23 Shipwright's Arms Hotel ... D6

Entertainment

24 Salamanca Arts Centre Courtyard ... B6
25 Theatre Royal ... C2

Royal Tasmanian Botanical Gardens Gardens

(03-6166 0451; www.rtbg.tas.gov.au; Lower Domain Rd, Queens Domain; 8am-6.30pm Oct-Mar, to 5.30pm Apr & Sep, to 5pm May-Aug) FREE On the eastern side of the Queen's Domain, these small but beguiling gardens hark back to 1818 and feature more than 6000 exotic and native plant species. Picnic on the lawns, check out the Subantarctic Plant House or grab a bite at the restaurant or cafe. Call to ask about guided tours.

ACTIVITIES

Mt Wellington Descent Cycling

(1800 064 726; www.underdownunder.com.au; adult/child $75/65; 10am & 1pm daily year-round, plus 4pm Dec-Feb) Take a van ride to the summit of kunanyi/Mt Wellington (1271m), and follow with 22km of downhill cruising (mostly – the last 5km are flat) on a mountain bike. It's terrific fun, with minimal energy output and maximum views! Tours start and end at 4 Elizabeth St on the Hobart waterfront, and last 2½ hours.

Roaring 40s Kayaking Kayaking

(0455 949 777; www.roaring40skayaking.com.au; Marieville Esplanade, Sandy Bay; adult/child $90/60; 10am daily Oct-Apr, plus 4pm Nov-Mar) Hobart is perhaps at its prettiest when viewed from the water. Take a safe, steady, 2½-hour guided paddle with Roaring 40s, named after the prevailing winds at these latitudes. You'll cruise from Sandy Bay past Battery Point and into the Hobart docks for some fish and chips while you float, before returning to Sandy Bay.

TOURS

Pennicott Wilderness Journeys Boating

(03-6234 4270; www.pennicottjourneys.com.au; Dock Head Bldg, Franklin Wharf; tours adult/child from $225/155; 7am-6.30pm) Pennicott offers half-a-dozen outstanding boat trips around key southern Tasmanian sights, including trips to Bruny Island, Tasman Island, the Tasman Peninsula, D'Entrecasteaux Channel, and the Iron Pot Lighthouse south of Hobart.

Hobart Historic Tours Walking

(03-6234 5550; www.hobarthistorictours.com.au; tours from $30) Informative, entertaining 90-minute walking tours of Hobart and historic Battery Point. There's also an Old Hobart Pub Tour available, which sluices through some waterfront watering holes, and a three-hour Grand Hobart Walk. Call

GRANT DIXON/GETTY IMAGES ©

Handmark Gallery

or see the website for times and bookings. Reduced winter schedule.

Gourmania Walking
(☎0419 180 113; www.gourmaniafoodtours.com.au; tours from $89) Fabulous, flavour-filled walking tours around Salamanca Place and central Hobart, with plenty of opportunities to try local foods and chat to restaurant, cafe and shop owners.

SHOPPING

Fullers Bookshop Books
(☎03-6234 3800; www.fullersbookshop.com.au; 131 Collins St; ⏲8.30am-6pm Mon-Fri, 9am-5pm Sat, 10am-4pm Sun) Hobart's best bookshop has a great range of literature and travel guides, plus regular launches and readings, and the writerly Afterword Cafe in the corner. A real hub of the Hobart literary scene for around 70 years.

Cool Wine Wine
(☎03-6231 4000; www.coolwine.com.au; shop 8, MidCity Arcade, Criterion St; ⏲9.30am-6.30pm Mon-Sat) Excellent selection of Tasmanian wine, spirits and craft beers (plus a few global interlopers, if they're up to scratch). Open Sunday by appointment.

Handmark Gallery Art
(☎03-6223 7895; www.handmark.com.au; 77 Salamanca Pl; ⏲10am-5pm) A key tenant at the Salamanca Arts Centre (p185), Handmark has been here for 30 years, displaying unique ceramics, glass, woodwork and jewellery, plus paintings and sculpture – 100% Tasmanian.

EATING

Farm Gate Market Market $
(☎03-6234 5625; www.farmgatemarket.com.au; Bathurst St, btwn Elizabeth & Murray Sts; ⏲8.30am-1pm Sun) The waterfront Salamanca Market has dominated for decades, but this hyperactive foodie street-mart is giving it a run for its money. Trading commences with the ding of a big brass bell: elbow your way in for the best fruit, veg, honey, wine, baked goods, beer, smoked meats, coffee,

cheese, nuts, oils, cut flowers, jams… Terrific!

Jackman & McRoss Bakery $
(03-6223 3186; 57-59 Hampden Rd, Battery Point; items $4-14; 7am-5pm Mon-Sat) Make sure to stop by this neighbourhood bakery-cafe, even if it's just to gawk at the display cabinet full of delectable pies, tarts, baguettes and pastries. Early-morning cake and coffee may evolve into a quiche for lunch, or perhaps a duck, cranberry and walnut sausage roll. Staff stay cheery despite being run off their feet.

Retro Cafe Cafe $
(03-6223 3073; 31 Salamanca Pl; mains $11-17; 7.30am-6pm Mon-Fri, 8am-4pm Sat & Sun) So popular it hurts, funky Retro is ground zero for Saturday brunch among the market stalls (or any day, really). Masterful breakfasts, bagels, salads and burgers interweave with laughing staff, chilled-out jazz and the whirr and bang of the coffee machine. A classic Hobart cafe.

Flippers Fish & Chips $
(03-6234 3101; www.flippersfishandchips.com.au; Constitution Dock; meals $10-28; 9.30am-8.30pm) There are quite a few floating fish punts moored in Constitution Dock, selling fresh-caught seafood either uncooked or cooked. Our pick is Flippers, an enduring favourite with a voluptuous fish-shaped profile. Fillets of flathead and curls of calamari – straight from the deep blue sea and into the deep fryer. The local seagulls will adore you.

Pilgrim Coffee Cafe $$
(03-6234 1999; www.pilgrimcoffee.com; 48 Argyle St; mains $15-20; 6.30am-4.30pm Mon-Fri, 8am-2pm Sat & Sun) With exposed bricks, timber beams and distressed walls, L-shaped Pilgrim is Hobart's hippest cafe. Expect wraps, panini and interesting mains (Bolivian breakfast bowl!), plus expertly prepared coffee. Fall into conversation with the locals at big shared tables.

Templo Italian $$
(03-6234 7659; www.templo.com.au; 98 Patrick St; mains $24-32; noon-3pm & 6pm-late Thu-Mon) Unpretentious little Templo, on a nondescript reach of Patrick St, has assumed the mantle of Hobart's 'must-do' restaurant. With only about 20 seats (bookings essential), and only three or four Italian-inspired mains to choose from, Templo is an exercise in selectivity and sharing (your personal space, and your food). Survey the pricey-but-memorable wine list at the cute bar.

Annapurna Indian $$
(03-6236 9500; www.annapurnaindiancuisine.com; 305 Elizabeth St, North Hobart; mains $16-18, banquets $22-32; noon-3pm & 5-10pm Mon-Fri, 5-10pm Sat & Sun;) It seems like

Hobart for Children

The free Friday-night Rektango (p185) music event in the courtyard at the Salamanca Arts Centre is a family-friendly affair, while the street performers and buskers at Saturday's Salamanca Market (p185) captivate. There's always something going on around the waterfront (p188) – fishing boats chugging in and out, yachts tacking in Sullivans Cove…and you can feed the tribe on a budget at the floating fish punts on Constitution Dock.

Rainy-day attractions to satisfy your child (or inner child) include the Tasmanian Museum & Art Gallery (p188) and the excellent Mawson's Huts Replica Museum (p189).

Hobart is an active kinda town: take a boat cruise up or down the river; assail the heights of kunanyi/Mt Wellington (p188); or hire a bike and explore the cycling paths.

If you're in need of a romantic dinner for two, contact the **Mobile Nanny Service** (0437 504 064, 03-6273 3773; www.mobilenannyservice.com.au).

Sydney to Hobart Yacht Race

Arguably the world's greatest and most treacherous open-ocean yacht race, the **Sydney to Hobart Yacht Race** (www.rolexsydneyhobart.com; ⌚Dec) winds up at Hobart's Constitution Dock some time around New Year's Eve. As the storm-battered maxis limp across the finish line, champagne corks pop and weary sailors turn the town upside down. On New Year's Day, find a sunny spot by the harbour, munch some lunch from the Taste of Tasmania food festival and count spinnakers on the river. New Year's resolutions? What New Year's resolutions?

Racing yachts
ALVOV/SHUTTERSTOCK ©

half of Hobart lists Annapurna as their favourite eatery (you'd better book). Northern and southern Indian options are served with absolute proficiency: the *masala dosa* (south Indian crepe filled with curried potato) is a crowd favourite. Takeaways, too. Hard to top.

Tricycle Cafe & Bar Cafe $$
(☎03-6223 7228; 77 Salamanca Pl; mains $12-20; ⌚8.30am-4pm Mon-Sat) This cosy red-painted nook inside the Salamanca Arts Centre (p185) serves up a range of cafe classics (BLTs, toasties, scrambled free-range eggs, salads, house-brewed chai and Fair Trade coffee), plus awesome daily specials (braised Wagyu rice bowl with jalapeño cream – wow!). Wines by the glass from the bar.

Aloft Modern Australian $$$
(☎03-6223 1619; www.aloftrestaurant.com; Brook St Pier; mains $34-35, Fri set lunch $30, banquets from $70; ⌚6pm-late Tue-Sat) Staking a bold claim as Hobart's top restaurant, Aloft occupies a lofty eyrie in the floating Brook Street Pier. Menu hits include the likes of yellow fish curry with beetroot and fennel, and steamed oysters with fermented chilli. If you can drag your gaze away from the view, service and presentation are both excellent, in an unpretentious Hobart kinda way.

Astor Grill Steak $$$
(☎03-6234 3122; www.astorgrill.com.au; 157 Macquarie St; mains $29-65; ⌚noon-4pm & 5.30-11.45pm Mon-Fri, 5.30-11.45pm Sat) Indulge in old-school meaty treats at this sumptuous stalwart, in a blood-coloured 1920s brick building on the CBD fringe. Start with some oysters, then choose your prime cut, or perhaps the wallaby fillets with onion mash, beetroot and pepperberry sauce.

DRINKING & NIGHTLIFE

New Sydney Hotel Pub
(☎03-6234 4516; www.newsydneyhotel.com.au; 87 Bathurst St; ⌚noon-10pm Mon, to midnight Tue-Sat, 4-9pm Sun) This low-key city pub is the best boozer in the CBD, with open fires, creative pub food (think duck tongue tortilla!; mains $14 to $35) and a terrific 15-tap beer selection, including an ever-changing array of island craft beers (try the Seven Sheds Paradise Pale). Irish jam session at 2pm on Saturdays, if you're lucky.

T-Bone Brewing Co Craft Beer
(☎0407 502 521; www.tbonebrewing.com.au; 308 Elizabeth St, North Hobart; ⌚4pm-late Wed & Thu, 2pm-late Fri-Sun) Obsessively brewed real ales steal the show at this new North Hobart brew-bar, a stylish black beer-bunker reviving an old corner shop, just a short wobble from the main Elizabeth

St action. Sit by the fold-back windows, or play peek-a-boo with the beer vats, bubbling beyond a hole in the wall. Tasting flights $16.

Winston Pub

(☎03-6231 2299; www.thewinstonbar.com; 381 Elizabeth St, North Hobart; ⏰4pm-late) The grim old art deco Eaglehawk pub has been transformed into the Winston, a hipster-driven, US-style craft-beer alehouse. Grab a pint of the house stout from one of the beardy guys behind the bar and check out the wall of US registration plates near the pool table. Calorific bar food and live music, too.

Jack Greene Bar

(☎03-6224 9655; www.jackgreene.com.au; 49 Salamanca Pl; ⏰11.30am-late) The gourmet burgers here nudge $20, but atmospheric Jack Greene (a European hunting lodge on the run?) is worthwhile if you're a wandering beer fan. Glowing racks of bottled brews fill the fridges, and there are at least 16 beers on tap from around Australia and New Zealand. Occasional acoustic troubadours perch next to the stairs.

Willing Bros Wine Bar

(☎03-6234 3053; www.facebook.com/willingbros; 390 Elizabeth St, North Hobart; ⏰3pm-late Tue-Sun) Hey – a classy wine bar! Just what NoHo ordered. Pull up a window seat at the front of the skinny room and sip something hip from the tightly edited menu of reds, whites and bubbles. The food on offer drifts from Moroccan fish cakes to spicy lamb *empanadas* – perfect fodder for a post-movie debrief.

Glass House Cocktail Bar

(☎0437 245 540; www.theglass.house; Brooke St Pier; ⏰noon-10pm Mon & Tue, to midnight Wed-Sun) The very fancy Glass House sits in the prow of the floating Brooke Street Pier, a huge window-wall affording uninterrupted views down the Derwent River estuary. Put on your best duds, order a Hobartian Sidecar and soak it all in. Fab bar food, too (small plates $18 to $30).

Waterfront area (p188)

 ENTERTAINMENT

State Cinema Cinema

(☎03-6234 6318; www.statecinema.com.au; 375 Elizabeth St, North Hobart; ⏰10am-late Mon-Fri, 9.30am-late Sat & Sun) Saved from the wrecking ball in the 1990s, the multiscreen State (built in 1913) shows independent and art-house flicks from local and international film-makers. There's a great cafe and bar on-site, plus a rooftop screen, a browse-worthy bookshop and the foodie temptations of North Hobart's restaurants right outside.

Republic Bar & Café Live Music

(☎03-6234 6954; www.republicbar.com; 299 Elizabeth St, North Hobart; ⏰11am-late; 📶) The Republic is a raucous art deco pub hosting live music every night (often free entry). It's the number-one live-music pub around town, with an always-interesting line-up, including international acts. Loads of different beers and excellent food (mains $24 to $36; try the Jack Daniels–marinated scotch fillet!) – just the kind of place you'd love to call your local.

Theatre Royal Theatre

(☎03-6233 2299, 1800 650 277; www.theatreroyal.com.au; 29 Campbell St; ⏰box office 9am-5pm Mon-Fri) This venerable old stager is Australia's oldest continuously operating theatre, with actors first cracking the boards here back in 1837 (the foundation stone says 1834, but it took them a few years to finish it). Expect a range of music, ballet, theatre, opera and university revues. Guided tours available.

 INFORMATION

MEDICAL SERVICES

City Doctors & Travel Clinic (☎03-6231 3003; www.citydoctors.com.au; 188 Collins St; ⏰9am-5pm Mon-Fri) General medical appointments and travel immunisations. Book online or call.

My Chemist Salamanca (☎03-6224 9994; www.mychemist.com.au; 6 Montpelier Retreat; ⏰8.30am-6pm Mon-Fri, to 5pm Sat, 10am-4pm Sun) Handy chemist just off Salamanca Place.

Taste of Tasmania food festival

Royal Hobart Hospital (☎03-6222 8423; www.dhhs.tas.gov.au; 48 Liverpool St; ⏰24hr) Accident and emergency, running round the clock.

TOURIST INFORMATION

Hobart Visitor Information Centre (☎03-6238 4222; www.hobarttravelcentre.com.au; cnr Davey & Elizabeth Sts; ⏰9am-5pm) Information, maps and state-wide tour, transport and accommodation bookings.

GETTING THERE & AWAY

Hobart's 'international' airport has only domestic flights, with services operated by **Qantas** (www.qantas.com.au), **Virgin Australia** (www.virginaustralia.com.au), **Jetstar** (www.jetstar.com.au) and **Tiger Air** (www.tigerair.com.au).

GETTING AROUND

BICYCLE

There are a number of bike-hire options around the city. Try **Hobart Bike Hire** (☎0447 556 189; www.hobartbikehire.com.au; 35 Hunter St; bike hire per day/overnight from $25/35; ⏰9am-5.30pm).

BUS

The local bus network is operated by **Metro Tasmania** (☎13 22 01; www.metrotas.com.au), which is reliable but infrequent outside of business hours. The **Metro Shop** (☎13 22 01; www.metrotas.com.au; 22 Elizabeth St; ⏰8am-6pm Mon-Fri, 9.30am-2pm Sat) handles ticketing and enquiries: most buses depart from this section of Elizabeth St, or from nearby Franklin Sq.

- One-way cash ticket prices on Metro Tasmania buses vary with the number of zones travelled: one zone $3.30, two zones $4.60, or all zones $6.90.
- Buy a rechargeable Greencard in store or online from the Metro Shop for a 20% discount on regular fares.
- One-way tickets can be bought from the Metro Shop, the driver (exact change required), or ticket agents (newsagents and post offices).

CAR & MOTORCYCLE

Timed, metered parking predominates in the CBD and tourist areas such as Salamanca Place and the waterfront. For longer-term parking, large CBD garages (clearly signposted) offer inexpensive rates.

The big-boy rental firms have airport desks and city offices. Cheaper local firms offer daily rental rates from as low as $30.

TAXI

131008 Hobart (☎13 10 08; www.131008hobart.com) Standard taxis.

Maxi-Taxi Services (☎13 32 22; www.hobartmaxitaxi.com.au) Wheelchair-accessible vehicles, and taxis for groups.

McLaren Vale (p204)

PETER WALTON PHOTOGRAPHY/GETTY IMAGES ©

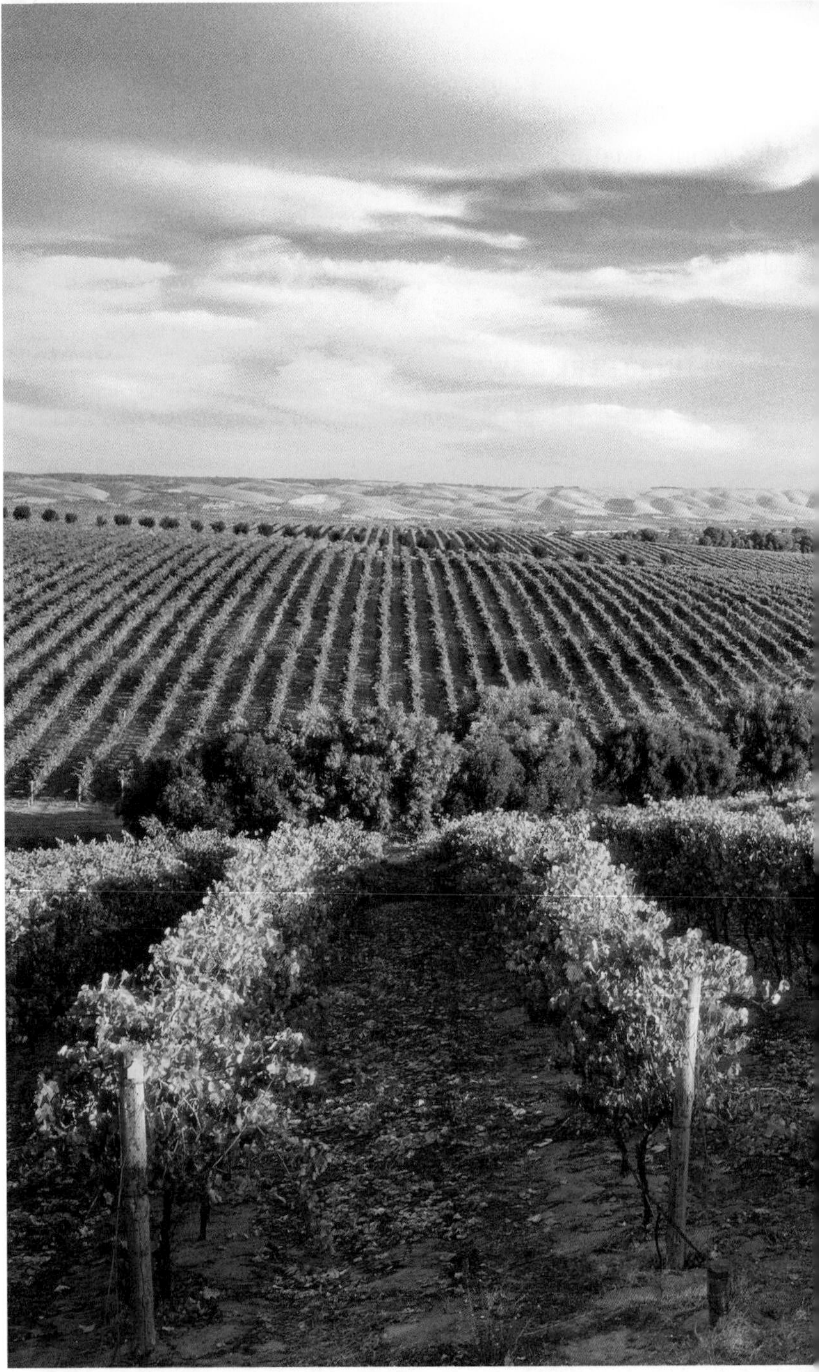

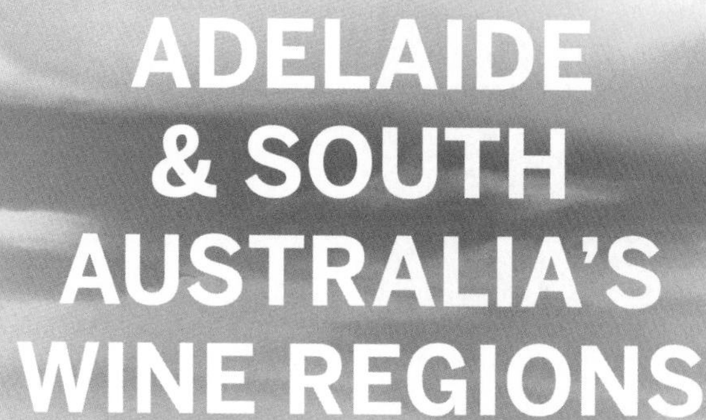

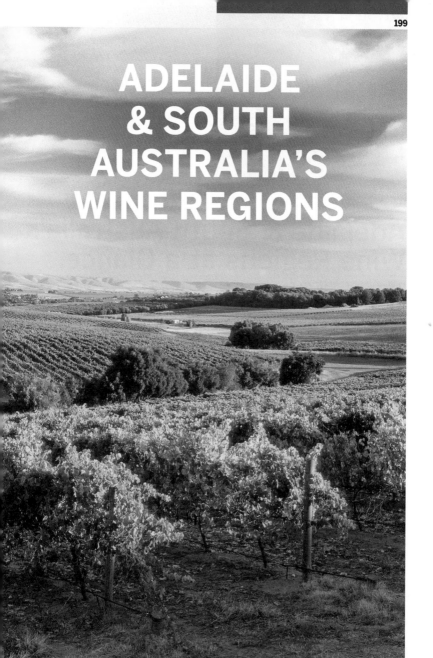

ADELAIDE & SOUTH AUSTRALIA'S WINE REGIONS

In this Chapter

Adelaide & South Australia's Wine Regions at a Glance...

Restrained, dignified, neat-casual – the staid self-image Adelaide has traditionally projected, a nod to the days of free colonisation without the 'penal colony' taint. But these days, things are much more hip in this Unesco 'City of Music', with multicultural restaurants, pumping arts and live-music scenes, savvy laneway bars and a packed festival calendar.

Day trips away are to the world-class Barossa Valley and McLaren Vale wine regions (superb shiraz), plus the utterly photogenic Adelaide Hills – a rolling landscape of cool-climate wineries, cosy pubs and historic stone villages.

Adelaide & South Australia's Wine Regions in Two Days

Head to Adelaide's **Central Market** (p208) early for breakfast, then take a tour – a **RoofClimb** (p211) or at ground-level – of **Adelaide Oval** (p208). Wander through the estimable **Art Gallery of South Australia** (p208), the hit the bars around Peel St. On day two, day-trip into the **Adelaide Hills** (p206): wineries, historic villages, koalas and viewpoints.

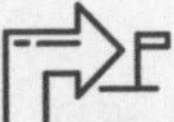

Adelaide & South Australia's Wine Regions in Four Days

On day three, broaden your SA adventure with a visit to either the **McLaren Vale** (p204) or **Barossa Valley** (p202) wine regions, both an hour or less from the city. On day four, take the tram to **Glenelg** (p212) for some beach time and sunset fish and chips by the sea. Drinks on Rundle St back in the city await.

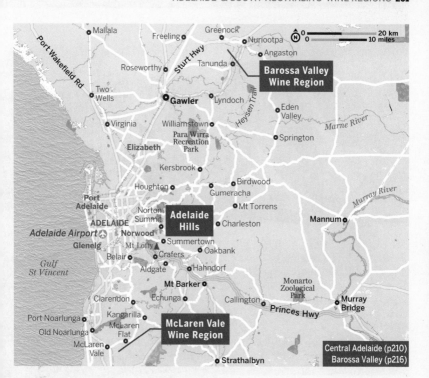

Central Adelaide (p210)
Barossa Valley (p216)

Arriving in Adelaide & South Australia's Wine Regions

Adelaide Airport (p214) The airport is 7km west of the CBD; taxis ($30), shuttles ($35) and Metro buses ($3 to $5) are on hand.

Adelaide Central Bus Station (p214) The main bus station is in the city centre.

Adelaide Parklands Terminal (p214) The interstate train station is 1km southwest of the city centre.

From the city, it's a day-trip drive or tour to the Adelaide Hills and wine regions.

Where to Stay

Most Adelaide accommodation is in the city centre, but in a grid-town this easy to navigate, staying outside the CBD is viable. North Adelaide is under the flight path, but it's otherwise low-key. For beachside accommodation, try Glenelg. In the Barossa and McLaren Vale you'll find B&Bs and luxe stays; the Adelaide Hills have slick pub rooms and yet more B&Bs.

Preparing for winemaking

Barossa Valley Wine Region

With hot, dry summers and cool, moderate winters, the Barossa is one of the world's great wine regions – an absolute must for anyone keen on a good drop.

Great For...

☑ Don't Miss

The view over the valley from Mengler's Hill Lookout (p216).

Big Reds, Aromatic Whites

The Barossa is best known for shiraz, with riesling the dominant white. There are around 80 vineyards here and 60 cellar doors, ranging from boutique wine rooms to monstrous complexes. The long-established 'Barossa Barons' hold sway – big, brassy operators – while spritely young boutique wineries are harder to sniff out. The pick of the bunch:

Penfolds Winery

(☎08-8568 8408; www.penfolds.com; 30 Tanunda Rd, Nuriootpa; ⏰9am-5pm) You know the name: Penfolds is a Barossa legend. Book ahead for the Make Your Own Blend tour ($65), or the Taste of Grange tour ($150).

Rockford Wines Winery

(☎08-8563 2720; www.rockfordwines.com.au; 131 Krondorf Rd, Tanunda; ⏰11am-5pm) Our favourite boutique Barossa winery, this 1850s cellar door sells traditionally made, small-range wines, including sparkling reds.

Henschke Winery

(☎08-8564 8223; www.henschke.com.au; 1428 Keyneton Rd, Keyneton; ⏰9am-4.30pm Mon-Fri, to noon Sat) Detour 10km southeast of Angaston to the Eden Valley, where old-school Henschke bottles its iconic Hill of Grace red.

ℹ Need to Know

Just 65km northeast of Adelaide, the Barossa makes an easy day trip from the city.

✂ Take a Break

Fino Seppeltsfield (p218) is one of the best restaurants in Australia, hands down.

★ Top Tip

Cycling is a great way to see the valley: roll into the Barossa Cycle Hub (p216).

Peter Lehmann Wines Winery

(☎08-8565 9555; www.peterlehmannwines.com.au; Para Rd, Tanunda; ⏰9.30am-5pm Mon-Fri, 10.30am-4.30pm Sat & Sun) The shiraz and riesling vintages here are probably the most consistent and affordable Barossa wines.

St Hallett Winery

(☎08-8563 7070; www.sthallett.com.au; St Hallett Rd, Tanunda; ⏰10am-5pm) Unpretentious St Hallett produces reasonably priced but consistently good whites (try the Poacher's Blend) and the excellent Old Block Shiraz.

Guided Tours

Wine-flavoured day tours departing either Adelaide or locally are bountiful; the Barossa Visitor Information Centre (p218) can help with bookings. Operators include the following:

Taste the Barossa (☎08-8357 1594; www.winetoursbarossa.com.au; full-day tours $129)

Barossa Wine Lovers Tours (☎08-8270 5500; www.wineloverstours.com.au; tours incl lunch from $90)

Barossa Epicurean Tours (☎0457 101 487; www.barossatours.com.au; half-/full-day tours from $150/180)

McLaren Vale Wine Region

Most people come to McLaren Vale – just a 40-minute drive south of Adelaide – to cruise the 80-plus wineries here: you could spend days doing nothing else!

Great For...

☑ Don't Miss

Nosing your way into some sublime shiraz at McLaren Vale's many cellar doors.

Seriously Good Wineries

If the Barossa Valley is SA wine's old school, then McLaren Vale is the upstart teenager smoking cigarettes behind the shed and stealing nips from mum's sherry bottle. The luscious vineyards around here have a Tuscan haze in summer, rippling down to a calm coastline that's similarly Ligurian. This is shiraz country – solid, punchy and seriously good. Quaff some at five of the region's best:

d'Arenberg Winery

(☎08-8329 4888; www.darenberg.com.au; Osborn Rd, McLaren Vale; ⏰10am-5pm) The wine labels are part of the character of this place: the Dead Arm shiraz and the Broken Fishplate sauvignon blanc are our faves.

DARREN TIERNEY/SHUTTERSTOCK ©

Alpha Box & Dice Winery

(☎08-8323 7750; www.alphaboxdice.com; 8 Olivers Rd, McLaren Vale; ⏰11am-5pm Mon-Fri, 10am-6pm Sat & Sun) One out of the box, this refreshing little gambler wins top billing for interesting blends, funky retro furnishings, quirky labels and laid-back staff.

Coriole Winery

(☎08-8323 8305; www.coriole.com; Chaffeys Rd, McLaren Vale; ⏰10am-5pm Mon-Fri, 11am-5pm Sat & Sun) Take your regional tasting platter out into the garden of this beautiful cottage cellar door (1860), made lovelier by a swill of the flagship chenin blanc.

Need to Know

Pick up a map of winery cellar doors at the McLaren Vale & Fleurieu Visitor Information Centre (p219).

Take a Break

Duck into **Blessed Cheese** (p219) for a coffee, burger, pastry or...some cheese!

★ Top Tip

Saturday morning? The effervescent, rootsy **Willunga Farmers Market** (☎08-8556 4297; www.willungafarmersmarket.com; Willunga Town Sq; ⏰8am-12.30pm Sat) is just 6km south.

Wirra Wirra Winery

(☎08-8323 8414; www.wirrawirra.com; cnr McMurtrie & Strout Rds, McLaren Vale; ⏰10am-5pm Mon-Sat, 11am-5pm Sun) Fancy some *pétanque* with your plonk? This barnlike, 1894 cellar door has a grassy picnic area, and there's a roaring fire inside in winter.

SC Pannell Winery

(☎08-8323 8000; www.pannell.com.au; 60 Olivers Rd, McLaren Vale; ⏰11am-5pm) With one of the best views in the business, SC Pannell (Steve, to his mates) produces excellent reds you can drink young.

Guided Tours

Most tours can be taken from Adelaide, or, for a few dollars less, from McLaren Vale itself. Operators include the following:

Adelaide's Top Food & Wine Tours (☎08-8386 0888; www.topfoodandwinetours.com.au)

Chook's Little Winery Tours (☎0414 922 200; www.chookslittlewinerytours.com.au; per person from $100)

McLaren Vale Wine Tours (☎0414 784 666; www.mclarenvaletours.com.au)

ANDREY MOISSEYEV/GETTY IMAGES ©

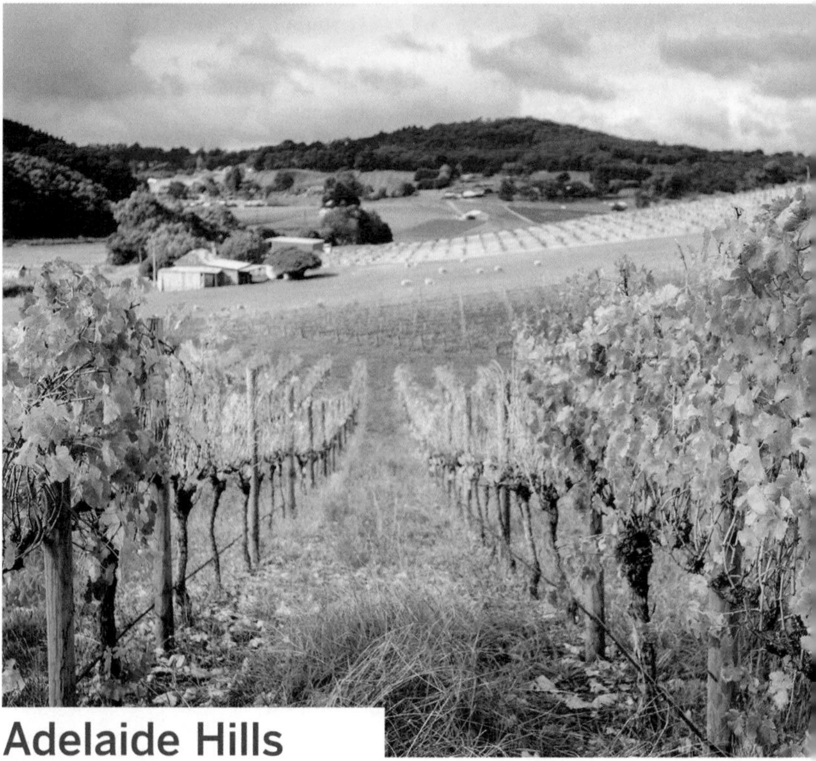

Adelaide Hills Wine Region

The Hills make a brilliant day trip from Adelaide: hop from town to town, passing stone pubs, old cottages, olive groves and wineries along the way.

Great For...

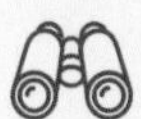

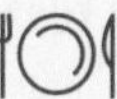

☑ Don't Miss

The view over the Adelaide Plains from Mt Lofty Summit (p220).

Cool-Climate Wineries

With night mists and reasonable rainfall, the Adelaide Hills' mid-altitude slopes sustain one of SA's cooler climates – perfect for producing some complex and truly top-notch white wines, especially chardonnays and sauvignon blancs. There are dozens of wineries in the Hills (see www.adelaidehillswine.com.au for details, or pick up the *Adelaide Hills Cellar Door Guide* brochure); January's Crush festival and Winter Reds in July celebrate this rich bounty. The pick of the bunch:

Shaw & Smith (☎08-8398 0500; www.shawandsmith.com; 136 Jones Rd, Balhannah; wine-flight tastings from $12; ⏰11am-5pm)

Bird in Hand (☎08-8389 9488; www.birdinhand.com.au; cnr Bird in Hand & Pfeiffer Rds,

Dinner at an Adelaide Hills restaurant

GREG ELMS/GETTY IMAGES ©

Woodside; 11am-5pm Mon-Fri, 10am-5pm Sat & Sun)

Deviation Road (08-8339 2633; www.deviationroad.com; 207 Scott Creek Rd, Longwood; 10am-5pm;)

The Lane (08-8388 1250; www.thelane.com.au; Ravenswood Lane, Hahndorf; 10am-4pm)

Pike & Joyce (08-8389 8102; www.pikeandjoyce.com.au; 730 Mawson Rd, Lenswood; 11am-5pm, to 4pm Jun-Aug)

Cheeky Overnighter?

Most travellers tackle the Adelaide Hills as a day trip from Adelaide – it's barely 15 minutes away. But if you want to stay the night, you'll find ritzy renovated pub rooms, historic hotels and some good B&Bs. If you feel like staying the night, both the **Stirling Hotel** (08-8339 2345; www.stirlinghotel.com.au; 52 Mt Barker Rd, Stirling; d from $280;) and **Crafers Hotel** (08-8339 2050; www.crafershotel.com.au; 8 Main St, Crafers; d from $180;) have stylish boutique rooms upstairs, while **Mt Lofty House** (08-8339 6777; www.mtloftyhouse.com.au; 74 Mt Lofty Summit Rd, Crafers; d/ste/cottage from $239/509/369;) is an 1850s stone mansion with show-stopping valley views.

Need to Know

Autumn is particularly atmospheric here: cool, misty weather and deciduous colours.

Take a Break

Seasonal Garden Cafe (p221) is the pick of Hahndorf's myriad options.

★ Top Tip

For a tailored Hills experience, take a day trip with **Ambler Touring** (0414 447 134; www.ambler.net.au; half-/full-day tours per person $99/155) or Tour Adelaide Hills (p220).

Fab Hills Festivals

Crush Wine

(www.crushfestival.com.au; Jan) Celebrating all things good about life in the Adelaide Hills, with food and wine at the fore. Lots of cellar-door events and tastings.

Winter Reds Wine

(www.winterreds.com.au; Jul) '*Brrr,* it's chilly. Pour me another shiraz.' Winter Reds celebrates the cold season in the Adelaide Hills, with winery tastings, hearty food and lots of open fires.

Adelaide

SIGHTS

Central Market Market
(08-8203 7494; www.adelaidecentralmarket.com.au; Gouger St; 7am-5.30pm Tue, 9am-5.30pm Wed & Thu, 7am-9pm Fri, 7am-3pm Sat) Satisfy your deepest culinary cravings at this 250-stall market. A sliver of salami from the Mettwurst Shop, a crumb of English Stilton from the Smelly Cheese Shop, a tub of blueberry yoghurt from the Yoghurt Shop – you name it, it's here. Adelaide's Chinatown is right next door. **Adelaide's Top Food & Wine Tours** (08-8386 0888; www.topfoodandwinetours.com.au) offers guided tours.

Adelaide Oval Landmark
(08-8205 4700; www.adelaideoval.com.au; King William Rd, North Adelaide; tours adult/child $22/12; tours 10am, 11am & 2pm daily, plus 1pm Sat & Sun) Hailed as the world's prettiest cricket ground, the Adelaide Oval hosts interstate and international cricket matches in summer, plus national AFL football and state football matches in winter. Guided 90-minute **tours** run on nongame days: call for bookings or book online. Also here is RoofClimb Adelaide Oval (p211).

Art Gallery of South Australia Gallery
(08-8207 7000; www.artgallery.sa.gov.au; North Tce; 10am-5pm) FREE Spend a few hushed hours in the vaulted, parquetry-floored gallery that represents the big names in Australian art. Permanent exhibitions include Australian, Aboriginal and Torres Strait Islander, Asian, European and North American art – 20 bronze Rodins! There are free guided tours at 11am and 2pm daily, and a lovely cafe out the back.

South Australian Museum Museum
(08-8207 7500; www.samuseum.sa.gov.au; North Tce; 10am-5pm) FREE Dig into SA's history with the museum's special exhibits on whales and Antarctic explorer Sir Douglas Mawson. The Aboriginal Cultures Gallery displays artefacts of the Ngarrindjeri people. Free tours depart 11am

Adelaide Botanic Gardens

weekdays and 2pm and 3pm weekends. Good cafe, too!

National Wine Centre of Australia Winery
(08-8313 3355; www.wineaustralia.com.au; cnr Botanic & Hackney Rds; 8am-6pm Mon-Thu, to 9pm Fri, 9am-9am Sat, to 6pm Sun) FREE Check out the free self-guided, interactive Wine Discovery Journey exhibition at this very sexy wine centre. Explore the Cellar Door with cleverly automated tastings (from $2.50).

Adelaide Zoo Zoo
(08-8267 3255; www.zoossa.com.au; Frome Rd; adult/child/family $34.50/19/88.50; 9.30am-5pm) Around 1800 exotic and native mammals, birds and reptiles roar, growl and screech at Adelaide's wonderful zoo, dating from 1883. There are free **walking tours** half-hourly. You can take a river cruise to the zoo on **Popeye** (0400 596 065; www.thepopeye.com.au; return adult/child $15/8, one-way $10/5; 10am-4pm, reduced winter hours).

Adelaide Botanic Gardens Gardens
(08-8222 9311; www.botanicgardens.sa.gov.au; cnr North Tce & East Tce; 7.15am-sunset Mon-Fri, from 9am Sat & Sun) FREE Meander, jog or chew through your trashy airport novel in these lush city-fringe gardens. Free 1½-hour **guided walks** depart at 10.30am daily. The classy **Botanic Gardens Restaurant** (08-8223 3526; www.botanicgardensrestaurant.com.au; off Plane Tree Dr, Adelaide Botanic Gardens; 2-/3-courses $55/72; noon-2.30pm Tue-Sun, 6.30-9pm Fri & Sat) is here too.

ACTIVITIES

Adventure Kayaking SA Kayaking
(08-8295 8812; www.adventurekayak.com.au; tours adult/child from $50/25, kayak hire per 3hr 1-/2-/3-seater $40/60/80) Family-friendly guided kayak tours around the Port River estuary (dolphins, mangroves, shipwrecks) near Port Adelaide.

Mad March

Adelaide hosts a string of world-class festivals...but why do most of them have to be in March?

Adelaide Fringe (www.adelaidefringe.com.au; Feb/Mar) This annual independent arts festival in February and March is second only to the Edinburgh Fringe. Funky, unpredictable and downright hilarious. Get into it!

Adelaide Festival (www.adelaidefestival.com.au; Mar) Top-flight international and Australian dance, drama, opera, literature and theatre performances in March. Don't miss the hedonistic late-night club.

WOMADelaide (www.womadelaide.com.au; Mar) One of the world's best live-music events, with more than 300 musicians and performers from around the globe. Perfect for families and those with a new-age bent.

Performer at Adelaide Fringe
GREYBOOTS40/SHUTTERSTOCK ©

Escapegoat Mountain Biking
(0422 916 289; www.escapegoat.com.au) Careen down the slopes of 727m Mt Lofty into Adelaide below ($99), or take a day trip through McLaren Vale by bike ($129).

TOURS

Adelaide City Explorer Tours
(www.adelaidecityexplorer.com.au) Excellent new downloadable walking tours around the city. There are 15 themed trails in all

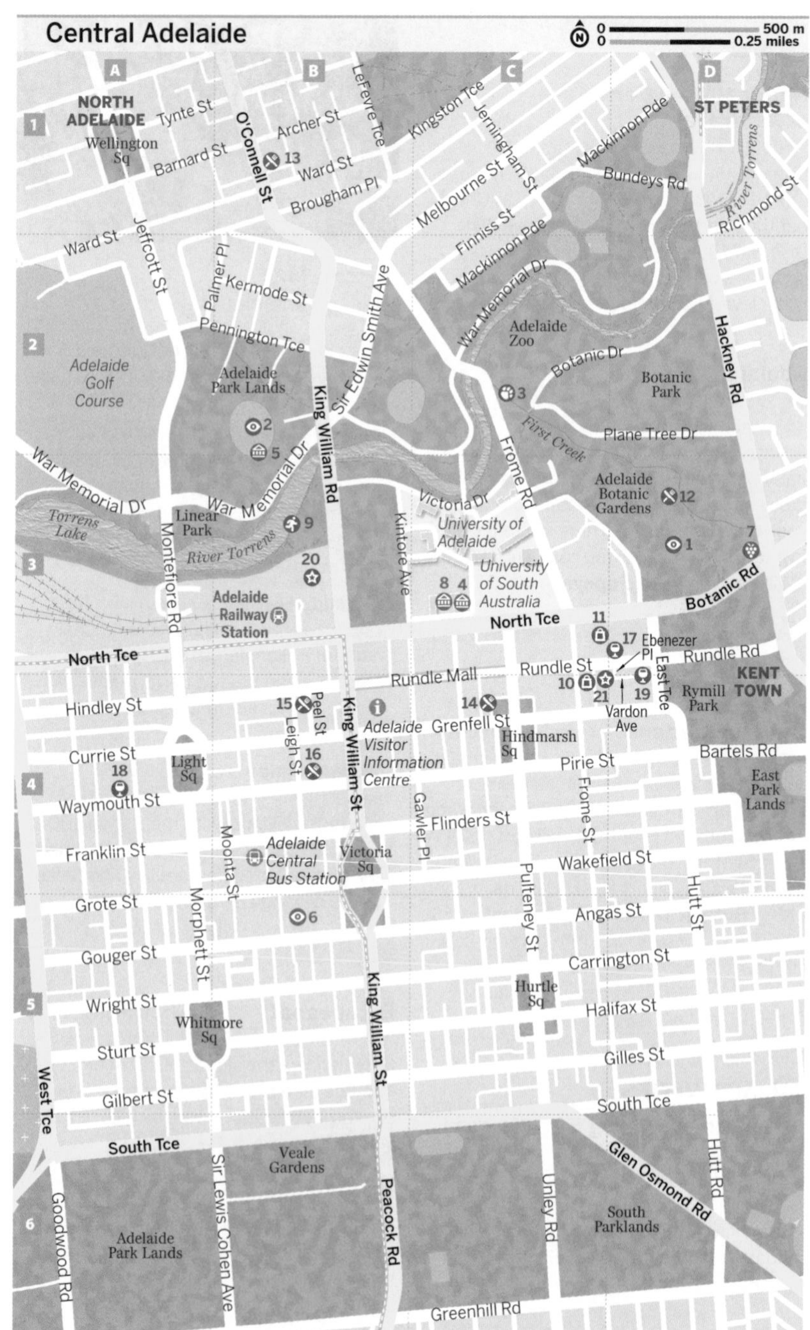
Central Adelaide
0 500 m
0 0.25 miles
NORTH ADELAIDE
Wellington Sq
Tynte St
Barnard St
Archer St
Ward St
Brougham Pl
O'Connell St
LeFevre Tce
Kingston Tce
Jerningham St
Melbourne St
Mackinnon Pde
Bundeys Rd
ST PETERS
River Torrens
Richmond St
Finniss St
Ward St
Jeffcott St
Palmer Pl
Kermode St
Pennington Tce
Sir Edwin Smith Ave
War Memorial Dr
Adelaide Zoo
Botanic Dr
Botanic Park
Hackney Rd
Adelaide Golf Course
Adelaide Park Lands
King William Rd
First Creek
Plane Tree Dr
Frome Rd
Adelaide Botanic Gardens
Torrens Lake
Linear Park
Victoria Dr
University of Adelaide
River Torrens
Kintore Ave
University of South Australia
Botanic Rd
Montefiore Rd
Adelaide Railway Station
North Tce
Ebenezer Pl
Rundle Rd
KENT TOWN
Rundle Mall
Rundle St
East Tce
Rymill Park
Vardon Ave
Hindley St
Peel St
Leigh St
King William St
Adelaide Visitor Information Centre
Grenfell St
Hindmarsh Sq
Currie St
Light Sq
Pirie St
Bartels Rd
East Park Lands
Waymouth St
Gawler Pl
Flinders St
Frome St
Franklin St
Moonta St
Adelaide Central Bus Station
Victoria Sq
Wakefield St
Pulteney St
Hutt St
Grote St
Angas St
Morphett St
Gouger St
Carrington St
Hurtle Sq
Wright St
Halifax St
Whitmore Sq
Sturt St
Gilles St
West Tce
Gilbert St
South Tce
South Tce
Glen Osmond Rd
Veale Gardens
Sir Lewis Cohen Ave
Peacock Rd
Unley Rd
Hutt Rd
Goodwood Rd
South Parklands
Adelaide Park Lands
Greenhill Rd

Central Adelaide

Sights

1 Adelaide Botanic Gardens D3
2 Adelaide Oval B2
3 Adelaide Zoo C2
4 Art Gallery of South Australia C3
5 Bradman Collection B2
6 Central Market B5
7 National Wine Centre of Australia D3
8 South Australian Museum C3

Activities, Courses & Tours

9 Popeye B3
RoofClimb Adelaide Oval .... (see 2)

Shopping

10 Miss Gladys Sym Choon C4
11 Streetlight C3

Eating

12 Botanic Gardens Restaurant D3
13 Gin Long Canteen B1
14 Jasmin Indian Restaurant C4
Lucia's Pizza & Spaghetti Bar .... (see 6)
15 Peel Street B4
16 Press B4

Drinking & Nightlife

17 Exeter Hotel D3
18 Grace Emily Hotel A4
Maybe Mae .... (see 15)
19 Nola D4

Entertainment

20 Adelaide Festival Centre B3
21 Palace Nova Eastend Cinemas C4

– art deco, pubs, North Tce, outdoor art, trees etc – get 'em on your phone and get walking.

RoofClimb Adelaide Oval Climbing

(☎08-8331 5222; www.roofclimb.com.au; Adelaide Oval, King William Rd, North Adelaide; day/twilight adult $99/109, child $69/79) Scale the lofty rooftops of the Adelaide Oval – the views are astonishing! Climbers must be at least 120cm tall, and at most 136kg. Better yet, watch Port Adelaide play a quarter of AFL football from the roof ($225).

Adelaide Sightseeing Tours

(☎1300 769 762; www.adelaidesightseeing.com.au) Runs a half-day city highlights tour ($58). Full-day city and Adelaide Hills tours also available ($98), plus jaunts to the Barossa Valley and McLaren Vale.

SHOPPING

Streetlight Books, Music

(☎08-8227 0667; www.facebook.com/streetlightadelaide; 2/15 Vaughan Pl; ⏰10am-6pm Mon-Thu & Sat, to 9pm Fri, noon-5pm Sun) Lefty, arty and subversive in the best possible way, Streetlight is the place to find that elusive Miles Davis disc or Charles Bukowski poetry compilation.

Miss Gladys Sym Choon Fashion & Accessories

(☎08-8223 1500; www.missgladyssymchoon.com.au; 235a Rundle St; ⏰9.30am-6pm Mon-Thu, to 9pm Fri, 10am-5.30pm Sat, 11am-5.30pm Sun) Named after a famed Rundle St trader from the 1920s, this hip shop is the place for fab frocks, rockin' boots, street-beating sneakers, jewellery, watches and hats.

EATING

Lucia's Pizza & Spaghetti Bar Italian $

(☎08-8231 2303; www.lucias.com.au; Shop 3, Central Western Mall, Central Market; meals $8-15; ⏰7am-4pm Mon-Thu & Sat, to 9pm Fri) This little slice of Italy in the Central Market has been around since Lucia was a lot younger. All her pasta, sauces and pizzas are authentically homemade – perfection any time of day.

Peel Street Modern Australian, Asian $$

(☎08-8231 8887; www.peelst.com.au; 9 Peel St; mains $20-35; ⏰7.30am-10.30pm Mon & Wed-Fri, 7.30am-4.30pm Tue, 6-10.30pm Sat) Peel St is a super cool cafe/bistro/wine bar that just keeps packing 'em in: glam city girls sit at window seats nibbling

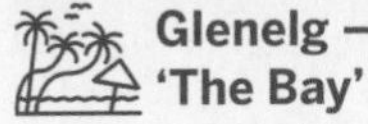

Glenelg – 'The Bay'

Glenelg, or 'the Bay' – the site of SA's colonial landing – is Adelaide at its most LA. Glenelg's beach faces towards the west, and as the sun sinks into the sea, the pubs and bars burgeon with surfies, backpackers and sun-damaged sexagenarians. The tram rumbles in from the city, past the Jetty Rd shopping strip to the alfresco cafes around Moseley Sq.

The **Glenelg Visitor Information Centre** (08-8294 5833; www.glenelgsa.com.au; Glenelg Town Hall, Moseley Sq; 9am-5pm Mon-Fri, 10am-2pm Sat & Sun, reduced winter hours) has the local lowdown, including information on diving and sailing opportunities and Aboriginal heritage.

From the city, take the tram or bus 167, 168 or 190 to get here.

Glenelg beach
IVO ANTONIE DE ROOIJ/SHUTTERSTOCK ©

parmesan-crumbed parsnips and turkey meatballs with preserved lemon. Killer wine list.

Gin Long Canteen Asian $$
(08-7120 2897; www.ginlongcanteen.com.au; 42 O'Connell St, North Adelaide; small plates $9-15, mains $18-45; noon-2.30pm Tue-Fri, 5.30pm-late Tue-Sat) This energetic food room is a winner. Chipper staff allocate you a space at the communal tables (bookings only for six or more) and take your order pronto. The food arrives just as fast: fab curries, slow-braised Thai beef and pork, netted spring rolls, Malay curry puffs...

Jasmin Indian Restaurant Indian $$
(08-8223 7837; www.jasmin.com.au; Basement level, 31 Hindmarsh Sq; mains $17-29; noon-2.30pm Thu & Fri, 5.30-9pm Tue-Sat) Enter this basement wonderland for magical north Indian curries and consummately professional staff. There's nothing too surprising about the menu, but it's done to absolute perfection.

Press Modern Australian $$$
(08-8211 8048; www.pressfoodandwine.com.au; 40 Waymouth St; mains $16-46; noon-late Mon-Sat) Press is super-stylish (brick, glass, lemon-coloured chairs) and not afraid of offal (pan-fried lamb's brains, sweetbreads, grilled calf's tongue) or things raw (beef carpaccio, gravlax salmon). Tasting menu $68 per person. Book a table upstairs, or they'll fit you in downstairs near the bar.

DRINKING & NIGHTLIFE

Exeter Hotel Pub
(08-8223 2623; www.theexeter.com.au; 246 Rundle St; 11am-late) This legendary boozer attracts an eclectic brew of postwork, punk and uni drinkers, shaking the day off their backs. Pull up a bar stool or nab a table in the grungy beer garden and settle in for the evening. Original music nightly.

Nola Bar
(www.nolaadelaide.com; 28 Vardon Ave; 4pm-midnight Tue-Thu, noon-2am Fri & Sat, 11am-midnight Sun) Craft beers, American and Australian whiskies (no Scotch!), Cajun cooking (gumbo, oysters, jambalaya, fried chicken) and regular live jazz – a bit of saucy Deep South in Adelaide's East End.

Maybe Mae Bar
(0421 405 039; www.maybemae.com; 15 Peel St; 5pm-late Mon-Fri, 6pm-late Sat & Sun) If you can't find the door here, you won't be the first thirsty punter to wander away looking confused. But once you're inside, let the good times roll: classic rock, cool staff, booth seats and brilliant beers. Love it!

Grace Emily Hotel Pub
(☎08-8231 5500; www.graceemilyhotel.com.au; 232 Waymouth St; ⏰4pm-late) The 'Gracie' has live music most nights (alt-rock, country, acoustic, open-mike nights), kooky '50s-meets-voodoo decor, open fires and great beers.

ENTERTAINMENT

Governor Hindmarsh Hotel Live Music
(☎08-8340 0744; www.thegov.com.au; 59 Port Rd, Hindmarsh; ⏰11am-late) Ground zero for live music in Adelaide, 'The Gov' hosts some legendary local and international acts. The main room hosts rock, folk, jazz, blues, salsa, reggae and dance.

Palace Nova Eastend Cinemas Cinema
(☎08-8232 3434; www.palacecinemas.com.au; 250-51 Rundle St; tickets adult/child $19.50/15.50; ⏰10am-late) Facing-off across Rundle St, both these cinema complexes screen 'sophisticated cinema': new-release art-house, foreign-language and independent films as well as some mainstream flicks.

Adelaide Festival Centre Performing Arts
(☎08-8216 8600; www.adelaidefestivalcentre.com.au; King William Rd; ⏰box office 9am-6pm Mon-Fri) The hub of performing arts in SA, this crystalline white Festival Centre opened in June 1973, four proud months before the Sydney Opera House! The State Theatre Company (www.statetheatrecompany.com.au) is based here.

INFORMATION

Adelaide Visitor Information Centre (☎1300 588 140; www.adelaidecitycouncil.com; 9 James Pl, off Rundle Mall; ⏰9am-5pm Mon-Fri, 10am-4pm Sat & Sun, 11am-3pm public holidays) Adelaide-specific information, plus abundant info on SA including fab regional booklets.

Royal Adelaide Hospital (☎08-8222 4000; www.rah.sa.gov.au; 275 North Tce; ⏰24hr) Emergency department. By the time you read this, the

Rower on River Torrens

DIANA MAYFIELD/GETTY IMAGES ©

AMOPHOTO_AU/SHUTTERSTOCK ©

From left: Blue King Brown perform at the Governor Hindmarsh Hotel (p213); Tram at Moseley Square stop; Cycling along River Torrens

new RAH, at the junction of North Tce and Port Rd, will probably be up and running.

 GETTING THERE & AWAY

AIR

International and interstate flights service **Adelaide Airport** (ADL; ☎08-8308 9211; www.adelaideairport.com.au; 1 James Schofield Dr), 7km west of the city centre. Domestic operators flying direct to most capitals include **Jetstar** (www.jetstar.com.au), **Qantas** (www.qantas.com.au), **Tiger Air** (www.tigerair.com.au) and **Virgin Australia** (www.virginaustralia.com.au).

BUS

Adelaide Central Bus Station (☎08 8221 5080; www.adelaidemetro.com.au/bussa; 85 Franklin St; ⏱6am-9.30pm) is the hub for interstate bus services. Note: there is no Adelaide–Perth bus service.

Firefly Express (☎1300 730 740; www.fireflyexpress.com.au) Runs between Sydney, Melbourne and Adelaide.

Greyhound Australia (☎1300 473 946; www.greyhound.com.au) Runs between Adelaide and Melbourne, Canberra, Sydney, Alice Springs and Darwin.

V/Line (☎1800 800 007; www.vline.com.au) Bus and bus/train services between Adelaide and Melbourne.

TRAIN

Interstate trains run by **Great Southern Rail** (☎1800 703 357, 08 8213 4401; www.greatsouthernrail.com.au) grind into the **Adelaide Parklands Terminal** (Railway Tce, Keswick; ⏱6am-5pm Mon & Fri, 6.30am-5.30pm Tue, 9am-5pm Wed, to 7pm Thu, 8.30am-1pm Sun), 1km southwest of the city centre. Services:

The Ghan to Alice Springs (from $799, 19 hours)

The Ghan to Darwin (from $1499, 47 hours)

The Indian Pacific to Perth (from $1189, 39 hours)

The Indian Pacific to Sydney (from $589, 25 hours)

The Overland to Melbourne (from $149, 11 hours)

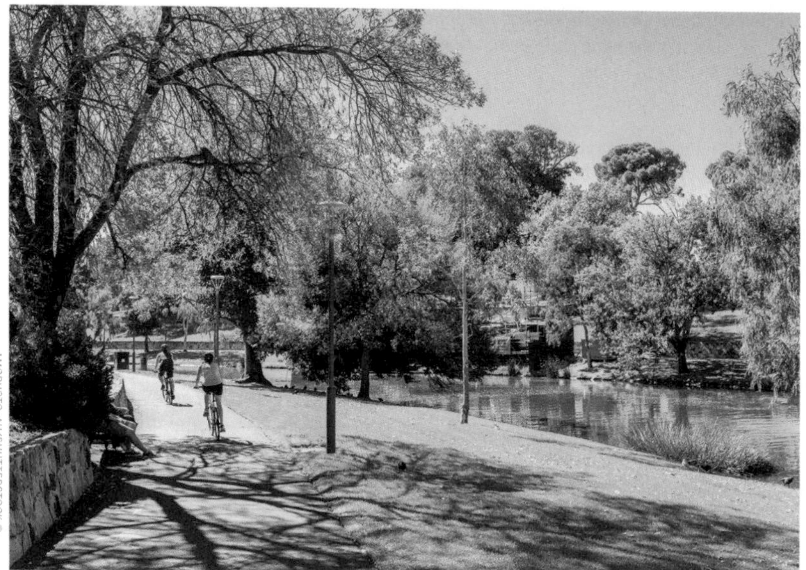
AMOPHOTO_AU/SHUTTERSTOCK ©

GETTING AROUND

TO/FROM THE AIRPORT

Prebooked **Adelaide Airport Flyer** (☎08-8353 5233, 1300 856 444; www.adelaideairportflyer.com) minibuses run door-to-door between the airport and the city ($35).

Adelaide Metro **JetExpress and JetBus** (www.adelaidemetro.com.au/timetables/special-services; $3.20-5.10; ⊙6.30am-11pm Mon-Fri, 7.15am-11pm Sat & Sun) bus services – routes J1, J1X, J3, J7 and J8 – connect the airport with Glenelg and the CBD; standard Metro fares apply.

Taxis charge around $30 into the city.

BICYCLE

Adelaide is pizza-flat: great for cycling! With a valid passport or driver's licence you can borrow an **Adelaide Free Bike** from **Bicycle SA** (☎08-8168 9999; www.bikesa.asn.au; 53 Carrington St; ⊙9am-5pm Mon-Fri, 8am-5pm Sat & Sun). There are a couple of dozen locations around town.

Down at the beach, try **Glenelg Bicycle Hire** (☎08-8376 1934; www.glenelgbicyclehire.com.au; Norfolk Motel, 71 Broadway, Glenelg South; bikes per day $25, tandems per hour/day $25/50).

PUBLIC TRANSPORT

Adelaide Metro (☎1300 311 108; www.adelaidemetro.com.au; cnr King William & Currie Sts; ⊙8am-6pm Mon-Fri, 9am-5pm Sat, 11am-4pm Sun) runs Adelaide's integrated bus, train and tram network.

Tickets can be purchased on board, at staffed train stations and in delis and newsagents across the city. Ticket types include day trip ($10), two-hour peak ($5.30) and two-hour off-peak ($3.40). A three-day, unlimited-travel visitor pass is $26. Save at least $1 per trip with a rechargeable multi-trip Metrocard.

BUS

Adelaide's buses start around 6am and run until midnight.

Every 30 minutes, **Free City Loop buses** (☎1300 311 108; www.adelaidemetro.com.au/timetables/special-services; ⊙9am-7.15pm Sat-Thu, to 9.15pm Fri) – routes 98A and 98C – run clockwise and anticlockwise around the CBD, passing North Tce, Victoria Sq, Hutt St, the Central Market and North Adelaide. The 99A and 99C buses ply the same route (minus North Adelaide), Monday to Friday.

TRAIN

Adelaide's trains depart from **Adelaide Station** (www.railmaps.com.au/adelaide.htm; North Tce), plying five suburban routes (Belair, Gawler, Grange, Noarlunga and Outer Harbour). Trains run between 6am and midnight (some start at 4.30am).

TRAM

Adelaide's trams follow a single track from Glenelg, through the city and along North Tce to the Adelaide Entertainment Centre. Trams run every 10 to 15 minutes from 5.30am to midnight. Standard Metro fares apply; the section between South Tce and the Adelaide Entertainment Centre is free.

Cycling the Barossa

From Tanunda, a 14km **rail trail** continues through Nuriootpa to Angaston, passing plenty of wineries. Pick up the *Barossa by Bike* brochure at the **Barossa Visitor Information Centre** (p218), or download one from its website.

Based in Nuriootpa, **Barossa Bike Hire** (☎0400 537 770; www.barossabikehire.com; 5 South Tce; 9am-5pm) rents out quality cycles/tandems from $40/70 per day (pick-up price; bikes can be delivered for $10/20 extra). In Tanunda, the **Barossa Cycle Hub** (☎08-8563 0600, 1300 852 982; www.barossa.com; 70 Murray St; 9am-5pm Mon-Fri, to 4pm Sat, 10am-4pm Sun) has bikes per half-/full day for $30/44. **Angaston Hardware** (☎08-8564 2055; www.angastonhardware.com.au; 5 Sturt St; 8.30am-5.30pm Mon-Fri, 9am-4pm Sat, 10am-4pm Sun) also rents out bikes for $25/35 per half-/full day. **Uber Cycle Adventures** (☎08-8563 1148; www.ubercycle.com.au; 2hr/half-day/full-day tours $95/145/195) runs cycling tours from two hours to a full day.

TAXI

Suburban Taxis (☎13 10 08; www.suburbantaxis.com.au) Taxis, all suburbs.

Yellow Cabs (☎13 22 27; www.yellowcabgroup.com.au) Regular cabs (most of which are white!).

Barossa Valley

The Barossa is a compact valley – just 25km long – yet it manages to produce 21% of Australia's wine. The local towns – Tanunda, Angaston and Nuriootpa are the big three – have a distinctly German heritage, dating back to 1842. Fleeing religious persecution in Prussia and Silesia, settlers (bringing their vine cuttings with them) created a Lutheran heartland where German traditions endure today (...a passion for oom-pah bands, wurst, pretzels and sauerkraut).

SIGHTS

Mengler's Hill Lookout Viewpoint
(Menglers Hill Rd) From Tanunda, take the scenic route to Angaston via Bethany for hazy valley views. The road tracks through beautiful rural country, studded with huge eucalyptuses.

Keg Factory Factory
(☎08-8563 3012; www.thekegfactory.com.au; 25 St Hallett Rd; 8am-4pm Mon-Fri, 11am-4pm Sat & Sun) FREE Watch honest-to-goodness coopers make and repair wine barrels, 4km south of town. Amazing!

TOURS

Barossa Explorer Tours
(☎0423 376 155; www.barossaexplorer.com; per person/family $30/100; 10am-5pm Thu-Sun) Jump aboard this hop-on, hop-off tourist bus, which loops past nine handy Barossa sites. Do the whole loop in an hour, or take your own sweet time about it. Tickets are valid for 24 hours.

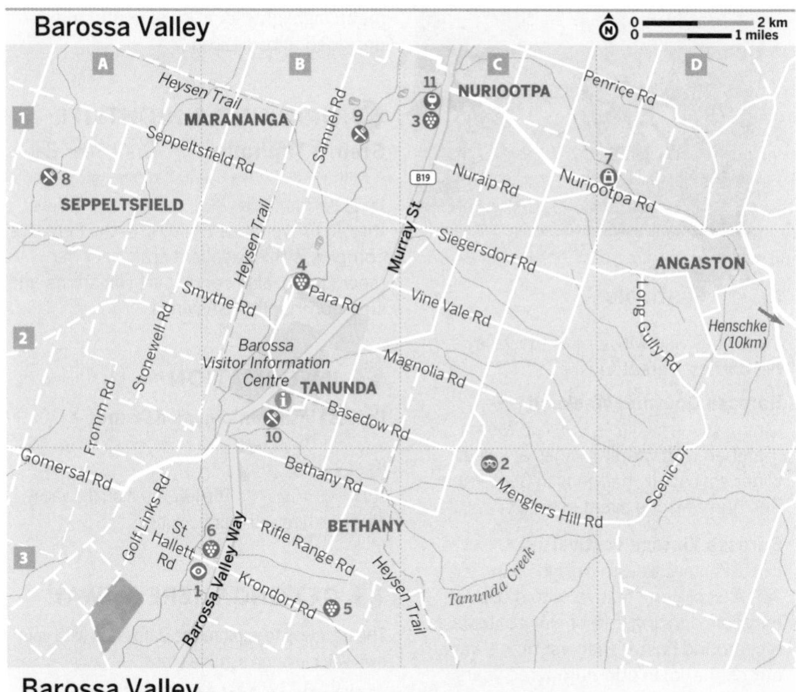

Barossa Valley

Sights

1 Keg Factory A3
2 Mengler's Hill Lookout C3
3 Penfolds C1
4 Peter Lehmann Wines B2
5 Rockford Wines B3
6 St Hallett B3

Shopping

7 Barossa Farmers Market D1

Eating

8 Fino Seppeltsfield A1
9 Maggie Beer's Farm Shop B1
10 Red Door Espresso B2

Drinking & Nightlife

11 Stein's Taphouse C1

SHOPPING

Barossa Farmers Market Market

(☎0402 026 882; www.barossafarmersmarket.com; cnr Stockwell & Nuriootpa Rds; ⊙7.30-11.30am Sat) Happens in the big farm shed behind Vintners Bar & Grill every Saturday. Expect hearty Germanic offerings, coffee, flowers, lots of local produce and questionable buskers.

EATING

Maggie Beer's Farm Shop Deli $

(☎08-8562 4477; www.maggiebeer.com.au; 50 Pheasant Farm Rd; items $5-20, picnic baskets from $16; ⊙10.30am-5pm) Celebrity SA gourmet Maggie Beer has been hugely successful with her range of condiments, preserves and pâtés (and TV appearances!). Stop by for some gourmet tastings, an ice cream or a takeaway hamper of delicious bites.

Barossa Festivals

Time your visit with one of the valley's big parties – great fun!

Barossa Gourmet Weekend (www.barossagourmet.com; Sep) Fab food matched with winning wines at select wineries; usually happens in September. The number-one event in the valley.

Barossa Vintage Festival (www.barossavintagefestival.com.au; Mar/Apr) A week-long festival with music, maypole dancing, tug-of-war contests etc; around Easter (harvest time – very atmospheric) in odd-numbered years.

SVITLANA BOYKO/SHUTTERSTOCK ©

Red Door Espresso Cafe $$
(08-8563 1181; www.reddoorespresso.com; 79 Murray St; mains breakfast $8-26, lunch $12-30; 7.30am-4pm Mon, to 5pm Wed-Sat, 9.30am-4pm Sun;) It's rare in the Barossa for good cafe food, coffee, staff, music and atmosphere to come together this well. The avocado and basil-infused eggs Benedict is a winner. Live music over weekend brunch; wine, cheese and antipasto in the afternoons.

Fino Seppeltsfield Modern Australian $$$
(08-8562 8528; www.fino.net.au; 730 Seppeltsfield Rd, Seppeltsfield; small/large plates from $22/46; noon-3pm daily, 6-8.30pm Fri & Sat) Fino is one of Australia's best restaurants, ensconced in the gorgeous 1851 Seppeltsfield estate west of Tanunda. Food from the understated, deceptively simple menu highlights local ingredients, and is designed to be shared.

DRINKING & NIGHTLIFE

Stein's Taphouse Craft Beer, Bar
(08-8562 2899; www.steinstaphouse.com.au; 18-28 Barossa Valley Way; noon-late) Inside the old Provenance Building in the Penfolds complex is this excellent craft beer bar (sacrilege?), also serving artisan spirits and small-production SA wines.

INFORMATION

Barossa Visitor Information Centre (1300 852 982, 08-8563 0600; www.barossa.com; 66-68 Murray St; 9am-5pm Mon-Fri, to 4pm Sat, 10am-4pm Sun;) The low-down on the valley, plus bike hire and tour bookings.

GETTING THERE & AWAY

The best way to explore the Barossa is with your own vehicle or on a guided tour.

Alternatively, **Adelaide Metro** (www.adelaidemetro.com.au) runs regular daily trains from Adelaide to Gawler ($5.30, one hour), from where **LinkSA** (www.linksa.com.au) buses run to Tanunda ($10.10), Nuriootpa ($12.80) and Angaston ($15.60).

GETTING AROUND

Tanunda, Angaston and Nuriootpa are all a 10-minute drive from each other.

Barossa Taxis (0411 150 850; www.barossataxis.com.au; 24hr) Taxis for up to nine people.

McLaren Vale

On the Fleurieu Peninsula, flanked by the wheat-coloured Willunga Scarp and striated with vines, McLaren Vale is just 40 minutes south of Adelaide. Servicing the wine industry, it's an energetic, utilitarian town with some great eateries and easy access to some truly excellent winery cellar doors.

ACTIVITIES

Shiraz Trail Cycling, Walking

(www.walkingsa.org.au) Get the McLaren Vale vibe on this 8km walking/cycling track, along an old railway line between McLaren Vale and Willunga. Hire a bike from **Oxygen Cycles** (08-8323 7345; www.oxygencycles.com; 143 Main Rd; bike hire per half-day/full day/overnight $15/25/40; 10am-6pm Tue-Fri, 9am-5pm Sat, plus Sun & Mon Dec-Feb); ask the visitor information centre for a map.

EATING

Blessed Cheese Cafe, Deli $

(08-8323 7958; www.blessedcheese.com.au; 150 Main Rd; mains $11-18; 8am-4pm Mon-Fri, to 5pm Sat, 9am-4pm Sun) The staff at this blessed cafe crank out great coffee, croissants, wraps, salads, tarts, burgers, cheese platters, massive cakes and funky sausage rolls. Sniff the aromas emanating from the cheese counter – deliciously stinky!

Salopian Inn Modern Australian $$$

(08-8323 8769; www.salopian.com.au; cnr Main & McMurtrie Rds; mains $30-33; noon-3.30pm daily, 6pm-late Thu-Sat) This old vine-covered inn has been here since 1851. Its latest incarnation features super Mod Oz offerings with an Asian twist: launch into the Berkshire pork buns or blue swimmer crab and prawn dumplings, with a bottle of something local which you can hand-select from the cellar.

INFORMATION

McLaren Vale & Fleurieu Visitor Information Centre (1800 628 410, 08-8323 9944; www.mclarenvale.info; 796 Main Rd; 9am-5pm Mon-Fri, 10am-4pm Sat & Sun) Winery info, plus the *McLaren Vale Heritage Trail* brochure for a historic walk around town.

GETTING THERE & AWAY

It is possible to get here via public transport via train then bus, but hey, life's too short. Drive or take a tour instead.

McLaren Vale wine region

Accordian player next to the German Village Shop in Hahndorf

Adelaide Hills

When the Adelaide plains are desert-hot in the summer months, the Adelaide Hills (technically the Mt Lofty Ranges) are always a few degrees cooler, with crisp air, woodland shade and labyrinthine valleys. Early colonists built stately summer houses around Stirling and Aldgate, and German settlers escaping religious persecution also arrived, infusing towns like Hahndorf with European values and architecture.

SIGHTS

Mt Lofty Summit Viewpoint

(08-8370 1054; www.environment.sa.gov.au/parks; Mt Lofty Summit Rd, Crafers; 24hr) FREE From Cleland Wildlife Park you can bushwalk (2km) or drive up to Mt Lofty Summit (a surprising 727m), which has show-stopping views across Adelaide. **Mt Lofty Summit Visitor Information Centre** (9am-5pm) has info on local attractions and walking tracks, including the steep Waterfall Gully Track (8km return, 3½ hours).

Cleland Wildlife Park Wildlife Reserve

(08-8339 2444; www.clelandwildlifepark.sa.gov.au; 365 Mt Lofty Summit Rd, Crafers; adult/child/family $25/12/56; 9.30am-5pm, last entry 4.30pm) Within the steep **Cleland Conservation Park** (08-8278 5477; www.environment.sa.gov.au/parks; 24hr) FREE, this place lets you interact with all kinds of Australian beasts. There are keeper talks and feeding sessions throughout the day, plus occasional Night Walks (adult/child $50/40) and you can have your mugshot taken with a koala.

TOURS

Tour Adelaide Hills Tours

(08-8563 1000; www.touradelaidehills.com; full-day tours per person $155) Full-day tours through the Hills with views, vines and fine food (chocolate, strawberries and cheese... not all at once).

SHOPPING

Stirling Markets Market

(☎0488 770 166; www.stirlingmarket.com.au; Druid Ave, Stirling; ⏰10am-4pm 4th Sun of the month, 3rd Sun in Dec) Market stalls fill oak-lined Druid Ave: much plant-life, busking, pies, cakes, affluent locals with dogs and Hills knick-knackery (not many druids...).

EATING

Seasonal Garden Cafe Cafe $$

(☎08-8388 7714; www.facebook.com/theseasonalgardencafe; 100 Main St, Hanhdorf; mains $10-25; ⏰7.30am-4.30pm Mon-Fri, to 5.30pm Sat & Sun;) This zero-waste cafe is adorned with piles of pumpkins and strings of chubby chillies. Food-wise, it has good coffee, grass-green smoothies and lots of local, seasonal and organic ingredients (try the potted baked eggs with house-made beans).

Fred Eatery Cafe $$

(☎08-8339 1899; www.fredeatery.com.au; 220 Mt Barker Rd, Aldgate; mains $11-26; ⏰7.30am-4pm Tue-Sun, plus 6-9pm Fri;) Fred is a rather urbane fellow, decked out in green, black and white, with a savvy cityside menu, killer coffee and great staff. The bodacious Reuben sandwich is calorific heaven.

DRINKING & NIGHTLIFE

Prancing Pony Brewery

(☎08-8398 3881; www.prancingponybrewery.com.au; 42 Mt Barker Rd, Totness; ⏰10am-6pm Mon-Thu, to 10pm Fri & Sat, to 8pm Sun) Prize-winning craft beers, burgers, platters, bar snacks and live troubadours all make an appearance at this funky beer shed, on the road out of Mt Barker heading for Hahndorf.

INFORMATION

Adelaide Hills Visitor Information Centre

(☎1800 353 323, 08-8388 1185; www.adelaidehills.org.au; 68 Main St; ⏰9am-5pm Mon-Fri, 10am-4pm Sat & Sun) The usual barrage of brochures, plus accommodation bookings. In Hahndorf.

ULURU & THE OUTBACK

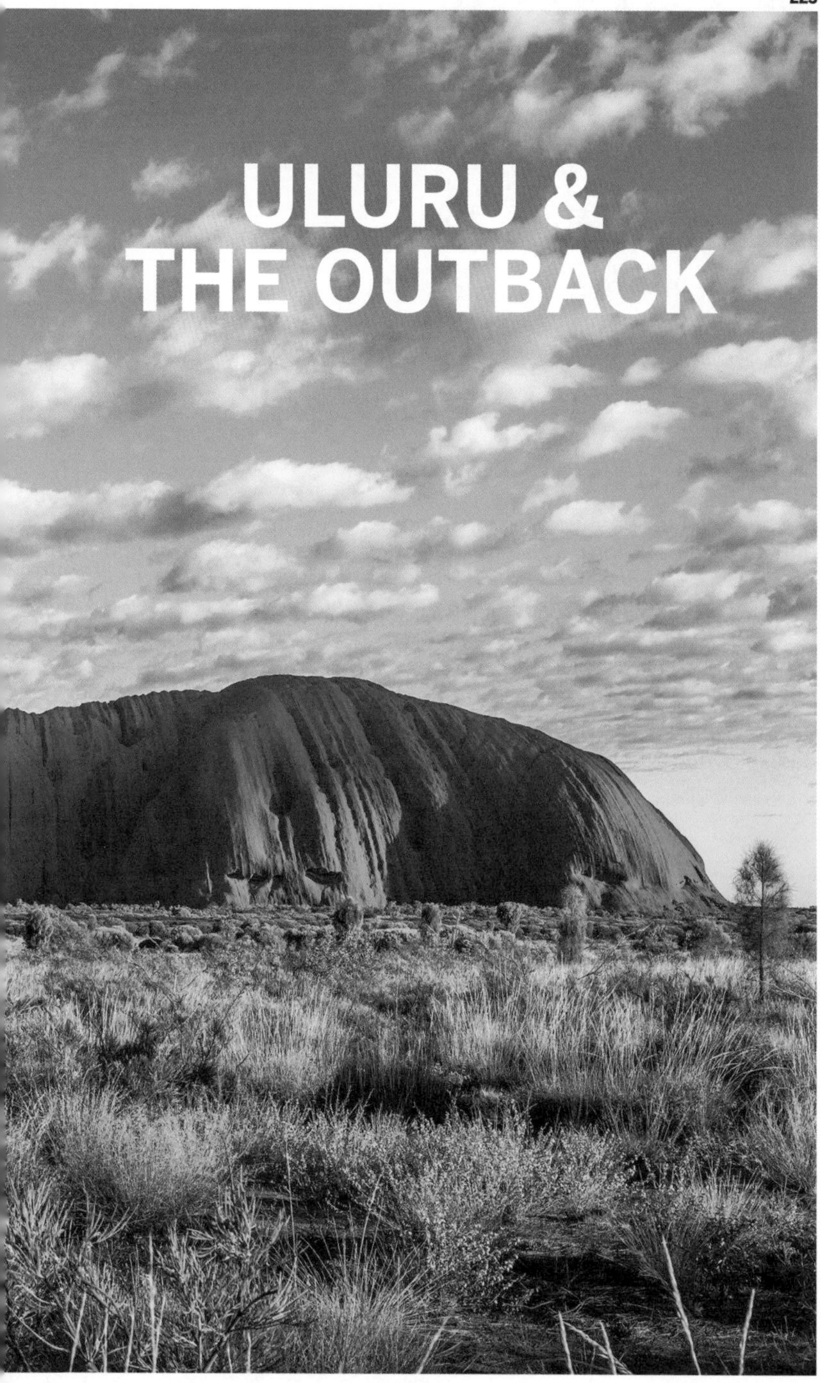

In this Chapter

Uluru & the Outback at a Glance...

Nothing can prepare you for the immensity, grandeur, changing colours and stillness of Uluru – a sight that will sear itself onto your mind. This World Heritage–listed icon has attained pilgrimage status for many Australians. There's plenty to see and do once you get here: walks, bike rides, cultural tours...

Equally impressive Kata Tjuta and the surrounding desert are of deep cultural significance to the traditional Anangu owners.

Alice Springs is the biggest town in the Australian Outback – an urban oasis – while Yulara is Uluru's busy service town, 20km from 'the Rock'.

Uluru & the Outback in Two Days

Fly directly to **Yulara** (p232) to maximise your time in **Uluru-Kata Tjuta National Park** (p227). Head straight to the **Uluru-Kata Tjuta Cultural Centre** (p226) and book yourself onto a ranger-led tour of Uluru. Head to the **sunset viewing area** (p228) at dusk to see the desert colours shift. On day two, take a tour or a drive to explore **Kata Tjuta** (p230).

Uluru & the Outback in Four Days

With four days to play with, you might want to do some bike riding around Uluru, sign up for a **scenic flight** (p229), or at least tackle a couple of **independent walks** (p231). **Alice Springs** (p233) is also worth a visit – a unique, isolated desert town with a brilliant **wildlife park** (p237) and excellent Aboriginal art galleries.

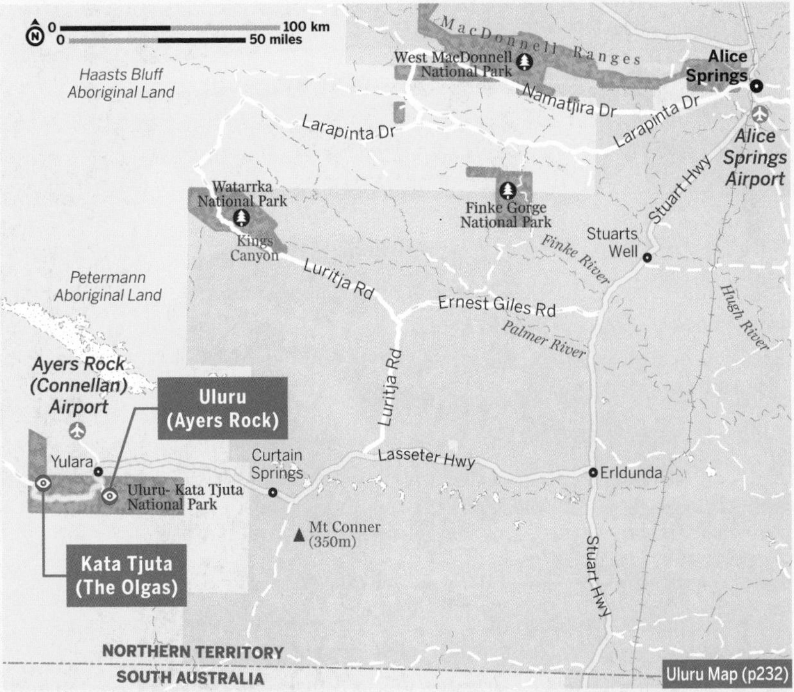

Uluru Map (p232)

Arriving in Uluru & the Outback

Yulara Gateway to the park, Yulara has an airport with flights from major Australian cities. It's also serviced by buses and tours from Alice Springs. If you're driving, the sealed route from Alice Springs (447km) is via the Stuart and then Lasseter Hwys.

Alice Springs Well connected by air to capital cities. Also accessible by train and bus.

Where to Stay

Alice Springs has plenty of hotels, motels and resorts if you're spending any time there. Out at Uluru, the only accommodation is at Yulara, 20km away. There are 5000 beds here – campgrounds, a hostel, apartments and resort-style hotels – but you still need to book ahead through a central reservations system. Expect premium prices, reflecting the remote locale.

View of Uluru at sunrise from the back of a van

Uluru (Ayers Rock)

The first sighting of Uluru on the horizon will astound even the most jaded traveller. Solitary and prodigious, it's 3.6km long and towers 348m above the surrounding scrub.

Great For...

☑ Don't Miss

Wonderful rock art in shelters along the Mala Walk and Kuniya Walk to Mutitjulu Waterhole.

The Big Rock

Uluru is undeniably huge, but it's believed that two-thirds of the rock lies beneath the sand! Close inspection reveals a wondrously contoured surface concealing numerous sacred sites of particular significance to the Anangu.

If your first look at Uluru is in the afternoon, it appears to be ochre-brown, scored and pitted by dark shadows. As the sun sets, it illuminates the rock in burnished orange, then a series of deeper reds before it fades into charcoal. A performance in reverse, with marginally fewer spectators, is given at dawn.

Exploring Uluru

Uluru-Kata Tjuta Cultural Centre (☎08-8956 1128; www.parksaustralia.gov.au/uluru/do/

Dot painting

SHAANA MCNAUGHT/TOURISM NT ©

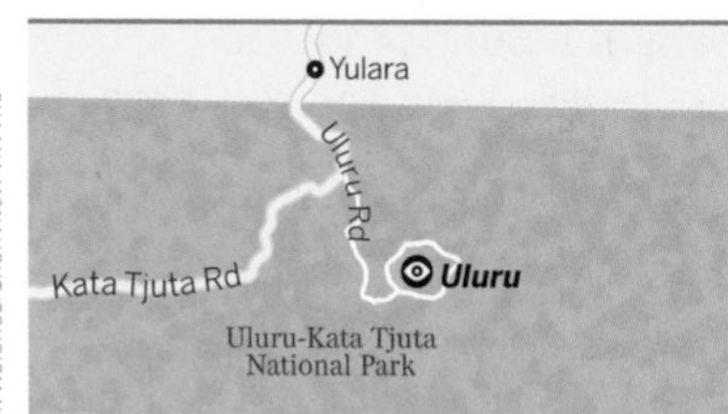

Need to Know

Uluru-Kata Tjuta National Park; www.parksaustralia.gov.au/uluru; adult/child 3-day pass $25/free; sunrise-sunset

Take a Break

The **Tali Wiru** (02-8296 8010; www.ayersrockresort.com.au; per person $325; Apr–mid-Oct) outdoor dining experience (atop a dune!) can be magical.

★ Top Tip

The sunset viewing area is the best place for those classic, saffron-red rock shots.

cultural-centre.html; 7am-6pm) is 1km before Uluru on the road from Yulara and should be your first stop. Displays and exhibits focus on *tjukurpa* (Aboriginal law, religion and custom) and the history and management of the national park. The information desk in the Nintiringkupai building is staffed by park rangers who supply the informative *Visitor Guide & Maps*, leaflets and walking notes.

Walks

There are several established walking tracks around Uluru. Ranger-led walks explain the area's plants, wildlife, geology and cultural significance. The excellent *Visitor Guide & Maps* brochure from the Cultural Centre details a few self-guided walks.

Base Walk This track (10.6km, three to four hours) circumnavigates the rock, passing caves, paintings, sandstone folds and geological abrasions along the way.

Liru Walk Links the Cultural Centre with the start of the Mala walk and climb, and winds through strands of mulga before opening up near Uluru (4km return, 1½ hours).

Mala Walk From the base of the climbing point (2km return, one hour), interpretive signs explain the *tjukurpa* of the Mala (hare-wallaby people), which is significant to the Anangu, as well as fine examples of rock art. A ranger-guided walk (free) along this route departs at 10am (8am from October to April) from the car park.

Kuniya Walk A short walk (1km return, 45 minutes) from the car park on the southern side leads to the most permanent waterhole, Mutitjulu, home of the ancestral watersnake. Great birdwatching and some excellent rock art are highlights of this walk.

Sunset & Sunrise Views

About halfway between Yulara and Uluru, the sunset viewing area has plenty of car and coach parking for that familiar postcard view. The Talinguru Nyakunytjaku sunrise viewing area is perched on a sand dune and captures both Uluru and Kata Tjuta in all their glory. It also has two great interpretive walks (1.5km) about women's and men's business. There's a shaded viewing area, toilets and a place to picnic.

A Question of Climbing

Many visitors consider climbing Uluru to be a highlight of a trip to the Centre, and even a rite of passage. But for the traditional owners, the Anangu, Uluru is a sacred place. The path up the side of Uluru is part of the route taken by the Mala ancestors on their arrival at Uluru and has great spiritual significance – and is not to be trampled by human feet. When you arrive at Uluru you'll see a sign from the Anangu saying 'We don't climb', and a request that you don't climb either.

The Anangu are the custodians of Uluru and take responsibility for the safety of visitors. Any injuries or deaths that occur are a source of distress and sadness to them. For similar reasons of public safety, Parks Australia would prefer that people didn't climb. It's a very steep ascent, not to be taken lightly, and each year there are several air rescues, mostly from people suffering heart attacks.

A commitment has been made to close the climb for good, but only when there are adequate new visitor experiences in place or when the proportion of visitors climbing

Helicopter view of Uluru

falls below 20%. Until then, it remains a personal decision and a question of respect. Before deciding, visit the Cultural Centre and perhaps take an Anangu guided tour.

Tours of Uluru

Sounds of Silence Tours

(☎08-8957 7448; www.ayersrockresort.com.au/sounds-of-silence; adult/child $195/96) Waiters serve champagne and canapés on a desert dune with stunning sunset views of Uluru and Kata Tjuta. Then it's a buffet dinner (with emu, croc and roo) beneath the southern sky, which, after dinner, is dissected and explained with the help of a telescope. If you're more of a morning person, try the similarly styled **Desert Awakenings 4WD Tour** (☎1300 134 044; www.ayersrockresort.com.au/experiences/detail/desert-awakenings-tour; adult/child $185/145). Neither tour is suitable for children under 10 years.

Uluru Aboriginal Tours Cultural Tour

(☎0447 878 851; www.facebook.com/Uluru-Aboriginal-Tours-248457278623328; guided tours from $99) Owned and operated by Anangu from the Mutitjulu community, this company offers a range of trips to give you an insight into the significance of the Rock through the eyes of the traditional owners. Tours depart from the Cultural Centre, Yulara Ayers Rock Resort and from Alice Springs.

Ayers Rock Helicopters Scenic Flights

(☎08-8956 2077; www.new.helicoptergroup.com/arh-index; 20/40/60min scenic flight per person $115/230/360) One of the most memorable ways to see the Rock; you'll need the 40-minute flight to also take in Kata Tjuta.

Seit Outback Australia Bus

(☎08-8956 3156; www.seitoutbackaustralia.com.au) This small-group tour operator has dozens of Uluru and Kata Tjuta tours, including sunset tours around Uluru and sunrise tours at Kata Tjuta.

AAT Kings Bus

(☎08-8956 2171; www.aatkings.com) Operating the largest range of coach tours to Uluru, AAT offers a range of half- and full-day tours from Yulara.

On Your Bike

A wonderful new way of experiencing the rock is by bike, available for hire at the Cultural Centre (p226).

SHAANA MCNAUGHT/TOURISM NT ©

Tours from Alice Springs

Several bus/tour companies can take you from Alice to Uluru and back in a day: try Emu Run Experience (p235) or Gray Line (p237).

Kata Tjuta at sunset

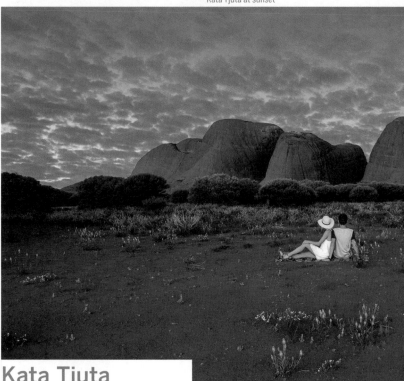

Kata Tjuta (The Olgas)

No journey to Uluru is complete without a visit to Kata Tjuta, a striking group of domed rocks huddled together about 35km west of the Rock.

Great For...

☑ Don't Miss

Kata Tjuta at sunset, when the boulders are at their glorious, blood-red best.

Big Boulders

There are 36 boulders shoulder to shoulder here, forming deep valleys and steep-sided gorges. The tallest rock, namesake Kata Tjuta (aka Mt Olga; 546m, 1066m above sea level) is approximately 200m higher than Uluru, and indeed, many visitors find them even more captivating than their prominent neighbour...but why choose?

Trails weave in among the red rocks, leading to pockets of silent beauty and spiritual gravitas. Kata Tjuta is of great *tjukurpa* significance (relating to Aboriginal law, religion and custom), particularly for Indigenous men, so stick to the tracks.

As an aside (astound friends around the campfire), the English name for Kata Tjuta, the Olgas, was bestowed in 1872 by Ernest Giles, in honour of Russian Queen Olga of Württemberg, daughter of Tsar Nicholas I.

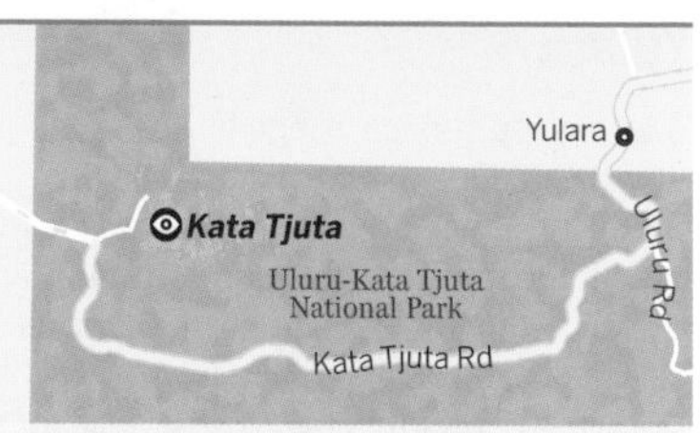

Need to Know

Uluru-Kata Tjuta National Park; www.parksaustralia.gov.au/uluru; adult/child 3-day pass $25/free; sunrise-sunset

Take a Break

There's a picnic and sunset-viewing area with toilet facilities just off the access road.

★ Top Tip

The Valley of the Winds walk sidesteps the crowds and rewards hikers with sensational views.

Indigenous Significance

The name 'Kata Tjuta' in the Pitjantjatjara language means 'many heads'. Sacred to the Anangu people, the 500-million-year-old rocks are said to be the home of the snake king Wanambi, who only comes down from his fastness atop Mt Olga in the dry season. This is, however, by no means the only legend told about the site. The majority of myths about Kata Tjuta, and the ceremonies still practised by its traditional owners, are off-limits to women and outsiders.

Walks

The 7.4km Valley of the Winds loop (two to four hours) is one of the most challenging and rewarding bushwalks in the park. It winds through the gorges giving excellent views of the surreal domes and traversing varied terrain. It's not particularly arduous, but wear sturdy shoes and take plenty of water. Starting this walk at first light often rewards you with solitude, enabling you to appreciate the sounds of the wind and bird calls carried up the valley. When the weather gets too hot, trail access is often closed by late morning.

The short signposted track beneath towering rock walls into pretty Walpa Gorge (2.6km return, 45 minutes) is especially beautiful in the afternoon, when sunlight floods the gorge. Watch for rock wallabies in the early morning or late afternoon.

Tours

Unless you're on a tour, you'll need your own wheels to reach Kata Tjuta. Many companies offering tours of Uluru can also take you to Kata Tjuta, including Seit Outback Australia (p229), Sounds of Silence (p229) and Ayers Rock Helicopters (p229).

Yulara

Yulara is the service village for the Uluru-Kata Tjuta National Park and has effectively turned one of the world's least hospitable regions into a comfortable place to stay. Lying just outside the national park, 20km from Uluru and 53km from Kata Tjuta, the complex is the closest base for exploring the park. Yulara supplies the only accommodation, food outlets and other services available in the region.

EATING

Outback Pioneer Barbecue Barbecue $$

(Outback Pioneer Hotel & Lodge; burgers $20, meat $32, salad bar $18; ⏲6-9pm) For a fun, casual night out, this lively tavern is the popular choice for everyone from backpackers to grey nomads. Choose between kangaroo skewers, prawns, veggie burgers, steaks and emu sausages, and grill them yourself at the communal BBQs. The deal includes a salad bar.

Geckos Cafe Mediterranean $$

(Town Sq; mains $19-25; ⏲noon-2.30pm & 6.30-9pm; 🍷) For great value, a warm atmosphere and tasty food, head to this buzzing licensed cafe. The wood-fired pizzas, pulled pork sliders and kangaroo burgers go well with a carafe of sangria, and the courtyard tables are a great place to enjoy the desert night air. There are several veggie and gluten-free options, plus meals can be made to take away.

Bough House Australian $$$

(Outback Pioneer Hotel & Lodge; mains $35-45; ⏲6.30-10am & 6.30-9.30pm) This family-friendly, country-style place overlooks the pool at the Outback Pioneer. Intimate candlelit dining is strangely set in a barnlike dining room. Bough House specialises in native ingredients such as lemon myrtle, kakadu plums and bush tomatoes. The

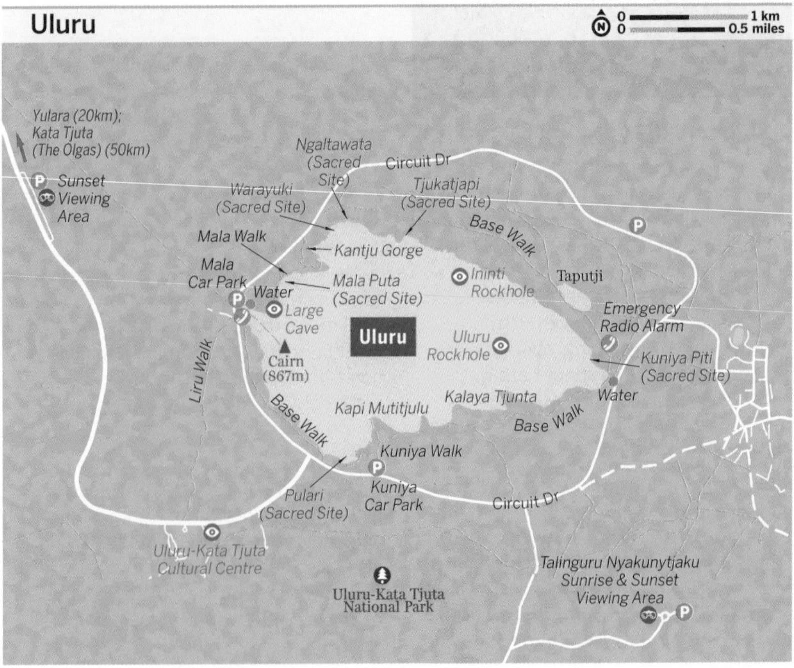

Uluru

entrée or buffet dessert is free with your main course or you can opt for the whole three courses.

Walpa Lobby Bar Modern Australian $$$
(Sails in the Desert; mains $35; 11am-10pm) If you want to treat yourself, this is the place to try. With a recent makeover, and the feel of a Hilton Hotel bar, the excellent food and friendly service make up for the slight sterility. Hot and cold seafood platters are a treat and most dishes feature Australian bush ingredients. Salads and antipasto are also available.

INFORMATION

Tour & Information Centre (08-8957 7324; Resort Shopping Centre; 8am-7pm) Most tour operators and car-hire firms have desks at this centre.

Visitor Information Centre (08-8957 7377; Town Sq; 8.30am-4.30pm) Contains displays on the geography, wildlife and history of the region. There's a short audio tour ($2) if you want to learn more. It also sells books and regional maps.

GETTING THERE & AWAY

AIR

Yulara's **Connellan Airport** (08-8956 2266), serviced by a number of **Qantas** (13 13 13; www.qantas.com.au), **Virgin Australia** (13 67 89; www.virginaustralia.com) and **Jetstar** (www.jetstar.com) flights, is about 4km north from Yulara.

BUS

Emu Run (p235) has cheap daily connections between Alice Springs and Yulara (one-way adult/child $135/80).

CAR & MOTORCYCLE

One route from Alice to Yulara is sealed all the way, with regular food and petrol stops. It's 200km from Alice to Erldunda on the Stuart Hwy, where you turn west for the 245km journey along the Lasseter Hwy. The journey takes four to five hours.

GETTING AROUND

A free shuttle bus meets all flights (pick-up is 90 minutes before your flight) and drops off at all accommodation points around the resort.

Uluru Express (08-8956 2152; www.uluruexpress.com.au; adult/child $45/15) falls somewhere between a shuttle-bus service and an organised tour. It provides return transport from the resort to Uluru and Kata Tjuta.

Hiring a car will give you the flexibility to visit Uluru and Kata Tjuta whenever you want. Car-rental offices are at the Tour & Information Centre and Connellan Airport.

Alice Springs

Alice Springs wouldn't win a beauty contest, but there's a lot more going on here than first meets the eye. Alice is shaped by its mythical landscapes, vibrant Aboriginal culture (where else can you hear six uniquely Australian languages in the main street?) and tough pioneering past. The town is a natural base for exploring central Australia, with Uluru-Kata Tjuta National Park a relatively close four-hour drive away.

SIGHTS

Araluen Arts Centre Gallery
(08-8951 1122; www.araluenartscentre.nt.gov.au; cnr Larapinta Dr & Memorial Ave; 10am-4pm) For a small town, Alice Springs has a thriving arts scene and the Araluen Arts Centre is at its heart. There is a 500-seat **theatre**, and four galleries with a focus on art from the central desert region. The Albert Namatjira Gallery features works by the artist, who began painting watercolours in the 1930s at Hermannsburg. The exhibition draws comparisons between Namatjira and his initial mentor, Rex Battarbee, and other Hermannsburg School artists.

SARENA HYLAND/TOURISM NT ©

JOHN HENSHALL/TOURISM NT ©

From left: Emu; bush tucker display; Tourists at Anzac Hill

Museum of Central Australia Museum
(☎08-8951 1121; www.dtc.nt.gov.au; cnr Larapinta Dr & Memorial Ave; ⏲10am-5pm Mon-Fri) The natural history collection at this compact museum recalls the days of megafauna – when hippo-sized wombats and 3m-tall flightless birds roamed the land. Among the geological displays are meteorite fragments and fossils. There's a free audio tour, narrated by a palaeontologist, which helps bring the exhibition to life.

Anzac Hill Landmark
For a tremendous view, particularly at sunrise and sunset, take a hike (use Lions Walk from Wills Tce) or a drive up to the top of Anzac Hill, known as Untyeyetweleye in Arrernte. From the war memorial there is a 365-degree view over the town down to Heavitree Gap and the MacDonnell Ranges.

Desert Star-Gazing

Get an eyeful of astonishing central desert stars just outside Alice Springs with **Earth Sanctuary** (☎08-8953 6161; www.earth-sanctuary.com.au; astronomy tours adult/child $36/25), who run terrific nightly astronomy tours. Tours last for an hour and the informative guides have high-powered telescopes to get you up close and personal with the stars. You'll need to ring ahead – they'll know by 4pm if clear skies are forecast.

They also run food-themed events and tours like outback dinners and bush-tucker tours.

TOURS

Dreamtime Tours Cultural
(☎08-8955 5095; 72 Hillside Garden; adult/child $85/42, self-drive $66/33; ⏲8.30-11.30am) Runs the three-hour Dreamtime & Bushtucker Tour, where you meet Warlpiri Aboriginal people and learn a little about their traditions. As it caters for large bus groups it can be impersonal, but you can tag along with your own vehicle.

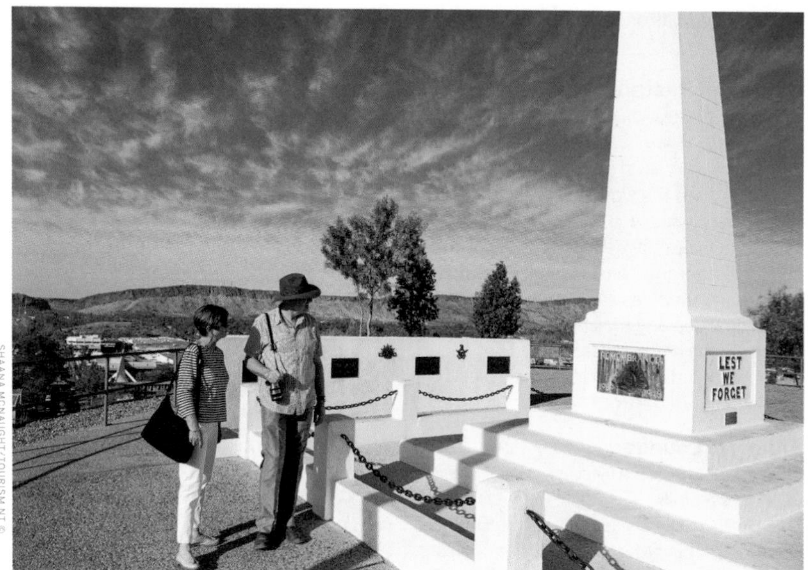

SHAANA MCNAUGHT/TOURISM NT ©

Foot Falcon Walking

(0427 569 531; www.footfalcon.com; tours $35; 3.30pm Apr-Sep, 4.30pm Oct-Mar) Local historian, author and teacher Linda Wells leads two-hour walks around town with insights into Alice's Indigenous past and the history of white settlement.

Emu Run Experience Tours

(08-8953 7057, 1800 687 220; www.emurun.com.au; 72 Todd St) Operates day tours to Uluru ($226) and two-day tours to Uluru and Kings Canyon ($536). Prices include park entry fees, meals and accommodation. There are also recommended, small-group day tours through the West MacDonnell Ranges (from $119).

SHOPPING

Papunya Tula Artists Art

(08-8952 4731; www.papunyatula.com.au; Todd Mall; 9am-5pm Mon-Fri, 10am-2pm Sat) This stunning gallery showcases artworks from the Western Desert communities of Papunya, Kintore and Kiwikurra – even if you're not buying, it's worth stopping by to see the magnificent collection.

Red Kangaroo Books Books

(08-8953 2137; www.redkangaroobooks.com; 79 Todd Mall; 9am-5pm Mon-Fri, 9am-3pm Sat & Sun) Excellent bookshop specialising in central Australian titles: history, art, travel, novels, guidebooks and more. It also has a small but excellent wildlife section.

EATING

Piccolo's Cafe $

(08-8953 1936; Shop 1, Cinema Complex 11, Todd Mall; breakfast from $12; 7am-3pm Mon-Fri, 7am-2pm Sat, 8am-noon Sun) This modern cafe is popular with locals for its excellent food and probably Alice's best coffee. Try the toasties or one of the breakfast rolls.

Montes Modern Australian $$

(08-8952 4336; www.montes.net.au; cnr Stott Tce & Todd St; mains $13-26; 11am-late) Travelling circus meets outback homestead. It's family friendly with a play area for kids, and the food ranges from gourmet burgers, pizzas and tapas to curries and seafood. Sit in the leafy beer garden (with a range of beers) or intimate booth seating. Patio heaters keep patrons warm on cool desert nights.

Hanuman Restaurant Thai $$
(08-8953 7188; www.hanuman.com.au; Doubletree by Hilton, 82 Barrett Dr; mains $25-36; noon-10pm Mon-Fri, 6pm-midnight Sat, 6-10pm Sun;) You won't believe you're in the outback when you try the incredible Thai- and Indian-influenced cuis-ine at this stylish restaurant. The delicate Thai entrées are a real triumph as are the seafood dishes, particularly the Hanuman prawns. Although the menu is ostensibly Thai, there are enough Indian dishes to satisfy a curry craving.

Epilogue Lounge Tapas $$
(08-8953 4206; www.facebook.com/epiloguelounge; 58 Todd Mall; mains $16-25; 8am-11.30pm Wed-Sat, 8am-3pm Sun & Mon) This urban, retro delight is definitely the coolest place to hang in town. With a decent wine list, food served all day and service with a smile, it is a real Alice Springs standout. Expect dishes like haloumi burgers or steak sandwiches and a cooling breeze under the shade cover. It also has live music some nights.

Overlanders Steakhouse Steak $$$
(08-8952 2159; 72 Hartley St; mains $32-55; 6pm-late) The place for steaks, big succulent cuts of beef – and crocodile, camel, kangaroo or emu. Amid the cattle station decor you can try Stuart's Tucker Bag: a combo of croc, kangaroo, emu and camel.

INFORMATION

Alice Springs Hospital (08-8951 7777; Gap Rd) For medical care.

Tourism Central Australia Visitor Information Centre (1800 645 199, 08-8952 5800; www.discovercentralaustralia.com; cnr Todd Mall & Parsons St; 8.30am-5pm Mon-Fri, 9.30am-4pm Sat & Sun;) This helpful centre can load you up with stacks of brochures and the free visitors guide. Weather forecasts and road conditions are posted on the wall. National parks information is also available. Ask about the unlimited kilometre deals if you are thinking of renting a car.

Overlanders Steakhouse

SHAANA MCNAUGHT/TOURISM NT ©

 GETTING THERE & AWAY

AIR

Alice Springs is well connected, with **Qantas** (☎13 13 13, 08-8950 5211; www.qantas.com.au) and **Virgin Australia** (☎13 67 89; www.virginaustralia.com) operating regular flights to and from capital cities.

BUS

Emu Run (p235) Has daily connections between Alice Springs and Yulara (one-way $120).

Gray Line (☎1300 858 687; www.grayline.com; Capricornia Centre 9, Gregory Tce) Runs between Alice Springs and Yulara (one-way $120) .

Greyhound Australia (☎1300 473 946; www.greyhound.com.au; Shop 3, 113 Todd St) Has regular services to/from Alice Springs.

CAR & MOTORCYCLE

All the major companies have offices in Alice Springs, and many have counters at the airport. Talk to the Tourism Central Australia Visitor Information Centre (p236) about its unlimited kilometres deal before you book. A conventional (2WD) vehicle will get you to Uluru via sealed roads (watch out for wildlife).

TRAIN

A classic way to enter or leave the Territory is by the *Ghan*, which can be booked through **Great Southern Rail** (☎13 21 47; www.greatsouthernrail.com.au).

GETTING AROUND

TO/FROM THE AIRPORT

Alice Springs airport is 15km south of the town; it's about $50 by taxi. The **airport shuttle** (☎08-8952 2111; Gregory Tce; one-way $18) meets all flights and drops off passengers at city accommodation.

BUS

The public bus service, **Asbus** (☎08-8944 2444), departs from outside the Yeperenye Shopping Centre. The visitor information centre has timetables.

Alice Springs Desert Park

If you haven't glimpsed a spangled grunter or marbled velvet gecko on your travels, head to the excellent **Alice Springs Desert Park** (☎08-8951 8788; www.alicespringsdesertpark.com.au; Larapinta Dr; adult/child $32/16, nocturnal tours $44/28; ⏲7.30am-6pm, last entry 4.30pm, nocturnal tours 7.30pm Mon-Fri), where the creatures of central Australia are all on display in one place. The predominantly open-air exhibits faithfully re-create the animals' natural environments in a series of habitats: inland river, sand country and woodland. It's an easy 2.5km cycle to the park. Pick up a free audio guide (available in various languages) or join one of the free ranger-led talks throughout the day.

Try to time your visit with the terrific birds of prey show, featuring free-flying Australian kestrels, kites and awesome wedge-tailed eagles. To catch some of the park's rare and elusive animals, such as the bilby, visit the excellent nocturnal house. If you like what you see, come back at night and spotlight endangered species on the guided nocturnal tour (bookings essential).

Ranger-led talk at Alice Springs Desert Park
PETER EVE/TOURISM NT ©

TAXI

Taxis congregate near the visitor information centre. To book one, call ☎13 10 08 or ☎08-8952 1877.

DANIELA CONSTANTINESCU/SHUTTERSTOCK ©

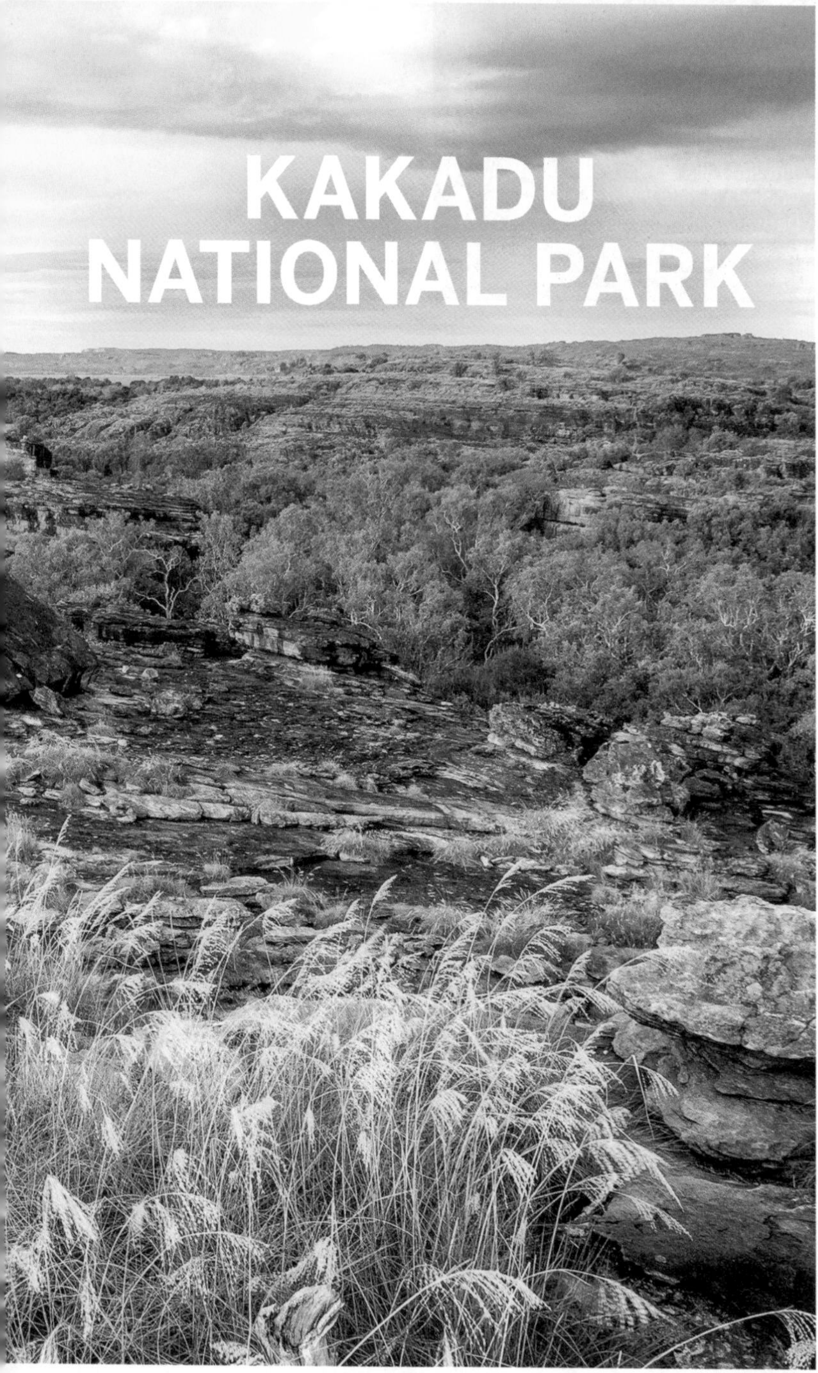

KAKADU NATIONAL PARK

In this Chapter

Kakadu National Park at a Glance...

Kakadu is more than a national park: it's also a vibrant, living acknowledgement of the elemental link between Aboriginal custodians and the country they've nurtured for millennia. Encompassing almost 20,000 sq km, it's a truly spectacular ecosystem, overrun with wildlife and dotted with waterfalls and mind-blowing ancient rock art.

Your access point is Darwin, Australia's only tropical capital. Closer to Bali than Bondi, Darwin can certainly feel removed from the rest of the country – just the way the locals like it! More than 50 nationalities are represented here, clearly represented in the city's wonderful markets.

Kakadu in Two Days

Just two days in this glorious national park seems like an error in judgement. But if time is tight, do the essentials: wildlife spotting with **Yellow Water Cruises** (p254), a hike to see the rock art at spectacular **Nourlangie** (p243), and an Indigenous-led guided tour at **Ubirr** (p243), with views from Nardab Lookout.

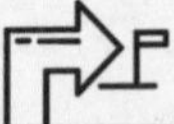

Kakadu in Four Days

Spend three days in Kakadu, ticking off the big-ticket sights then exploring some of the more remote locations such as **Jim Jim Falls and Twin Falls** (p246). Recover in **Darwin** (p247) with a visit to the Museum & Art Gallery of the Northern Territory and drinks and nocturnal shenanigans along Mitchell St.

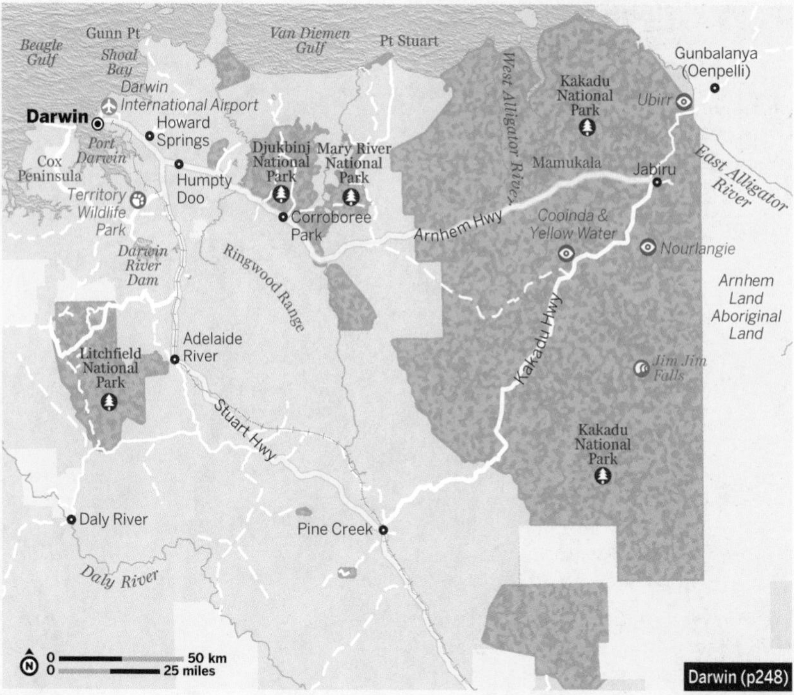

Darwin (p248)

Arriving in Kakadu

Many people access Kakadu on a tour from Darwin (253km to Jabiru), seeing the major sights with the minimum of hassles, but it's just as easy with your own wheels. Note that some sights (eg Jim Jim Falls and Twin Falls) are 4WD-access only.

Jabiru Greyhound Australia (p254) runs buses from Darwin to Jabiru ($75, 3½ hours).

Darwin (p254) The international airport has connections to all capital cities.

Where to Stay

If you want to stay within Kakadu (as opposed to just day-tripping in from Darwin – not recommended!), Jabiru has the best choice of accommodation within the park, including a couple of good resorts. The resort at Cooinda and wilderness lodge near Ubirr are also worthwhile. Booking ahead is essential, especially from June to September.

See p253 for more information on accommodation.

Nourlangie rock art, Kakadu National Park

Indigenous Rock Art

Kakadu is one of Australia's richest, most accessible repositories of Aboriginal rock art. There are more than 5000 sites here, which date from 20,000 years to 10 years ago.

Great For...

☑ **Don't Miss**

Touring Ubirr with an Indigenous guide and hearing Dreaming stories.

Significance & Preservation

For local Aboriginal people, Kakadu's ancient rock-art sites are a major source of traditional archival knowledge. Some older paintings are believed by many Aboriginal people to have been painted by mimi spirits, connecting people with creation legends and the development of Aboriginal lore.

As the paintings are all rendered with natural, water-soluble ochres, they are very susceptible to water damage. Drip lines of clear silicon rubber have been laid on the rocks above the paintings to divert rain. As the most accessible sites receive up to 4000 visitors a week, boardwalks have been erected to keep the dust down and to keep people at a suitable distance from the paintings.

Ubirr

It'll take a lot more than the busloads of visitors here to disturb the inherent majesty and grace of **Ubirr** (⌚8.30am-sunset Apr-Nov, from 2pm Dec-Mar). Layers of rock-art paintings, in various styles and from various centuries, command a mesmerising stillness. Part of the main gallery reads like a menu, with images of kangaroos, tortoises and fish painted in X-ray, the dominant style about 8000 years ago. Look for the yam-head figures, which date back around 15,000 years.

The magnificent Nardab Lookout is a 250m scramble from the main gallery. Surveying the billiard-table-green floodplain and watching the sun set and the moon rise, like they're on an invisible set of scales, is glorious, to say the least.

🛈 Need to Know

Kakadu's climate is complex – more than just four seasons! The dry, unhumid April to August period allows best access.

✗ Take a Break

Little **Border Store** (☎08-8979 2474; www.facebook.com/ubirrborderstore; mains $28; ⌚8.30am-8pm Jun-Oct) near Ubirr has good coffee, cakes and awesome Thai food.

★ Top Tip

The outstanding Nanguluwur Gallery sees fewer visitors than nearby Nourlangie: it's a 3.5km return walk.

Ubirr is 39km north of the Arnhem Hwy via a sealed road.

Nourlangie

The sight of this looming outlier of the Arnhem Land escarpment makes it easy to understand its ancient importance to Aboriginal people. Its long red-sandstone bulk, striped in places with orange, white and black, slopes up from surrounding woodland to fall away at one end in stepped cliffs. Below is Kakadu's best-known collection of rock art.

The 2km looped **walking track** (⌚8am-sunset) takes you first to the Anbangbang Shelter, used for 20,000 years as a refuge and canvas. Next is the Anbangbang Gallery, featuring Dreaming characters repainted in the 1960s. Look for the virile Nabulwinjbulwinj, a dangerous spirit who likes to eat females after banging them on the head with a yam. From here it's a short walk to Gunwarddehwarde Lookout, with views of the Arnhem Land escarpment.

Crocodile

Native Wildlife

Kakadu is home to 60 mammal species, 280-plus bird species, 120 species of reptile, 25 frog species, 55 freshwater fish species and at least 10,000 different kinds of insect.

Great For...

☑ **Don't Miss**

The weird alien 'cities' formed by the cathedral termite mounds found right through Kakadu.

Birds

Abundant waterbirds are a Kakadu highlight. This is one of the chief refuges in Australia for several species, including the magpie goose, green pygmy goose and Burdekin duck. Other waterbirds include pelicans, brolgas and the jabiru – technically the black-necked stork, Australia's only stork – with distinctive red legs and long beak. Herons, egrets, cormorants, wedge-tailed eagles, whistling kites and black kites are common. Open woodlands harbour rainbow bee-eaters, kingfishers and the endangered bustard. Majestic white-breasted sea eagles are seen near inland waterways. At night, you might hear barking owls calling – they sound just like dogs – or the plaintive wail of the bush stone curlew. The

Brolga

PARKS AUSTRALIA ©

raucous call of the spectacular red-tailed black cockatoo is often considered the signature sound of Kakadu.

Mammals

Several types of kangaroo and wallaby inhabit the park; the shy black wallaroo is unique to Kakadu and Arnhem Land – look for them at Nourlangie Rock. At Ubirr, short-eared rock wallabies can be spotted in the early morning. You may see a sugar glider or a shy dingo in wooded areas in the daytime. Kakadu has 26 bat species, four of them endangered.

Reptiles

Twin Falls and Jim Jim Falls have resident freshwater crocodiles, which have narrow snouts and rarely exceed 3m, while the dangerous saltwater variety is found throughout the park.

Kakadu's other reptiles include the frilled lizard, 11 species of goanna, and five freshwater turtle species, of which the most common is the northern snake-necked turtle. Kakadu has many snakes, though most are nocturnal and rarely encountered. The striking Oenpelli python was first recorded by non-Aboriginal people in 1976. The odd-looking file snake lives in billabongs and is much sought after as bush tucker. They have square heads, tiny eyes and saggy skin covered in tiny rough scales (hence 'file'). They move very slowly, eating only once a month and breeding once every decade.

Fish

You can't miss the silver barramundi, which creates a distinctive swirl near the water's surface. Renowned sportfish, 'barra' can grow to more than 1m long.

Need to Know

Insects aside, most visitors see only a fraction of Kakadu's creatures: many are shy and/or nocturnal.

Take a Break

In between croc-spotting jaunts, the **Jabiru Sports & Social Club** (08-8979 2326; www.jabirusportsandsocialclub.com.au; Lakeside Dr; mains $16-35; 6-8.30pm Mon-Sat, noon-2pm & 6-8.30pm Sun) is a top spot for a beer.

★ Top Tip

Dawn and dusk are the prime times for Kakadu wildlife spotting.

Jabiru

It may seem surprising to find a town of Jabiru's size and structure in the midst of a wilderness national park, but it exists solely because of the nearby Ranger uranium mine. It's Kakadu's major service centre, with a bank, newsagent, medical centre, supermarket, bakery and service station. You can even play a round of golf here. It also has some good accommodation and simple restaurants, making it an agreeable if relatively unexciting base.

Jim Jim Falls & Twin Falls

Remote and spectacular, these two falls epitomise the rugged Top End. Jim Jim Falls, a sheer 215m drop, is awesome after rain (when it can only be seen from the air), but its waters shrink to a trickle by about June. Twin Falls flows year-round (no swimming), but half the fun is getting here, involving a little **boat trip** (adult/child $15/free, 7.30am-5pm, last boat 4pm) and an over-the-water boardwalk.

Kakadu National Park Admission

Admission to the park is via a seven-day **Park Pass** (www.parksaustralia.gov.au/kakadu; adult/child/family Apr-Oct $40/20/100, Nov-Mar $25/12.50/65). Passes can be bought online or at various places around the park including display-rich **Bowali Visitor Information Centre** (08-8938 1121; https://parksaustralia.gov.au/kakadu/plan-your-trip/visitor-centres.html; Kakadu Hwy, Jabiru; 8am-5pm), where you can also pick up the excellent *Visitor Guide* booklet. Carry your pass with you at all times as rangers conduct spot checks – penalties apply for nonpayment.

These two iconic waterfalls are reached via a 4WD track, closed during wet season (and off limits to most rental vehicles). Jim Jim Falls is about 56km from the turn-off (the last 1km on foot); it's a further five cor-

From left: Jim Jim woodlands; Jim Jim Falls; displays in the Museum & Art Gallery of the Northern Territory

JAMES HUNT ©

PARKS AUSTRALIA ©

rugated kilometres to Twin Falls. A couple of tour companies make trips here in the Dry.

Cooinda & Yellow Water

Cooinda is one of the main tourism hubs in Kakadu. A slick resort has grown up around the wetlands, known as Yellow Water (or to give it's rather challenging Indigenous name, Ngurrungurrundjba). The cruises (p254) here, preferably around sunrise or sunset, are true Kakadu highlights.

About 1km from the resort (an easy 15 minutes' walk), the **Warradjan Aboriginal Cultural Centre** (www.kakadutourism.com; 9am-5pm) FREE depicts Creation stories and has an excellent permanent exhibition. You'll be introduced to the moiety system (the law of interpersonal relationships), languages and skin names, and there's a minitheatre with a huge selection of films from which to choose. A mesmeric soundtrack of chants and didgeridoos plays in the background.

The turn-off to the Cooinda accommodation complex and Yellow Water wetlands is 47km down the Kakadu Hwy from the Arnhem Hwy intersection.

Darwin

Gazing out confidently across the Timor Sea, Darwin has plenty to offer travellers. Tables spill out of street-side restaurants and bars, innovative museums celebrate the city's past, and galleries showcase the region's rich Indigenous art.

Nature fills Darwin's backyard – the famous national parks of Kakadu and Litchfield are only a few hours' drive away. Cosmopolitan and youthful, it's a city on the move, but retains a laconic small-town vibe that fits easily with the tropical climate.

SIGHTS

Museum & Art Gallery of the Northern Territory Museum
(MAGNT; 08-8999 8264; www.magnt.net.au; 19 Conacher St, Fannie Bay; 9am-5pm Mon-Fri, 10am-5pm Sat & Sun) FREE This superb museum and gallery boasts beautifully presented galleries of Top End–centric exhibits.

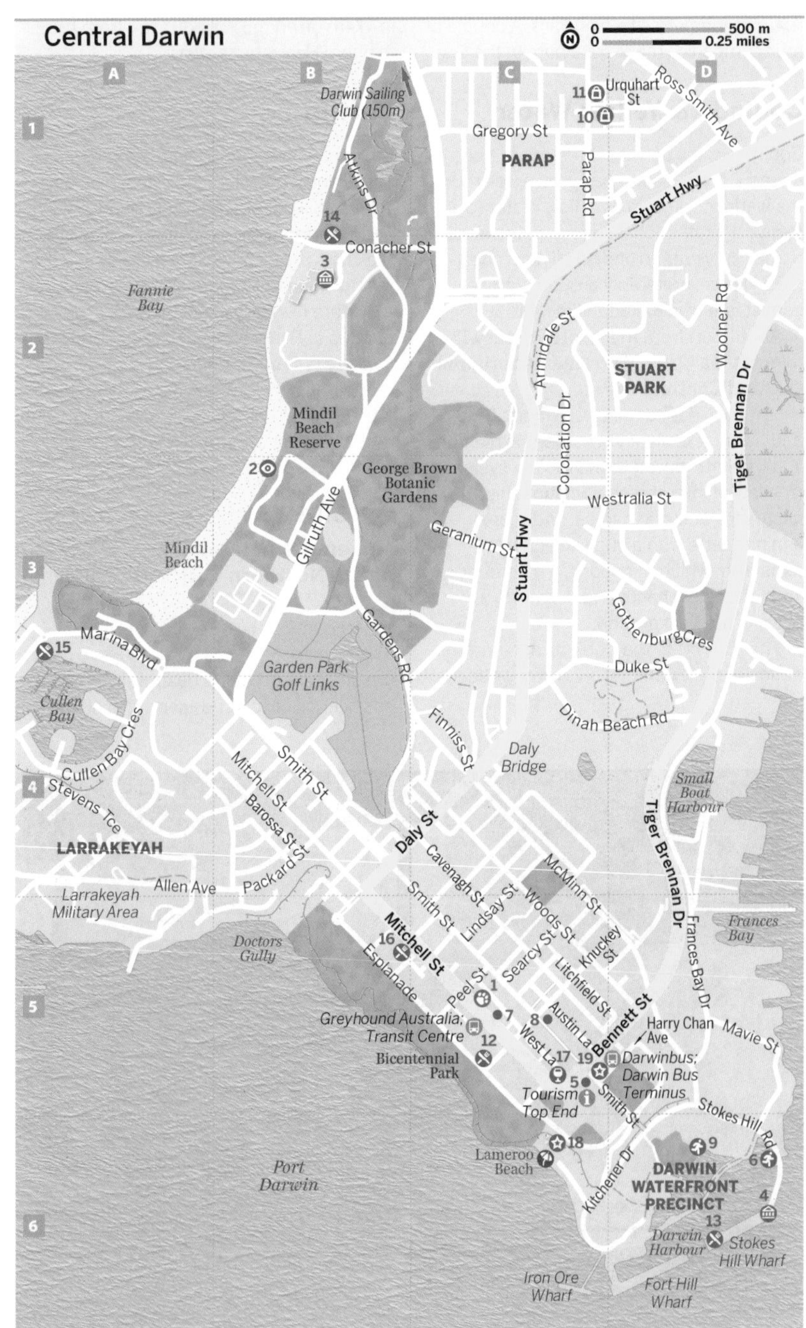
Central Darwin
0 500 m
0 0.25 miles
A
B
C
D
1
2
3
4
5
6
Darwin Sailing Club (150m)
Urquhart St
Ross Smith Ave
Gregory St
PARAP
Parap Rd
Stuart Hwy
Atkins Dr
Conacher St
Fannie Bay
Armidale St
STUART PARK
Woolner Rd
Tiger Brennan Dr
Coronation Dr
Mindil Beach Reserve
George Brown Botanic Gardens
Gilruth Ave
Westralia St
Geranium St
Stuart Hwy
Mindil Beach
Gothenburg Cres
Gardens Rd
Marina Blvd
Duke St
Garden Park Golf Links
Cullen Bay
Cullen Bay Cres
Finniss St
Dinah Beach Rd
Daly Bridge
Smith St
Mitchell St
Stevens Tce
Barossa St
Small Boat Harbour
Tiger Brennan Dr
LARRAKEYAH
Daly St
Packard St
Cavenagh St
McMinn St
Allen Ave
Larrakeyah Military Area
Smith St
Lindsay St
Woods St
Frances Bay
Doctors Gully
Mitchell St
Knuckey St
Searcy St
Esplanade
Litchfield St
Frances Bay Dr
Peel St
Austin La
Greyhound Australia; Transit Centre
Bennett St
Harry Chan Ave
Mavie St
West La
Bicentennial Park
Darwinbus; Darwin Bus Terminus
Tourism Top End
Smith St
Stokes Hill Rd
Lameroo Beach
Kitchener Dr
DARWIN WATERFRONT PRECINCT
Port Darwin
Darwin Harbour
Stokes Hill Wharf
Iron Ore Wharf
Fort Hill Wharf
1
2
3
4
5
6
7
8
9
10
11
12
13
14
15
16
17
18
19

Central Darwin

Sights
1 Crocosaurus Cove C5
2 Mindil Beach Sunset Market B3
3 Museum & Art Gallery of the Northern Territory B2
4 Royal Flying Doctor Service D6

Activities, Courses & Tours
5 Darwin Explorer C5
6 Darwin Harbour Cruises D6
7 Darwin Walking Tours C5
8 Tour Tub C5
9 Wave & Recreation Lagoons D6

Shopping
10 Outstation Gallery C1
11 Parap Village Market C1

Eating
12 Aboriginal Bush Traders Cafe C5
13 Crustaceans D6
14 Darwin Ski Club B1
15 Exotic North Indian Cuisine A3
16 Hanuman B5

Drinking & Nightlife
17 Deck Bar C5

Entertainment
18 Deckchair Cinema C6
19 Happy Yess C5

The Aboriginal art collection is a highlight, with carvings from the Tiwi Islands, bark paintings from Arnhem Land and dot paintings from the desert. An entire room is devoted to Cyclone Tracy, in a display that graphically illustrates life before and after the disaster.

Crocosaurus Cove — Zoo

(08-8981 7522; www.crocosauruscove.com; 58 Mitchell St; adult/child $32/20; 9am-6pm, last admission 5pm) If the tourists won't go out to see the crocs, then bring the crocs to the tourists. Right in the middle of Mitchell St, Crocosaurus Cove is as close as you'll ever want to get to these amazing creatures. Six of the largest crocs in captivity can be seen in state-of-the-art aquariums and pools, while an eco **boat cruise** (adult/child $14/7) takes you out on the water with them.

Royal Flying Doctor Service — Museum

(08-8983 5700; www.flyingdoctor.org.au; Stokes Hill Wharf; adult/child/family $26/16/70; 9.30am-6pm, last entry 5pm) This outstanding new museum on Stokes Hill Wharf is the way all museums should be. There's a 55-seat hologram cinema, virtual-reality glasses that enable you to relive in vivid detail the 1942 Japanese bombing raid on Darwin Harbour, a decommissioned Pilatus PC-12 aircraft from the Royal Flying Doctor Service (RFDS), a live map showing the current location of RFDS planes, and a series of touch screens that take you through the story of the RFDS and Darwin during WWII.

Territory Wildlife Park — Zoo

(08-8988 7200; www.territorywildlifepark.com.au; 960 Cox Peninsula Rd; adult/child/family $32/16/54.50; 9am-5pm) This excellent park, 60km from Darwin, showcases the best of Aussie wildlife. Pride of place must go to the aquarium, where a clear walk-through tunnel puts you among giant barramundi, stingrays, sawfish and saratogas, while a separate tank holds a 3.8m saltwater crocodile.

ACTIVITIES

Wave & Recreation Lagoons — Water Park

(08-8985 6588; www.waterfront.nt.gov.au; Wave Lagoon adult/child $9/6; Wave Lagoon 10am-6pm) Darwin's hugely popular waterfront Wave Lagoon is a hit with locals and travellers alike. There are 10 different wave patterns produced, along with lifeguards, a kiosk and a strip of lawn to bask on. Adjacent is the Recreation Lagoon with a sandy beach and lifeguards.

TOURS

Darwin Harbour Cruises Cruise

(☎08-8942 3131; www.darwinharbourcruises.com.au) Variety of cruises from Stokes Hill Wharf. The 20m schooner *Tumlaren* does a 'Tastes of the Territory' sunset cruise (adult/child $74/45), and there are day and evening cruise options aboard the *Charles Darwin*, a tri-level catamaran.

Darwin Walking Tours Walking

(☎08-8981 0227; www.darwinwalkingtours.com; 50 Mitchell St; adult/child $25/free) Two-hour guided history walks around the city, plus fishing, adventure and wildlife tours available from the Darwin Tours Shop.

Darwin Explorer Bus

(☎0416 140 903; www.theaustralianexplorer.com.au; 24hr ticket adult/child $40/25) Open-top bus tours that explore Darwin's major sights – hop-on/hop-off with either a 24-hour or 48-hour ticket. Departs every 30 minutes or so from the visitor centre (p254).

Kakadu Tours from Darwin

See also the box on p254 for tours departing within Kakadu National Park.

Northern Territory Indigenous Tours Cultural Tour

(☎1300 921 188; www.ntitours.com.au; day tours adult/child from $249/124) Upmarket Indigenous tours to Kakadu and Litchfield National Park.

Sacred Earth Safaris Adventure

(☎08-8536 2234; www.sacredearthsafaris.com.au; ⏱May-Oct) Multiday, small-group 4WD camping tours around Kakadu. Two-day tours start at $850.

Kakadu Dreams Tours

(☎1800 813 269; www.kakadudreams.com.au) Backpacker-biased day tours to Litchfield ($149), and boisterous two-/three-day trips to Kakadu ($445/665).

Yellow Water sunrise cruise (p254)

PARKS AUSTRALIA ©

SHOPPING

Outstation Gallery Art

(☎08-8981 4822; www.outstation.com.au; 8 Parap Pl; ⊙10am-1pm Tue, 5pm Wed-Fri, 2pm Sat) One of Darwin's best galleries of Indigenous art, Outstation presents the works of nine different Aboriginal art centres from across the NT, from Arnhem Land to the Western Desert.

Parap Village Market Market

(www.parapvillage.com.au; Parap Shopping Village, Parap Rd, Parap; ⊙8am-2pm Sat) This compact, crowded food-focused market is a local favourite. There's the full gamut of Southeast Asian cuisine, as well as plenty of ingredients to cook up your own tropical storm. It's open year-round.

EATING

Aboriginal Bush Traders Cafe Cafe, Australian $

(☎09-8942 4023; www.aboriginalbushtraders.com; cnr Esplanade & Knuckey St; mains & light meals $9.50-17; ⊙7.30am-2pm) In historic Lyons Cottage, this fine little cafe has some really tasty dishes inspired by Aboriginal bush tucker from the desert. In addition to more conventional dishes such as gourmet toasted rolls, try the damper with jam (Kakadu plum or wild rosella jam), the kutjera (wild tomato) and aniseed myrtle feta damper, or the saltbush dukkah, avocado and feta smash.

Darwin Ski Club Modern Australian $$

(☎08-8981 6630; www.darwinskiclub.com.au; Conacher St, Fannie Bay; mains $18-28; ⊙noon-10pm) This place just keeps getting better. Already Darwin's finest location for a sunset beer, it now does seriously good tucker too. The dishes are well prepared, and the menu is thoughtful and enticing. We had the red curry and were impressed.

Exotic North Indian Cuisine Indian $$

(☎08-8941 3396; www.exoticnorthindiancuisine.com.au; Cullen Bay Marina; mains $14-23; ⊙5-10pm) Offering outstanding value for quality Indian cuisine, this place has taken over the mantle of Darwin's best Indian restaurant. It's positioned right on the waterfront at

Litchfield National Park

It's not as famous as Kakadu, but **Litchfield** (☎08-8976 0282; www.nt.gov.au) is one of the best places in the NT for walking, camping and swimming. Just 115km south of Darwin, it makes a brilliant day trip or tour: try **Ethical Adventures** (☎0488 442 269; www.ethicaladventures.com).

The 1500-sq-km national park encloses much of the Tabletop Range, a wide sandstone plateau with waterfalls pouring off the edge, feeding crystal-clear, croc-free plunge pools.

Entering the park from Batchelor, the tombstones you see after 17km are, in fact, magnetic termite mounds.

Another 6km in is the turn-off to Buley Rockhole (2km), with a series of rock pools. This turn-off also takes you to Florence Falls (5km), accessed by a 15-minute, 135-step descent to a deep pool surrounded by forest. About 18km beyond the turn-off is another turn-off to spectacular Tolmer Falls. A 1.6km loop track affords beaut views.

It's a further 7km along the main road to the turn-off for Litchfield's big-ticket Wangi Falls ('wong-guy'; 1.6km). The falls flow year-round, filling an enormous swimming hole bordered by rainforest. Bring your goggles!

Swimming at Florence Falls

MANFRED GOTTSCHALK/GETTY IMAGES ©

GRAHAM MONRO/GM PHOTOGRAPHICS/GETTY IMAGES ©

From left: Deckchair Cinema; Mindil Beach (p255); Darwin Waterfront Precinct

ANDREW WATSON/GETTY IMAGES ©

Cullen Bay, making for extremely pleasant waterside dining in the evening. The service is attentive, there are high chairs for young 'uns and, unusually for Darwin, you can BYO wine.

Hanuman Indian, Thai **$$**
(☎08-8941 3500; www.hanuman.com.au; 93 Mitchell St; mains $13-36; ⊙noon-2.30pm, dinner from 6pm; ✎) Ask locals about fine dining in Darwin and they'll usually mention Hanuman. It's sophisticated but not stuffy. Enticing aromas of innovative Indian and Thai nonya dishes waft from the kitchen to the stylish open dining room and deck. The menu is broad, with exotic vegetarian choices, and banquets also available. Respect the sign on the door: 'we appreciate neat attire'.

Crustaceans Seafood **$$$**
(☎08-8981 8658; www.crustaceans.net.au; Stokes Hill Wharf; mains $26-65; ⊙5.30-11pm) This casual, licensed restaurant features fresh fish, Moreton Bay bugs, lobster, oysters, even crocodile, as well as succulent steaks. It's all about the location, perched right at the end of Stokes Hill Wharf with sunset views over Frances Bay. The cold beer and a first-rate wine list seal the deal.

Pee Wee's at the Point Modern Australian **$$$**
(☎08-8981 6868; www.peewees.com.au; Alec Fong Lim Dr, East Point Reserve; mains $41-68; ⊙from 6.30pm) With Hahndorf venison striploin kicking in at $68 a serve, this is indeed a place for a treat. One of Darwin's finest restaurants, it is well worth shelling out for the experience. Enjoy your double-roasted duckling among tropical palms at East Point Reserve, right on the waterfront.

DRINKING & NIGHTLIFE

Darwin Sailing Club Sports Bar
(☎08-8981 1700; www.dwnsail.com.au; Atkins Dr, Fannie Bay; ⊙noon-2pm & 5.30-9pm) More upmarket than the ski club (p251), the sailing club is always filled with yachties enjoying a sunset beer overlooking the Timor Sea. Tunes on the sound system are surprisingly un-yacht club (no Christopher Cross or Rod

DANIELA CONSTANTINESCU/SHUTTERSTOCK ©

Stewart). Sign in as a visitor at the door (bring some ID).

Deck Bar Bar

(www.thedeckbar.com.au; 22 Mitchell St; 11am-late) At the nonpartying parliamentary end of Mitchell St, the Deck Bar still manages to get lively with happy hours, pub trivia and regular live music. Blurring the line between indoors and outdoors brilliantly, the namesake deck is perfect for people-watching.

ENTERTAINMENT

Deckchair Cinema Cinema

(08-8981 0700; www.deckchaircinema.com; Jervois Rd, Waterfront Precinct; adult/child $16/8; box office from 6.30pm Apr-Nov) During the Dry, the Darwin Film Society runs this fabulous outdoor cinema below the southern end of the Esplanade. Watch a movie under the stars while reclining in a deckchair. There's a licensed bar serving food or you can bring a picnic (no BYO alcohol). There are usually double features on Friday and Saturday nights (adult/child $24/12).

Happy Yess Live Music

(www.happyyess.tumblr.com; Brown's Mart, 12 Smith St; 6pm-midnight Thu-Sat) A not-for-profit venue for musicians run by musicians, you won't hear cover bands in here. Original, sometimes weird, always fun.

Where to Stay

You can stay in Kakadu itself – there are resorts, safari-tent lodges and lots of fab camping sites. If you're booked on a tour, your accommodation will probably be included at one of these operators. Back in Darwin, most accommodation is right in the city centre, close to all the restaurants and nightlife, or in quieter Larrakeyah just to the north of the CBD. Cullen Bay is another option, with lots of apartments and some good waterside eateries, though it's not really walking distance to any of the action.

Tours in Kakadu

See also p250 for tours departing from Darwin.

Yellow Water Cruises (☎1800 500 401; www.kakadutourism.com; per person $72-99) Cruise the South Alligator River and Yellow Water Billabong spotting wildlife. Purchase tickets from Gagudju Lodge, Cooinda; a shuttle bus will take you from here to the tour's departure point. Two-hour cruises depart at 6.45am, 9am and 4.30pm; 1½-hour cruises leave at 11.30am, 1.15pm and 2.45pm.

Kakadu Air (☎08-8941 9611, 1800 089 113; www.kakaduair.com.au; adult/child 30min flight $150/120, 60min flight $250/200, 45/60min helicopter flight adult $485/650) Offers fixed-wing and helicopter scenic flights; both are a wonderful way to get a sense of the sheer scale and beauty of Kakadu and Arnhem Land.

Kakadu Animal Tracks (☎0409 350 842; www.animaltracks.com.au; adult/child $220/110; ⏰1pm) Based at Cooinda, this outfit runs seven-hour tours with an Indigenous guide combining a wildlife safari and Aboriginal cultural tour. You'll see thousands of birds, get to hunt, gather, prepare and consume bush tucker and crunch on some green ants.

Ayal Aboriginal Tours (☎0429 470 384; www.ayalkakadu.com.au; adult/child $220/99) Full-day Indigenous-run tours around Kakadu, with former ranger and local, Victor Cooper, shining a light on art, culture and wildlife.

INFORMATION

Tourism Top End (☎1300 138 886, 08-8980 6000; www.tourismtopend.com.au; cnr Smith & Bennett Sts; ⏰8.30am-5pm Mon-Fri, 9am-3pm Sat & Sun) Helpful office with hundreds of brochures; books tours and accommodation.

Royal Darwin Hospital (☎08-8920 6011; www.health.nt.gov.au; 105 Rocklands Dr, Tiwi; ⏰24hr) Accident and emergency.

GETTING THERE & AWAY

AIR

Darwin International Airport (☎08-8920 1811; www.darwinairport.com.au; Henry Wrigley Dr, Marrara) is serviced by **Jetstar** (www.jetstar.com), **Qantas** (www.qantas.com.au) and **Virgin Australia** (www.virginaustralia.com), with flights (or connections) to all capital cities.

BUS

Greyhound Australia (☎1300 473 946; www.greyhound.com.au) operates long-distance bus services from the **Transit Centre** (www.enjoy-darwin.com/transit-bus.html; 69 Mitchell St). There's at least one service per day up/down the Stuart Hwy to Alice Springs ($265, 22 hours).

For Kakadu, there's a daily return service from Darwin to Jabiru ($75, 3½ hours).

CAR & CAMPERVAN

Most car-rental companies offer only 100km free, which won't get you far (you pay per kilometre beyond 100km). Rates start at around $40 per day for a small car with 100km per day. All the usual car-hire suspects operate here, or **JJ's Car Hire** (☎0427 214 229; www.jjscarhire.com.au; 7 Goyder Rd, Parap) is a good local operator.

There are also plenty of 4WD vehicles available in Darwin, but you have to book ahead and fees/deposits are higher than for 2WD vehicles.

TRAIN

The legendary *Ghan* train, operated by **Great Southern Rail** (☎08-8213 4401, 1800 703 357; www.greatsouthernrail.com.au), runs weekly (twice weekly May to July) between Adelaide and Darwin via Alice Springs.

GETTING AROUND

TO/FROM THE AIRPORT

A taxi fare from Darwin International Airport into the centre is about $40 (12km). **Darwin**

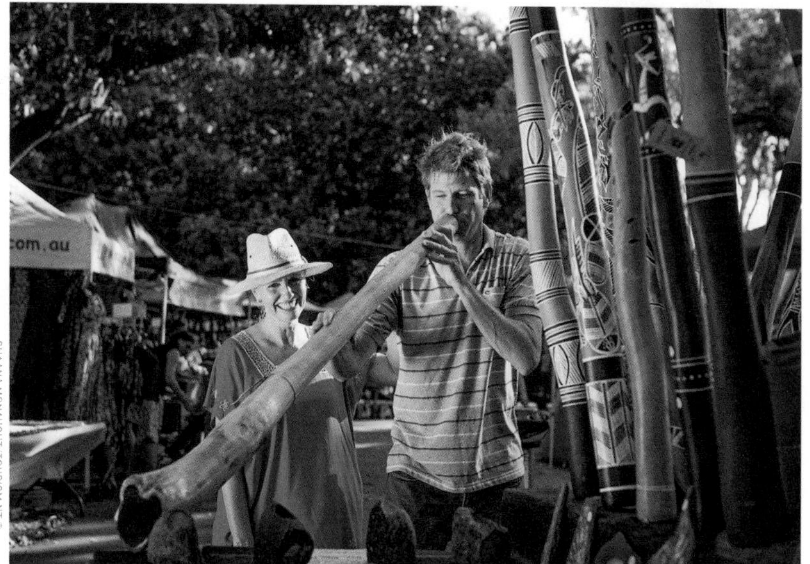

SHAANA MCNAUGHT/TOURISM NT ©

Practicing the didgeridoo at Mindil Beach Sunset Market

City Airport Shuttle Service (☎08-8947 3979; www.darwincityairportshuttleservice.com.au; per person $15) pick up/drop off almost anywhere in the centre.

PUBLIC TRANSPORT

Darwinbus (☎08-8944 2444; www.nt.gov.au/driving/public-transport-cycling) runs a comprehensive bus network that departs from the **Darwin Bus Terminus** (Harry Chan Ave), opposite Brown's Mart.

A $3 adult ticket gives unlimited travel on the bus network for three hours. Daily ($7) and weekly ($20) travel cards are also available.

Alternatively, the privately run **Tour Tub** (☎08-8985 6322; www.tourtub.com.au; Smith St Mall; adult/child $110/60) is a hop-on, hop-off minibus touring Darwin's sights.

TAXI

Call **Darwin Radio Taxis** (☎13 10 08; www.131008.com).

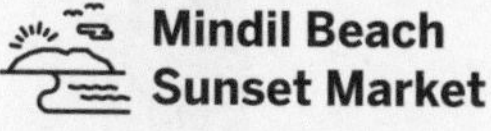

Mindil Beach Sunset Market

Food is the main attraction at this **market** (www.mindil.com.au; off Gilruth Ave; ⏲5-10pm Thu, 4-9pm Sun May-Oct) – from Thai, Sri Lankan, Indian, Chinese and Malaysian to Brazilian, Greek, Portuguese and more. Don't miss a flaming satay stick from Bobby's brazier. Top it off with fresh fruit salad, decadent cakes or luscious crepes.

But that's only half the fun! Arts and crafts stalls bulge with handmade jewellery, fabulous rainbow tie-dyed clothes, Aboriginal artefacts, and wares from Indonesia and Thailand.

Mindil Beach is about 2km from Darwin's city centre; an easy walk or hop on buses 4 or 6 which go past the market area.

City skyline view of Perth (p262) from Elizabeth Quay

ROB BAYER/SHUTTERSTOCK ©

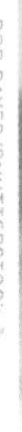

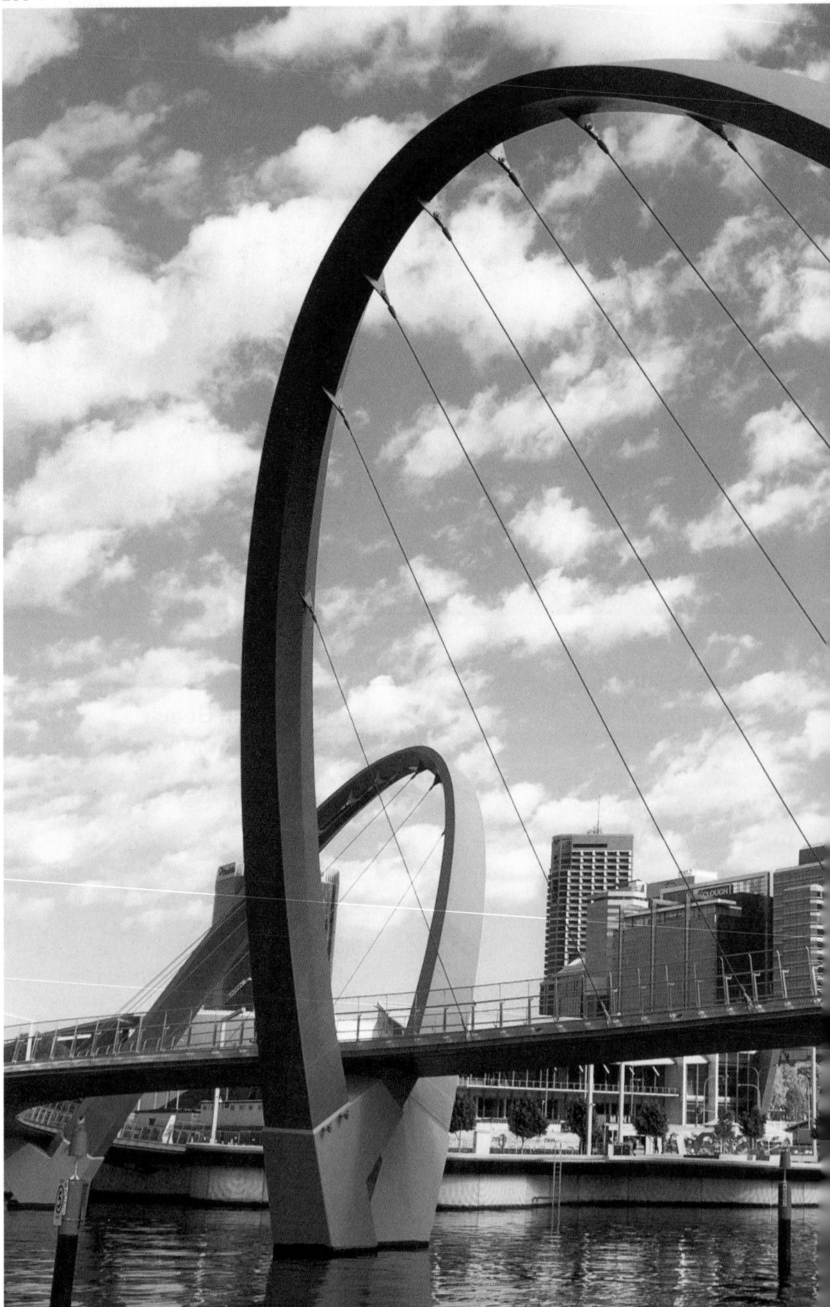

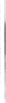

PERTH &
FREMANTLE
bhpbilliton
Deloitte
LAVAN LAVAN

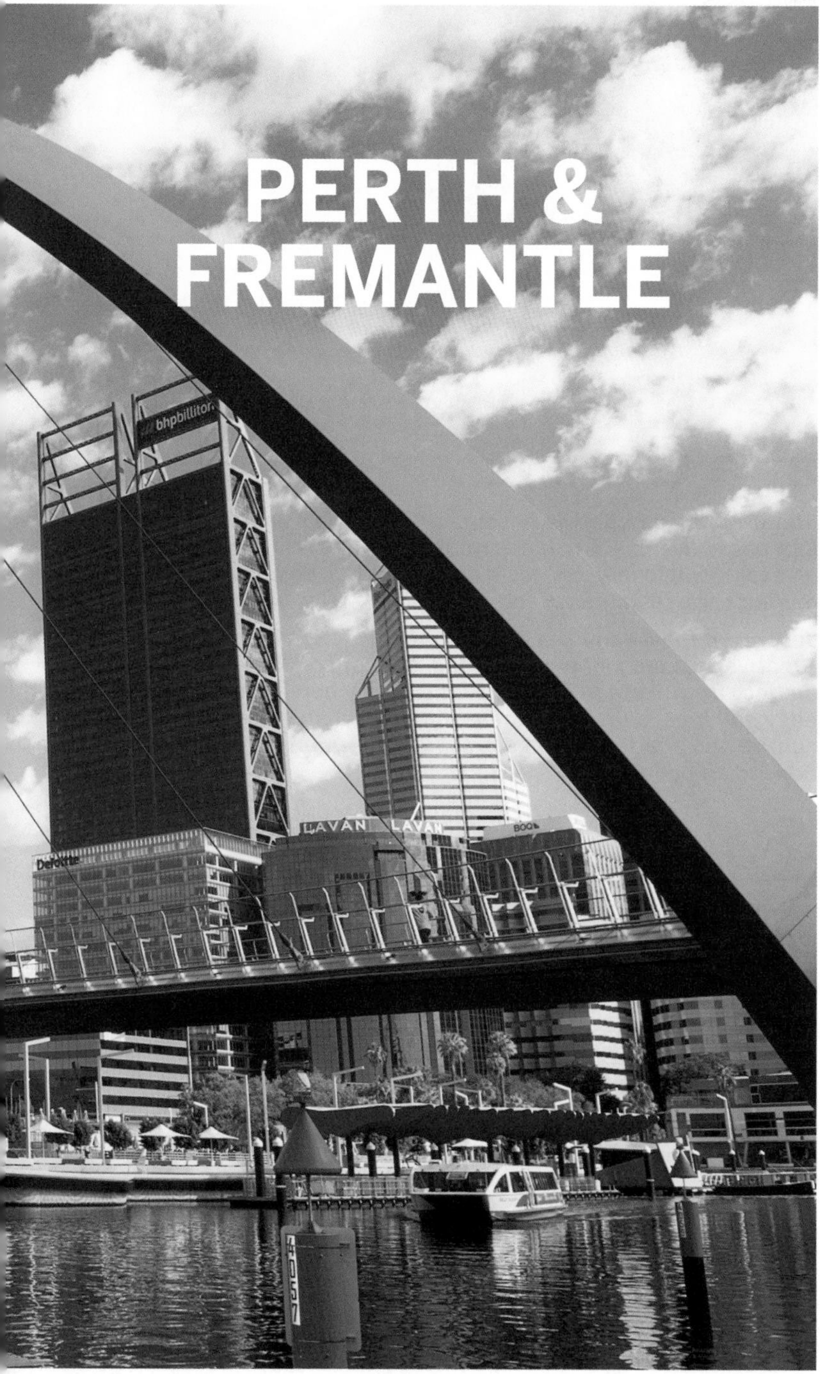

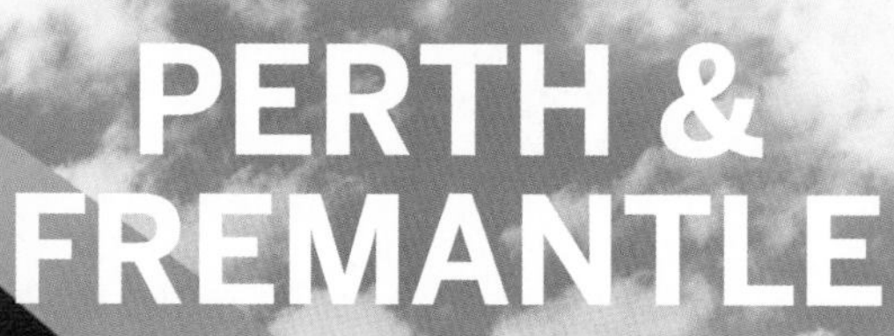

In this Chapter

Perth & Fremantle at a Glance...

About as close to Bali as to some of Australia's eastern cities, laid-back, 'liveable' Perth has wonderful weather, beaut beaches and an easy-going character. It's a sophisticated, cosmopolitan city, with myriad bars, restaurants and cultural activities all vying for attention.

Just down the Swan River is Fremantle, Western Australia's main port. Creative, relaxed and open-minded, the soul of 'Freo' spirit is entirely distinct from Perth's. There's a lot to enjoy here: fantastic museums, edgy galleries, pubs thrumming with live music, thriving coffee culture and a faded heritage precinct of formerly grand Victorian and Edwardian buildings.

Perth & Fremantle in Two Days

A day in Perth, a day in Fremantle: nice! Have breakfast in Mt Lawley or the CBD, then check out the **Art Gallery of Western Australia** (p262). Grab lunch in hip Leederville, explore view-friendly **Kings Park** (p260), then go drinking in Northbridge. Next day in Freo, visit the **Fremantle Markets** (p269), then go gothic at **Fremantle Prison** (p267). A beer and dinner at waterside **Little Creatures** (p272) is the ideal Freo sign-off.

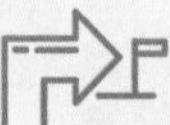

Perth & Fremantle in Four Days

With four days, pick up provisions for a picnic at **Cottesloe Beach** (p262), then detour north to the **Aquarium of Western Australia** (p262) to see what's under the sea. Next day, take a **cruise** (p263) on the Swan River, or if it's sunny a day trip to **Rottnest Island** (Wadjemup; 263), not far offshore.

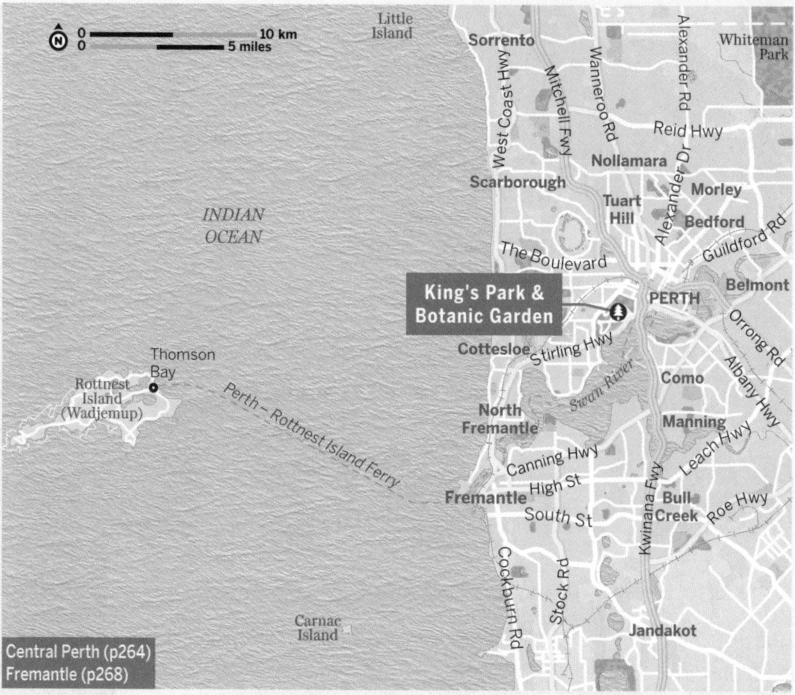

Central Perth (p264)
Fremantle (p268)

Arriving in Perth & Fremantle

Perth Airport (p266) About 10km east of the city, with flights winging in from overseas and other Australian capitals. A cab will cost around $45 into the centre. Connect (p266) runs shuttles ($15) to/from city accommodation.

Fremantle (p273) Thirty minutes from Perth by train or bus, or an easy drive.

Where to Stay

Perth CBD (hotels, apartments) and Northbridge (backpackers, boutique hotels) are close to public transport, making accessing inner-city suburbs such as Leederville and Mt Lawley straightforward. If you're a beach fan, consider staying at Cottesloe or Scarborough (although public transport is limited). Alternatively, head to Fremantle for a good mix of sleeping options: pubs, boutique hotels, B&Bs and hostels.

Kings Park

Kings Park & Botanic Garden

Rising above the Swan River on Perth's western flanks, the 400-hectare, bush-filled Kings Park is the city's pride and joy.

Great For...

☑ Don't Miss

The epic glass-and-steel bridge on the Lotterywest Federation Walkway.

Parklife

Kings Park is a top spot for a picnic or to let the kids off the leash. Its numerous tracks are popular with walkers and joggers, with an ascent of the steep stairs from the river rewarded with fab city views.

At the park's heart is the 17-hectare **Botanic Garden**, containing over 2000 plant species indigenous to WA. In spring there's an impressive display of WA's famed wildflowers.

Another highlight is the **Lotterywest Federation Walkway** (9am-5pm), a 620m path including a 222m-long glass-and-steel bridge that passes through the canopy of a stand of eucalypts.

Leading into the park, Fraser Ave is lined with towering lemon-scented gums that are dramatically lit at night. At its culmination are the State War Memorial, a cafe, a gift

Lotterywest Federation Walkway

MANEERAT SHOTIYANPITAK/SHUTTERSTOCK ©

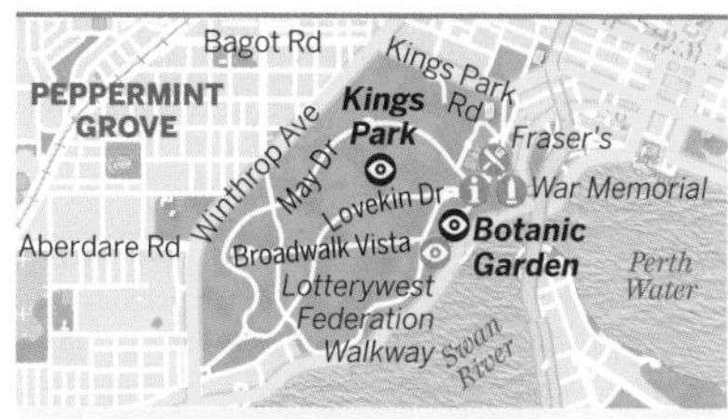

Need to Know

☎08-9480 3600; www.bgpa.wa.gov.au; ⌚guided walks 10am, noon & 2pm FREE

Take a Break

Fraser's (☎08-9481 7100; www.frasersrestaurant.com.au; Fraser Ave; mains $28-45; ⌚noon-late) plates up mod-American food in a beaut location at the top of Kings Park.

★ Top Tip

The hop-on, hop-off City Sightseeing Perth Tour (p263) bus rolls through the park, too...so hop off!

shop, Fraser's restaurant and the Kings Park Visitor Centre. Free **guided walks** leave from here.

Indigenous Heritage

The Noongar people knew the Kings Park area as *Kaarta Gar-up* and used it for thousands of years for hunting, food gathering, ceremonies, teaching and tool-making. A freshwater spring at the base of the escarpment, now known as Kennedy Fountain but before that as *Goonininup*, was a home of the Wargal, mystical snake-like creatures that created the Swan River and other waterways.

For today's Aboriginal perspective on Kings Park, sign up for an **Indigenous Heritage Tour** (☎0405 630 606; www.indigenouswa.com; adult/child $50/15; ⌚1.30pm Mon-Fri) – a 90-minute Indigenous-themed stroll around the park. Bookings essential.

Kings Park Festival

Held annually throughout September to coincide with the park's rampant wildflower blooms, the super-popular **Kings Park Festival** (www.kingsparkfestival.com.au; ⌚Sep) involves floral displays, workshops, exhibitions, artworks and installations, guided walks, family distractions and live music every Sunday. Running since 1964, the festival these days is a polished act.

Getting Here

Take bus 935 from St Georges Tce to near the visitor centre. You can also walk up (steep) Mount St from the city or climb Jacob's Ladder from Mounts Bay Rd.

Perth

 SIGHTS

Art Gallery of Western Australia Gallery

(☎08-9492 6622; www.artgallery.wa.gov.au; Perth Cultural Centre; ⊙10am-5pm Wed-Mon) FREE Founded in 1895, this excellent gallery houses the state's pre-eminent art collection. It contains important post-WWII works by Australian luminaries such as Arthur Boyd, Albert Tucker, Grace Cossington Smith, Russell Drysdale, Arthur Streeton and Sidney Nolan. The Indigenous-art galleries are also very well regarded. Check the website for info on free tours.

Cottesloe Beach Beach

(Marine Pde) The safest swimming beach, Cottesloe has cafes, pubs, pine trees and fantastic sunsets.

Aquarium of Western Australia Aquarium

(AQWA; ☎08-9447 7500; www.aqwa.com.au; Hillarys Boat Harbour, 91 Southside Dr; adult/child $30/18; ⊙10am-5pm) Dividing WA's vast coastline into five distinct zones, AQWA features a 98m underwater tunnel showcasing stingrays, turtles, fish and sharks.

Perth Zoo Zoo

(☎08-9474 0444; www.perthzoo.wa.gov.au; 20 Labouchere Rd; adult/child $29/14; ⊙9am-5pm) Part of the fun of a day at the zoo is getting there – taking the ferry across the Swan River from Elizabeth Quay Jetty to Mends Street Jetty (every half-hour) and walking up the hill. Zones include Reptile Encounter, African Savannah, Asian Rainforest and Australian Bushwalk.

ACTIVITIES

Spinway WA Cycling

(www.spinwaywa.bike) Spinway WA has 17 self-serve bicycle hire kiosks in city hot spots. Bikes, costing $11 for one hour, $22 for four hours, or $33 for 24 hours, can be rented in central Perth, Kings Park, South Perth, Scarborough and Fremantle.

Fijian crested iguana at Perth Zoo

TOURS

Captain Cook Cruises Cruise

(08-9325 3341; www.captaincookcruises.com.au; adult/child from $40/23) Cruises to the Swan Valley or Fremantle, with an array of add-ons such as meals, craft beer, wine tastings and tram rides. Departures are from Barrack Street Jetty.

City Sightseeing Perth Tour Bus

(08-9203 8882; www.citysightseeingperth.com; adult/child from $32/12) Hop-on, hop-off double-decker bus tour, with loop routes taking in the central city, Kings Park and Northbridge. Tickets are valid for up to two days.

SHOPPING

Future Shelter Homewares

(08-9228 4832; www.futureshelter.com; 56 Angove St; 10am-5pm Mon-Sat, noon-3pm Sun) Quirky clothing, gifts and homewares designed and manufactured locally. Surrounding Angove St is an emerging hip North Perth neighbourhood with other cafes and design shops worth browsing.

Aboriginal Art & Craft Gallery Art

(08-9481 7082; www.aboriginalgallery.com.au; Fraser Ave; 10.30am-4.30pm Mon-Fri, 11am-4pm Sat & Sun) Work from around WA; more populist than high end or collectable.

EATING

Toastface Grillah Cafe $

(0409 115 909; www.toastfacegrillah.com; Grand Lane; sandwiches $7-10; 7am-4pm Mon-Fri, 9am-4pm Sat, 10am-4pm Sun) Vibrant street art, excellent coffee and a sneaky laneway location combine with interesting toasted sandwiches such as the 'Pear Grillz' with blue cheese, pear and lime chutney.

Brika Greek $$

(0455 321 321; www.brika.com.au; 3/177 Stirling St; meze & mains $9-27; noon-3pm & 5pm-late Fri-Sun, 5pm-late Mon-Thu) Presenting a stylish spin on traditional Greek cuisine, Brika is one of Perth's most appealing restaurants. The whitewashed interior is enlivened by colourful traditional fabrics, and menu highlights include creamy smoked-eggplant dip, slow-cooked lamb, and prawns with fried *saganaki* cheese.

Rottnest Island (Wadjemup)

'Rotto' has long been the family-holiday playground of choice for Perth locals. Although it's only about 19km offshore from Fremantle, this car-free, off-the-grid slice of paradise, ringed by secluded beaches and bays, feels a million miles away. A day trip spent cycling around the 11km-long, 4.5km-wide island is a real pleasure: you're bound to spot quokkas, the island's famed native mammals.

Rottnest Express (1300 467 688; www.rottnestexpress.com.au) runs ferries from Perth's Barrack Street Jetty (adult/child $105.50/58, 1¾ hours, once daily) and Fremantle (adult/child $85.50/48.50, 30 minutes, five times daily).

Bikes can be booked through **Rottnest Island Bike Hire** (08-9292 5105; www.rottnestisland.com; cnr Bedford Ave & Welch Way; bikes per half-/full-day from $16/30; 8.30am-4pm, to 5.30pm summer). The ferry companies and island visitor centre also hire bikes.

Quokka

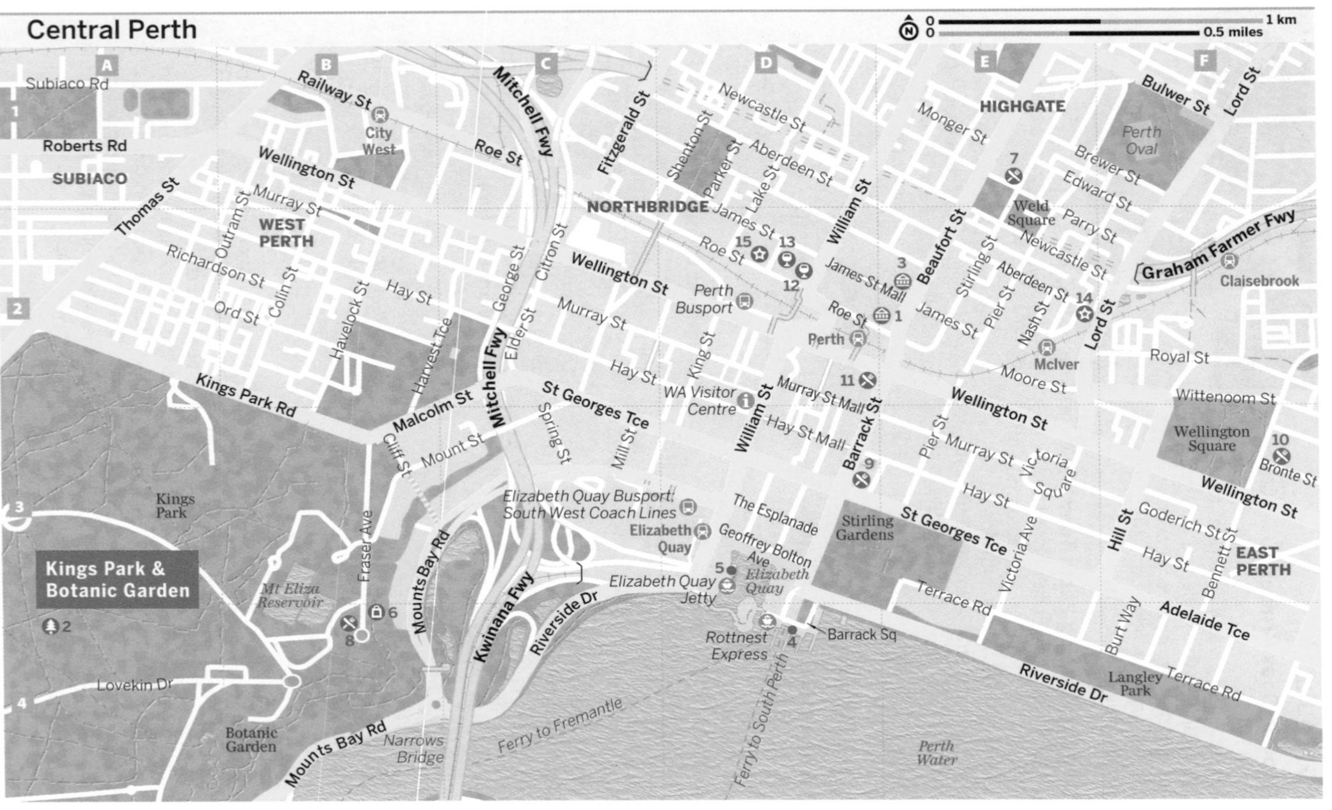

Central Perth
0
0
1 km
0.5 miles
A
B
C
D
E
F
1
2
3
4
Subiaco Rd
Roberts Rd
SUBIACO
Railway St
City West
Roe St
Mitchell Fwy
Fitzgerald St
Newcastle St
Shenton St
Parker St
Aberdeen St
Lake St
Monger St
HIGHGATE
Bulwer St
Lord St
Perth Oval
Brewer St
Edward St
7
Weld Square
Parry St
Newcastle St
Graham Farmer Fwy
Claisebrook
Wellington St
Thomas St
Murray St
Outram St
WEST PERTH
NORTHBRIDGE
James St
William St
Beaufort St
Stirling St
Aberdeen St
Richardson St
Colin St
Ord St
Havelock St
Hay St
George St
Citron St
Wellington St
Roe St
15
13
12
James St Mall
3
Perth Busport
Roe St
1
James St
Pier St
Nash St
14
Lord St
Murray St
Elder St
Perth
McIver
Royal St
Harvest Tce
Mitchell Fwy
King St
Hay St
11
Moore St
Wittenoom St
Kings Park Rd
Malcolm St
St Georges Tce
WA Visitor Centre
William St
Murray St Mall
Barrack St
Wellington St
Hay St Mall
Pier St
Murray St
Wellington Square
10
Bronte St
Cliff St
Mount St
Spring St
Mill St
9
Victoria Square
Hay St
Wellington St
Kings Park
Elizabeth Quay Busport; South West Coach Lines
The Esplanade
Stirling Gardens
St Georges Tce
Hill St
Goderich St
Elizabeth Quay
Geoffrey Bolton Ave
Victoria Ave
Hay St
Bennett St
EAST PERTH
Kings Park & Botanic Garden
Fraser Ave
Mounts Bay Rd
5
Elizabeth Quay
Mt Eliza Reservoir
Kwinana Fwy
Elizabeth Quay Jetty
Terrace Rd
Burt Way
Adelaide Tce
6
2
Riverside Dr
8
Rottnest Express
4
Barrack Sq
Riverside Dr
Langley Park
Terrace Rd
Lovekin Dr
Ferry to Fremantle
Ferry to South Perth
Botanic Garden
Mounts Bay Rd
Narrows Bridge
Perth Water

Central Perth

Sights
1 Art Gallery of Western Australia E2
2 Kings Park & Botanic Garden A4
3 Western Australian Museum – Perth E2

Activities, Courses & Tours
4 Captain Cook Cruises D4
5 Little Ferry Co D3

Shopping
6 Aboriginal Art & Craft Gallery B4

Eating
7 Brika E1
8 Fraser's B4
9 Long Chim D3
10 Restaurant Amusé F3
11 Toastface Grillah D2

Drinking & Nightlife
12 Ezra Pound D2
Petition Beer Corner .... (see 9)
13 Sneaky Tony's D2

Entertainment
14 Badlands Bar E2
15 Rooftop Movies D2

Long Chim Thai $$$
(08-6168 7775; www.longchimperth.com; State Buildings, cnr St Georges Tce & Barrack St; mains $28-45; noon-late;) Australian chef David Thompson is renowned for respecting the authentic flavours of Thai street food, and with dishes like a fiery chicken *laap* (warm salad with fresh herbs) and roast curry of red duck, there's definitely no dialling back on the flavour for Western palates.

Restaurant Amusé Modern Australian $$$
(08-9325 4900; www.restaurantamuse.com.au; 64 Bronte St; degustation with/without wine pairing $210/130; 6.30pm-late Tue-Sat) The critics have certainly been amused by this degustation-only establishment, regularly rated as one of Australia's finest. Ongoing accolades include being dubbed WA's number-one eatery by *Gourmet Traveller* magazine every year since 2010. Book ahead.

DRINKING & NIGHTLIFE

Sneaky Tony's Bar
(www.facebook.com/sneakytonys; Nicks Lane; 4pm-midnight) On Friday and Saturday you'll need the password to get into this unmarked bar amid street art and Chinese restaurants – don't worry, it's revealed weekly on Sneaky Tony's Facebook page. Try the refreshing Dark & Stormy with ginger beer and lime. The entrance is behind 28 Roe St.

Petition Beer Corner Craft Beer
(08-6168 7773; www.petitionperth.com/beer; State Buildings, cnr St Georges Tce & Barrack St; 11.30am-late Mon-Sat, from noon Sun) Distressed walls provide the backdrop for craft brews at this spacious bar. There's a rotating selection of beers on tap – check out Now Tapped on Petition's website – and it's a great place to explore the more experimental side of the Australian craft-beer scene.

Ezra Pound Bar
(0415 757 666; www.ezrapound.com.au; 189 William St; 3pm-midnight Tue-Sat,1-10pm Sun) Down a much-graffitied lane leading off William St, Ezra Pound is favoured by Northbridge's bohemian set. It's the kind of place where you can settle into a red-velvet chair and sip a Tom Collins out of a jam jar. Earnest conversations about Kerouac and Kafka are strictly optional.

ENTERTAINMENT

Badlands Bar Live Music
(08-9225 6669; www.badlands.bar; 3 Aberdeen St; 7pm-2am) Located on the fringes of Northbridge, Badlands has shrugged off its previous incarnation as a retro 1950s-inspired nightclub to be reborn as the city's best rock venue.

JAMESTEOHART/SHUTTERSTOCK ©

INGEHOGENBIJL/SHUTTERSTOCK ©

From left: Seafood dish; Lunching alfresco; Elizabeth Quay

Rooftop Movies Cinema
(08-9227 6288; www.rooftopmovies.com.au; 68 Roe St; $16; Tue-Sun late Oct-late Mar) Art-house and classic movies screen under the stars on the 6th floor of a Northbridge car park. Deckchairs, pizza and craft beer all combine for a great night out. Book online.

INFORMATION

WA Visitor Centre (1800 812 808, 08-9483 1111; www.bestofwa.com.au; 55 William St; 9am-5.30pm Mon-Fri, 9.30am-4.30pm Sat, 11am-4.30pm Sun) Excellent resource for information across WA.

Royal Perth Hospital (08-9224 2244; www.rph.wa.gov.au; Victoria Sq) In central Perth.

GETTING THERE & AWAY

AIR

The domestic and international terminals at **Perth Airport** (08-9478 8888; www.perthairport.com.au) are 10km and 13km east of Perth respectively, near Guildford. A free transfer bus links the terminals.

Connect (www.perthairportconnect.com.au; one-way/return $15/30) runs shuttles to/from city accommodation (every 50 minutes).

Transperth buses 36, 37 and 40 travel to the domestic airport ($4.60, 40 minutes).

BUS

Transwa (1300 662 205; www.transwa.wa.gov.au) operates services around the state from the bus terminal at East Perth train station.

South West Coach Lines (08-9261 7600; www.southwestcoachlines.com.au) services the southwestern corner of WA from **Elizabeth Quay Busport**.

TRAIN

The Indian Pacific rolls into Perth from the east coast; see www.greatsouthernrail.com.au.

 GETTING AROUND

PUBLIC TRANSPORT

Transperth (13 62 13; www.transperth.wa.gov.au) operates Perth's public buses, trains and ferries. Fares and zones:

Free Transit Zone (FTZ) Covers the central commercial area.

Zone 1 City centre and inner suburbs ($3).

Zone 2 Fremantle, Guildford and the beaches as far north as Sorrento ($4.60).

DayRider Unlimited travel after 9am weekdays and all day on the weekend in any zone ($12.40).

FamilyRider Lets two adults and up to five children travel for $12.40 on weekends, after 6pm weekdays and after 9am on weekdays during school holidays.

BUS

Most Transperth buses leave from the city's new **Perth Busport** (www.transperth.wa.gov.au). There are also three free **Central Area Transit** (CAT) services.

FERRY

A ferry runs every 20 to 30 minutes between t new **Elizabeth Quay Jetty** and Mends Street Jetty in South Perth (for the zoo). The **Little Ferry Co** (0488 777 088; www.littleferryco.com.au; adult/child single $10/12, return $22/1 9.30am-5.30pm) links Elizabeth Quay and Claisebrook Cove.

TRAIN

Transperth has five train lines: Armadale Thornl Fremantle, Joondalup, Mandurah and Midland.

TAXI

The two main companies are **Swan Taxis** (13 13 30; www.swantaxis.com.au) and **Black & White** (13 10 08; www.bwtaxi.com.au).

Fremantle

 SIGHTS

Fremantle Prison Historic Building
(08-9336 9200; www.fremantleprison.com.au 1 The Terrace; adult/child single day tours $20/1 combined day tours $28/19, Torchlight Tour $26/16, Tunnels Tour $60/40; 9am-5.30pm)

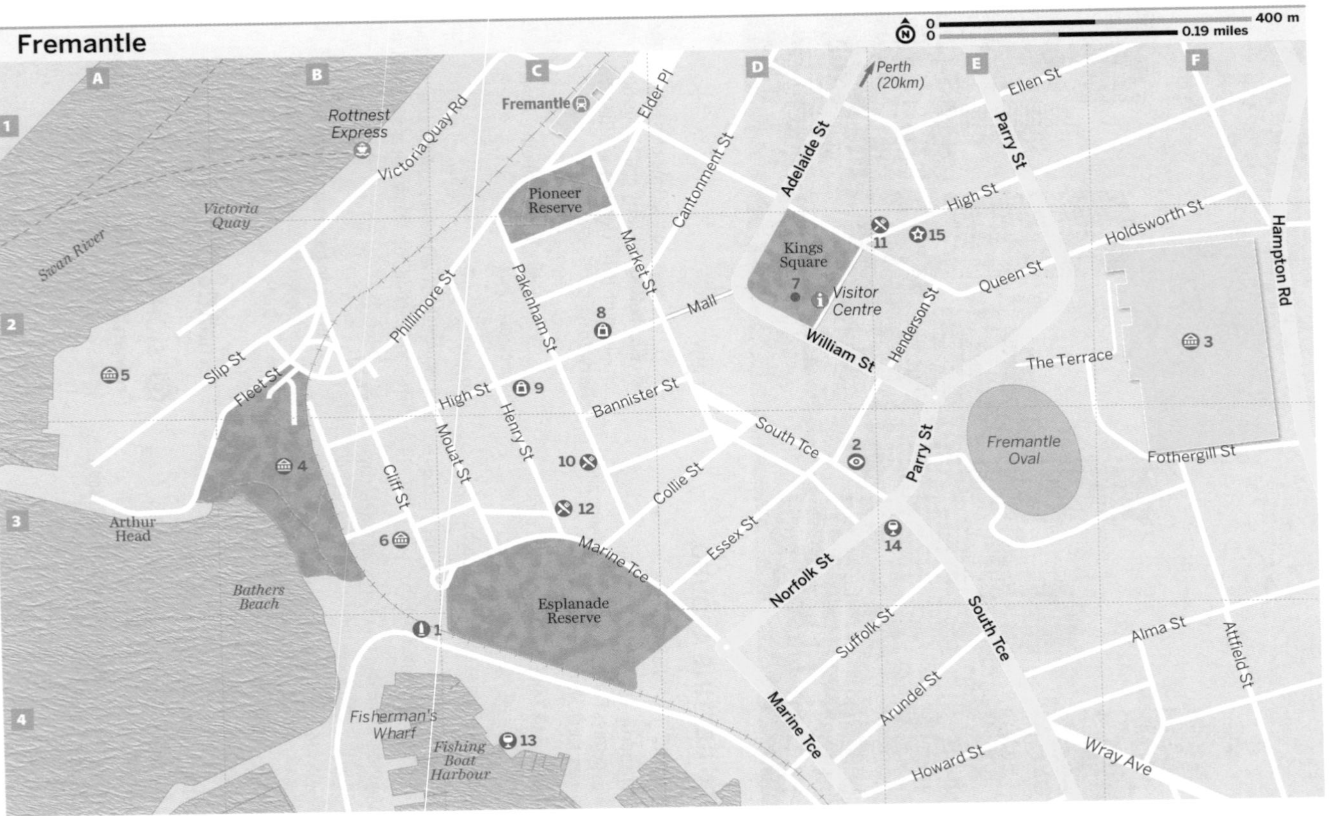
Fremantle
400 m
0.19 miles
Perth (20km)
Rottnest Express
Victoria Quay Rd
Fremantle
Elder Pl
Cantonment St
Adelaide St
Ellen St
Parry St
High St
Holdsworth St
Hampton Rd
Pioneer Reserve
Victoria Quay
Swan River
Kings Square
Visitor Centre
Queen St
Market St
Mall
William St
Henderson St
Phillimore St
Pakenham St
The Terrace
Slip St
Fleet St
High St
Bannister St
South Tce
Henry St
Mouat St
Cliff St
Collie St
Parry St
Fremantle Oval
Fothergill St
Arthur Head
Essex St
Marine Tce
Norfolk St
Bathers Beach
Esplanade Reserve
Suffolk St
South Tce
Alma St
Attfield St
Arundel St
Fisherman's Wharf
Fishing Boat Harbour
Marine Tce
Howard St
Wray Ave

Fremantle

Sights
1 Bon Scott Statue B4
2 Fremantle Markets D3
3 Fremantle Prison F2
4 Round House B3
5 Western Australian Museum – Maritime A2
6 Western Australian Museum – Shipwreck Galleries B3

Activities, Courses & Tours
7 Fremantle Tram Tours D2

Shopping
8 Common Ground Collective C2
9 Japingka C2

Eating
10 Bread in Common C3
11 Manuka Woodfire Kitchen E2
12 Moore & Moore C3

Drinking & Nightlife
13 Little Creatures C4
14 Norfolk Hotel E3

Entertainment
15 Fly by Night Musicians Club E2

With its foreboding 5m-high walls, the old convict-era prison still dominates Fremantle. Daytime tour options include the Doing Time Tour, taking in the kitchens, men's cells and solitary-confinement cells. Book ahead for the Torchlight Tour, focusing on macabre aspects of the prison's history, and the 2½-hour Tunnels Tour (minimum age 12 years), which includes an underground boat ride.

Western Australian Museum – Maritime Museum

(08 1300 134 081; www.museum.wa.gov.au; Victoria Quay; adult/child museum $15/free, submarine $15/7.50, museum & submarine $25/7.50; 9.30am-5pm) Housed in an intriguing sail-shaped building on the harbour, just west of the city centre, the maritime museum is a fascinating exploration of WA's relationship with the ocean. Tours leave every half-hour from 10am to 3.30pm. Booking ahead is recommended.

Western Australian Museum – Shipwreck Galleries Museum

(1300 134 081; www.museum.wa.gov.au; Cliff St; admission by donation; 9.30am-5pm) Located within an 1852 commissariat store, the Shipwreck Galleries are considered the finest display of maritime archaeology in the southern hemisphere. The highlight is the **Batavia Gallery**, where a section of the hull of Dutch merchant ship *Batavia*, wrecked in 1629, is displayed.

Round House Historic Building

(08-9336 6897; www.fremantleroundhouse.com.au; Captains Lane; admission by donation; 10.30am-3.30pm) Built from 1830 to 1831, this 12-sided stone prison is WA's oldest surviving building. On the hilltop outside is the Signal Station, where at 1pm daily a time ball and cannon blast were used to alert seamen to the correct time. The ceremony is re-enacted daily; book ahead if you want to fire the cannon.

Fremantle Markets Market

(www.fremantlemarkets.com.au; cnr South Tce & Henderson St; 8am-8pm Fri, to 6pm Sat & Sun) FREE Originally opened in 1897, these colourful markets were reopened in 1975 and today draw slow-moving crowds combing over souvenirs. The fresh-produce section is a good place to stock up on snacks and there's an excellent food court featuring lots of global street eats.

ACTIVITIES

Fremantle Trails Walking

(www.visitfremantle.com.au) Pick up trail cards from the visitor centre (p273) for 11 self-guided walking tours, covering various themes (Art and Culture, Fishing Boat Harbour, Hotels and Breweries etc).

Live Music in Freo

Fly by Night Musicians Club (☎08-9430 5208; www.flybynight.org; 179 High St) Variety is the key at Fly by Night, a not-for-profit club that's been run by musos for musos for years. All kinds perform, and many local bands made a start here.

Mojos (☎08-9430 4010; www.mojosbar.com.au; 237 Queen Victoria St; ⏰7pm-late) Local and national bands (mainly Aussie rock and indie) and DJs play at this small place, and there's a sociable beer garden out the back. First Friday of the month is reggae night; every Monday is open-mike night.

TOURS

Fremantle Tram Tours Bus

(☎08-9433 6674; www.fremantletrams.com.au; city circuit adult/child $28/5, Ghostly Tour $85/65) Looking like a heritage tram, this bus departs from the Town Hall on an all-day hop-on, hop-off circuit around the city. The Ghostly Tour, departing 6.45pm to 10.30pm Friday, visits the prison, Round House and Fremantle Arts Centre (former asylum) by torchlight.

Two Feet & a Heartbeat Walking

(☎1800 459 388; www.twofeet.com.au; per person $45-60; ⏰10am) Operated by a young, energetic crew, tours focus on Fremantle's often rambunctious history. The three-hour 'Sailors' Guide to Fremantle' option includes a couple of drink stops. **Perth** (☎1800 459 388; www.twofeet.com.au; per person $35-55) tours also available.

SHOPPING

Common Ground Collective Design

(☎0418 158 778; www.facebook.com/cmmngrnd; 82 High St; ⏰9am-5pm Mon-Sat, 10am-4pm Sun) An eclectic showcase of jewellery, apparel and design, mainly from local Fremantle artisans and designers. The coffee at the in-house cafe is pretty damn good too.

From left: Signal cannon at Round House (p269); Fremantle Town Hall; Thai chicken wrap from Fremantle Markets (p269); exterior of Fremantle Markets

EA GIVEN/SHUTTERSTOCK ©

ROB RAYWORTH/ALAMY STOCK PHOTO ©

Japingka Art
(☎08-9335 8265; www.japingka.com.au; 47 High St; ⏲10am-5.30pm Mon-Fri, noon-5pm Sat & Sun) Specialising in Aboriginal fine art from WA and beyond. Purchases come complete with extensive notes about the works and the artists who created them.

EATING

Ootong & Lincoln Cafe $
(☎08-9335 6109; www.ootongandlincoln.com.au; 258 South Tce; mains $12-23; ⏲6am-5pm; 🖉) Catch the free CAT bus to South Fremantle for a top breakfast spot. Join the locals grabbing takeaway coffee or beavering away on their laptops, and start the day with macadamia-and-dukkah porridge or pop in from noon for Mexican corn croquettes.

Manuka Woodfire Kitchen Barbecue, Pizza $$
(☎08-9335 3527; www.manukawoodfire.com.au; 134 High St; shared plates $11-38, pizzas $19-21; ⏲5-9pm Tue-Fri, noon-3pm & 5-9pm Sat & Sun) Centred on a wood-fired oven, the kitchen at Manuka is tiny, but it's still big enough to turn out some of the tastiest food in town. Pretty well everything is cooked in the oven and the seasonal menu could include Esperance octopus, roast chicken with miso sauce or peppers and basil pesto.

Bread in Common Bistro, Bakery $$
(☎08-9336 1032; www.breadincommon.com.au; 43 Pakenham St; shared platters $15-21, mains $19-26; ⏲9am-10pm Sun-Thu, to 11pm Fri & Sat) Be lured by the comforting aroma of the in-house bakery before staying on for cheese and charcuterie platters, or larger dishes such as lamb ribs, octopus or pork belly. Big shared tables and a laid-back warehouse ambience encourage conversation over WA wines and Aussie craft beers and ciders.

Mantle South American $$
(www.themantle.com.au; cnr Beach & James Sts; mains $18-30; ⏲4.30-11pm Tue-Fri, 11am-11pm Sat & Sun) Filling a heritage warehouse, the Mantle's three businesses make it worth the 1.5km schlep from central Fremantle. Don Tapa combines South American and

EA GIVEN/SHUTTERSTOCK ©

EQROY/SHUTTERSTOCK ©

From left: Fishing Boat Harbour; Bon Scott (2009) by artist Greg James; Little Creatures brewery

Asian flavours, Magna Pizza creates good wood-fired pizza amid the Mantle's rustic industrial ambience, and Alter Ego's hipster bar crew concocts inventive cocktails and serves up frosty craft beer best enjoyed in the raffish, compact courtyard.

Moore & Moore Cafe **$$**

(08-9335 8825; www.mooreandmoorecafe.com; 46 Henry St; mains $13-22; 7am-4pm;) An urban-chic cafe that spills into the adjoining art gallery and overflows into a flagstoned courtyard. With great coffee, good cooked breakfasts, pastries, wraps and free wi-fi, it's a great place to linger.

RIP Bon Scott

The most popular of Fremantle's public sculptures is Greg James's statue of **Bon Scott** (1946–80), strutting on a Marshall amplifier in Fishing Boat Harbour. The AC/DC singer moved to Fremantle with his family in 1956; his ashes are interred in **Fremantle Cemetery** (Carrington St).

DRINKING & NIGHTLIFE

Little Creatures Brewery

(1800 308 388; www.littlecreatures.com.au; Fishing Boat Harbour, 40 Mews Rd; 10am-midnight) Try the Little Creatures Pale Ale and Pilsner, and other beers and ciders under the White Rabbit and Pipsqueak labels. Keep an eye out for one-off Shift Brewers' Stash beers. It's chaotic at times, but the wood-fired pizzas ($19 to $24) are worth the wait.

Norfolk Hotel Pub

(08-9335 5405; www.norfolkhotel.com.au; 47 South Tce; 11am-midnight Mon-Sat, to 10pm Sun) Slow down to Freo pace at this 1887 pub. Interesting guest beers create havoc for the indecisive drinker, and the food and pizzas are very good. The heritage limestone courtyard is a treat. Downstairs, the Odd Fellow channels a bohemian small-bar vibe and has live music Wednesday to Saturday.

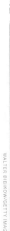

Mrs Browns Bar
(☎08-9336 1887; www.mrsbrownbar.com.au; 241 Queen Victoria St; ⏲4.30pm-midnight Tue-Thu, noon-midnight Fri-Sun) Exposed bricks and a copper bar combine with retro and antique furniture to create North Fremantle's most atmospheric drinking den. The music could include all those cult bands you thought were *your* personal secret, and an eclectic menu of beer, wine and tapas targets the more discerning, slightly older bar hound.

INFORMATION

Fremantle Hospital (☎08-9431 3333; www.fhhs.health.wa.gov.au; Alma St) At the edge of central Fremantle.

Visitor Centre (☎08-9431 7878; www.visitfremantle.com.au; Town Hall, Kings Sq; ⏲9am-5pm Mon-Fri, 9am-4pm Sat, 10am-4pm Sun) Accommodation and tour bookings, and bike rental.

GETTING THERE & AWAY

BOAT

A pleasant way to get here from Perth is by taking the 1¼-hour river cruise run by Captain Cook Cruises (p263).

PUBLIC TRANSPORT

Fremantle is 30 minutes from Perth by train (Zone 2). Buses routes include 103, 106, 107, 111 and 158.

GETTING AROUND

It's easy enough to travel by foot or on the free CAT bus service, which loops past the major sights every 10 minutes from 7.30am to 6.30pm on weekdays, until 9pm on Friday and 10am to 6.30pm on the weekend.

Bicycles (Fremantle Visitor Centre, Kings Sq; ⏲9am-5pm Mon-Fri, 9am-4pm Sat, 10am-4pm Sun) can be rented for free at the visitor centre (refundable bond $200).

Brighton Beach huts, Melbourne (p141)

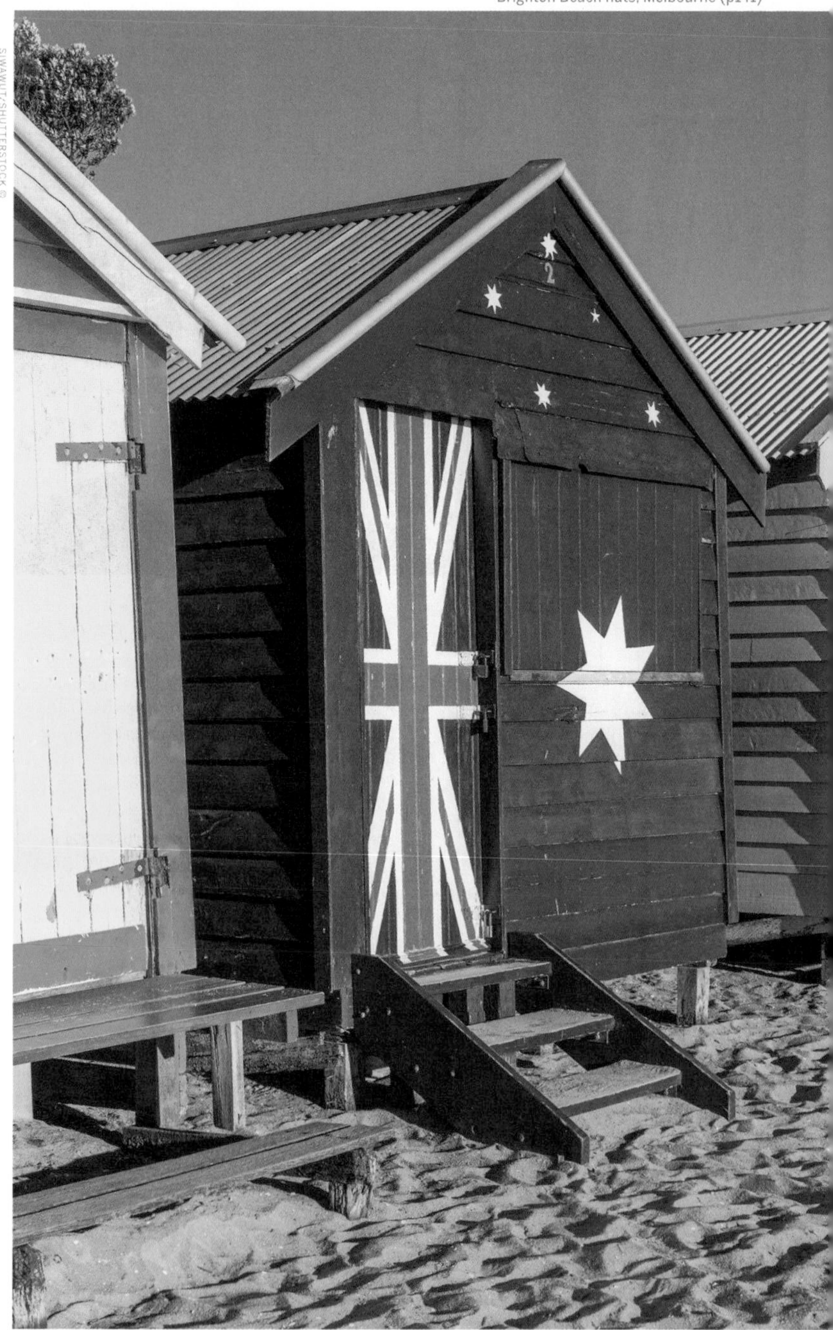

SIWAWUT/SHUTTERSTOCK ©

In Focus

Flinders Street Station (p152), Melbourne

Australia Today

Australia seems caught between the populist disaffection sweeping Western countries and the innate optimism of its people – which will win? In the meantime, those touchstones and preoccupations of modern Australian life – the relationship between Indigenous and non-Indigenous Australians; the economy; the future of multicultural Australia – all still hold centre stage. If only the country's politicians could get their act together...

Indigenous Australians

Australia's treatment of Indigenous Australians has come a long way since the days of 'terra nullius' – the legal fiction declaring Australia devoid of human settlement that the British empire used to prop up its colonisation – and needing a referendum to grant the most basic citizenship rights to its first inhabitants. Indigenous owners now own roughly half of the Northern Territory's land, for example, and many Aboriginal communities have negotiated lucrative royalty deals with mining companies working on traditional lands. But many (though by no means all) Aboriginal communities remain in crisis – poorly governed and beset with problems of alcohol, petrol-sniffing, high crime levels and the concomitant high levels of incarceration. The correct balance between self-determination and government intervention is one that no one in Australian policy circles has ever quite worked out.

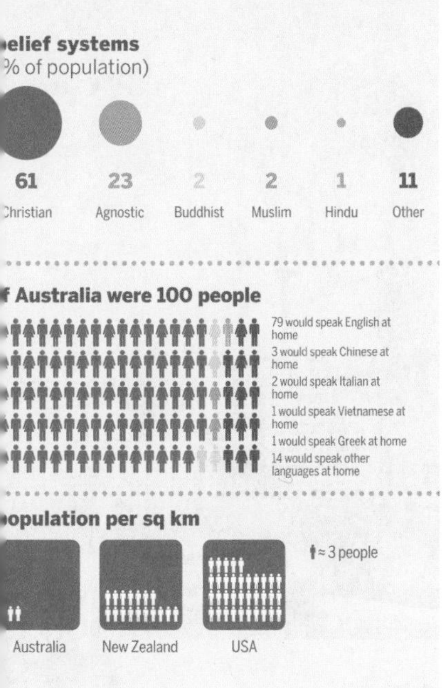

In the meantime, there have been moves towards greater legal recognition: in 2017 both Victoria and South Australia began formal treaty negotiations with local Indigenous communities, and there appears to be bipartisan support for a formal referendum seeking constitutional recognition of Indigenous Australians as Australia's first people. But with Indigenous Australians suffering disproportionately when compared to non-Indigenous Australians – from life expectancy and key health indicators to unemployment and economic disadvantage – there remains a long way to go.

The Rise of Populism?

With the world still reeling from the UK's Brexit referendum and the election of US President Donald Trump, many Australians are wondering what their political future holds. There appear to be no obviously Trump-like candidates with nationwide appeal ready and able to take up the mantle of populist anger, but there are signs that disaffection with mainstream politics is growing. Independents are a growing and increasingly powerful force in Australian politics. Pauline Hanson, last seen in 1998 when she lost her seat in Federal Parliament, has returned to the fore, calling for caps on immigration from Muslim countries and even a Royal Commission into Islam. Other names advocating a similar line include Tasmanian independent senator Jacqui Lambie and South Australian senator Cory Bernardi, who in early 2017 left the Liberal Party to form his own party, the Australian Conservatives. In the absence of an economic downturn, such views remain on the fringe (albeit with a vocal voice in parliament) and have yet to penetrate the mainstream. They are, however, increasingly a feature of the national conversation.

Economy & Environment

Australia's economy continues its remarkable story of prosperity. Having weathered the GFC with barely a blip, the country continues to enjoy low unemployment, low inflation and generally high wages – though the cost of living has soared to levels that threaten to leave behind a generation of would-be home owners and the days of the great mining boom are definitely over. But for now at least, the economy is forging onwards and upwards, thankfully paying little heed to the shenanigans of its political leaders from both sides of Parliament.

At the same time, environmentalists worry that the Australian government will continue to keep environmental protection as a low policy priority, from new coal mines in Queensland and policies which environmentalists argue pose serious threats to the Great Barrier Reef – the government even picked a fight on this with Ellen DeGeneres – to the dismantling of the country's carbon tax.

HMS Endeavour replica, Sydney (p35)

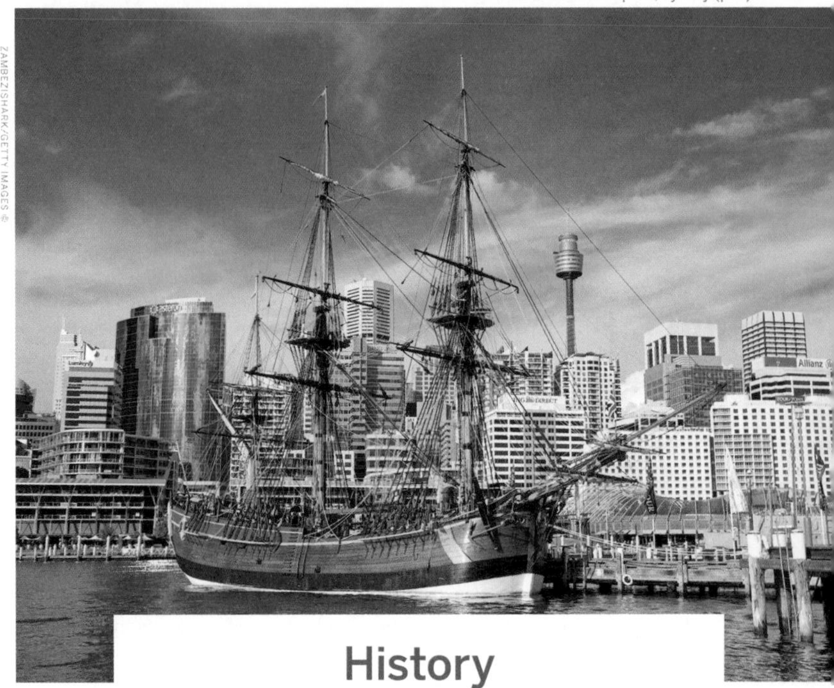

History

Australia: where the New World meets the Old in a clash of two very different versions of history. Only recently has the story of Indigenous Australians – here for more than 50,000 years before British colonisation – come to occupy its rightful place at centre stage. It is a further sign, perhaps, that this dynamic, sometimes progressive and laid-back country is really starting to grow up.

80 million years ago
Continental Australia breaks free from the Antarctic landmass and drifts north.

50,000 years ago
The first Australians arrive by sea to northern Australia.

1606
Dutch Navigator Willem Janszoon makes the first authenticated European landing on Australian soil.

Indigenous rock art (p242)

PETER EVE/TOURISM NT ©

First Australians

Human contact with Australia is thought by many to have begun around 60,000 years ago, when Aboriginal people journeyed across the straits from what is now Indonesia and Papua New Guinea. Aboriginal people, however, believe they have always inhabited the land. Undoubtedly, Indigenous life in Australia marked the beginning of the world's longest continuous cultural history.

Across the continent, Aboriginal peoples traded goods, items of spiritual significance, songs and dances across central Australia and beyond, using routes that followed the paths of ancestors from the Dreaming, the complex system of country, culture and beliefs that defines Indigenous spirituality.

An intimate understanding of plant ecology and animal behaviour ensured that food shortages were rare. Even central Australia's hostile deserts were occupied year-round, thanks to scattered permanent wells. Fire-stick farming was practised in forested areas,

1770
First Lieutenant James Cook claims the entire east coast of Australia for England.

1788
Captain Arthur Phillip and the First Fleet – 11 ships and about 1350 people – arrive at Botany Bay.

1835
John Batman negotiates a land deal with the Kulin nation; Melbourne is settled that same year.

★ Best Convict History

Museum of Sydney (p51)

Hyde Park Barracks Museum (p49)

Cascades Female Factory Historic Site (p189)

Fremantle Prison (p267)

Fremantle Prison (p267)

EA GIVEN/SHUTTERSTOCK ©

involving the burning of undergrowth and dead grass to encourage new growth, to attract game and reduce the threat of bushfires.

For more information on Aboriginal Australia, see p286.

Intruders Arrive

In April 1770, Aboriginal people standing on a beach in southeastern Australia saw an astonishing spectacle out at sea. It was an English ship, the *Endeavour,* under the command of then-Lieutenant James Cook. His gentleman passengers were English scientists visiting the Pacific to make astronomical observations and to investigate 'new worlds'. As they sailed north along the edge of this new-found land, Cook began drawing the first British chart of Australia's east coast. This map heralded the beginning of conflicts between European settlers and Indigenous peoples.

A few days after that first sighting, Cook led a party of men ashore at a place known to the Aboriginal people as Kurnell. Though the Kurnell Aboriginal people were far from welcoming, the *Endeavour*'s botanists were delighted to discover that the woods were teeming with unfamiliar plants. To celebrate this profusion, Cook renamed the place Botany Bay.

When the *Endeavour* reached the northern tip of Cape York, Cook and his men could smell the sea route home. And on a small, hilly island (Possession Island), Cook raised the Union Jack. Amid volleys of gunfire, he claimed the eastern half of the continent for King George III.

Cook's intention was not to steal land from the Aboriginal peoples. In fact he rather idealised them. 'They are far more happier than we Europeans', he wrote. 'They think themselves provided with all the necessaries of Life and that they have no superfluities.'

Convict Beginnings

Eighteen years after Cook's arrival, in 1788, the English were back to stay. They arrived in a fleet of 11 ships, packed with supplies including weapons, tools, building materials and livestock. The ships also contained 751 convicts and more than 250 soldiers, officials and

1851
A gold rush in central Victoria brings settlers from across the world. Democracy is introduced in the eastern colonies.

1880
Bushranger Ned Kelly is hanged as a criminal – and remembered as a folk hero.

1901
The Australian colonies form a federation of states. The federal parliament sits in Melbourne.

their wives. This motley 'First Fleet' was under the command of a humane and diligent naval captain, Arthur Phillip. As his orders dictated, Phillip dropped anchor at Botany Bay. But the paradise that had so delighted Joseph Banks filled Phillip with dismay. So he left his floating prison and embarked in a small boat to search for a better location. Just a short way up the coast, his heart leapt as he sailed into the finest harbour in the world. There, in a small cove, in the idyllic lands of the Eora people, he established a British penal settlement. He renamed the place after the British Home Secretary, Lord Sydney.

Phillip's official instructions urged him to colonise the land without doing violence to the local inhabitants. Among the Indigenous people he used as intermediaries was an Eora man named Bennelong, who adopted many of the white people's customs and manners. But Bennelong's people were shattered by the loss of their lands. Hundreds died of smallpox, and many of the survivors, including Bennelong himself, succumbed to alcoholism and despair.

In 1803, English officers established a second convict settlement in Van Diemen's Land (now Tasmania). Soon, reoffenders filled the grim prison at Port Arthur on the beautiful and wild coast near Hobart.

From Shackles to Freedom

At first, Sydney and the smaller colonies depended on supplies brought in by ship. Anxious to develop productive farms, the government granted land to soldiers, officers and settlers. After 30 years of trial and error, the farms began to flourish. The most irascible and ruthless of these new landholders was John Macarthur.

Macarthur was a leading member of the Rum Corps, a clique of powerful officers who bullied successive governors (including William Bligh of *Bounty* fame) and grew rich by controlling much of Sydney's trade, notably rum. But the Corps' racketeering was ended in 1810 by a tough new governor named Lachlan Macquarie. Macquarie laid out the major roads of modern-day Sydney, built some fine public buildings (many of which were designed by talented convict-architect Francis Greenway) and helped to lay the foundations for a more civil society. Macquarie also championed the rights of freed convicts, granting them land and appointing several to public office.

Southern Settlements

In the cooler grasslands of Van Diemen's Land, sheep farmers were thriving. In the 1820s they waged a bloody war against the island's Indigenous population, driving them to the brink of extinction. Now these settlers were hungry for more land.

In 1835 an ambitious young man named John Batman sailed to Port Phillip Bay on mainland Australia. On the banks of the Yarra River, he chose the location for Melbourne, famously announcing 'This is the place for a village'. Batman persuaded local Aboriginal peoples to 'sell' him their traditional lands (a whopping 250,000 hectares) for a crate of blankets, knives

1915
The Anzacs join a British invasion of Turkey: this military disaster spawns a nationalist legend.

1939
Prime Minister Robert Menzies announces that Britain is at war; 'as a result, Australia is also at war'.

1942
The Japanese bomb Darwin, the first of numerous air strikes on the northern capital.

and knick-knacks. Back in Sydney, Governor Bourke declared the contract void, not because it was unfair, but because the land officially belonged to the British Crown.

At the same time, a private British company settled Adelaide in South Australia. Proud to have no links with convicts, these God-fearing folk instituted a scheme under which their company sold land to well-heeled settlers, and used the revenue to assist poor British labourers to emigrate. When these worthies earned enough to buy land from the company, that revenue would in turn pay the fare of another shipload of labourers.

Gold & Rebellion

Transportation of convicts to eastern Australia ceased in the 1840s. This was just as well: in 1851, prospectors discovered gold in New South Wales and central Victoria, including at Ballarat. The news hit the colonies with the force of a cyclone. Young men and some women from every social class headed for the diggings. Soon they were caught up in a great rush of prospectors, publicans and prostitutes. In Victoria the British governor was alarmed – both by the way the Victorian class system had been thrown into disarray, and by the need to finance the imposition of law and order on the goldfields. His solution was to compel all miners to buy an expensive monthly licence.

But the lure of gold was too great and in the reckless excitement of the goldfields, the miners initially endured the thuggish troopers who enforced the government licence. After three years, though, the easy gold at Ballarat was gone, and miners were toiling in deep, water-sodden shafts. They were now infuriated by a corrupt and brutal system of law that held them in contempt. Under the leadership of a charismatic Irishman named Peter Lalor, they raised their own flag, the Southern Cross, and swore to defend their rights and liberties. They armed themselves and gathered inside a rough stockade at Eureka, where they waited for the government to make its move.

In the predawn of Sunday 3 December 1854, a force of troopers attacked the stockade. It was all over in 15 terrifying minutes. The brutal and one-sided battle claimed the lives of 30 miners and five soldiers. But democracy was in the air and public opinion sided with the miners. The eastern colonies were already in the process of establishing democratic parliaments, with the full support of the British authorities.

The Long Walk to Ballarat

During the 1850s gold rush in Victoria, the town of Robe in South Australia came into its own when the Victorian government whacked a $10-per-head tax on Chinese gold miners arriving to work the goldfields. Thousands of Chinese miners dodged the tax by landing at Robe instead, then walking the 400-odd kilometres to Bendigo and Ballarat: 10,000 arrived in 1857 alone. But the flood stalled as quickly as it started when the SA government instituted its own tax on the Chinese.

1945
Australia's motto: 'Populate or Perish!'. During the next 30 years more than two million immigrants arrive.

1948
Cricketer Don Bradman retires with an unsurpassed test average of 99.94 runs.

1956
The Olympic Games are held in Melbourne: the flame is lit by running champion Ron Clarke.

Meanwhile, in the West...

Western Australia lagged behind the eastern colonies by about 50 years. Though Perth was settled by genteel colonists back in 1829, its material progress was handicapped by isolation, Aboriginal resistance and the arid climate. It was not until the 1880s that the discovery of remote goldfields promised to gild the fortunes of the isolated colony. At the time, the west was just entering its own period of self-government, and its first premier was a forceful, weather-beaten explorer named John Forrest. He saw that the mining industry would fail if the government did not provide a first-class harbour, efficient railways and reliable water supplies. Ignoring the threats of private contractors, he appointed the brilliant engineer CY O'Connor to design and build each of these as government projects.

It's Just not Cricket

The year 1932 saw accusations of treachery on the cricket field. The English team, under captain Douglas Jardine, employed a violent new bowling tactic known as 'bodyline'. The aim was to unnerve Australia's star batsman, the devastatingly efficient Donald Bradman. The bitterness of the tour provoked a diplomatic crisis with Britain and became part of Australian legend. Bradman batted on. When he retired in 1948 he had a still-unsurpassed career average of 99.94 runs.

Nationhood

On 1 January 1901, Australia became a federation. When the members of the new national parliament met in Melbourne, their first aim was to protect the identity and values of a European Australia from an influx of Asians and Pacific Islanders. The solution was a law that became known as the White Australia Policy. It became a racial tenet of faith in Australia for the next 70 years.

For whites who lived inside the charmed circle of citizenship, this was to be a model society, nestled in the skirts of the British Empire. Just one year later, white women won the right to vote in federal elections. In a series of radical innovations, the government introduced a broad social welfare scheme and it protected Australian wage levels with import tariffs.

Entering the World Stage

Living on the edge of a dry and forbidding land, isolated from the rest of the world, most Australians took comfort in the knowledge that they were a dominion of the British Empire. When war broke out in Europe in 1914, thousands of Australian men rallied to the Empire's call. They had their first taste of death on 25 April 1915, when the Australian and New Zealand Army Corps (the Anzacs) joined thousands of other British and French troops in an assault

1965
Menzies commits Australian troops to the American war in Vietnam, and divides the nation.

1967
In a national referendum, white Australians vote overwhelmingly to give citizenship to Indigenous people.

1975
Against a background of reform and inflation, Governor General Sir John Kerr sacks the Whitlam government.

★ Best History Museums

Rocks Discovery Museum (p48)

Melbourne Museum (p153)

National Museum of Australia (p84)

Australian War Memorial (p85)

Melbourne Museum (p153)

on the Gallipoli Peninsula in Turkey. It was eight months before the British commanders acknowledged that the tactic had failed. By then 8141 young Australians were dead. Before long the Australian Imperial Force was fighting in the killing fields of Europe. By the time the war ended, 60,000 Australians had died.

In the 1920s Australia embarked on a decade of chaotic change. The country careered wildly through the 1920s until it collapsed into the abyss of the Great Depression in 1929. World prices for wheat and wool plunged. Unemployment brought its shame and misery to one in three households.

War with Japan

After 1933, the economy began to recover. Daily life was hardly dampened when Hitler hurled Europe into a new war in 1939. Though Australians had long feared Japan, they took it for granted that the British navy would keep them safe. In December 1941, Japan bombed the US Fleet at Pearl Harbor. Weeks later, the 'impregnable' British naval base in Singapore crumbled.

As the Japanese swept through Southeast Asia and into Papua New Guinea, the British announced that they could not spare any resources to defend Australia. But US commander General Douglas MacArthur saw that Australia was the perfect base for American operations in the Pacific. In fierce sea and land battles, Allied forces turned back the Japanese advance. Importantly, it was the USA, not the British Empire, who saved Australia. The days of alliance with Britain alone were numbered.

Visionary Peace

When WWII ended, a new slogan rang out: 'Populate or Perish!'. The Australian government embarked on a scheme to attract thousands of immigrants. People flocked from Britain and non-English-speaking countries. They included Greeks, Italians, Serbs, Croatians and Dutch, followed by Turks and many others.

1992
The High Court of Australia recognises the principle of native title in the Mabo decision.

2000
The Sydney Olympic Games are a triumph of spectacle and goodwill.

2007
Kevin Rudd is elected prime minister and says 'Sorry' to Australia's Indigenous peoples.

In addition to growing world demand for Australia's primary products (wool, meat and wheat), there were jobs in manufacturing and on major public works, notably the mighty Snowy Mountains Hydro-Electric Scheme in the mountains near Canberra.

This era of growth and prosperity was dominated by Robert Menzies, the founder of the Liberal Party of Australia, and Australia's longest-serving prime minister. Menzies was steeped in British tradition, and was also a vigilant opponent of communism. As Asia succumbed to the chill of the Cold War, Australia and New Zealand entered a formal military alliance with the USA – the 1951 Anzus security pact. When the USA jumped into a civil war in Vietnam, Menzies committed Australian forces to battle. The following year Menzies retired, leaving his successors a bitter legacy.

In an atmosphere of youthful rebellion and new-found nationalism, the Labor Party was elected to power in 1972 under an idealistic lawyer named Gough Whitlam. In four short years his government transformed the country, ending conscription and abolishing university fees. He introduced a free universal health scheme, no-fault divorce, and the principles of Indigenous land rights and equal pay for women.

By 1975, the Whitlam government was rocked by inflation and scandal. At the end of 1975 his government was infamously dismissed from office by the governor general.

Modern Challenges

Today Australia faces new challenges. After two centuries of development, the strains on the environment are starting to show – on water supplies, forests, soil and the oceans.

Under the conservative John Howard, Australia's second-longest serving prime minister (1996–2007), the country grew closer to the USA, joining the Americans in their war in Iraq. The government's harsh treatment of asylum seekers, its refusal to acknowledge the reality of climate change, its anti-union reforms and the prime minister's lack of empathy with Indigenous peoples dismayed many liberal-minded Australians. But Howard presided over a period of economic growth and won continuing support in middle Australia.

In 2007, Howard was defeated by the Labor Party's Kevin Rudd, an ex-diplomat who immediately issued a formal apology to Indigenous Australians for the injustices they had suffered over the past two centuries. Though it promised sweeping reforms in environment and education, the Rudd government found itself faced with a crisis when the world economy crashed in 2008; by June 2010 it had cost Rudd his position. Incoming prime minister Julia Gillard, the first woman to hold the position, battled slow economic recovery and diminishing party support, eventually losing her job to a resurgent Rudd in June 2013. Rudd was then ousted again by his right-wing adversary Tony Abbott and the Liberal–National Party Coalition in the 2013 federal election. With *his* poll numbers slipping, Abbott then fell to Liberal Party colleague Malcolm Turnbull in 2015 – Australia's fifth incoming Prime Minister in as many years.

2010
Kevin Rudd is ousted as prime minister by Julia Gillard, the first woman to hold the office.

2015
Tony Abbott is replaced by Malcolm Turnbull in a Liberal Party leadership spill. Five prime ministers in five years!

2016
Prime Minister Turnbull narrowly wins a federal election and returns to power with a wafer-thin majority in parliament.

Kuku Yalanji man applying ochre markings to his arm

Aboriginal Australia

A visit to Australia would not be complete without experiencing the rich cultures of Aboriginal and Torres Strait Islander peoples. Visitors have an opportunity to learn and interact with the oldest continuous cultures in the world and share a way of life that has existed for more than 50,000 years.

History of Aboriginal Australia

First Australians

Many academics believe Indigenous Australians came here from somewhere else, with scientific evidence placing them on the continent at least 40,000 to 60,000 years ago. Aboriginal people, however, believe they have always inhabited the land.

At the time of European contact, the Aboriginal population was grouped into 300 or more different nations, with distinct languages and land boundaries. Most Aboriginal people did not have permanent shelters but moved within their territory and followed seasonal patterns of animal migration and plant availability. The diversity of landscapes in

Australia meant that each nation varied in their lifestyles; although they were distinct cultural groups, there were also many common elements, and each nation had several clans or family groups who were responsible for looking after specific areas.

From the desert to the sea, Aboriginal people shaped their lives according to their environments and developed different skills and a wide body of knowledge on their territory.

Colonised

The effects of colonisation started immediately after the Europeans arrived. It began with the appropriation of land and water resources and an epidemic of diseases – smallpox killed around half of the Indigenous people who were native to Sydney Harbour. A period of resistance occurred as Aboriginal people fought back to retain their land and way of life; as violence and massacres swept the country, many were pushed away from their traditional lands. Over a century, the Aboriginal population was decimated by 90%.

The Stolen Generations

When Australia became a Federation in 1901, a government policy known as the 'White Australia policy' was put in place. It was implemented mainly to restrict nonwhite immigration to Australia but the policy also had a huge impact on Indigenous Australians. Assimilation into the broader society was encouraged by all sectors of government, with the intent to eventually 'fade out' the Aboriginal race. A policy of forcibly removing Aboriginal and Torres Strait Islander children from their families operated from 1909 to 1969. It is estimated that around 100,000 Indigenous children – or one in three – were taken from their families: they became known as the Stolen Generations.

On 13 February 2008 Kevin Rudd, then prime minister of Australia, offered a national apology to the Stolen Generations.

Rights & Reconciliation

The relationship between Indigenous Australians and other Australians hasn't always been an easy one. Over the years several systematic policies have been put in place, but these have often had underlying and conflicting motives that include control over the land, decimating the population, protection, assimilation, self-determination and self-management.

The history of forced resettlement, removal of children, and the loss of land and culture can never be erased, even with governments addressing some of the issues. Current policies focus on 'closing the gap' and centre on better delivery of essential services to improve lives, but there is still great disparity between Indigenous Australians and the rest of the population, including lower standards of education, employment, health and living conditions; high incarceration and suicide rates; and a lower life expectancy.

Throughout all of this, Aboriginal people have managed to maintain their identity and link to country and culture. Although there is a growing recognition and acceptance of Indigenous Australians' place in this country, there is still a long way to go.

Aboriginal Culture

Aboriginal culture has never been static, and continues to evolve with the changing times and environment. New technologies and mediums are now used to tell Aboriginal stories, and cultural tourism and hospitality ventures where visitors can experience an Aboriginal perspective have been established. You can learn about ancestral beings at particular natural landmarks, look at rock art that is thousands of years old, taste traditional foods or attend an Aboriginal festival or performance.

★ Indigenous Art Encounters

National Gallery of Australia (p84), Canberra

Rock art, Kakadu National Park (p242)

Art Gallery of NSW (p49)

Koorie Heritage Trust (p142), Melbourne

Art Gallery of Western Australia (p262)

Aboriginal artworks

JOHN BORTHWICK/GETTY IMAGES ©

The Land

Aboriginal culture views humans as part of the ecology, not separate from it. Everything is connected – a whole environment that sustains the spiritual, economic and cultural lives of the people. In turn, Aboriginal people have sustained the land over thousands of years, through knowledge passed on in ceremonies, rituals, songs and stories. Land is intrinsically connected to identity and spirituality; all land in Australia is reflected in Aboriginal lore but particular places may be significant for religious and cultural beliefs. Sacred sites can be parts of rocks, hills, trees or water and are associated with an ancestral being or an event that occurred. Often these sites are part of a Dreaming story and link people across areas.

The Arts

Aboriginal art has impacted the Australian landscape, and is now showcased at national and international events and celebrated as a significant part of Australian culture. It still retains the role of passing on knowledge but today it is also important for economic, educational and political reasons. In many Indigenous communities, art has become a major source of employment and income.

Rock Art

Rock art is the oldest form of human art and Aboriginal rock art stretches back thousands of years. Rock art is found in every state of Australia and many sites are thousands of years old. There are a number of different styles of rock art across Australia. These include engravings in sandstone and stencils, prints and drawings in rock shelters.

Some of the oldest examples of engravings can be found in the Pilbara in Western Australia and in Olary in South Australia, where there is an engraving of a crocodile. All national parks surrounding Sydney have rock engravings and can be easily accessed and viewed. At Gariwerd (the Grampians) in Victoria there are handprints and hand stencils.

In the Northern Territory many of the rock-art sites have patterns and symbols that appear in paintings, carvings and other cultural material. Kakadu National Park has over 5000 recorded sites but many more are thought to exist.

Contemporary Art

The National Gallery of Australia (p84) in Canberra has a fantastic collection, but contemporary Aboriginal art can also be viewed at any public art gallery or in one of the many independent galleries dealing in Aboriginal work. The central desert area is still a hub for Aboriginal art and Alice Springs is one of the best places to see and buy art. Cairns is another hotspot for innovative Aboriginal art.

Torres Strait Islanders

Aboriginal society is a diverse group of several hundred sovereign nations. Torres Strait Islanders are a Melanesian people with a separate culture from that of Aboriginal Australians, though they have a shared history. Together, these two groups form Australia's Indigenous peoples.

Music

Music has always been a vital part of Aboriginal culture. Songs were important for teaching and passing on knowledge, and musical instruments were often used in healing, ceremonies and rituals. The most well-known instrument is the *yidaki* or didgeridoo, which was traditionally only played by men in northern Australia.

This rich musical heritage continues today with a very strong contemporary music industry. Contemporary artists such as Dan Sultan and Jessica Mauboy have crossed over successfully into the mainstream and have won major music awards, and can be seen regularly on popular programs and at major music festivals.

Performing Arts

Dance and theatre are a vital part of social and ceremonial life and important elements in Aboriginal culture. Historically, dances often told stories to pass on knowledge. Like other art forms, dance has adapted to the modern world and contemporary dance companies and groups have merged traditional forms into a modern interpretation. The most well-known dance company is the internationally acclaimed Bangarra Dance Theatre (p39).

Theatre also draws on the storytelling tradition. Currently there are two major Aboriginal theatre companies, Ilbijerri (www.ilbijerri.com) in Melbourne and Yirra Yaakin (www.yirrayaakin.com.au) in Perth. Traditionally drama and dance came together in ceremonies or corroborees and this still occurs in many contemporary productions.

TV, Radio & Film

Aboriginal people have developed an extensive media network of radio, print and television services. There are over 120 Aboriginal radio stations and programs operating across Australia in cities, rural areas and remote communities. From its base in Brisbane, the National Indigenous Radio Service (NIRS; www.nirs.org.au) broadcasts four radio channels of Aboriginal content. There's also Radio Larrakia (www.radiolarrakia.org) in Darwin and Koori Radio (www.kooriradio.com) in Sydney.

There is a thriving Aboriginal film industry and in recent years feature films including *The Sapphires*, *Bran Nue Day*, *Samson and Delilah* and *Putuparri and the Rainmakers* have had mainstream success. Since the first Aboriginal television channel, NITV (www.nitv.org.au), was launched in 2007, there has been a large rise in the number of filmmakers wanting to tell their stories.

Baby wombat in Tasmania

Environment

Australia's plants and animals are just about the closest things to alien life you are likely to encounter on earth. That's because Australia has been isolated from the other continents for a very long time: around 80 million years. The result today is the world's most distinct natural realm – and one of the most diverse.

Dr Tim Flannery

Fundamentally Different

There are two important factors that go a long way towards explaining nature in Australia: its soils and its climate. Both are unique.

In recent geological times, on other continents, processes such as volcanism, mountain building and glacial activity have been busy creating new soil. All of these soil-forming processes have been almost absent from Australia. Under such conditions no new soil is created and the old soil is leached of all its goodness by the rain, and is blown and washed away. It is an old, infertile landscape and life in Australia has been adapting to these conditions for aeons.

Australia's misfortune in respect to soils is echoed in its climate. Most of Australia experiences seasons – sometimes severe ones – yet life does not respond solely to them.

This can clearly be seen by the fact that although there's plenty of snow and cold country in Australia, there are almost no trees that shed their leaves in winter, nor do many Australian animals hibernate. Instead there is a far more potent climatic force that Australian life must obey: El Niño.

El Niño is a complex climatic pattern that can cause major weather shifts around the South Pacific. The cycle of flood and drought that El Niño brings to Australia is profound. Our rivers – even the mighty Murray River, the nation's largest river, which runs through the southeast – can be miles wide one year, yet you can literally step over its flow the next. This is the power of El Niño, and its effect, when combined with Australia's poor soils, manifests itself compellingly.

Shark!

Despite media hype (and a particularly bad year in 2014, with five deaths), Australia has averaged just one shark-attack fatality per year since 1791 – a remarkably low number considering how many beaches there are around the coastline. Sydney in particular has a bad rep. Attacks here peaked between 1920 and 1940, but since shark net installation began in 1937 there's only been one fatality (1963), and dorsal-fin sightings are rare enough to make the nightly news. Realistically, you're more likely to get hit by a bus – so look both ways before crossing the road on the way to the beach!

Fuel-Efficient Fauna

Australia is, of course, famous as the home of the kangaroo (aka just plain 'roo') and other marsupials. Have you ever wondered why kangaroos hop? It turns out that hopping is the most efficient way of getting about at medium speeds. This is because the energy of the bounce is stored in the tendons of the legs – much like in a pogo stick – while the intestines bounce up and down like a piston, emptying and filling the lungs without needing to activate the chest muscles.

Marsupials are so energy efficient that they need to eat one-fifth less food than equivalent-sized placental mammals (everything from bats to rats, whales and ourselves). But some have taken energy efficiency much further: if you visit a wildlife park or zoo, you might notice that faraway look in a koala's eyes. Several years ago biologists announced that koalas are the only living creatures that have brains that don't fit their skulls. Instead they have a shrivelled walnut of a brain that rattles around in a fluid-filled cranium. We now believe that the koala has sacrificed its brain to energy efficiency – brains cost a lot to run. Koalas eat gum leaves, which are so toxic that they use 20% of their energy just detoxifying this food. This leaves little energy for the brain, but fortunately living in the treetops – where there are so few predators – means that they can get by with few wits at all.

The peculiar constraints of the Australian environment have not made everything dumb. The koala's nearest relative, the wombat (of which there are three species), has a large brain for a marsupial. These creatures live in complex burrows and can weigh up to 35kg, making them the largest herbivorous burrowers on earth.

Two unique monotremes (egg-laying mammals) live in Australia: the bumbling echidna, something akin to a hedgehog but bigger and spikier; and the platypus, a bit like an otter, with webbed feet and a ducklike bill. Echidnas are common along bushland trails, but platypuses are elusive, seen at dawn and dusk in quiet rivers and streams.

Relatively few of Australia's birds are seasonal breeders, and few migrate – instead, they breed when the rain comes. A large percentage are nomads, following the rain across the breadth of the continent.

Dish from Cullen Wines restaurant, Margaret River

Food & Drink

Not so long ago, Australians proudly survived on a diet of 'meat and three veg'. Fine fare was a Sunday roast, and lasagne or croissants were considered exotic. Not any more. These days Australian gastronomy is keen to break rules, backed up by award-winning wines, world-class coffee, an organic revolution in the importance of fresh produce and a booming craft beer scene.

Mod Oz?

The phrase Modern Australian (Mod Oz) has been coined to classify contemporary Australian cuisine: a melange of East and West; a swirl of Atlantic and Pacific Rim; a flourish of authentic French and Italian.

Immigration has been the key to this culinary concoction. An influx of immigrants since WWII, from Europe, Asia, the Middle East and Africa, introduced new ingredients and new ways to use staples. Vietnamese, Japanese, Fijian – no matter where it's from, there are expat communities and interested locals keen to cook and eat it. You'll find Jamaicans using Scotch bonnet peppers and Tunisians making *tajine*.

As the Australian appetite for diversity and invention grows, so does the food culture surrounding it. Cookbooks and foodie magazines are bestsellers, and Australian celebrity chefs – highly sought-after overseas – reflect Australia's multiculturalism in their backgrounds and dishes. Cooking TV shows, both competitions and foodie travel documentaries, have become mandatory nightly viewing.

If all this sounds overwhelming, never fear. The range of food in Australia is a true asset. You'll find that dishes are characterised by bold and interesting flavours and fresh ingredients. All palates are catered for: the chilli metre spans gentle to extreme, seafood is plentiful, meats are full-flavoured and vegetarian needs are considered (especially in the cities).

Vegemite

Vegemite: you'll either love it or hate it (...for reference, Barack Obama diplomatically called it 'horrible'). It's certainly an acquired taste – a black salty spread slathered onto toast with butter – but Australians consume more than 22 million jars of the stuff every year. And they're particularly pleased as ownership of this national icon recently returned to Australian hands for the first time since 1928.

Cafes & Coffee

Cafes in Australia generally serve good-value food: they're usually more casual than restaurants and you can get a decent meal for around $20, although many only open for breakfast and lunch. Kids are usually more than welcome.

Coffee has become a nationwide addiction: there are Italian-style espresso machines in virtually every cafe, boutique roasters are all the rage and, in urban areas, the qualified barista (coffee-maker) is the norm. Sydney and even subtropical Brisbane have borne generations of coffee snobs, but Melbourne takes top billing as Australia's caffeine capital. The cafe scene here rivals the most vibrant in the world: the best way to dunk yourself in it is by wandering the city centre's cafe-lined lanes.

Fire Up the Barbie

The iconic Australian barbecue (BBQ or 'barbie') is a near-mandatory cultural experience. In summer locals invite their friends around at dinnertime and fire up the barbie, grilling burgers, sausages ('snags'), steaks, seafood, and veggie, meat or seafood skewers. If you're invited to a BBQ, bring some meat and cold beer. Year-round the BBQ is wheeled out at weekends for quick-fire lunches. There are plenty of free electric or gas BBQs in parks around the country, too – a terrific traveller-friendly option.

Cheers!

No matter what your poison, you're in the right country if you're after a drink.

Wine

Long recognised as among the finest in the world, Australian wine is now one of the country's top exports. In fact, if you're in the country's cooler southern climes (particularly in South Australia, and even in southeast Queensland), you're probably not far from a wine region. Some regions have been producing wines from the early days of settlement more than 220 years ago. Most wineries have small cellar-door sales where you can taste for a nominal fee (or often free). Although plenty of good wine comes from big producers with economies of scale on their side, the most interesting wines are usually made by smaller, family-run wineries.

★ Best Wine Tasting

National Wine Centre of Australia (p209), Adelaide, South Australia

McLaren Vale (p204), South Australia

Barossa Valley (p202), South Australia

Yarra Valley (p164), Victoria

Domain Chandon winery (p164), Yarra Valley

WALTER BIBIKOW/GETTY IMAGES ©

Beer

As the public develops a more sophisticated palate, local craft beers are rising to the occasion. There's a growing wealth of microbrewed flavours and varieties on offer, challenging the nation's entrenched predilection for mass-produced lager. Have a look at www.findabrewery.com.au for brewery listings. Most beers have an alcohol content between 3.5% and 5.5% – less than many European beers but more than most in North America.

The terminology used to order beer varies state by state. In New South Wales you ask for a schooner (425mL) if you're thirsty and a middy (285mL) if you're not quite so dry. In Victoria the 285mL measure is called a pot; in Tasmania it's called a 10-ounce. Pints can either be 425mL or 568mL, depending on where you are. Mostly you can just ask for a beer and see what turns up.

Spirits

In recent years, Tasmania – with its chilly Scotland-like highlands and clean water – has become a whisky-producing hotspot. There are about a dozen distillers around the state now, bottling superb single malt for a growing international market. Keep an eye out for excellent drops from Sullivans Cove Whisky, Nant Distillery and Hellyers Road Distillery. Gins from Kangaroo Island Spirits in South Australia and Melbourne's Four Pillars are also impressive.

Etiquette

At the bar, 'shouting' is a revered custom, where people take turns to pay for a round of drinks. Leaving before it's your 'shout' won't win you many friends! Once the drinks are distributed, a toast of 'Cheers!' is standard practice: everyone should touch glasses and look each other in the eye as they clink – failure to do so purportedly results in seven years' bad sex.

Collingwood Magpies vs Brisbane Lions AFL match

NEALE COUSLAND/SHUTTERSTOCK ©

Sport

Whether they're filling stadiums, glued to a pub's big screen or on the couch, Australians invest heavily in sport – both fiscally and emotionally. The federal government kicks in more than $300 million every year – enough for Australia to hold its own against formidable international sporting opponents. But it's the local football codes that really excite Aussies and tap into primal passions.

Australian Rules Football

Australia's number-one watched sport is Australian Rules football. Originally exclusive to Victoria, the Australian Football League (AFL; www.afl.com.au) has expanded into South Australia, Western Australia and even rugby-dominated New South Wales and Queensland. Long kicks, high marks and brutal collisions whip crowds into fevered frenzies: the roar of 50,000-plus fans yelling 'Carn the [insert team nickname]' and '*Baaalll!!!!*' upsets dogs in suburban backyards for kilometres around. Every September it culminates in the AFL Grand Final at Melbourne's MCG stadium – one of Australia's most-watched sporting events.

Rugby

The National Rugby League (NRL; www.nrl.com.au) is the most popular football code north of the Murray River, with the season highlight the annual State of Origin series between

★ Best Sporting Experiences

AFL football, Melbourne Cricket Ground (p148)

Surfing (p98), Byron Bay

Cricket, Sydney Cricket Ground (p70)

Sydney to Hobart Yacht Race (p194)

Sydney to Hobart Yacht Race (p194)

ALVOV/SHUTTERSTOCK ©

NSW and Queensland. To watch an NRL game is to fully appreciate Newton's laws of motion – bone-crunching! Meanwhile, the national rugby union team, the Wallabies, won the Rugby World Cup in 1991 and 1999 and was runner-up in 2003 (to England) and 2015 (to eternal rivals New Zealand). Between World Cups, Bledisloe Cup games against New Zealand are hotly contested.

Soccer

Australia's national soccer team, the Socceroos, won the 2015 Asian Cup and qualified for the 2006, 2010 and 2014 World Cups, after a long history of almost-but-not-quite getting there. Results were mixed, but national pride in the team remains undiminished. The national A-League (www.a-league.com.au) has enjoyed increased popularity in recent years.

Cricket

The Aussies dominated world test and one-day cricket for much of the 2000s, but the retirements of once-in-a-lifetime players like Shane Warne and Ricky Ponting exposed a leaky pool of second-tier talent. A 'rebuilding phase' ensued, accompanied by several test series losses to arch-rivals England. But things are looking up: after winning the 2015 one-day cricket World Cup, the team is returning to a level of success to which the viewing public has become accustomed, although world domination is no longer assured.

Tennis

Every January, tennis shoes melt in the Melbourne heat at the Australian Open (www.ausopen.com), one of tennis' four Grand Slam tournaments. In the men's comp, following the retirement of former world number one Lleyton Hewitt, Australians don't quite know what to make of the talented-but-flawed enfants terribles, Nick Kyrgios and Bernard Tomic. In the women's game, Australian Sam Stosur won the US Open in 2011 and has been hovering around the top-20 player rankings ever since.

Horse Racing

Australian's love to bet on the 'nags' – in fact, betting on horse racing is almost a national hobby! On the first Tuesday in November the nation stops for a world-famous horse race, the Melbourne Cup (www.melbournecup.com). In Victoria it's cause for a holiday. Australia's most famous cup winner was Phar Lap, who won in 1930, and later died of a mystery illness in the USA. Makybe Diva is a more recent star, winning three Melbourne Cups in a row before retiring in 2005.

Woman hiking in the Blue Mountains (p74)

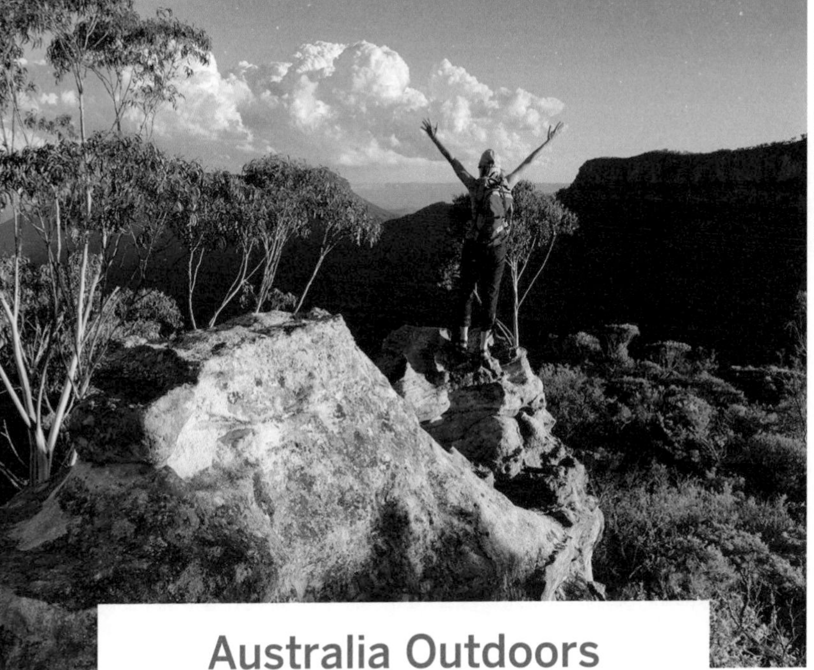

LEAH-ANNE THOMPSON/SHUTTERSTOCK ©

Australia Outdoors

A vast, underpopulated nation, Australia serves up plenty of excuses to just sit back and roll your eyes across the varied landscape. But that same landscape lends itself to boundless outdoor pursuits – whether it's getting active on wilderness trails, bike tracks and ski slopes on dry land, or riding ocean swells and diving on reefs offshore.

Bushwalking

Bushwalking (aka hiking, trekking or tramping, depending on where you're from) is supremely popular in Australia, with national parks and vast tracts of untouched scrub and forest providing ample opportunity. June to August are the best walking months up north; down south, summer (December to February) is better.

Lonely Planet's *Walking in Australia* provides detailed information and trail notes for Australia's best bushwalks. Online, look at www.bushwalkingaustralia.org. The book *Sydney's Best Harbour & Coastal Walks* details the excellent 5.5km Bondi to Coogee Clifftop Walk and the 10km Manly Scenic Walkway, in addition to wilder walks.

★ Best Surf Spots

Byron Bay (p98), New South Wales
Bells Beach (p172), Victoria
Sydney's northern beaches (p56)
Anglesea (p172), Victoria

Surfing at Tamarama Beach (p46)

RUGLIG/SHUTTERSTOCK ©

Other good sources of bushwalking information and trail descriptions are outdoor stockists and the websites of the various state government national parks departments. Online, see www.lonelyplanet.com/australia/things-to-do/bushwalking-in-australia.

Cycling

Cyclists in Australia have access to plenty of cycling routes and can tour the country for days, weekends or even multiweek trips. Or you can just rent a bike for a few hours and wheel around a city.

Standout longer routes include the Murray to the Mountains Rail Trail and the East Gippsland Rail Trail in Victoria. In Western Australia the Munda Biddi Trail offers 900km of mountain biking, or you can rampage along the same distance on the Mawson Trail in South Australia. The 480km Tasmanian Trail is a north–south mountain-bike route across the length of the island state.

Rental rates charged by most outfits for road or mountain bikes start at around $25/50 per hour/day. Most states have bicycle organisations that can provide maps and advice.

Online, www.bicycles.net.au is a useful resource; in print, there's Lonely Planet's *Cycling Australia*.

Diving & Snorkelling

Professional Association of Diving Instructors (PADI) dive courses are offered throughout the country. Courses range from two to five days and cost anything between $350 and $850. Alternatively, hiring a mask, snorkel and fins is an affordable way to get underwater.

In Queensland, the Great Barrier Reef has more dazzling dive sites than you can poke a fin at. There are coral reefs off some mainland beaches and around many islands. Many day trips to the reef include snorkelling gear for free.

North of Sydney in New South Wales, try Broughton Island near Port Stephens, and, further north, Fish Rock Cave off South West Rocks is renowned for its excellent diving, with shells, schools of clownfish and humpback whales. On the NSW south coast popular diving spots include Jervis Bay, Montague Island and Merimbula.

In WA, Ningaloo Reef is every bit as interesting as the east-coast coral reefs, without the tourist numbers. Rapid Bay jetty off the Gulf St Vincent coast in SA is renowned for its abundant marine life, while in Tasmania the Bay of Fires and Eaglehawk Neck are popular spots.

Check out www.diveoz.com.au online for nationwide info.

Skiing & Snowboarding

Australia has a small but enthusiastic skiing industry, with snowfields straddling the NSW–Victoria border. The season is relatively short, however, running from about mid-June to early September, with unpredictable snowfalls. The top places to ski are in the Snowy Mountains in NSW (Perisher Valley and Thredbo snowfields), and Mt Buller, Falls Creek and Mt Hotham in Victoria's High Country. Tasmania has a couple of very low-key options, at Mt Field and Ben Lomond.

See www.ski.com.au for ski-cams, forecasts and reports.

Surfing

World-class waves can be found all around Australia. If you've never surfed before, a lesson or two will get you started.

In NSW, Sydney is strewn with ocean beaches with decent breaks. Further north, Crescent Head is the longboard capital of Australia, and there are brilliant breaks at Lennox Head and Byron Bay. On the south coast, try Jervis Bay and Ulladulla.

There are magical breaks along Queensland's southeastern coast, notably at Coolangatta, Burleigh Heads, Surfers Paradise, North Stradbroke Island and Noosa.

Victoria's Southern Ocean coastline has impressive surf. Bells Beach hosts the annual Rip Curl Pro comp. For the less experienced, there are surf schools in Victoria at Anglesea, Lorne and Phillip Island.

Southern WA is a surfing mecca (head for Margaret River), while SA's Cactus Beach is remote but internationally lauded. Tasmania's cold-water surf spots include legendary Shipstern Bluff, Australia's heaviest wave.

See www.coastalwatch.com for forecasts and surf-cams.

Wildlife Watching

Wildlife is one of Australia's top selling points. Most national parks are home to native fauna, although much of it is nocturnal so you may need good flashlight skills to spot it. Australia is also a twitcher's haven.

In NSW there are platypuses and gliders in New England National Park, and 120 bird species in Dorrigo National Park. Border Ranges National Park is home to a quarter of all of Australia's bird species. Koalas are everywhere around Port Macquarie. In Victoria, Wilsons Promontory National Park teems with wildlife – wombats seem to have right of way!

In Queensland, head to Malanda for birdlife, turtles and pademelons; Cape Tribulation for even better birdlife; Magnetic Island for koalas; Fraser Island for dingoes; and the Daintree for cassowaries. In SA, Flinders Chase National Park on Kangaroo Island has platypuses, kangaroos and New Zealand fur seals.

In Tasmania, Maria Island is another twitcher's paradise (Tasmanian devils, too!), while Mt William and Mt Field National Parks and Bruny Island teem with native fauna. In the Northern Territory, head to Kakadu National Park for birdlife and crocodiles.

Western Australia has whale sharks and manta rays at Ningaloo Marine Park, fur seals and sea lions at Rottnest Island, Esperance and Rockingham, and all manner of sea creatures at Monkey Mia. Canberra has the richest birdlife of any Australian capital city, plus grey kangaroos at Namadgi National Park.

Whale-watching hot spots include Victor Harbor and Head of Bight in SA, Warrnambool in Victoria, Hervey Bay in Queensland and out on the ocean beyond Sydney Harbour. If you're lucky enough to be out on the water with one of them, give them a wide berth – humanity owes them a little peace and quiet!

LEV KROPOTOV/SHUTTERSTOCK ©

Survival Guide

Directory A–Z

Accommodation

Australia has accommodation for all budgets, but you still need to book ahead – especially through summer (December to February), over Easter and during school holidays, when prices are at their highest. Outside these times you'll find useful discounts and lower walk-in rates. Notable exceptions include central Australia, the Top End and Australia's ski resorts, where summer is the low season and prices drop substantially.

B&Bs

Australian bed-and-breakfast options include restored miners' cottages, converted barns, rambling old houses, upmarket country manors and beachside bungalows. Tariffs are typically in the midrange bracket, but can be higher. In areas that attract weekenders – historic towns, wine regions, accessible forest regions such as the Blue Mountains in New South Wales and the Dandenongs in Victoria – B&Bs are often upmarket, charging small fortunes for weekend stays in high season.

Online resources:

Beautiful Accommodation (www.beautifulaccommodation.com) A select crop of luxury B&Bs and self-contained houses.

Hosted Accommodation Australia (www.australianbedandbreakfast.com.au) Listings for B&Bs, farmstays, cottages and homesteads.

OZ Bed and Breakfast (www.ozbedandbreakfast.com) Nationwide website.

Book Your Stay Online

For more accommodation reviews by Lonely Planet writers, check out http://hotels.lonelyplanet.com/australia. You'll find independent reviews, as well as recommendations on the best places to stay. Best of all, you can book online.

Holiday Apartments

Holiday apartments are particularly common in coastal areas, with reservations often handled by local real estate agents or online booking engines.

Costs For a two-bedroom flat, you're looking at anywhere from $150 to $250 per night, but you will pay much more in high season and for serviced apartments in major cities.

Facilities Self-contained holiday apartments range from simple, studiolike rooms with small kitchenettes, to two-bedroom apartments with full laundries and state-of-the-art entertainment systems: great value for multinight stays.

Hotels

Hotels in Australian cities or well-touristed places are generally of the business or luxury-chain variety (midrange to top end): comfortable, anonymous, mod-con-filled rooms in multistorey blocks. For these hotels we quote 'rack rates' (official advertised rates – usually upwards of $160 a night), though significant discounts can be offered when business is quiet.

Motels

Drive-up motels offer comfortable midrange accommodation and are found all over Australia, often on the edges of urban centres. They rarely offer a cheaper rate for singles, so are better value for couples or groups of three. You'll mostly pay between $120 and $180 for a simple room with a kettle, fridge, TV, air-con and bathroom.

Pubs

Many Australian pubs (from the term 'public house') were built during boom times, so they're often among the largest, most extravagant buildings in town. Some have been restored, but generally rooms remain small and weathered, with a long amble down the hall to the bathroom. They're usually central and cheap –

singles/doubles with shared facilities from $60/100, more if you want a private bathroom.

Resorts

Australia does a nice line in resorts and other forms of accommodation that represent destinations in their own right. Most work so well because their locations are prized patches of real estate, often on private concessions in remote areas that are for the exclusive enjoyment of guests. Rates are high – up to $3000 per night – and most have minimum stays, but prices usually include all meals and activities.

Customs Regulations

For detailed information on customs and quarantine regulations, contact the **Department of Immigration and Border Protection** (☎1300 363 263, 02-6275 6666; www.border.gov.au).

When entering Australia you can bring most articles in free of duty provided that customs is satisfied they are for personal use and that you'll be taking them with you when you leave. Duty-free quotas per person (note the unusually low figure for cigarettes):

Alcohol 2.25L (over the age of 18)

Cigarettes 50 cigarettes (over the age of 18)

Dutiable goods Up to the value of $900 ($450 for people under 18)

Narcotics, of course, are illegal, and customs inspectors and their highly trained hounds are diligent in sniffing them out. Quarantine regulations are strict, so you *must* declare all goods of animal or vegetable origin – wooden spoons, straw hats, the lot. Fresh food (meat, cheese, fruit, vegetables etc) and flowers are prohibited. There are disposal bins located in airports where you can dump any questionable items if you don't want to bother with an inspection. You must declare currency in excess of $10,000 (including foreign currency).

Climate

Cairns

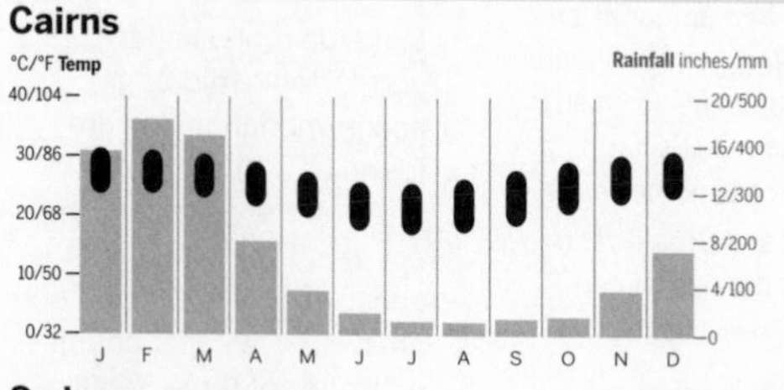

Sydney

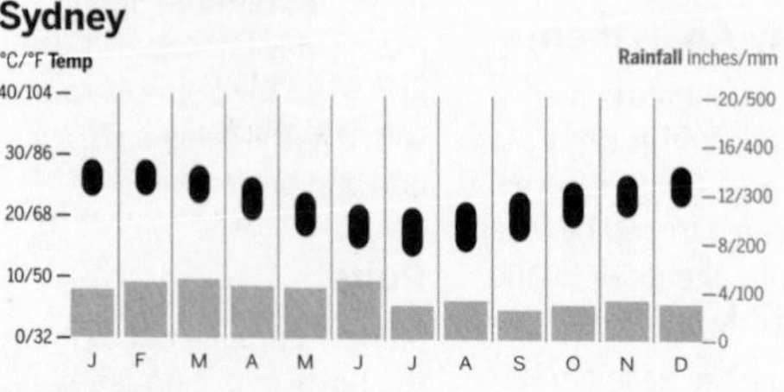

Melbourne

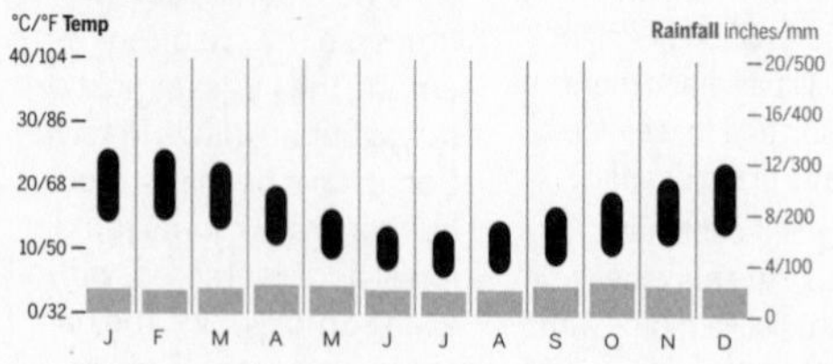

Discount Cards

Travellers over the age of 60 with some form of identification (eg a state-issued seniors card or overseas equivalent) are sometimes eligible for concession prices for public transport.

The internationally recognised **International Student Identity Card** (ISIC; www.isic.org) is available to full-time students aged 12 and over. The card gives the bearer discounts on accommodation, transport and admission to various attractions. Similar are the International Youth Travel Card (IYTC), issued to nonstudents under 26 years of age; and the International Teacher Identity Card (ITIC), available to teaching professionals. All three cards are available online and from student travel companies ($30).

Electricity

Type I
230V/50Hz

Food

See the Food & Drink chapter (p292) for more information.

The following price ranges refer to a standard main course:

$ Less than $15

$$ $15–32

$$$ More than $32

GLBTI Travellers

Australia is a popular destination for gay and lesbian travellers, with the so-called 'pink tourism' appeal of Sydney especially big, thanks largely to the city's annual, high-profile and spectacular Sydney Gay & Lesbian Mardi Gras. In general, Australians are open-minded about homosexuality, but the further from the cities you get, the more likely you are to run into suspicion or hostility.

Throughout the country, but particularly on the east coast, there are tour operators, travel agents and accommodation places that make a point of welcoming gay men and lesbians.

Same-sex acts are legal in all states, but the age of consent varies.

Major Gay & Lesbian Events

Midsumma Festival, Melbourne (www.midsumma.org.au)

Sydney Gay & Lesbian Mardi Gras (www.mardigras.org.au)

Feast Festival, Adelaide (www.feast.org.au)

PrideFest, Perth (www.pridewa.com.au)

Brisbane Pride Festival (www.brisbanepride.org.au)

Resources

Major cities have gay newspapers, available from clubs, cafes, venues and newsagents. Gay and lesbian lifestyle magazines include *DNA*, *Lesbians on the Loose (LOTL)* and the Sydney-based *SX*. In Melbourne look for *MCV;* in Queensland look for *Queensland Pride*. Perth has the free *OutinPerth* and Adelaide has *Blaze*.

Gay & Lesbian Tourism Australia (Galta; www.galta.com.au) General information on gay-friendly businesses, places to stay and nightlife.

Same Same (www.samesame.com.au) News, events and lifestyle features.

Gay Stay Australia (www.gaystayaustralia.com) A useful resource for accommodation.

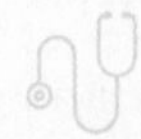

Health

Health-wise, Australia is a remarkably safe country in which to travel, considering that such a large portion of it lies in the tropics. Few travellers to Australia will experience anything worse than an upset stomach or a bad hangover and, if you do fall ill, the standard of hospitals and health care is high.

Availability & Cost of Health Care

Facilities Australia has an excellent health-care system. It's a mixture of privately run medical clinics and hospitals alongside a system of public hospitals funded by the Australian government.

Medicare The Medicare system covers Australian residents for some health-care costs. Visitors from countries with which Australia has a reciprocal health-care agreement – New Zealand, the Republic of Ireland, Sweden, the Netherlands, Finland, Italy, Belgium, Malta, Slovenia, Norway and the UK – are eligible for benefits specified under the Medicare program. See www.humanservices.gov.au/customer/subjects/medicare-services.

Medications Painkillers, antihistamines for allergies, and skincare products are widely available at chemists throughout Australia. You may find that medications readily available over the counter in some countries are only available in Australia by prescription. These include the oral contraceptive pill, some medications for asthma and all antibiotics.

Resources

There's a wealth of travel health advice on the internet. **Lonely Planet** (www.lonelyplanet.com) is a good place to start, while the **World Health Organization** (www.who.int/ith) publishes *International Travel and Health*, which is revised annually and available free online. **MD Travel Health** (www.mdtravelhealth.com) provides complete travel-health recommendations for every country, updated daily.

Where the Wild Things Are

Australia's profusion of dangerous creatures is legendary, but travellers needn't be alarmed – you're unlikely to see many of these creatures in the wild, much less be attacked by one.

Crocodiles Around the northern Australian coastline, saltwater crocodiles (salties) are a real danger. They also inhabit estuaries, creeks and rivers, sometimes a long way inland. Observe safety signs or ask locals before plunging in.

Jellyfish With venomous tentacles up to 3m long, box jellyfish (aka sea wasps or stingers) and their tiny, lethal relatives the irukandji inhabit Australia's tropical waters. They're most common during the wet season (October to March). Stinger nets are in place at some beaches, but never swim unless you've checked. If you are stung, wash the skin with vinegar then get to a hospital.

Sharks Despite extensive media coverage, the risk of shark attack in Australia is no greater than in other countries with extensive coastlines. Check with surf life-saving groups about local risks.

Snakes Australia has some of the world's most venomous snakes. Most common are brown and tiger snakes, but few species are aggressive. If you are bitten, prevent the spread of venom by applying pressure to the wound and immobilising the area with a splint or sling. Stay put and get someone else to go for help.

Spiders The deadly funnel-web spider lives in NSW (including Sydney) – bites are treated as per snake bites (pressure and immobilisation before transferring to a hospital). Redback spiders live throughout Australia; bites cause pain, sweating and nausea. Apply ice or cold packs, then transfer to hospital. White-tailed spider bites may cause an ulcer that's slow and difficult to heal. Clean the wound and seek medical assistance. The disturbingly large huntsman spider is harmless.

Government travel-health websites:

Australia (www.smartraveller.gov.au)

Canada (www.hc-sc.gc.ca)

UK (www.nhs.uk/livewell/travelhealth/pages/travelhealthhome.aspx)

USA (www.cdc.gov/travel)

Vaccinations

Visit a physician four to eight weeks before departure. Ask your doctor for an *International Certificate of Vaccination* (aka the 'yellow booklet'), which will list the vaccinations you've received.

Upon entering Australia you'll be required to fill out a 'travel history card' detailing any visits to Ebola-affected regions within the last 21 days.

If you're entering Australia within six days of having stayed overnight or longer in a yellow-fever-infected country, you'll need proof of yellow-fever vaccination. For a full list of these countries visit **Centers for Disease Control & Prevention** (www.cdc.gov/travel).

The **World Health Organization** (www.who.int) recommends that all travellers should be covered for diphtheria, tetanus, measles, mumps, rubella, chicken pox and polio, as well as hepatitis B, regardless of their destination. While Australia has high levels of childhood vaccination coverage, outbreaks of these diseases do occur.

Insurance

Worldwide travel insurance is available at www.lonelyplanet.com/travel-insurance. You can buy, extend and claim online anytime – even if you're already on the road.

Level of Cover A good travel insurance policy covering theft, loss and medical problems is essential. Some policies specifically exclude designated 'dangerous activities' such as scuba diving, skiing and even bushwalking. Make sure the policy you choose fully covers you for your activity of choice.

Health You may prefer a policy that pays doctors or hospitals directly rather than requiring you to pay on the spot and claim later. If you have to claim later make sure you keep all documentation. Check that the policy covers ambulances and emergency medical evacuations by air.

Internet Access

Wi-fi

Wi-fi is increasingly the norm in urban Australian accommodation (often free for guests). Cafes, bars and even some public gardens and town squares also provide wi-fi access. Local tourist offices should have details of public wi-fi hotspots.

Even so, there remain a surprising number of black spots without mobile or internet coverage. Most of these are in rural or outback areas. In such areas, hotel wi-fi may be your saviour.

Access

There are fewer internet cafes around these days than there were five years ago (thanks to the advent of iPhones/iPads and wi-fi), but you'll still find them in most sizeable towns. Most accommodation is phasing out internet terminals and kiosks in favour of wi-fi, although most hostels still have a public computer.

Most public libraries have internet access, but generally it's provided for research needs, not for travellers to check Facebook – so book ahead or find an internet cafe.

Legal Matters

Most travellers will have no contact with Australia's police or legal system; if they do, it's most likely to be while driving.

Driving There's a significant police presence on Australian roads, and police have the power to stop your car, see your licence (you're required to carry it), check your vehicle for roadworthiness and insist that you take a breath test for alcohol (and sometimes illicit drugs).

Drugs First-time offenders caught with small amounts of illegal drugs are likely to receive a fine rather than go to jail, but the recording of a conviction against you may affect your visa status.

Visas If you remain in Australia beyond the life of your visa, you'll officially be an 'overstayer' and could face detention and then be prevented from returning to Australia for up to three years.

Arrested? It's your right to telephone a friend, lawyer or relative before questioning begins. Legal aid is available only in serious cases; for Legal Aid office info see www.nationallegalaid.org. However, many solicitors do not charge for an initial consultation.

Money

Australia's currency is the Australian dollar, comprising 100 cents. There are 5c, 10c, 20c, 50c, $1 and $2 coins, and $5, $10, $20, $50 and $100 notes. Prices in shops are often marked in single cents then rounded to the nearest 5c when you come to pay.

ATMs & Eftpos

ATMs Australia's 'big four' banks – ANZ, Commonwealth, National Australia Bank and Westpac – have ATMs all over Australia. Most ATMs accept cards issued by other banks (for a fee) and are linked to international networks.

Eftpos Most service stations, supermarkets, restaurants, cafes and shops have Electronic Funds Transfer at Point of Sale (Eftpos) facilities, allowing you to make purchases and even draw out cash with your credit or debit card.

Fees Bear in mind that withdrawing cash through ATMs or Eftpos may attract significant fees – check the associated costs with your bank first.

Credit Cards

Credit cards such as Visa and MasterCard are widely accepted for everything from a hostel bed or a restaurant meal to an adventure tour, and are pretty much essential (in lieu of a large deposit) for hiring a car. Diners Club and American Express (Amex) are not as widely accepted.

Lost credit-card contact numbers:

American Express (☎1300 132 639; www.americanexpress.com.au)

Diners Club (☎1300 360 060; www.dinersclub.com.au)

MasterCard (☎1800 120 113; www.mastercard.com.au)

Visa (☎1800 450 346; www.visa.com.au)

Debit Cards

A debit card allows you to draw money directly from your home bank account using ATMs, banks or Eftpos machines. Any card connected to the international banking network – Cirrus, Maestro, Plus and Eurocard – should work with your PIN. Expect substantial fees.

Companies such as Travelex offer debit cards with set withdrawal fees and a balance you can top up from your personal bank account while on the road.

Exchanging Money

Changing foreign currency (or travellers cheques, if you're still using them) is usually no problem at banks throughout Australia, or at licensed moneychangers such as Travelex or Amex in cities and major towns.

Taxes & Refunds

Goods & Services Tax The GST is a flat 10% tax on all goods and services – accommodation, eating out, transport, electrical and other goods, books, furniture, clothing etc. There are exceptions, however, such as basic foods (milk, bread, fruit and vegetables etc). By law the tax is included in the quoted or shelf price, so all prices are GST-inclusive.

Refund of GST If you purchase goods with a total minimum value of $300 from any one supplier no more than 30 days before you leave Australia, you are entitled under the Tourist Refund Scheme (TRS) to a

Practicalities

DVDs Australian DVDs are encoded for Region 4, which includes Mexico, South America, Central America, New Zealand, the Pacific and the Caribbean.

Newspapers Leaf through the daily *Sydney Morning Herald* (www.smh.com.au), Melbourne's *Age* (www.theage.com.au) or the national *Australian* broadsheet newspaper (www.theaustralian.com.au).

Radio Tune in to ABC radio; check out www.abc.net.au/radio for local frequencies.

Smoking Banned on public transport, in pubs, bars and eateries, and in some public outdoor spaces.

TV The main free-to-air TV channels are the government-sponsored ABC, multicultural SBS and the three commercial networks – Seven, Nine and Ten. Numerous free spin-off and local channels enrich the viewing brew.

Weights & Measures Australia uses the metric system.

refund of any GST paid. Check out www.border.gov.au/trav/ente/tour/are-you-a-traveller for details.

Opening Hours

Business hours vary from state to state, but the following is a guide. Note that nearly all attractions across Australia are closed on Christmas Day; many also close on New Year's Day and Good Friday.

Banks 9.30am to 4pm Monday to Thursday; until 5pm on Friday.

Cafes All-day affairs opening from around 7am until around 5pm.

Petrol stations and roadhouses Usually 8am to 10pm; some are 24-hour.

Post offices 9am to 5pm Monday to Friday; some also 9am to noon on Saturday.

Pubs Usually serving food from noon to 2pm and 6pm to 8pm. Pubs and bars often open for drinking at lunchtime and continue well into the evening, particularly from Thursday to Saturday.

Restaurants Open around noon to 2.30pm for lunch and 6pm to 8.30pm for dinner. Eateries in major cities keep longer hours.

Shops and businesses 9am to 5pm or 6pm Monday to Sunday. In larger cities, doors stay open until 9pm on Fridays.

Supermarkets Generally open from 7am until at least 8pm; some open 24 hours.

Post

Australia Post (www.auspost.com.au) runs very reliable national and worldwide postal services; see the website for details.

Public Holidays

Timing of public holidays can vary from state to state: check locally for precise dates. Some holidays are only observed locally within a state.

National

New Year's Day 1 January

Australia Day 26 January

Easter (Good Friday to Easter Monday inclusive) Late March/early April

Anzac Day 25 April

Queen's Birthday Second Monday in June (last Monday in September in WA)

Christmas Day 25 December

Boxing Day 26 December

Australian Capital Territory

Canberra Day Second Monday in March

Bank Holiday First Monday in August

Labour Day First Monday in October

New South Wales

Bank Holiday First Monday in August

Labour Day First Monday in October

Northern Territory

May Day First Monday in May

Show Day (Alice Springs) First Friday in July; (Darwin) fourth Friday in July

Picnic Day First Monday in August

Queensland

Labour Day First Monday in May

Royal Queensland Show Day (Brisbane) Second or third Wednesday in August

South Australia

Adelaide Cup Day Third Monday in May

Labour Day First Monday in October

Proclamation Day Last Monday or Tuesday in December

Tasmania

Regatta Day (Hobart) 14 February

Eight Hours Day First Monday in March

Bank Holiday Tuesday following Easter Monday

Hobart Show Day Thursday preceding fourth Saturday in October

Victoria

Labour Day Second Monday in March

Melbourne Cup Day First Tuesday in November

Western Australia

Labour Day First Monday in March

Foundation Day First Monday in June

School Holidays

The Christmas/summer school holidays run from mid-December to late January.

Three shorter school holiday periods occur during the year, varying by a week or two from state to state. They fall roughly from early to mid-April (usually including Easter), late June to mid-July, and late September to early October.

Safe Travel

Australia is a relatively safe place to travel by world standards – crime- and war-wise at any rate – but natural disasters regularly wreak havoc. Bushfires, floods and cyclones decimate parts of most states and territories, but if you pay attention to warnings from local authorities and don't venture into affected areas, you should be fine.

Telephone

Australia's main telecommunication companies:

Telstra (☎13 22 00; www.telstra.com.au)

Optus (☎1800 780 219; www.optus.com.au)

Vodafone (☎1300 650 410; www.vodafone.com.au)

Virgin (☎1300 555 100; www.virginmobile.com.au)

International Calls

From payphones Most payphones allow International Subscriber Dialling (ISD) calls, the cost and international dialling code of which will vary depending on which international phonecard provider you are using. International phone cards are readily available from internet cafes and convenience stores.

From landlines International calls from landlines in Australia are also relatively cheap and often subject to special deals; rates vary with providers.

Codes When calling overseas you will need to dial the international access code from Australia (☎0011 or 0018), the country code and then the area code (without the initial 0). So for a London telephone number you'll need to dial ☎0011-44-20, then the number. If dialling Australia from overseas, the country code is 61 and you need to drop the 0 in state/territory area codes.

Local Calls

Local calls cost 50c from public phones, and 25c from private phones (although it depends on the provider) – there are no time limits. Calls to/from mobile phones cost more and are timed.

Long-Distance Calls & Area Codes

Long-distance calls (over around 50km) are timed. Australia uses four Subscriber Trunk Dialling (STD) area codes. These STD calls can be made from any public phone and are cheaper during off-peak hours (generally between 7pm and 7am, and on weekends). Broadly, the main area codes are as follows:

State/ Territory	Area code
ACT	☎02
NSW	☎02
NT	☎08
QLD	☎07
SA	☎08
TAS	☎03
VIC	☎03
WA	☎08

Mobile (Cell) Phones

Numbers Numbers with the prefix 04xx xxx xxx belong to mobile phones.

Networks Australia's digital network is compatible with GSM 900 and 1800 (used in Europe), but generally not with the systems used in the USA or Japan.

Reception Australia's mobile networks service more than 90% of the population, but leave vast tracts of the country uncovered.

Providers Buy a starter kit from one of the main service providers (Telstra, Optus, Virgin and Vodafone), which may include a phone or, if you have your own phone, a SIM card and a prepaid charge card.

Phonecards & Public Phones

Phonecards A variety of phonecards can be bought at newsagents, hostels and post offices for a fixed-dollar value (usually $10, $20 etc) and can be used with any public or private phone by dialling a toll-free access number and then the PIN number on the card.

Public Phones Most of the few public phones that remain use phonecards; some also accept credit cards. Old-fashioned coin-operated public phones are becoming increasingly rare.

Toll-Free & Information Calls

Many businesses have either a toll-free 1800 number, dialled from anywhere within Australia for free, or a 13 or 1300 number, charged at a local call rate. None of these numbers can be dialled from outside Australia (and often can't be dialled from mobile phones within Australia).

To make a reverse-charge (collect) call from any public or private phone, dial 1800 738 3773 or 12 550.

Numbers starting with 190 are usually recorded information services, charged at anything from 35c to $5 or more per minute (more from mobiles and payphones).

Time

Zones Australia is divided into three time zones: Western Standard Time (GMT/UTC plus eight hours), covering Western Australia; Central Standard Time (plus 9½ hours), covering South Australia and the Northern Territory; and Eastern Standard Time (plus 10 hours), covering Tasmania, Victoria, NSW, the ACT and Queensland.

Daylight saving Clocks are put forward an hour. This system operates in some states during the warmer months (October to early April), but Queensland, WA and the NT stay on standard time.

Tourist Information

Tourism Australia (www.australia.com) is the national government tourist body and has a good website for pretrip research. The website also lists reliable travel agents in countries around the world to help you plan your trip, plus visa, work and customs information.

Almost every major town in Australia has a tourist office of some type and they can be super helpful, with chatty staff (often retiree volunteers) providing local info not readily available from the state offices.

Travellers with Disabilities

Download Lonely Planet's free **Accessible Travel guide** from http://lptravel.to/accessibletravel.

- Disability awareness in Australia is high and getting higher.
- Legislation requires that new accommodation meets accessibility standards for mobility-impaired travellers, and discrimination by tourism operators is illegal.
- Many of Australia's key attractions, including many national parks, provide access for those with limited mobility and a number of sites also address the needs of visitors with visual or hearing impairments.
- Tour operators with vehicles catering to mobility-impaired travellers operate from most capital cities.
- Facilities for wheelchairs are improving in accommodation, but there are still many older establishments where the necessary upgrades haven't been done.

Resources

Deaf Australia (www.deafaustralia.org.au)

e-Bility (www.ebility.com)

National Information Communication & Awareness Network (www.nican.com.au) Australia-wide directory providing information on access, accommodation, sports and recreational activities, transport and specialist tour operators.

Vision Australia (☎1300 847 466; www.visionaustralia.org.au)

Air Travel

Qantas entitles a disabled person with high-support needs and the carer travelling with them to a discount on full economy fares; contact **Nican** (☎1300 655 535, 02 6241 1220; www.nican.com.au) for eligibility info and an application form.

Guide dogs travel for free on Qantas, Jetstar, Virgin Australia and their affiliated carriers. All of Australia's major airports have dedicated parking spaces, wheelchair access to terminals, accessible toilets, and skychairs to convey passengers onto planes via air bridges.

Train Travel

In NSW, CountryLink's XPT trains have at least one carriage (usually the buffet car) with a seat removed for a wheelchair, and an accessible toilet. Queensland Rail's *Tilt Train* from Brisbane to Cairns has a wheelchair-accessible carriage.

All of Australia's suburban rail networks are wheelchair-accessible and guide dogs and hearing dogs are permitted on all public transport.

In Victoria, **Public Transport Victoria** (☎1800 800 007; www.ptv.vic.gov.au) offers a free travel pass to visually impaired people and wheelchair users for transport around Melbourne.

Visas

There are several different visas available, depending on your nationality and what kind of visit you're contemplating. See the website of the **Department of Immigration & Border Protection** (☎1300 363 263, 02-6275 6666; www.border.gov.au) for info and application forms (also available from Australian diplomatic missions overseas and travel agents), plus details on visa extensions, Working Holiday Visas (417) and Work and Holiday Visas (462).

Government Travel Advice

The following government websites offer travel advisories and information for travellers.

Australian Department of Foreign Affairs & Trade (www.smartraveller.gov.au)

Canadian Department of Foreign Affairs & International Trade (www.voyage.gc.ca)

UK Foreign & Commonwealth Office (www.gov.uk/foreign-travel-advice)

US Department of State (www.travel.state.gov)

eVisitor (651)

- Many European passport holders are eligible for a free eVisitor visa, allowing stays in Australia for up to three months within a 12-month period.
- eVisitor visas must be applied for online (www.border.gov.au). They are electronically stored and linked to individual passport numbers, so no stamp in your passport is required.
- It's advisable to apply at least 14 days prior to the proposed date of travel to Australia.

Electronic Travel Authority (ETA; 601)

- Passport holders from eight countries that aren't part of the eVisitor scheme – Brunei, Canada, Hong Kong, Japan, Malaysia, Singapore, South Korea and the USA – can apply for either a visitor or business ETA.
- ETAs are valid for 12 months, with stays of up to three months on each visit.
- You can apply for an ETA online (www.border.gov.au), which attracts a nonrefundable service charge of $20.

Visitor (600)

- Short-term Visitor visas have largely been replaced by the eVisitor and ETA. However, if you're from a country not covered by either, or you want to stay longer than three months, you'll need to apply for a Visitor visa.
- Standard Visitor visas allow one entry for a stay of up to three, six or 12 months, and are valid for use within 12 months of issue.
- Apply online at www.border.gov.au.

Volunteering

Lonely Planet's *Volunteer: A Traveller's Guide to Making a Difference Around the World* provides useful information about volunteering.

Women Travellers

Australia is generally a safe place for women travellers, although the usual sensible precautions apply.

Night-time Avoid walking alone late at night in any of the major cities and towns – keep enough money aside for a taxi back to your accommodation.

Pubs Be wary of staying in basic pub accommodation unless it looks safe and well managed.

Sexual harassment Rare, though some macho Aussie males still slip – particularly when they've been drinking.

Rural areas Stereotypically, the further you get from the big cities, the less enlightened your average Aussie male is probably going to be about women's issues. Having said that, many women travellers say that they have met the friendliest, most down-to-earth blokes in outback pubs and remote roadhouse stops.

Hitchhiking Hitching is not recommended for anyone. Even when travelling in pairs, exercise caution at all times.

Drugged drinks Some pubs in Sydney and other big cities post warnings about drugged or 'spiked' drinks. It's probably not cause for paranoia, but play it safe if someone offers you a drink in a bar.

Transport

Getting There & Away

Australia is a long way from just about everywhere – getting there usually means a long-haul flight. If you're short on time on the ground, consider internal flights – they're affordable (compared with petrol and car-hire costs), can usually be carbon offset, and will save you some *looong* days in the saddle. Flights, tours and rail tickets can be booked online at www.lonelyplanet.com/bookings.

Entering the Country

Arrival in Australia is usually straightforward and efficient, with the usual customs declarations.

There are no restrictions for citizens of any particular foreign countries entering Australia. If you have a current passport and visa, you should be fine.

Air

Airlines & Airports

Most major international airlines fly to/from Australia. Australia's international carrier is **Qantas** (☎13 13 13; www.qantas.com.au), which has an outstanding safety record (...as Dustin Hoffman said in *Rainman*, 'Qantas never crashed').

Australia has numerous international gateways, with Sydney and Melbourne being the busiest.

Adelaide Airport (ADL; ☎08-8308 9211; www.adelaideairport.com.au; 1 James Schofield Dr)

Brisbane Airport (www.bne.com.au; Airport Dr)

Cairns Airport (☎07-4080 6703; www.cairnsairport.com; Airport Ave)

Darwin International Airport (☎08-8920 1811; www.darwinairport.com.au; Henry Wrigley Dr, Marrara)

Gold Coast Airport (www.goldcoastairport.com.au; Longa Ave, Bilinga)

Melbourne Airport (MEL; ☎03-9297 1600; www.melbourneairport.com.au; Departure Rd, Tullamarine)

Perth Airport (☎08-9478 8888; www.perthairport.com.au)

Sydney Airport (☎02-9667 9111; www.sydneyairport.com.au; Airport Dr, Mascot)

Getting Around

Air

Australia's main domestic airlines service the large centres with regular flights. The major players:

Qantas (☎13 13 13; www.qantas.com.au)

Virgin Australia (☎13 67 89; www.virginaustralia.com)

Jetstar (☎131 538; www.jetstar.com)

Tiger Air (www.tigerair.com.au)

Air Passes

Qantas (☎13 13 13; www.qantas.com.au) offers a discount-fare **Walkabout Air Pass** (www.qantas.com/travel/airlines/walkabout/us/en) for passengers flying into Australia from overseas with Qantas or American Airlines. The pass allows you to link up around 80 domestic Australian destinations for less than you'd pay booking flights individually.

Bicycle

Australia has much to offer cyclists, from bike paths winding through most major cities, to thousands of kilometres of good country roads where you can wear out your sprockets.

Hire Bike hire in cities is easy, but if you're riding for more than a few hours or even a day, it's more economical to invest in your own wheels.

Legalities Bike helmets are compulsory in all states and territories, as are white front lights and red rear lights for riding at night.

Weather In summer carry plenty of water. Wear a helmet with a peak (or a cap under your helmet), use sunscreen and avoid cycling in the middle of the day. Beware summer northerly winds that can make life hell for a northbound cyclist. Southeasterly trade winds blow in April, when you can have (theoretically) tail winds all the way to Darwin. It can get very cold in Victoria, Tasmania, southern SA and the NSW mountains, so pack appropriate clothing.

Transport If you're bringing in your own bike, check with your airline for costs and the degree of dismantling or packing required. Within Australia, bus companies require you to dismantle your bike and some don't guarantee that it will travel on the same bus as you.

Resources

Each state and territory has a cycling organisation that can help with cycling information and put you in touch with touring clubs. **Bicycles Network Australia** (www.

Climate Change & Travel

Every form of transport that relies on carbon-based fuel generates CO_2, the main cause of human-induced climate change. Modern travel is dependent on aeroplanes, which might use less fuel per kilometre per person than most cars but travel much greater distances. The altitude at which aircraft emit gases (including CO_2) and particles also contributes to their climate change impact. Many websites offer 'carbon calculators' that allow people to estimate the carbon emissions generated by their journey and, for those who wish to do so, to offset the impact of the greenhouse gases emitted with contributions to portfolios of climate-friendly initiatives throughout the world. Lonely Planet offsets the carbon footprint of all staff and author travel.

bicycles.net.au) offers information, news and links.

Bicycle NSW (www.bicyclensw.org.au)

Bicycle Network Tasmania (www.biketas.org.au)

Bicycle Network Victoria (www.bicyclenetwork.com.au)

Bicycle Queensland (www.bq.org.au)

Bicycle Transportation Alliance (www.btawa.org.au) In WA.

Bike SA (www.bikesa.asn.au)

Cycling Northern Territory (www.nt.cycling.org.au)

Pedal Power ACT (www.pedalpower.org.au)

Bus

Australia's extensive bus network is a reliable way to get around, though bus travel isn't always cheaper than flying and it can be tedious over huge distances. Most buses are equipped with air-con, toilets and videos; all are smoke-free and some have wi-fi. There are no class divisions on Australian buses (very democratic), and the vehicles of the different companies all look pretty similar.

Small towns eschew formal bus terminals for a single drop-off/pick-up point (post office, newsagent, corner shop etc). Major companies:

Greyhound Australia (☎02-6211 8545; www.greyhound.com.au; ⏰6am-6pm) Runs a national network (notably not across the Nullarbor Plain between Adelaide and Perth, nor Perth to Broome). Book online for the cheapest fares.

Firefly Express (☎1300 730 740; www.fireflyexpress.com.au) Runs between Sydney, Canberra, Melbourne and Adelaide.

Premier Motor Service (☎133 410; www.premierms.com.au) Greyhound's main competitor along the east coast.

V/Line (☎1800 800 007; www.vline.com.au) Connects Victoria with NSW, SA and the ACT.

Bus Passes

If you're planning on doing a lot of travel in Australia, a Greyhound Australia bus pass will save you money. Bus-pass discounts of 10% apply to YHA- and student-card holders, and children under 14. For a full list of passes, check out www.greyhound.com.au/passes.

Costs

Following are the average one-way bus fares along some well-travelled routes, booked online.

Route	Fare
Adelaide–Alice Springs	$155
Adelaide–Melbourne	$60
Brisbane–Cairns	$320
Cairns–Sydney	$429
Sydney–Brisbane	$109
Sydney–Melbourne	$120

Car & Motorcycle

Driving Licence

To drive in Australia you'll need to hold a current driving licence issued in English from your home country. If the licence isn't in English, you'll also need to carry an International Driving Permit, issued in your home country.

Choosing a Vehicle

2WD Depending on where you want to travel, a regulation 2WD vehicle might suffice. They're cheaper to hire, buy and run than 4WDs and are more readily available. Most are fuel efficient and easy to repair and sell. Downsides: no off-road capability and no room to sleep!

4WD Good for outback travel as they can access almost any track for which you get a hankering, and there might even be space to sleep in the back. Downsides: poor fuel economy, awkward to park and more expensive to hire/buy.

Campervan Creature comforts at your fingertips: sink, fridge, cupboards, beds, kitchen and space to relax. Downsides: slow and often not fuel-efficient, not great on dirt roads and too large for nipping around the city.

Motorcycle The Australian climate is great for riding, and bikes are handy in city traffic. Downsides: Australia isn't particularly bike-friendly in terms of driver awareness, there's limited luggage capacity, and exposure to the elements.

Renting a Vehicle

Larger car-rental companies have offices in major cities and towns. Most companies require drivers to be over the age of 21, though in some cases it's 18 and in others 25.

Suggestions to assist in the process:

- Read the contract cover to cover.
- Bond: some companies may require a signed credit-card slip, while others may actually charge your credit card. If the latter is the case, find out when you'll get a refund.
- Ask if unlimited kilometres are included and, if not, what the extra charge per kilometre is.
- Find out what excess you'll have to pay if you have an accident, and if it can be lowered by an extra charge per day (this option will usually be offered to you whether you ask or not). Check if your personal travel insurance covers you for vehicle accidents and excess.
- Check for exclusions (hitting a kangaroo, damage on unsealed roads etc) and whether you're covered on unavoidable unsealed roads (eg accessing campsites). Some companies also exclude parts of the car from cover, such as the underbelly, tyres and windscreen.
- At pick-up inspect the vehicle for any damage. Make a note of anything on the contract before you sign.
- Ask about breakdown and accident procedures.
- If you can, return the vehicle during business hours and insist on an inspection in your presence.

The usual big international companies (Avis, Budget, Europcar, Hertz, Thrifty) all operate in Australia. The following websites offer last-minute discounts and the opportunity to compare rates between the big operators:

- www.carhire.com.au
- www.drivenow.com.au
- www.webjet.com.au

4WDs

The major car-hire companies have 4WDs. Something like a Nissan X-Trail (which can get you through most, but not all, tracks) costs around $100 to $150 per day; for a Toyota Landcruiser you're looking at around $150 up to $200, which should include unlimited kilometres.

Check the insurance conditions, especially the excess (the amount you pay in the event of accident and which can be up to $5000), as they can be onerous. A refundable bond is also often required – this can be as much as $7500.

Campervans

Companies for campervan hire – with rates from around $90 (two-berth) or $150 (four-berth) per day, usually with minimum five-day hire and unlimited kilometres – include:

Apollo (☎1800 777 779; www.apollocamper.com) Also has a backpacker-focused brand called Hippie Camper.

Britz (☎1300 738 087; www.britz.com.au)

Jucy (☎1800 150 850; www.jucy.com.au)

Maui (☎1800 827 821; www.maui.com.au)

Mighty Campers (☎1800 821 824; www.mightycampers.com.au)

Spaceships (☎1300 132 469; www.spaceshipsrentals.com.au)

Travelwheels (☎0412 766 616; www.travelwheels.com.au)

One-Way Relocations

Relocations are usually cheap deals, although they don't allow much time flexibility. Most of the large hire companies offer deals, or try the following operators:

imoova (www.imoova.com)

Transfercar (www.transfercar.com.au)

See also www.hippiecamper.com and www.drivenow.com.au.

Insurance

Third-party insurance With the exception of NSW and Queensland, third-party personal-injury insurance is included in the vehicle registration cost, ensuring that every registered vehicle carries at least minimum insurance (if registering in NSW or Queensland you'll need to arrange this privately). We recommend extending that minimum to at least third-party property insurance – minor collisions can be amazingly expensive.

Rental vehicles When it comes to hire cars, understand your liability in the event of an accident. Rather than risk paying out thousands of dollars, consider taking out comprehensive car insurance or paying an additional daily amount to the rental company for excess reduction (this reduces the excess payable in the event of an accident from between $2000 and $5000 to a few hundred dollars).

Exclusions Be aware that if travelling on dirt roads you usually will not be covered by insurance for your rental vehicle unless you have a 4WD (read the fine print); some agreements even specify specific roads/tracks that you're not allowed to drive on. Also, many companies' insurance won't cover the cost of damage to glass (including the windscreen) or tyres.

Auto Clubs

Under the auspices of the **Australian Automobile Association** (AAA; ☎02-6247 7311; www.aaa.asn.au) are automobile clubs in each state, handy when it comes to insurance, regulations, maps and roadside assistance. Club membership (around $100 to $150) can save you a lot of trouble if things go wrong mechanically. If you're a member of an auto club in your home country, check if reciprocal rights are offered in Australia.

The major Australian auto clubs generally offer reciprocal rights in other states and territories:

Automobile Association of the Northern Territory (AANT; ☎08 8925 5901; www.aant.com.au; ⊙9am-5pm Mon-Fri, to 12.30pm Sat)

NRMA (☎13 11 22; www.mynrma.com.au) NSW and the ACT.

RACQ (☎13 19 05; www.racq.com.au) Queensland.

RACV (☎13 72 28; www.racv.com.au) Victoria.

Royal Automobile Club of Tasmania (RACT; ☎03-6232 6300, roadside assistance 13 11 11; www.ract.com.au; cnr Murray & Patrick Sts, Hobart; ⊙8.45am-5pm Mon-Fri)

Royal Automobile Club of Western Australia (RAC; ☎13 17 03; www.rac.com.au)

Road Rules

Australians drive on the left-hand side of the road and all cars are right-hand drive.

Give way An important road rule is 'give way to the right' – if an intersection is unmarked (unusual), and at roundabouts, you must give way to vehicles entering the intersection from your right.

Speed limits The general speed limit in built-up and residential areas is 50km/h. Near schools, the limit is usually 25km/h (sometimes 40km/h) in the morning and afternoon. On the highway it's usually 100km/h or 110km/h; in the NT it's either 110km/h or 130km/h. Police have speed radar guns and cameras and are fond of using them in strategic locations.

Seat belts and car seats It's the law to wear seat belts in the front and back seats; you're likely to get a fine if you don't. Small children must be belted into an approved safety seat.

Drink-driving Random breath tests are common. If you're caught with a blood-alcohol level of more than 0.05%, expect a fine and the loss of your licence. Police can randomly pull any driver over for a breathalyser or drug test.

Mobile phones Using a mobile phone while driving is illegal in Australia (excluding hands-free technology).

Fuel

Fuel types Unleaded and diesel fuel is available from service stations sporting well-known international brand names. LPG (liquefied petroleum gas) is not always stocked at more remote roadhouses – if you're on gas it's safer to have dual-fuel capacity.

Costs Prices vary from place to place, but at the time of writing unleaded was hovering between $1.20 and $1.50 in the cities. Out in the country, prices soar – in outback NT, SA, WA and Queensland you can pay as much as $2 per litre.

Availability In cities and towns petrol stations proliferate, but distances between fill-ups can be long in the outback. That said, there are only a handful of tracks where you'll require a long-range fuel tank. On main roads there'll be a small town or roadhouse roughly every 150km to 200km. Many petrol stations, but not all, are open 24 hours.

Local Transport

All of Australia's major towns have reliable, affordable public bus networks, and there are suburban train lines in Sydney, Melbourne, Brisbane, Adelaide and Perth. Melbourne also has trams (Adelaide has one!), and Sydney has harbour ferries and a light rail line. Taxis operate Australia-wide.

Tours

Backpacker-style and more formal bus tours offer a convenient way to get from A to B and see the sights on the way. Following are some multistate operators; there are also smaller companies operating within individual states and territories.

AAT Kings (☎1300 556 100; www.aatkings.com) Big coach company (popular with the older set) with myriad tours all around Australia.

Adventure Tours Australia (☎1300 654 604; www.adventuretours.com.au) Affordable, young-at-heart tours in all states.

Autopia Tours (☎03-9393 1333; www.autopiatours.com.au) One- to three-day trips from Melbourne, Adelaide and Sydney.

Groovy Grape Tours (☎1800 661 177, 08-8440 1640; www.groovygrape.com.au) Small-group, SA-based operator running one-day to one-week tours ex-Adelaide, Melbourne and Alice Springs.

Nullarbor Traveller (☎1800 816 858; www.thetraveller.net.au) Small company running relaxed minibus trips across the Nullarbor Plain between SA and WA.

Oz Experience (☎1300 300 028; www.ozexperience.com) Backpacker tour covering central, northern and eastern Australia in a U-shaped route – Cairns, Brisbane, Sydney, Melbourne, Adelaide, Alice Springs and Darwin – utilising Greyhound bus services.

Train

Long-distance rail travel in Australia is something you do because you really want to – not because it's cheap, convenient or fast. That said, trains are more comfortable than buses, and there's a certain long-distance 'romance of the rails' that's alive and kicking. Shorter-distance rail services within most states are run by state rail bodies, either government or private.

The most important long-distance rail links:

Great Southern Rail (☎08-8213 4401, 1800 703 357; www.greatsouthernrail.com.au) Operates the *Indian Pacific* between Sydney and Perth, the *Overland* between Melbourne and Adelaide, and the *Ghan* between Adelaide and Darwin via Alice Springs.

Queensland Rail (☎1300 131 722; www.queenslandrailtravel.com.au) Runs the high-speed *Spirit of Queensland* service between Brisbane and Cairns.

NSW TrainLink (☎13 22 32; www.nswtrainlink.info) Trains from Sydney to Brisbane, Melbourne and Canberra.

V/Line (☎1800 800 007; www.vline.com.au) Trains within Victoria, linking up with buses for connections into NSW, SA and the ACT.

Behind the Scenes

Acknowledgements

Climate map data adapted from Peel MC, Finlayson BL & McMahon TA (2007) 'Updated World Map of the Köppen-Geiger Climate Classification', Hydrology and Earth System Sciences, 11, 1633–44.

Illustration pp42–3 by Javier Zarracina.

This Book

This 2nd edition of Lonely Planet's *Best of Australia* guidebook was curated by Charles Rawlings-Way and researched and written by Charles Rawlings-Way, Brett Atkinson, Cristian Bonetto, Peter Dragicevich, Anthony Ham, Paul Harding, Trent Holden, Kate Morgan, Tamara Sheward, Tom Spurling, Andy Symington and Donna Wheeler. We would also like to thank the following people for their contributions to this guide: Dr Michael Cathcart, Cathy Craigie and Dr Tim Flannery.

This guidebook was produced by the following:

Destination Editor Tasmin Waby

Product Editor Alison Ridgway

Senior Cartographer Julie Sheridan

Book Designer Virginia Moreno

Assisting Editors Janet Austin, Katie Connolly, Melanie Dankel, Vicky Smith, Gabrielle Stefanos, Amanda Williamson

Assisting Cartographer Michael Garrett

Assisting Book Designers Meri Blazevski, Nicholas Colicchia, Mazzy Prinsep

Cover Researcher Naomi Parker

Thanks to William Allen, Liz Heynes, Jenna Myers, Catherine Naghten, Kirsten Rawlings, Tony Wheeler

Send Us Your Feedback

We love to hear from travellers – your comments keep us on our toes and help make our books better. Our well-travelled team reads every word on what you loved or loathed about this book. Although we cannot reply individually to postal submissions, we always guarantee that your feedback goes straight to the appropriate authors, in time for the next edition. Each person who sends us information is thanked in the next edition, the most useful submissions are rewarded with a selection of digital PDF chapters.

Visit lonelyplanet.com/contact to submit your updates and suggestions or to ask for help. Our award-winning website also features inspirational travel stories, news and discussions.

Note: We may edit, reproduce and incorporate your comments in Lonely Planet products such as guidebooks, websites and digital products, so let us know if you don't want your comments reproduced or your name acknowledged. For a copy of our privacy policy visit lonelyplanet.com/privacy.

A–Z Index

000 Map pages

D

E

F

G

H

I

J

K

L

M

N

O

P

Q

000 Map pages

Symbols & Map Key

Look for these symbols to quickly identify listings:

- Sights
- Activities
- Courses
- Tours
- Festivals & Events
- Eating
- Drinking
- Entertainment
- Shopping
- Information & Transport

These symbols and abbreviations give vital information for each listing:

Sustainable or green recommendation

FREE No payment required

- Telephone number
- Opening hours
- Parking
- Nonsmoking
- Air-conditioning
- Internet access
- Wi-fi access
- Swimming pool
- Bus
- Ferry
- Tram
- Train
- English-language menu
- Vegetarian selection
- Family-friendly

Find your best experiences with these Great For... icons.

Art & Culture

Beaches

Budget

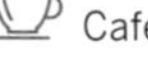
Cafe/Coffee

Cycling

Detour

Drinking

Entertainment

Events

Family Travel

Food & Drink

History

Local Life

Nature & Wildlife

Photo Op

Scenery

Shopping

Short Trip

Sport

Walking

Winter Travel

Sights

- Beach
- Bird Sanctuary
- Buddhist
- Castle/Palace
- Christian
- Confucian
- Hindu
- Islamic
- Jain
- Jewish
- Monument
- Museum/Gallery/Historic Building
- Ruin
- Shinto
- Sikh
- Taoist
- Winery/Vineyard
- Zoo/Wildlife Sanctuary
- Other Sight

Points of Interest

- Bodysurfing
- Camping
- Cafe
- Canoeing/Kayaking
- Course/Tour
- Diving
- Drinking & Nightlife
- Eating
- Entertainment
- Sento Hot Baths/Onsen
- Shopping
- Skiing
- Sleeping
- Snorkelling
- Surfing
- Swimming/Pool
- Walking
- Windsurfing
- Other Activity

Information

- Bank
- Embassy/Consulate
- Hospital/Medical
- Internet
- Police
- Post Office
- Telephone
- Toilet
- Tourist Information
- Other Information

Geographic

- Beach
- Gate
- Hut/Shelter
- Lighthouse
- Lookout
- Mountain/Volcano
- Oasis
- Park
- Pass
- Picnic Area
- Waterfall

Transport

- Airport
- BART station
- Border crossing
- Boston T station
- Bus
- Cable car/Funicular
- Cycling
- Ferry
- Metro/MRT station
- Monorail
- Parking
- Petrol station
- Subway/S-Bahn/Skytrain station
- Taxi
- Train station/Railway
- Tram
- Tube Station
- Underground/U-Bahn station
- Other Transport

Peter Dragicevich

After a successful career in niche newspaper and magazine publishing, both in his native New Zealand and in Australia, Peter finally gave into Kiwi wanderlust, giving up staff jobs to chase his diverse roots around much of Europe. Over the last decade he's written literally dozens of guidebooks for Lonely Planet on an oddly disparate collection of countries, all of which he's come to love. He once again calls Auckland, New Zealand his home – although his current nomadic existence means he's often elsewhere.

Anthony Ham

Anthony is a freelance writer and photographer who specialises in Spain, East and Southern Africa, the Arctic and the Middle East. When he's not writing for Lonely Planet, Anthony writes about and photographs Spain, Africa and the Middle East for newspapers and magazines in Australia, the UK and US.

Paul Harding

As a writer and photographer, Paul has been travelling the globe for the best part of two decades, with an interest in remote and offbeat places, islands and cultures. He's an author and contributor to more than 50 Lonely Planet guides to countries and regions as diverse as India, Iceland, Belize, Vanuatu, Iran, Indonesia, New Zealand, Finland, Philippines and – his home patch – Australia.

Trent Holden

A Geelong-based writer, located just outside Melbourne, Trent has worked for Lonely Planet since 2005. He's covered 30-plus guidebooks across Asia, Africa and Australia. With a penchant for megacities, Trent's in his element when assigned to cover a nation's capital – the more chaotic the better – to unearth cool bars, art, street food and underground subculture. On the flipside he also writes books to idyllic tropical islands across Asia, in between going on safari to national parks in Africa and the subcontinent. When not travelling, Trent works as a freelance editor and reviewer, and spends all his money catching live gigs.

Kate Morgan

Having worked for Lonely Planet for over a decade now, Kate has been fortunate enough to cover plenty of ground working as a travel writer on destinations such as Shanghai, Japan, India, Russia, Zimbabwe, the Philippines and Phuket. She has done stints living in London, Paris and Osaka but these days is based in one of her favourite regions in the world – Victoria, Australia. In between travelling the world and writing about it, Kate enjoys spending time at home working as a freelance editor.

Tamara Sheward

After years of freelance travel writing, rock'n'roll journalism and insalubrious authordom, Tamara leapt at the chance to join the Lonely Planet ranks in 2009. Since then, she's worked on guides to an incongruous jumble of countries including Montenegro, Australia, Serbia, Russia, the Samoas, Bulgaria and Fiji. She's written a miscellany of travel articles for the BBC, *The Independent, Sydney Morning Herald* et al; she's also fronted the camera as a documentary presenter for Lonely Planet TV, Nat Geo and Al-Jazeera.

Tom Spurling

Tom is an Australian LP guidebook author and high school teacher currently based in Hong Kong in search of the long-lost expatriate package. He's worked on 13 LP titles, including Japan, China, Central America, Turkey, India, South Africa and Australia. When not chasing his tail, he enjoys tucking it under his crossed legs for minutes on end.

Andy Symington

Andy has written or worked on more than a hundred books and other updates for Lonely Planet (especially in Europe and Latin America) and other publishing companies, and has published articles on numerous subjects for a variety of newspapers, magazines and websites. He part-owns and operates a rock bar, has written a novel and is currently working on several fiction and non-fiction writing projects. Andy, from Australia, moved to Northern Spain many years ago.

Donna Wheeler

Donna has written guidebooks for Lonely Planet for over ten years, including the Italy, Norway, Belgium, Africa, Tunisia, Algeria, France, Austria and Melbourne titles. She is the author of *Paris Precincts,* a curated photographic guide to the city's best bars, restaurants and shops and is reporter for Italian contemporary art publisher My Art Guides. Donna's work on contemporary art, architecture and design, food, wine, wilderness areas and cultural history also can be found in a variety of other publications.

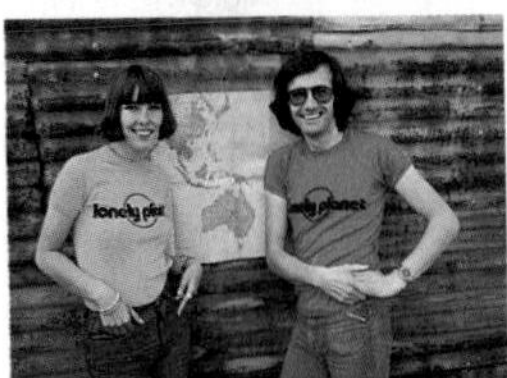

Our Story

A beat-up old car, a few dollars in the pocket and a sense of adventure. In 1972 that's all Tony and Maureen Wheeler needed for the trip of a lifetime – across Europe and Asia overland to Australia. It took several months, and at the end – broke but inspired – they sat at their kitchen table writing and stapling together their first travel guide, *Across Asia on the Cheap*. Within a week they'd sold 1500 copies. Lonely Planet was born.

Today, Lonely Planet has offices in Franklin, London, Melbourne, Oakland, Dublin, Beijing and Delhi, with more than 600 staff and writers. We share Tony's belief that 'a great guidebook should do three things: inform, educate and amuse'.

Our Writers

Charles Rawlings-Way

Charles is a veteran travel writer who has penned 30-something titles for Lonely Planet – including guides to Singapore, Toronto, Sydney, Tasmania, New Zealand, the South Pacific and Australia – and numerous articles. After dabbling in the dark arts of architecture, cartography, project management and busking for some years, Charles hit the road for LP in 2005 and hasn't stopped travelling since.

Brett Atkinson

Brett Atkinson is based in Auckland, New Zealand, but is frequently on the road for Lonely Planet. He's a full-time travel and food writer specialising in adventure travel, unusual destinations, and surprising angles on more well-known destinations. Craft beer and street food are Brett's favourite reasons to explore places, and he is featured regularly on the Lonely Planet website, and in newspapers, magazines and websites across New Zealand and Australia. Since becoming a Lonely Planet author in 2005, Brett has covered areas as diverse as Vietnam, Sri Lanka, the Czech Republic, New Zealand, Morocco, California and the South Pacific.

Cristian Bonetto

Cristian has contributed to more than 30 Lonely Planet guides to date, including *New York City, Italy, Venice & the Veneto, Naples & the Amalfi Coast, Denmark, Copenhagen, Sweden* and *Singapore*. Lonely Planet work aside, his musings on travel, food, culture and design appear in numerous publications around the world, including *The Telegraph* (UK) and *Corriere del Mezzogiorno* (Italy). When not on the road, you'll find the reformed playwright and TV scriptwriter slurping espresso in his beloved hometown, Melbourne.

More Writers

STAY IN TOUCH LONELYPLANET.COM/CONTACT

AUSTRALIA The Malt Store, Level 3, 551 Swanston St, Carlton, Victoria 3053 ☎ 03 8379 8000, fax 03 8379 8111

IRELAND Unit E, Digital Court, The Digital Hub, Rainsford St, Dublin 8, Ireland

USA 124 Linden Street, Oakland, CA 94607 ☎ 510 250 6400, toll free 800 275 8555, fax 510 893 8572

UK 240 Blackfriars Road, London SE1 8NW ☎ 020 3771 5100, fax 020 3771 5101

twitter.com/lonelyplanet

facebook.com/lonelyplanet

instagram.com/lonelyplanet

youtube.com/lonelyplanet

lonelyplanet.com/newsletter